Upholding Democracy

UPHOLDING DEMOCRACY

The United States Military Campaign in Haiti, 1994–1997

John R. Ballard

with a Foreword by
General John J. Sheehan

Westport, Connecticut
London

Library of Congress Cataloging-in-Publication Data

Ballard, John R., 1957–
    Upholding democracy : the United States military campaign in
Haiti, 1994–1997 / John R. Ballard ; foreword by General John J. Sheehan.
        p.   cm.
    Includes bibliographical references (p.   ) and index.
    ISBN 0–275–96237–7 (alk. paper)
    1. Haiti—History—American intervention, 1994–1995. I. Title.
    F1928.2.B35   1998
    972.9407′3—dc21   98–5239

British Library Cataloguing in Publication Data is available.

Library of Congress Catalog Card Number: 98–5239
ISBN: 0–275–96237–7

First published in 1998

Praeger Publishers, 88 Post Road West, Westport, CT 06881
An imprint of Greenwood Publishing Group, Inc.

Printed in the United States of America

The paper used in this book complies with the
Permanent Paper Standard issued by the National
Information Standards Organization (Z39.48–1984).

10 9 8 7 6 5 4 3 2 1

For Sergeant First Class Gregory Cardott, U.S. Army,
Killed at a checkpoint in Gonaives, Haiti,
January 12, 1995

Military service is the ultimate form of patriotism

Contents

List of Maps and Charts

List of Photographs

Photographs follow page 130

Foreword

Since the end of the Cold War the nature of security for the United States and other nations of the industrialized world has changed. Security is no longer defined entirely in a military dimension: the political, economic, and cultural aspects of security have now gained prominence. Within that larger context, terrorism, drug smuggling, and illegal migration are viewed today as threats by many Americans. Conditions in many developing world countries spawn these problems, and they can ultimately affect the United States. The U.S. military is adapting to deal with these new threats through changes in missions, organization, and training.

Recent operations in Haiti reflect the U.S. military's capacity to respond to operations across the spectrum of conflict, including operations other than war resulting from political and economic instability. Operation Uphold Democracy demonstrated military flexibility by transitioning from an assault operation in the initial execution phase to an unopposed intervention. Subsequent operations in Haiti established a stable and secure environment, which permitted the restoration of the legitimate government and follow-on democratic elections. United States joint task force commanders in Haiti successfully commanded a multinational force and completed a variety of tasks that enabled the transition to a United Nations military force. These wide-ranging actions in Haiti provided valuable experiences, from which we can learn, and important lessons, which we can build upon, for success in future operations. Uphold Democracy was not a template for coming operations, for they will all be unique, but this operation clearly demonstrated the appropriate use of the unique capabilities of today's U.S. armed forces in a complex and changeable environment.

As Americans, we should all reflect upon the challenges facing the men and women of our armed forces today so that we can act within the democratic process to determine when and how military force should be used. The key events of operation Uphold Democracy may never reoccur in exactly the same way, but the actions of U.S. military personnel in Haiti serve well as a study of the complexity of modern military operations, to inform and engage our fellow citizens.

JOHN J. SHEEHAN
General, USMC (Ret.)

Preface

In the late evening hours of September 18, 1994, operation Uphold Democracy began with one of the most challenging requests ever made by a U.S. President of a military commander. After over a year of planning, Admiral Paul D. Miller was directed to stop an airborne and amphibious invasion of over 100 aircraft and nearly 20,000 troops assembling from all over the United States, and recraft his operations so that Lieutenant General Hugh Shelton could enter Haiti peacefully to "cooperate" with the man formerly designated as his enemy. Within a space of 2 hours preceding the planned assault time, Miller, Shelton and their staffs successfully coordinated with other military agencies to halt the largest airborne strike since operation Market Garden in World War II. Early the next morning, Shelton flew into Haiti to negotiate the end of years of oppression within the country, using only the threat of his military power. What followed was a unique and ever-challenging campaign that illustrates well the difficult role that the United States now plays as the world's single superpower.

When General Shelton answered the phone in the combat operations center of the USS *Mount Whitney* on that night before the invasion, he did not expect the change in his campaign but was prepared with multiple options just in case the situation shifted. Turning back the assault force and crafting a humanitarian operation without combat appeared to be a herculean effort. But it was a task that the U.S. military was able to accomplish rapidly, without loss of momentum or resolve. Many other challenges also followed in Haiti as the United States worked for over 3 years to preserve regional stability in a nation with a complex and often violent past. Change has always been tough in Haiti, but the actions of the United States and its allies *have* made a difference there. This book is the story of that multifaceted campaign and an analysis of the factors that made actions in Haiti successful.

Military operations in Haiti demonstrated many of the significant changes that have occurred within the U.S. Department of Defense since the end of the Vietnam conflict. Lessons from the 1970s and early 1980s pointed out key areas that needed reform, and military leaders at all levels responded with improvements in force composition and readiness. The U.S. Congress, as the institution that makes the rules and regulations for the military, also participated in these changes. The efforts of these two institutions and the leadership of many concerned members of the executive branch eventually resulted in a smaller but more effective uniformed force. Increased effectiveness was the result of incorporating better technology, improved decision-making, and a concerted effort to inculcate joint concepts and synchronized capabilities within the armed services. The Persian Gulf War of 1990–1991 first demonstrated these new, emerging efficiencies. Operations in Somalia, 1992–1993, demonstrated additional benefits of the reforms as well as areas where improvement was still needed. This book outlines the Haitian Campaign of 1994–1997, which illustrated the success of these reforms in a different, yet still crucial, mode of military operations.

This study arose from my personal observations of the significant improvements made in U.S. military operations since the 1970s. As I witnessed the admirable professionalism of the present military, serving under very different circumstances from those it had experienced during the Cold War, I decided to investigate just how well the Haitian campaign fit within the parameters of U.S. national security strategy and the training that our service-members were receiving. What I discovered convinced me that Americans needed to better understand both the noncombat operations that so mark our current security environment and the capabilities that our military possess to accomplish them.

One of the primary purposes of this study is to provide the American people, students of military history, researchers, and interested members of the government with some of the valuable insights into the operation in Haiti. This understanding of the lessons learned in Uphold Democracy should help make any future commitment of American troops as safe and effective as possible. I also hope that these operational insights will aid in the continued refinement of joint tactics, techniques, and procedures, because these are now the heart of the American way of war. The campaign in Haiti was not a war, but the lives of many Americans were placed at risk during its execution. We must always learn as much we can from any military action in order to minimize risk in future operations.

Another of this book's primary goals is the explanation of the joint operations process that has contributed so significantly to the U.S. military's increased effectiveness in an era of constrained resources. Many of the inner workings of this joint process are still under development. Few outside the higher levels of the military have had an opportunity to observe how the United States prepares for and executes military operations short of war. However, such operations are growing in number and importance following the demise of the Soviet bloc, and therefore the American people they are designed to support should better understand them. As citizens of a democracy it is *we* who decide when and how military force should be employed, so therefore we must be cognizant of the benefits and dangers of committing our military forces.

Finally, the story of operation Uphold Democracy tells us much about U.S.–Haitian relations, our current national security strategy, strategic decision-making in America, and the evolving roles and missions of U.S. military forces. I hope that readers of military history and international affairs can derive from this book a deeper understanding of the contributions of today's servicemen and women and the conditions under which they serve our nation.

Acknowledgments

This book was written after my service as a member of the U.S. Atlantic Command's Joint Analysis and Assessment Team in Haiti and Norfolk, Virginia and while assigned to the faculty of the Armed Forces Staff College. For 6 years I have been privileged to work with some of the finest professionals in the Department of Defense. With the rise of every challenge these men and women have responded with dedication and unrelenting diligence to achieve consistently superb results. When their combined efforts have fallen short of the mark they have been even more inspiring, as they analyze, learn, improve, and progress to even greater challenges and better results. This special capacity of theirs to learn and be trained to ever-higher standards has inspired this book.

The information contained herein comes from various sources: personal observations, the compiled reports and interviews of individuals and organizations participating in operation Uphold Democracy, and the significant body of literature that has investigated the rich history and culture of the Haitian people. This study has also benefited from the dialogue and thoughtful questioning of a host of officer-students and the insights of my colleagues within the National Defense University. Finally, it has benefited from the example of a select group of leaders. Many of these leaders are general and flag officers, prominently among whom are Generals Jack Sheehan and Hugh Shelton and Admiral Hal Gehman; but many others are sergeants and petty officers working just as hard, often far from home, to keep our country safe.

The writing of this book would not have been possible without the support of many people. My special thanks must acknowledge the invaluable support provided by Gail Nicula and the staff of the Armed Forces Staff College Library: they have been ever helpful, ever patient, and always ready with an answer. Colonels Robert J. Fawcett, USMC, Donald W. Richardson, USA, and Robert J. Garner, USMC, provided the day-to-day guidance and the time that made writing this book possible; Drs. Nancy Wilds, Ralph Passarelli, and William McClintock provided valuable assistance, critique, and material support; and the members of the U.S. Atlantic Command staff and its Joint Analysis and Assessment Team gave me perspective and knowledge that was available nowhere else. The staff at Praeger, Heather Ruland and Robert Kowkabany, made final touches easier than I had thought possible.

Although it has benefited from a great deal of government information, this book does not reflect the opinions of the U.S. Department of Defense, the U.S. Atlantic Command, or the National Defense University, nor does it reflect their policies. The views expressed in this book are mine alone, as are any errors or omissions.

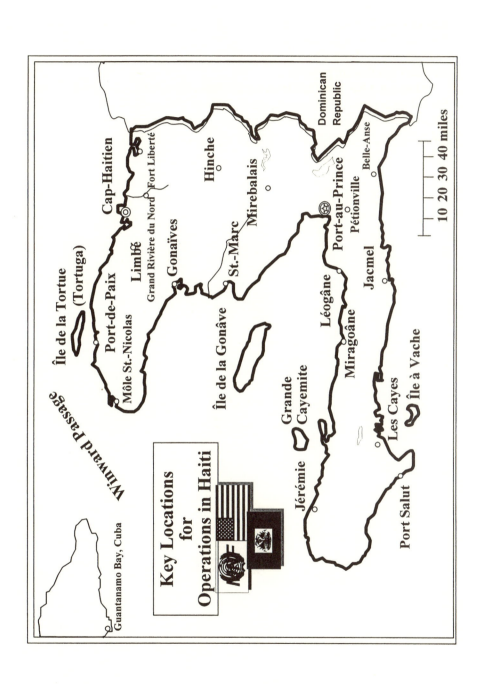

Key Locations for Operations in Haiti

Guantanamo Bay, Cuba

Windward Passage

Île de la Tortue (Tortuga)

Port-de-Paix

Môle St.-Nicolas

Cap-Haitien

Limbé

Grand Rivière du Nord

Fort Liberté

Gonaïves

Hinche

St.-Marc

Mirebalais

Dominican Republic

Île de la Gonâve

Belle-Anse

Port-au-Prince

Pétionville

Léogâne

Jacmel

Miragoâne

Grande Cayemite

Jérémie

Les Cayes

Île à Vache

Port Salut

10 20 30 40 miles

PART I

HISTORICAL BACKGROUND

"Haiti is imprisoned by its past."[1]

Robert D. Heinl

The internal conflict that resulted in the intervention of other nations into Haitian affairs in 1994 had deep roots in the culture and national character of Haiti. To place the military intervention in proper context, operation Uphold Democracy must be viewed from a perspective that includes Haiti's troubled past and America's extensive involvement in Haitian affairs. Although French in cultural tradition, Haiti has always had a strong, yet variable political and economic affiliation with the United States; and this long-standing relationship between the two nations had a dominant influence on planning and executing the operation.

Haiti has a unique heritage. No clear understanding of Haitian affairs can be gained without an appreciation of the traumatic history of this, the world's first black republic. This history begins with the initial Spanish colonization of Hispaniola and the subsequent development of the French colony of St. Domingue in Haiti. Haitian history took a radical turn when, spurred by the French Revolution, Toussaint L'Ouverture and his followers fought a war of independence against France. Thus, the first black republic issued from a bloody and divisive revolution, which profoundly marked its national character ever after.

Unfortunately, the natural resources that made the French colony so prosperous were rapidly depleted once Haiti gained its independence and the Haitian people began to suffer from a plague of internal strife. This dissension was so severe that it destroyed the richness of the land and the promise that independence had brought in 1804. A succession of regimes, poorly directed and ending in coups from the countryside, soon marked Haitian politics. During the nation's first century twenty-four rulers held sway in Port-au-Prince, yet only eight served a full term of office and only two retired peacefully.[2]

Very early in the twentieth century, the U.S. government began to view such instability as a threat to regional security and henceforward embarked on a more active role in Haitian affairs. These actions included the nineteen years of U.S. Marine nation-building from 1915 through 1934, on-again, off-again support of Haitian leaders following World War II, and intimate participation in the change of regimes after the fall of "Papa Doc" Duvalier in 1971. This American involvement colored perceptions of the United States in Haiti, drew key U.S. officials to Port-au-Prince on an increasingly frequent basis as the century wore on, and, when instability in Haiti grew chronic, eventually led to the operation entitled Uphold Democracy.

Relationships between nations are complex. Many factors have contributed to the multifaceted bond between Haiti and the United States: economics, shared democratic institutions, and certainly the close proximity of the two republics. Such close neighbors cannot coexist without frequently affecting each other's actions, but the United States and Haiti have developed special bonds resulting from a unique loveûhate relationship. The past had much to say about the reasons for American intervention in Haiti in 1994; the future will also bring new perceptions of the invasion. The events of 1994–1997 should be placed in proper perspective and must be well understood so that future Haitian–American relations will include no more conflict.

NOTES

1. Robert Debs Heinl and Nancy Gordon Heinl, *Written in Blood: The Story of the Haitian People, 1492–1971,* p. 6.
2. H. P. Davis, *Black Democracy: The Story of Haiti,* p. 324. See Appendix A for a listing of the rulers of Haiti.

CHAPTER 1

Colonial Haiti and Revolution

Haiti was one of the first locations discovered by Columbus on his voyage to the New World in 1492. When the *Santa Maria* ran hard aground east of the area where Cap-Haitien now stands, he was forced to leave part of the crew ashore, thereby establishing on Hispaniola the first Spanish settlement in the New World.[1] During the first century and a half of Hispaniola's colonization the Spanish did little with the western half of the island, concentrating instead on the eastern half, which appeared to be more lucrative. But the smaller island of Tortuga off the north coast of Hispaniola did become a haven for pirates, who preyed on the rich shipping trade of the region.[2] One of the significant results of this growth of piracy in the area was the beginning of a mixed island race, the product of pirate men and local black women purchased from traders or abducted from Spanish or English settlements. "These unions were responsible for the inception of the mulatto caste as a community, and for many years the majority of children born were of mixed white and Negro blood."[3] This early period was a time of European jockeying for possession of the rich lands of the Caribbean, and France soon superseded the influence of Spain in western Hispaniola.

The French, asserting their own rights within the region, soon saw the advantage of the island's location. France's foreign minister, Jean-Baptiste Colbert, chose Bertrand d'Ogeron de la Bouère, a former French officer and trader, to establish a settlement on the island in 1659. In d'Ogeron, Colbert found a capable and resourceful manager who was familiar with the area. As one of his first priorities, d'Ogeron brought cocoa, indigo, and perhaps most important, women to the region to further the development of a local economy. By 1681 d'Ogeron had established nearly 7000 planters in Haiti, but plenty of pirates still remained as well. The Treaty of Ryswick, which ended the War of the League of Augsburg in September 1697, established an initial boundary between the French and Spanish portions of Hispaniola: they were separated formally as the colonies of St. Domingue (French) and Santo Domingo (Spanish). Thus French became the official language of what is now Haiti.

The new colony of St. Domingue was to be ruled by a governor-general and an intendant, both working for the French Minister of Marine, who administered all of France's colonial possessions. The governor-general was the representative of the crown and head of the military; the intendant handled all administrative affairs, including justice, taxes, and revenues.[4] Unfortunately for France, the working relationship between the two men chosen for these key positions, and their contact with the mother country, was often not very close nor cordial. In addition, the only other organ of government for the colony was the colonial assembly, which was composed of the governor-general, the intendant, the attorney general, the navy commander, the chiefs of the militia, and the presidents of the provincial councils, none of whom effectively represented the colonists' interests.[5] This early colonial government began a process of poor administration that would grow more and more inadequate and disruptive in succeeding centuries in Haiti. Frequently insufficient to the task assigned and marked by inexperience and lack of understanding, the men "awarded" these positions inadvertently ensured that Haiti and France would eventually part, and that Haiti would be left with little or no working governmental structure.

Notably, these initial French settlers were planters and pirates but not slave owners. Slavery was first legally introduced into the new French colony in 1633, ostensibly to "gain souls for Christ."[6] The slave trade remained small until 1664, when the French Compaigne des Indes Occidentales began to transport Africans in ever-larger numbers to the New World. By 1700 there were nearly 10,000 slaves, and by the end of the century over 700,000 are estimated to have been working the land in Haiti.[7]

With such huge increases in the African population, the French in Haiti became more and more embroiled in the problems of slavery. To their credit, in March 1685 King Louis XIV issued one of the most liberal and fairest of all seventeenth-century laws concerning slavery. Known as the "Edit touchant la police des Isles de l'Amerique française," or Code Noir,[8] it actually provided for due process, restrictions on the break-up of families, limits on the authority of masters, and even the possibility of freedom for slaves. If exercised over the long term, the Code Noir could possibly have maintained a cooperative and viable society in St. Domingue by establishing a method of racial integration for the growing white and black populations. Unfortunately, the Code was soon largely ignored, and its liberal tenets served only to create racial conflict as black and white expectations were disappointed. The Code Noir did produce an additional faction within Haitian society: the "mulâtre" or "marron," the freed black.[9] As time progressed the presence of this third group would exacerbate all conflicts between whites and blacks, especially as many mulâtres became more prosperous than some whites.[10]

Large increases in the population resulted in the further settlement of Haiti during the colonial period. The population expanded generally south and then west from the area of Cap-Haitien, settling first near the better harbors. Port-au-Prince, first known as Port Royal, was founded in 1706 and became the capital 32 years later. St. Marc was founded in 1716, after Jacmel was founded in the south; Jérémie followed in the southwest in 1765. As a result of this growth, the interior was improved through the development of roads and stagelines connecting the major cities. The colony grew and prospered.

By the second half of the seventeenth century Haiti was understood by many Europeans to be a rich and quite delightful place. Unfortunately, its prosperity was but a thin veneer[11]—a layer as shallow as the 36,000 white elites overlaying the mass of nearly 700,000 blacks.[12] Although the colony supported much of Europe with sugar, coffee, and cocoa, life in Haiti was dehumanizing because of slavery.[13] A combination of poor administration, geographic expansion and population growth, rising prosperity for only a few, and internal conflict among the racial strata of the population soon began to traumatize the colony. Small revolts had begun as early as the mid-sixteenth century and, as the proportion of slaves in the colony increased, the frequency and seriousness of these revolts grew as well. This combination of threats and challenges soon resulted in measures designed to increase French controls within the colony. Such controls were focused primarily on the free black population—the mulâtres.

Formal reactions against the former slaves began as early as 1758, when the assembly of the colony passed a law prohibiting all colored people from carrying swords. Four years later all weapons were denied them. In 1767 the sale of any munitions to nonwhites was prohibited unless ordered by a white. In 1771 Louis XV's official "Instructions to Administrators" codified the maintenance of a line between the races.[14] By 1779 the local colonial laws had reached the point of resembling the Jim Crow laws of the nineteenth-century United States by restricting seating, dress, and occupations and even imposing a curfew on nonwhites.[15] Such a situation, in an age when liberal reforms were fanning revolutionary sentiment in many countries, was clearly a powder keg waiting to explode.

THE FRENCH REVOLUTION

The spark that burst the powder keg in Haiti was the same one that sealed the fate of Louis XVI in France: the French Revolution. The revolt that began in Paris in May 1789 eventually led to the reform of all French government institutions and the end of the Bourbon monarchy, and commenced nearly 20 years of war in Europe. But the implications of the French Revolution for Haiti were much greater than merely the change of government in the far-away mother country. The Revolution was accompanied by an overwhelming host of liberal ideas that modified forever the fundamental character of French culture—the same culture that nurtured life in Haiti. The greatest of these was the effort to institute social equality.

When the French revolutionary assembly proclaimed freedom for all Frenchmen in August 1789, that freedom included the slave populations in France's colonies. This granting of such freedom was easy for the men voting in the assembly hall in Paris; very few of them had even met a slave. The liberal sentiment for freedom was so strong in Paris that Mirabeau, one of the Revolution's greatest leaders, even chastised the representatives sent from Haiti to the National Assembly because they were all white![16] Mirabeau's reaction confounded the colonials, who not only were out of touch with the radical changes that had taken place in the French capital since May, but had little concept of representing the nonwhite population. Even so, a second delegation arriving in Paris later in the year *did* include mulâtres. Then 6 months later, on March 28, 1790, the French National Assembly gave the vote to all persons in the colony aged 25 and older who either owned property or who had paid taxes for 10 years. When the news arrived in the colony months later, the population was energized by the implications of the reform.

Unfortunately, freedom only set all the new citizens of Haiti on a collision course. The majority of whites foresaw the inevitable end of their way of life as they suddenly became a tiny minority of citizens immersed within the larger black colony.[17] Reforms from the Assembly in Paris particularly outraged many of the propertied elite in Haiti because they appeared to strike mortally at the economic basis of life in the colony, the plantation system. Liberty was a cherished ideal for slaves who had seen a glimpse of what life away from the fields could bring. But freedom for slaves also offended the freed blacks and mulattos, who felt that they had earned their freedom through guts and merit, and who would certainly risk the loss of their standard of living when the less prosperous and less educated slaves became their equals in rights. Although the law granting voting privileges passed in Paris, its implementation stalled in the Caribbean colony. The plantation owners strongly opposed giving the local population an opportunity at equality.

But on October 12, 1790 Vincent Ogé and his associate Jean-Baptiste Chavannes, both freed blacks who had been armed and financed by England and America, landed on the north coast of Haiti and formed the nucleus of a group intending to push for full execution of the Paris Assembly's decree. Ogé had been educated in France and encouraged by the association of the "Amis des Noirs" in Paris to work for full freedoms in the colony.[18] He and Chavannes tried to achieve their goal by asking the colonial assembly for full implementation of the National Assembly's declaration of expanded rights. When they were refused, they took to arms to demand those rights. Although they intended to bring about change in a peaceful manner, a white planter was killed in a resulting melee. As a result, their group was destroyed by the elites and both Ogé and Chavannes were tortured and killed, broken on the wheel in full public view.[19] Their deaths only convinced others that there could be no racial coexistence in Haiti.

These events established the pattern for a purely Haitian revolution. Internal conflict boiling under pressure, exacerbated by an infusion of liberal ideas during a period of rising prosperity, broke out into a condition of civil war. All these characteristics were similar to those that had created revolts in America in the 1770s and France in the 1780s, and would spark revolutions in Russia in the 1910s and China in the 1940s. But what made the revolution in Haiti different was the extreme disunity of the population. The other revolutions were bloody and disruptive, but due to a higher degree of homogeneity among the controlling populations that created the revolts in America, Europe, and Asia, they were not nearly as destructive as Haiti's.

The Ogé revolt was soon succeeded by another, led by a slave named Boukman. Boukman's supporters included men named Papillon, Biassou, Jeannot, and Toussaint L'Ouverture, the eventual "father of free Haiti." These men renounced peaceful approaches and soon had inflamed the whole of the north section of the colony by freeing slaves and destroying the property of recalcitrant whites. The savagery of this insurrection and the response it elicited from whites were unparalleled. A British historian visiting at the time noted that

to detail the various conflicts, skirmishes, massacres and slaughter which this exterminating war produced were to offer a disgusting and frightful picture. . . . Within two months after the revolt began, upwards of two thousand whites had been massacred, one hundred eighty sugar plantations and about nine hundred coffee, cotton and indigo settlements had been destroyed, and twelve hundred families reduced from opulence to abject destitution. Of the insurgents . . . upwards of ten thousand had perished by sword or famine and some hundreds by the hand of the executioner, many of these on the wheel.[20]

Boukman was soon captured and executed. But he was quickly succeeded by Jeannot, who was so savage in his approach that he was soon executed by Biassou. Haiti was rapidly consumed in fighting between black and white, poor and wealthy.

While the inhabitants of the colony were fighting one another, Britain and Spain took advantage of the opportunity to attack and expand their influence in the region at France's expense. With the entire colony under attack from within and without, the French commissioner in Port-au-Prince, Léger-Félicité Sonthonax, proclaimed the emancipation of the slaves in order to make an alliance with the current black commander in the north on August 29, 1793. That commander was L'Ouverture, who had initially proclaimed his goals as vengeance, then liberty and equality in St. Domingue.[21] Thus began the stormy relationship between Toussaint L'Ouverture and France. In September 1793 the British made landings in the port towns of Jérémie and Môle St. Nicholas, while forces from Santo Domingo advanced into the northeast region around Dondon. The Spanish also supported the slave revolts with arms and supplies.[22] The time was ripe for the emergence of a new leader.

Toussaint L'Ouverture was a 47-year-old former coachman and veterinarian at the plantation of Bréda in the northern region near Haut du Cap. He was gap-toothed (some say hence the name "l'ouverture," meaning "opening") and ugly, but literate, an excellent rider, and an active, effective leader. Two months later, after having first taken the pay and the cause of the Spanish to heart in order to gain his objectives in the north, he changed allegiances, saved Sonthonax from imprisonment, and became a "French" general.[23] Even with the help of L'Ouverture, however, over the following 10 months French fortunes fell steadily in Haiti, and the English finally conquered the capital of the colony in June 1794. Over the same period the fortunes of Toussaint L'Ouverture were rising dramatically, and with the fall of Port-au-Prince and French leader Robespierre's recall of Sonthonax, he and a man named André Rigaud[24] were the only "French" powers left on the island.

Sudden peace in mainland Europe caused the Spanish to stop fighting in Haiti, leaving Rigaud and L'Ouverture with only the English enemy in common and a clear disdain for each other. Haitians freed from conflict with the Spanish flocked to L'Ouverture's banner. Through 1796 the English troops suffered terribly from heat and disease, while the Haitians fought amongst themselves. Toussaint L'Ouverture steadily grew in power and prestige; he had been appointed lieutenant governor of Haiti for saving the life of Sonthonax in 1796 and a général de division in 1797 by the French Directory. Successive French administrators supported all efforts against the English and actually fanned the flames between Rigaud and L'Ouverture when it served their purposes. The English finally gave up on their Haitian campaign in October 1798, leaving the all-important question of Haitian leadership unresolved.

Open civil war began in Haiti later that same month when the last French administrator departed from Port-au-Prince, leaving L'Ouverture and Rigaud as coequal, independent commanders. In November 1798 L'Ouverture established relations with the United States. The platform for these relations comprised mutually beneficial trade supported by the American Navy, open ports for U.S. merchants in Haiti, and American arms for L'Ouverture's forces.[25] Haiti and the United States were natural allies at this point, both working to establish ties with former colonial masters and to develop important trade alliances in the western hemisphere. This relationship of mutual benefit would slowly evolve to the advantage of the United States, but at first the arrangement between the two powers was of much greater benefit to Haiti, and most significantly to Toussaint L'Ouverture.

The first U.S. consul general, Edward Stephens, arrived in the colony in March 1799, accredited not to Haiti, but to L'Ouverture personally. One result of this arrangement was a strict embargo, at L'Ouverture's request, of Rigaud's southern sector by the U.S. Navy.[26] War of the most brutal kind continued to ravage the country: thousands were shot, hung, starved to death, or burned alive as the forces of both sides ravaged the countryside. L'Ouverture did not hesitate to use any power at his disposal to attack Rigaud. Finally, in July 1800, after the decimation of his force, Rigaud elected to depart Haiti by ship, leaving L'Ouverture in control of the entire country. In response, Toussaint permitted the continued massacre of nearly 10,000 persons, for the most part mulattos, to subjugate the south completely. To everyone else, Toussaint L'Ouverture was a hero, his mission complete, "compared to Hercules, Alexander the Great, Napoleon Bonaparte and Bacchus."[27] But for L'Ouverture the victory was not complete; he needed to ensure that slavery and oppression would not return to Haiti, and to do that, he needed security in Hispaniola and freedom from France.

THE INCOMPLETE HAITIAN REVOLUTION

L'Ouverture then embarked on a concerted campaign to end any threat to Haitian freedoms. First, in May 1800 he ordered his forces into Santo Domingo and, within 6 months, had seized control of the entire island; then he turned his attention to reconstruction at home and efforts to keep the French at bay. Luckily for L'Ouverture, relations among the French, the Americans, and the English were again in crisis. For 2 years he had a relatively free hand in Haiti while the major powers were embroiled with other issues of commerce, freedom of the seas, and war in Europe between England and France. L'Ouverture focused his attentions on the development of a Haitian administrative system and resurrection of the local economy, which had been nearly destroyed by years of civil war.

The method he used to establish the new Haitian state is instructive. Because most of the skilled administrators, local or foreign, had been forced out during the revolt, Toussaint L'Ouverture had only his army to administer the state. Among his senior staff, most were noirs (blacks), many not even being Haitian-born, and several were undeniably vicious and vengeful.[28] Still, with only his military at hand, L'Ouverture divided the state into three districts and assigned one of his generals to each. The primary mission assigned to these generals was to restore the agricultural base of Haiti.

As an administrator, L'Ouverture demonstrated some promise, particularly given his limited experience. He chose moderation and reconciliation rather than continued vengeance and embarked upon a platform of black-ruled government supported by a strong Haitian agricultural base using the old plantation system. Forced labor was imposed on the people of Haiti, profits were divided among all, and a strict system of controls was developed for all workers.[29] He also retained a strong, military-like central government, with the army as the center of power. The chieftains of his army controlled the local districts, receiving their orders directly from L'Ouverture. To legalize the entire system he had the so-called "Constitution of 1801" concentrate all power in his hands and award to him alone the right to name his successor.[30] Thus he stamped Haiti with his personal image, molding it into a Caribbean Sparta—an image that would be resurrected time and time again by his successors, down to the rather unlikely General Cedras in the 1990s.

Unfortunately, L'Ouverture's vision was not very successful in practice. Although the initial results were promising and his creation of a black-ruled state demonstrated significant progress in the first year of peace, by 1801 the intricate web of deception and dominance he used to rule began to fall apart, both within and outside Haiti.[31] His favorite cohort and expected successor revolted against him and was executed. The international crisis that granted him some security in the Caribbean cooled: France began to take a stronger interest in its possessions after Napoleon consolidated his power as First Consul of France, and Britain lifted its blockade of the Caribbean. The lifting of the blockade permitted other nations to make contact with Haiti for the first time. Napoleon understood that Haiti was the French gateway to the Caribbean and hoped to use the colony as a staging base for French reconquest of parts of Louisiana.[32] The French ruler took advantage of an interim peace with his European enemies to send an expedition of 20,000 French soldiers to Haiti in an attempt to regain the colony and its strategic position in the Caribbean.

Napoleon chose his own brother-in-law, Victor-Emmanuel Leclerc, as the leader of this expedition. Leclerc's task was to smash resistance to France, pacify the hinterland, and then reestablish slavery. Napoleon's instructions were clear: Leclerc was to co-opt, use, and then cast off L'Ouverture and any others of influence in Haiti. All blacks were to be disarmed and put back to work; whites who supported L'Ouverture were to be sent to Guiana; women who had "prostituted" themselves with the local inhabitants were to be returned to Europe, stopping the mixing of races; and all public instruction was to be disestablished.[33] Leclerc's task was to return Haiti to docile servitude.

Leclerc arrived with a fleet of ships at the end of January 1802. At first, the weakening level of Haitian support for L'Ouverture was made clear by the lightening-fast advances made by the French. Although they were opposed by L'Ouverture's forces, the entire island fell quickly to the French from north to south, and L'Ouverture was forced to surrender after 3 short months of opposition. Although allowed at first to retire to his estate, he was soon deported to France, where he died, alone and without a hearing, in April 1803.

Yet the death of Toussaint L'Ouverture was not the end of the Haitian revolution. A combination of his example and the news that slavery had been reestablished in nearby French Guadeloupe inspired Haitians to greater resistance while, at the same time, disease and vicious fighting continually wore down French strength. These local factors, Napoleon's preoccupation with the war in Europe, and the support of arms, ammunition, and supplies provided by President Thomas Jefferson to the Haitians eventually caused Napoleon to abandon his campaign in the Caribbean. Rather than continue the costly effort, the French leader granted Haitian independence when the conflict in Europe erupted again in 1804. The Haitian campaign cost France almost the entire expeditionary force sent under Leclerc, which was mauled by disease and ruthless combat at the hands of L'Ouverture's successors, Jean-Jacques Dessalines, Henri Christophe, and Alexandre Pétion. Unfortunately for Haiti, independence from French rule did not lessen the burden of its problems much.

Although freedom had been proclaimed in Haiti, the revolution of Toussaint L'Ouverture was far from complete. In a practical sense, the French refused to recognize the new nation's independence and continued to posture as if a naval force might be returned to the island at any time. Much more detrimental for Haiti was the fact that it had not managed, even in so many years of conflict, to unite its people or develop an effective governmental system. Haiti was no longer subject to the rule of Europeans, but had a long way to go till it could demonstrate that it was the manager of its own national destiny.

SUMMARY

Four dominating factors can summarize the colonial period of Haitian history: economics, race, administration, and militarism. The colony's natural resources helped develop a strong trading economy based on a plantation system whereby a small percentage of elites managed the majority of the population as slave workers. Over time the Spanish, Indian, French, and African influences in Haiti mixed to produce a diverse population, with dominant African and French cultural links.

The colony was poorly administered and the local inhabitants were not well represented by their French political leaders. When the political firestorm of the French Revolution introduced egalitarianism to Haiti the bulk of the population rose up, seeking freedom, only to be beaten down by the local wealthy elites. Toussaint L'Ouverture stepped in to bring freedom to all of Haiti, using ruthless combat to rid the countryside of wealthy landowners and the French army. Although he was successful in his military effort to free Haiti, he found governance much more difficult, due primarily to a complete lack of managerial experience among his followers.

Although L'Ouverture did not live to see his nation recognized as an independent state, he did leave a strong legacy to Haiti. In the years following Haitian independence in 1804 his military assistants would dominate the new nation's government, establishing a Haitian political culture characterized by the use of military force, the growing divisiveness among the population, troubled financial programs, and inefficient administration. This legacy continues to plague Haiti today.

NOTES

1. Heinl notes that Martin Alonso Pinzo, captain of the *Pinta*, first sighted Haiti on November 30, 1492. Columbus arrived five days later at Môle St. Nicholas. Robert Debs Heinl and Nancy Gordon Heinl, *Written in Blood: The Story of the Haitian People, 1492–1971*, pp. 10–12.

2. From these pirates we get our term "buccaneers," from the French "filibustier," and the words for bacon and barbecue. Heinl, p. 16.

3. H. P. Davis, *Black Democracy: The Story of Haiti*, p. 19. Heinl cites "wenching" between white planters and maids as the source (Heinl, p. 26). James G. Leyburn, in his *The Haitian People*, p. 16, agrees with Heinl. The important point is that the mixed-race element in Haitian society grew to be accepted by both whites and blacks and eventually came to dominate Haiti.

4. Davis, p. 27.

5. Ibid.

6. Heinl, p. 25.

7. Ibid.

8. This "Proclamation concerning the Security of the French Islands in America" became known as the Black Code (Code Noir) because it focused so strongly on the relationships between the races in the region.

9. The term "marron" issued from *marronage*—the act of a domesticated animal running free. Heinl, p. 28.

10. Davis notes: "In 1789 it was estimated that mulattos possessed at least ten percent of the productive land and owned over 50,000 slaves" (Davis, p. 29).

11. Haiti was the single largest exporter of goods in the Caribbean between 1766 and 1791. Leyburn, p. 15.

12. These figures are from Leyburn, who estimated the number of free blacks in the 1780s at only 28,000. Leyburn, p. 16.

13. A planter's daughter wrote: "We are five whites . . . surrounded by over 200 slaves; from morning to night their faces stare at us. . . . Our talk is taken up with the health of slaves, the care they require, their schemes for revolt, and all our lives are bound up with these wretched beings." Heinl, p. 33.

14. Leyburn, p. 19.

15. Ibid, p. 20.

16. Heinl, p. 39. Later, in 1794, the colony sent a new delegation to Paris, composed of one white, one mulatto, and one black. The National Convention was thunderstruck by such apparent progress and voted the next day, February 4, 1794 to end slavery in all of France.

17. There are certain interesting parallels between the Haitian situation in the 1790s and that of South Africa following the end of British colonial rule. The immediate capability of the whites to control South Africa was clearly much stronger than in Haiti, but the end result—some degree of mutual accommodation—had to be the same.

18. Among several such groups spawned during the early months of the French Revolution, the "Amis des Noirs" or "Friends of the Blacks" was a prominent and well-financed group of liberals who worked to gain equality for the races.

19. Heinl, pp. 40–41.

20. Bryan Edwards, quoted in Davis, pp. 36–37.

21. Heinl, p. 67. The text of L'Ouverture's message reads: "I am Toussaint L'Ouverture; my name is perhaps known to you. I have undertaken to avenge your wrongs. It is my desire that liberty and equality shall reign in St. Domingue. I am striving to this end. Come and unite with us, brothers, and combat with us for the same cause." Also found in Davis, p. 49.

22. Heinl, pp. 63–64.

23. Heinl, p. 73.

24. André Rigaud was a veteran of the French volunteers in the War of American Independence who had also been commissioned a general in the French army in order to buy his military support. A "gen de couleur," or man of color, Rigaud initially fought against the French and against any effort to free the slaves in Haiti, which threatened the loss of relative mulatto power over the black-slave majority. The interests of the mixed-race inhabitants of Haiti were poised on the tightrope between whites' disdain of their lack of purity and blacks' resentment of their freedoms. Frequently, this meant that mulattos fought against both slave and rich white landowner.

25. George F. Tyson, Jr. (Ed.), *Toussaint L'Ouverture,* p. 17. Tyson gives American arms and vessels a central role in L'Ouverture's military successes in 1800.

26. Heinl, p. 86.

27. Heinl, p. 90.

28. Heinl, pp. 93–93.

29. Tyson, p. 18.

30. Ibid.

31. In L'Ouverture's defense, the economic situation would have challenged even the most practiced administrator.

32. Heinl, p. 99.

33. Heinl, p. 101.

CHAPTER 2

The Haitian Republic's Early Years

Haiti remains the second oldest democracy in the western hemisphere, yet it has seen more oppression and political instability in its history than freedom. This trend began with the succession of repressive regimes that followed the capture and death of Toussaint L'Ouverture. During this early period the nation quickly fell into damaging instability, internal strife, and economic distress, under the control of a succession of cruel local rulers. The first of these repressive leaders was perhaps the most damaging of all, for Jean-Jacques Dessalines took the centralized, military-based administration of Haiti's revered patriotic leader, Toussaint L'Ouverture, and ran it with greater vigor though unfortunately with none of his semi-enlightened attitudes.

The barbarity of Dessalines's 1804 campaign against the French exceeded even the bounds of Haiti's previous bloodthirsty reputation and razed any vestige of white ownership, inhabitation, or involvement in Haiti. As its ruler, he turned the state into an armed camp, marked by poverty and increasing dissension among the population, and consequently was ostracized by the world. Even sugar, indigo, and cotton, once staples of the colonial economy, were no longer exported.[1] Whatever limited economic viability Haiti had developed before, it plummeted under Dessalines's oppressive rule. For these and other reasons, Dessalines was eventually ambushed and fatally bayoneted in 1806. Dessalines gave Haiti little, but he at least kept the nation together in its misery. His murder brought about a power struggle between his would-be successors, Christophe and Pétion. Because Dessalines's rule had been so divisive, the competition between his political heirs resulted in a splitting of the nation between north and south, and between dark and light skin.

Christophe, never a slave, had been a general under L'Ouverture; he took control of the north of Haiti. Pétion, also a former soldier and then the President of the National Assembly, established himself in Port-au-Prince, supported by the educated elites. Over the following 14 years Haiti was two nations: an autocratic, if stable, northern state, and a more democratic but economically fractured southern state. This splitting of Haiti into two regions deepened the already acute divisions within the nation and left a strongly divisive legacy.

In the north, Christophe "combined the best qualities of Toussaint L'Ouverture and Dessalines with an enhanced appreciation of the nature and pressures of the international system. Dynamic, energetic, imaginative, and vain, Christophe consciously planned the economic development of his half of Haiti."[2] But he did so based on the servile labor of black agricultural workers and his own limitless ambition. His quest for power knew no bounds and took advantage of any opportunity. After naming himself king, Christophe continued his projects in order to glorify Haiti—projects that were marked by acceptance of white (normally British) advice and economic support. Over time, his kingdom prospered and returned to pre-L'Ouverture levels of exports and commercial productivity.[3] Overall, the north of the island was exceedingly prosperous, if growing ever more unforgiving of Christophe's personal ambition and love of luxury.

Unfortunately, in the south the more laissez-faire regime of Pétion did not progress as well economically as its northern neighbor. The southern state fell slowly into decay because its leader decided to reform the system of agriculture and subdivide the traditional large plantations into small plots. First, he reformed the tax system; then in 1809, for reasons unknown, he began to provide sections of government-owned land to his soldiers, so that all members of the army eventually received small plots. Certainly this effort brought some revenue to the state government, but it also destroyed the fabric of Haiti's plantation-based economy in the south. Smaller sections of the land were less productive than the plantations, even at first, and over time their owners lost any incentive to produce for export and turned their efforts to cottage farming. The end result was a happier population of small landowners, but a constantly downward-spiraling economy in southern Haiti.

Unlike vain Christophe, Pétion did not crown himself; he ruled in a democratic fashion. In fact, he was reelected in 1811 and again in 1815. Unfortunately, even liberal Pétion was unable to shield the democratic system against his personal temptations to usurp long-term rule, and he became president for life in 1816, thereby establishing an unfortunate precedent for many succeeding Haitian rulers to follow. Throughout the period he worked to install a mulatto-dominated system, favoring the educated and implementing the opposite of Christophe's heavy-handed rule.

Pétion died in 1818 and Christophe committed suicide in 1820 to avoid being captured alive as his oppressive regime was overthrown through an internal revolt. Thus the different national experiments of the successors to Toussaint L'Ouverture came to an end before either was completed. But short-lived as these experiments were, their legacies still influence Haiti. Tensions between autocracy and democracy, between affluent elites and the poor, between Port-au-Prince and the countryside—all nurtured during these early years—persisted as unresolved problems of Toussaint L'Ouverture's first Haitian revolution.

When Jean-Pierre Boyer, Pétion's secretary and successor, reunited the north and south in the 1820s, he hoped to combine the benefits of the regimes of his predecessors to produce a vibrant and contented Haiti. Boyer chose to rule using an unfortunate mixture of Christophe's military-supported, authoritarian style and Pétion's favoritism of the educated elites. He was also crippled by three inherited burdens to progress: Pétion's agricultural system of small freeholders; indebtedness to France; and the growing animosity between the darker- and lighter-skinned elements of Haitian society.[4] Even under Boyer's relatively effective rule, these problems overwhelmed Haitian hopes for real improvements in the quality of life.

In some ways, Haiti reached a national pinnacle of glory under Boyer, who marched outside the national borders in 1821 to conquer again the eastern half of the island—the newly independent Spanish Haiti. This united the island for the first time in the postcolonial era. Boyer also desired to end the animosity with France and the lingering perception that the French might return to reconquer the former colony. He therefore entered into negotiations with the French king, Charles X, only to find his initial offer of payment rejected, with Charles unilaterally deciding upon an indemnity 150 percent higher than Boyer's offer, to be paid in only five years! While Boyer dithered over the demand, the French king replied with an announcement of Haitian independence and the arrival of the entire French West Indian fleet, should Boyer reject his terms.

Boyer accepted and ruled independent Haiti for over 20 more years, until 1843, and even with internal tensions and debt, his administration still could have consolidated the best aspects of his predecessors' efforts. Unfortunately, his rule was plagued by instability, mostly due to his capricious attitude, fiscal irresponsibility, and his despotic approach towards governing. As the single source of power, he forced all echelons of government to defer to his wishes, and nothing could be managed without his intervention. The development of subordinate administrative structures was permanently arrested. Although he was revered by the people, his support

rested upon the acquiescence of the elite, the only temporary dampening of the class–color and sectional antagonisms, the apathy of the great mass of the apolitical peasants and, as he and his successors were pained to discover, the non-interference of the black-officered army. . . . Haiti was at peace but had little to show for it. The republic was backward, politically primitive and socially fragile.[5]

When his despotism finally exhausted the patience of the elites, Boyer's administration came to an end by musket and bayonet, setting a precedent for a future of change through military coups. The president abdicated, without defending Port-au-Prince, and left Haiti with his family and all the wealth he had accumulated while in power.

The legacy of these early rulers of Haiti was lasting. Many historians agree that, by the mid-nineteenth century, Haiti was shackled to a perilous future with little chance of overcoming its initial shortcomings.[6] Primarily, these shortcomings were economic. No small nation could have managed the debt that Boyer incurred while simultaneously rebuilding its economy by redistributing wealth. Yet economic woes could have been largely irrelevant for an island state cut off from most industrial advances during the century. The most serious problems for Haiti were cultural and administrative. If Haiti had remained poor, yet culturally united, it could have developed with some natural internal security and inner strength. If it could have developed a method of managing its internal affairs, Haiti might have slowly improved its economy and shared the moderate prosperity of many other Central American states. But with its internal divisions between dark and light, educated and military, north and south, the nation remained a breeding ground for internal conflict.[7] And, with no administrative cadre or enduring internal plan to guide it, Haiti was plagued by inefficiency, caprice, and even open theft by its leaders. Internal conflict and lack of administrative control was the sad beginning of Haiti in the nineteenth century.

HAITI DURING THE NINETEENTH CENTURY

The succession of leaders who ran Haiti after Boyer was removed from office was remarkable only for its negative impact on the country and its continuance of military despotism. Twenty-one rulers passed through the presidency in the 70 years between 1845 and 1915; most served 2 years or less.[8] Only one president of the period, Nissage Saget, served his full term, and his regime was "no less a military despotism than its predecessors."[9] With its other economic and cultural problems such instability at the top crippled Haiti, its negative effects compounding each of the weaknesses already present in Haitian society.

Economically, Haiti was burdened by both external and internal difficulties. Only France granted Haiti "most-favored" trade status, and even then, only with a 50 percent tariff on trade and a requirement that Haiti cede a controlling interest in its banking. Great Britain shared dominance with France and the United States of the Haitian foodstuff market, but all three were limited in their access to Haitian markets by Haitian objections to any white-owned or -operated business ventures in the country. Adding to this were other long-term problems, including dependence on a single major crop (coffee), inefficient marketing, an erratic tariff policy, debased currency, and an indifference to economic development on the part of the elite, educated minority who controlled the Haitian economy and had no real desire to improve the lot of the poor.[10]

Foreign relations outside of trade were also problematic. Haiti had developed such a poor international reputation that most nations considered it a pariah country. France treated Haiti as an errant stepchild. Although Holland, Prussia, Sweden, Denmark, and Great Britain recognized Haiti once France had settled the indemnity and acknowledged independence, few other nations did so. Spain had been angered by Haiti's annexation of Santo Domingo from 1821 to 1844 and refused to deal with the black republic. Even the United States refused to recognize its fellow "democracy" with full diplomatic relations until 1862, and then only due to American problems related to the Civil War.[11] Other South American nations were also reluctant to acknowledge Haiti. Brazil did so in 1865, but most others would hold off recognition until the middle of the next century. In short, Haiti was left to plod along without any help from other nations.

The United States did develop a military interest in Haiti's strategic position in the Caribbean during the post-Civil War period. President Grant angered Haiti by pressing for a base in Santo Domingo in 1870, and then attempted to secure the rights to Môle St. Nicholas as a naval base later in his administration. Haiti pursued this idea with the United States for over a decade, but internal unrest and duplicity between Haitian regimes eventually caused the negotiations to end in failure after a final deal fell through in 1891. After 1900 the United States turned its concern again to Haiti only when other nations postured to develop influence in its weak neighbor.

The late-nineteenth century saw Haitian politics continue down the path of successive coups until the nation became insolvent in 1910. Rather than see Haiti fall under the dominance of European powers, who then controlled the bulk of Haitian national assets, the American Secretary of State, Philander Knox, successfully demanded that the United States enter into with France and Germany a three-way customs receivership of Haiti's assets. If Haitian bases were not available to the United States, at least such economic control would ensure that Haiti's strategic position was not dominated by France—or worse, in 1910, a saber-rattling Germany.[12]

The same period witnessed a dramatic increase in U.S. involvement in Caribbean affairs. In 1898 the United States went to war over Cuba and kept the island under its control after forcing the Spanish out of the region. Five years later, American interest in the Panama Canal caused Americans to engineer the independence of Panama from Columbia; the following year, Theodore Roosevelt took control of the finances of the Dominican Republic as he enacted the Roosevelt corollary to the Monroe Doctrine.[13] In 1914, even liberal President Woodrow Wilson did not hesitate to land troops in Mexico when he felt that the Mexican government posed a security threat. Against this rising tide of U.S. involvement, and with the war in Europe beginning, Haiti's instability became increasingly problematic.

Meanwhile, Haiti changed presidents annually from 1910 to 1915. By 1915, the civil unrest was so bad that Woodrow Wilson felt he had to send the fleet to secure American lives and interests and add stability in the region.[14] The Haitian threat to the United States was exacerbated by a growing German commercial presence in Haiti and by very clear indications that the French were prepared to step in to preserve their national interests. Rather than permit a German foothold to grow, and to maintain the image that the United States was the sole arbiter of Caribbean affairs, Wilson ordered the U.S. fleet to head south towards Haiti. He did so just as another coup was being staged there.

The Haitian revolt of 1915 was typical of the pattern that had become the norm for overthrowing the government in Port-au-Prince. The Haitian president, then with only 2 months' experience in office, was named Joseph Davilmar Théodore; his rival was General Guillaume Sam, son of the former president from the period 1896–1902. Sam began his revolt in the north of the country in order to gather strength against the capital. First, he started by borrowing enough money (U.S. $30–50,000) to hire the bellicose Cacos[15] tribesmen as a private army. Then, after proclaiming himself "Chief of Executive Power," he marched with his mercenary army into Cap-Haitien in order to validate his movement as a "real revolution" in the eyes of the people. Once Cap-Haitien was taken, Sam drove his mercenary band south to lay siege to the town of St. Marc, midway to Port-au-Prince. If St. Marc could be taken, the government in power would most likely flee, since Port-au-Prince was habitually not defended. True to the pattern, when Sam's group took possession of St. Marc, Théodore gave up power and departed for personal exile with as much of the national treasure as he could carry. To many in Haiti, such actions were becoming a common part of political life. To President Wilson, the regional security situation had decayed beyond acceptable limits; he ordered in the U.S. Marines.

THE FIRST AMERICAN INTERVENTION

The internal political turmoil in Haiti that resulted in President Wilson's decision to land Marines in Haiti on July 28, 1915 was not new. As discussed earlier, it was simply one more in a long series of similar coups. The rationale behind Wilson's decision to intervene was related to the threats against the United States that could spring out of Haiti's instability.[16] It was a combination of regional and international factors, a complex mixture of Haitian internal and geopolitical problems and the international interest in the Caribbean by other nations that seemed to threaten U.S. dominance there, which drove the decision towards intervention. This complex causation is but one of several issues involved in this first U.S. incursion into Haitian territory that have relevance for a proper understanding of operation Uphold Democracy. The details of the 1915 operation thus warrant detailed discussion.

In this first twentieth-century incidence of American military intervention into Haitian affairs, the U.S. commander was 60-year-old Rear Admiral William B. Caperton, USN, newly named to command the Atlantic Fleet Cruiser Squadron. Caperton's squadron had only recently been assigned special duties as the military arm of U.S. diplomacy in the Caribbean to safeguard American interests and generally further the policies of Washington in the region. His operating area included not only Haiti but U.S. possessions stretching from Puerto Rico to the Panama Canal, including areas of special interest such as Nicaragua and Mexico and the U.S. protectorate in Cuba.

Caperton began a sailing tour of his region in January 1915 on board his flagship, the cruiser USS *Washington*. Entering the Port-au-Prince harbor in late January, Caperton observed the USS *Wheeling* at anchor and met with the U.S. ambassador, Arthur Bailly-Blanchard. Both the *Wheeling* and Ambassador Bailly-Blanchard had been quite busy for months. Marines had been landed in October of the previous year to try to stop Théodore from overthrowing his predecessor, President Zamor.[17] Then in December, the Marines had been landed again to take the gold reserves of the Haitian Bank to New York for "security" when Théodore's coup resulted in violence in Port-au-Prince. By the time Caperton arrived in the Haitian capital, it was President Théodore who was being attacked by another opponent, General Sam. Caperton asked for 650 additional Marines to secure the U.S. embassy as Sam marched south.

Sam arrived in St. Marc on February 5th and entered Port-au-Prince on the 25th. As was the custom, the winning general was formally elected president on March 4th. Things might have returned to normal following Sam's election except for two precautions taken by the new Haitian leader. First, Sam had all of his political rivals jailed; second, he ordered that they should all be killed in the event of another uprising. When in July the inevitable coup against Sam began and his presidential instructions were carried out, the city of Port-au-Prince rose up in violent objection to the killings, senselessly extreme even in Haitian eyes. As a result Sam was forced to flee to the protection of the French embassy. He was eventually taken by the mob, impaled, and then dismembered, before being publicly paraded in individual pieces through the capital city.[18] The mob continued to rampage through the city, invading even foreign legations and driving the diplomatic community to push Caperton to intervene as the only person capable of ensuring security for life and property in the city.

As Port-au-Prince was completely without order, Caperton, on his own initiative, stepped in to stabilize the city. He landed sailors and Marines in Port-au-Prince on July 28th[19]; met with the so-called "revolutionary council," a Haitian committee attempting to form a new government; disarmed everyone in the streets; and collected all weapons.[20] Over the following 10 days the Americans worked to calm the situation and help the interim government develop some return to normalcy; included in the prescription was gaining support from the press. Caperton received authorization from the State Department to act as he saw fit, while the admiral, concerned about the security of his troops ashore, requested reinforcements from nearby Guantanamo Bay, Cuba.[21]

Caperton appointed his chief of staff, Captain Edward L. Beach, USN, as his agent to coordinate with the revolutionary council, and Beach immediately took forceful steps to get the interim-ruling council to cooperate with the Americans. He also paid close attention to identifying a new Haitian leader who could work well with them. As no Haitian could muster an immediate majority within the national assembly and for once no local army was threatening the city, agreement to work under the security of the American force appeared to be advantageous to everyone. Caperton soon realized that delaying the decision for the next president permitted him to maneuver towards a pro-U.S. candidate. Over time, a solid working relationship developed, centered on Beach, Caperton, and Jacques Nicolas Léger, the former Haitian minister in Washington.

A major concern for Caperton was the attitude of the populace of Port-au-Prince. Faced with little real voice in affairs and clearly holding the potential to smother the American force, the people had to be won over. Overtures to the press had achieved some success, through a media campaign stressing that the Americans were only ashore for a short period to help with security during the government transition. Still, the large number of restless poor posed the greatest threat to the American force and Haitian internal stability, and Caperton chose a strategy oriented on food and work to help pacify the masses in the short term. He directed the Navy to donate food to the Catholic Church, which would feed the hungry as an intermediary, and even began a program of public-works construction projects to improve the general welfare and put the jobless to work.[22]

The arrival of a regiment of Marines in early August provided Caperton the manpower to secure the most crucial strategic locations in the Haitian capital. The cooperation of the commander of the presidential guard was obtained, and the Marines quickly moved on Casernes Dessalines and Fort National. Some influential Haitians were concerned that the growing control of the Americans was a threat to Haitian liberty, and Caperton himself understood that the signals he was sending were difficult to reconcile with a short stay. Yet he had to ensure security for his force, and only tight control could guarantee its safety.[23] Still, Caperton pressed for the election process to proceed publicly as a method of showing American impartiality and Haitian control, while asking Washington for additional guidance.[24] This said, he nonetheless had an undeniable interest in who might become the next president and worked to find a candidate both agreeable to the Haitians and amenable to U.S. control.

Eventually, Philippe Sudre Dartiguenave, President of the Haitian Senate, was approached by Captain Beach and agreed to become a candidate. Dartiguenave was a modest man and a realist; he understood that the U.S. presence in Haiti was not likely to be short-lived and that the next president must accept American involvement in Haitian affairs. Caperton had finally received detailed guidance from Washington, and the admiral made it clear that the United States expected to exercise financial control over Haiti, including control of Haitian customs. Even so, Dartiguenave agreed to run and eventually was elected on August 11th.

Following the election, Caperton received additional guidance from the State Department in the form of a treaty that outlined added U.S. controls over Haiti, including management of the national security force. Even though the new president and his legislature were outraged by the document, Caperton forced its acceptance through martial law, threats, and even bribes. In the fall of 1915 Haiti ratified the treaty, which was to remain in effect for 10 years and was renewable after expiration by either party for a second 10 years. In effect, the United States wanted and obtained a Haitian protectorate.[25]

Unfortunately, the American domination of Port-au-Prince was not quite sufficient to control the entire country and armed opposition broke out in several areas, most notably in the north, where the Cacos began a small-scale war against the Marines. In order to disarm the insurrectionists, Caperton offered to buy Caco rifles with dollars and the Marines eventually defeated the resistance movement. By autumn, Caperton had met all desired initial objectives and moved on to the creation of a new Haitian national security force, the gendarmerie, under control of the Marines. Major Smedley D. Butler, USMC, was named the gendarmerie commander with the rank of major general, while other Marine officers and non-commissioned officers assumed the remaining officer positions. Troops of the gendarmerie were recruited from the Haitian masses and were well paid by local standards; soon its size and power made it the dominant force in Haiti: "The gendarmerie officers took on many local functions: judge, paymaster, school superintendent, tax collector and police chief. Their authority was unchallenged, overriding that of local officials."[26]

The first U.S. military intervention in Haiti was skillfully and aggressively managed by Caperton, acting with minimal direction from Washington. The admiral managed to stabilize and establish a basis for security in a nation of over 2 million inhabitants using only a military force of little more than 2,000 U.S. Marines, and he did so in less than a year. He instituted an effective liaison with the Haitian government, developed a press-management scheme, used humanitarian means to gain popular support, added improvements to the Haitian infrastructure, and suppressed a revolt using both the carrot, in the form of dollars for guns, and the stick—armed Marines. In short, Caperton executed a very effective campaign while incurring minimal risk to either side. All of these techniques would also be used during operation Uphold Democracy, primarily because the fundamentals of Haitian society remain rooted in many of the same problems. But Caperton's job in 1915 was made immensely more easy because he endured little public scrutiny, had a more limited mission, and held relatively much more power over the key elements of Haitian society than would the commanders who restored President Aristide. The campaign of 1994 would be much more complex because of much greater international attention, the heavy presence of curious media using instantaneous visual communications, and the mission requirement to reestablish long-term stability in Haiti.

The one unfortunate aspect of the 1915 intervention concerned the operation's end objective. Caperton put a cap on the turmoil in Port-au-Prince by installing a puppet government and his own security force. This solution was not democratic and not acceptable to the Haitians; but the diplomatic policies of the United States in 1915 were much less concerned with Haitian desires than with the possible presence of German forces in the Caribbean. Be that as it may, the real mistake made by the United States in 1915 was the decision to remain militarily in Haiti past the point of Caperton's initial operational charter to restore order. The establishment of the gendarmerie and the initial customs receivership in Haiti was justifiable, given the eventual plan to turn over such capabilities to the Haitians once security in the region had been restored. Unfortunately, with the examples of Cuba and the Philippines recently in the American mind, U.S. involvement in Haiti took on a long-term focus, one that had detrimental effects for both sides.

NOTES

1. Robert I. Rotberg, *Haiti: The Politics of Squalor,* p. 56.

2. Rotberg, p. 58.

3. Rotberg quotes a London book written by William Woodis Harvey, who noted: "So striking, in short, was their improvement, that a foreigner would have found it difficult to persuade himself, on his first entering the place, that the people whom he now beheld so submissive, industrious, and contented, were the same who, a few years before,

had escaped from the shackles of slavery." William Woodis Harvey, *Sketches of Hayti: From the Expulsion of the French to the Death of Christophe* (London, 1827).

4. Boyer agreed to pay an indemnity to France for losses during the war of Haitian independence.

5. Rotberg, pp. 76–77.

6. This issue is best described in James G. Leyburn, *The Haitian People,* pp. 74–98, but Robert Debs Heinl and Nancy Gordon Heinl, *Written in Blood: The Story of the Haitian People, 1492–1971,* pp. 179–180, Selden Rodman, *Haiti: The Black Republic,* pp. 18–20, and Rotberg, pp. 62–64, agree that the Dessalines–Christophe–Pétion era left an indelible mark on Haiti.

7. An excellent treatment of the crystallization of the color lines in Haiti and its related impact on society is included in Leyburn's chapter, "The Drawing of Caste Lines," pp. 79–88.

8. See the list of Haiti's rulers in Appendix A.

9. Rotberg, p. 91.

10. See Leyburn, pp. 256–261.

11. Perhaps due to his domestic problems, President Lincoln made additional efforts to support Haiti economically in that year; unfortunately, these too failed to develop any real advances.

12. As early as 1912 the Wilson administration became worried that Germany was working through commercial surrogates in order to secure naval coaling facilities in Haiti. There was even a rumor at the time that Germany had a plan to make Haiti a protectorate. Heinl, p. 353.

13. Theodore Roosevelt's 1904 corollary to the Monroe Doctrine held that problems in Latin America might result in U.S. intervention in order to prevent European involvement in "American" problems. This explanation was also used by Presidents Taft and Wilson to justify U.S. actions in the Caribbean.

14. There was also a very clear financial and personal interest in Haiti, personified by Roger Farnham, "emissary of the National City Bank of New York and friend of important insiders in the State Department. By 1915, the National City Bank controlled the National Bank of Haiti." David Healy, "The U.S. Occupation of Haiti" in Georges A. Fauriol (Ed.), *Haitian Frustrations: Dilemmas for U.S. Policy,* pp. 36–45.

15. The Cacos were independent tribesmen from the north of Haiti known for their fighting skills. The origins of the people and their name are obscure, but their bellicose temperament and influence on Haitian politics grew over time to assume great proportions.

16. This entire incident is covered expertly in David Healy's book, *Gunboat Diplomacy in the Wilson Era: The U.S. Navy in Haiti, 1915–1916.*

17. Healy, *Gunboat Diplomacy,* pp. 31–33.

18. Healy, *Gunboat Diplomacy,* pp. 53–58.

19. See Appendix B for Caperton's operations order to his force.

20. See Healy, *Gunboat Diplomacy,* pp. 61–66.

21. The Americans were attempting to control a city of 60,000 with about 400 troops. Caperton was particularly worried about a possible attack from Cap-Haitien once the northern city learned of the U.S. intervention. Healy, *Gunboat Diplomacy,* p. 67.

22. The Secretary of the Navy, Josephus Daniels, took a dim view of this use of Navy funds to help the Haitians and eventually forced a curtailment in Caperton's plans. Healy, *Gunboat Diplomacy,* pp. 74–75.

23. Eventually, Caperton's Marines would disband the Haitian army forces and send all Cacos back to the hills to ensure security in the capital. Healy, *Gunboat Diplomacy,* pp. 92–93.

24. Healy, *Gunboat Diplomacy,* pp. 79–80.

25. Healy, "The U.S. Occupation of Haiti" in *Haitian Frustrations: Dilemmas for U.S. Policy,* p. 39.

26. Ibid, p. 40.

CHAPTER 3

The Garde d'Haiti and the Duvaliers

Thus, since 1915, but more particularly since 1922, Haiti has been a peculiarly intimate and quasi-dependent relation with the United States and the country has constituted in fact a unique laboratory for social, economic, political and administrative paternalism.[1]

Arthur C. Millspaugh
General Receiver of Haiti, 1927–1929

To ensure stability, the Marine force landed by Caperton stayed in Haiti until 1934. At first, the U.S. military provided only police functions; as time passed, however, its presence and activity supplanted more and more national capability, and in time, the United States found it hard to extract its forces. Over the years the Marines created an image so strong in Haiti that it remains nearly mythical to this day.[2] This temptation to become embroiled on a long-term basis in the affairs of the host nation is the ultimate challenge of any foreign-assistance effort. An overview of this period of American occupation provides an important backdrop for the Uphold Democracy operation because it sets the scene for Haitian expectations of American activities within the country and illustrates the fine line that must be walked to aid, but not replace, host capability.[3]

Admiral Caperton left Haiti in 1916, having completed his assigned objectives and established an interim American protectorate. Haitian President Dartiguenave was left with the difficult task of balancing American desires in Haiti with the strong national pride of his constituents. Unfortunately, his efforts were not well supported by the national legislature, which took a dim view of the American influence. Whenever possible, Dartiguenave ignored its objections; in fact, he even dissolved the Haitian legislature when faced with its refusal to impose a new constitution. But he could never erase the pain of some Haitian parliamentarians who lamented that Haitians were not in full control of their own affairs.

One major accomplishment of the United States was the formation of the national police force, or gendarmerie, later named the Garde d'Haiti.[4] Internal government opposition aside, the people of Haiti initially did not oppose the efforts of the gendarmerie; security, even at that price, was a healthy thing in Haiti. However, as time passed and the Marines began to make American value judgments about what Haiti needed, relations began to decay. Dissent naturally increased as the number of civic-improvement projects requiring Haitian labor rose and the presence of the Marines became more evident outside the capital. A turning point in this tenuous relationship between the Marines and the Haitian people was the discovery of an old Haitian law permitting forced labor for the development of roads. This work law, or "corvée" (the ancient name of the same law in France, cast out by the French Revolution) was instituted to enlist Haitian labor to improve the national infrastructure and had legal grounds. But its use soon generated fears of a return to slavery, as the gendarmerie pressed hundreds of citizens into road gangs to work on improvements throughout the country. The Americans, without the benefit of a French-based legal culture, not fully understanding the impact of white-dominated work gangs in black Haiti and without much concern about the traditional bases of power within the country soon found themselves confronted by a growing number of acts of opposition.

In the fall of 1918 Charlemagne Péralte, leader of the Cacos, began a true uprising against the national government, which focused on the Marines of the gendarmerie. This was the only real instance of actual combat during the intervention, but it focused the attention of Haitians and Americans on the unrest that was growing in the countryside. Péralte died in 1919, and with him passed the essence of the revolt's leadership. The conflict ended within the year, having produced losses of 3,000 Haitians and 16 Marines. But, more importantly, it resulted in the first real review of U.S. policy in Haiti.

By 1919 even Dartiguenave was weary of American heavy-handedness, and he soon became openly hostile to American initiatives. With the U.S. election of 1920 approaching, and postwar anti-imperialism beginning to peak within the U.S. Congress, the opposition of Dartiguenave to American activity and the recent Cacos combat in the north of Haiti generated a call for reform within the U.S. federal legislature. A 1921 Senate investigation demanded several specific improvements, including the appointment of a new U.S. high commissioner to oversee actions in Haiti. Apparently, the Senate's assumption was that a neutral administrator might develop a more even-handed approach in the country.

Interestingly, a Marine, Major General John H. Russell, was selected for the new post and served as High Commissioner from 1922 until 1930. Some viewed his assignment with concern, fearing that another Marine might not be capable of forming an appropriate partnership with Haitian leaders. Still, the assignment of the Marine general to the post did result in positive changes because Russell was able to form a trustworthy bond between the American forces and the government of Haiti. With Russell's enlightened perspective, a new chapter in the ongoing relationship between the two nations began. Also important to this renewed bond was the change of Haitian presidents. An embittered Dartiguenave left office in 1922 and was replaced by Louis Borno. Borno and Russell worked well together and soon formed a joint directory.

Overall, the reforms generated by Borno and Russell were well intentioned, but even they failed to help the development of the Haitian economy and brought in no new investment. Without an influx of money no gain in the lot of the local people could be realized. On the negative side, these reforms were also the cause of a few uninformed or mistaken actions that resulted in added discontent, particularly among the Haitian educated elites. For example, American racial biases, formed along U.S. color lines of the 1920s, reinforced Haitian antagonism, and an ill-conceived attempt to outlaw voodoo alienated the huge mass of Haitian society, which viewed the practice as a cultural heritage. The Russell–Borno team was also plagued by a traditional reformer's bane: unfulfilled expectations. As can frequently occur in societies working to reform and improve, sufficient advances were made in improving the lot of only a few. This small benefit served to tempt the population to press for more change, which was more difficult to achieve. Disappointment and blame replaced hope, thus creating a relative feeling of deprivation and an atmosphere of discontent leading to increased criticism of the government.

However, insufficient progress was not the only source of this discontent. The real problem was the clear dominance of Russell and the United States in Haitian affairs. Borno made no apologies for his acquiescence, alluding to the Christian responsibilities of one nation to another.[5] In reality, Borno was clearly out of touch with the feelings of many Haitians, and a growing patriotic movement was fueled by resentment of his weakness. A Haitian independence effort championed by the elites was announced in the press in 1922. This effort, along with other movements, grew in strength and became increasingly active, showing open opposition to Borno over a period of several years. One of the more influential writers of the patriotic, nationalist prose produced by the movement was journalist Duval Duvalier, the father of François Duvalier, the future president of Haiti.

The year 1929 represented a crucial turning point, as Borno decided to seek another term. He had canceled scheduled legislative elections in 1924 and 1926, preferring to rule without the growing opposition being presented in the legislature. The mid-1920s had also witnessed an economic downturn in Haiti, due largely to the collapse of the world coffee market, which was Haiti's major source of income. Even after a three-fold growth in American investments over nearly 15 years, Haiti had failed to make real economic improvements.[6] Finally, in 1929, a student strike over government funding of education set off a general anti-American and anti-Borno response by the citizenry. Russell convinced Borno not to run again, but the riots continued and martial law was decreed. Reinforcements from the United States were required to restore order. On December 6, an attack on a Marine detachment in Les Cayes caused the Marines to return fire in self-defense, which resulted in the killing of twelve Haitians and the injuring of twenty-three others. Once again Haiti erupted in protest. The "Cayes Massacre" was well covered in the U.S. press and had a decisive effect on U.S. policy in Washington. On December 7th, President Hoover asked for a commission to determine how the United States should leave Haiti.

After Sténio Vincent was elected to succeed Borno, the Forbes Commission sent to Haiti by President Hoover opened negotiations concerning the withdrawal of American troops. Dana G. Munro replaced Russell as the new American minister to Haiti. It was Munro who supervised the rapid exit of American forces after newly elected Franklin Delano Roosevelt approved an agreement in 1932 that permitted U.S. control over Haitian finances as long as the Marines departed by 1934.[7] The Haitian Legislature refused even this proposal, but Vincent implemented it by executive action in 1933. In truth, the tide had turned against continued American intervention worldwide, and the effects of the Nicaraguan insurgency led by Augusto César Sandino and his "Sandinistas" had reduced U.S. tolerance for conflict in the region. Clearly, it was time to leave.

A review of the U.S. occupation's results discloses the fundamental flaw of failing to focus on supporting long-term development in Haiti without replacing its national capability. Internal concerns and societal objectives were ignored in favor of more evident and achievable external improvements. While roadways, bridges, telephone systems, hospitals, and schools were improved, little investment in the quality of life or improvement in the efficacy of education was made. Maintenance of law and order took priority over economic growth, and little support for improvements was garnered in the countryside, where the majority of Haitians worked and lived. With few exceptions, no attempt was made to involve Haitians in the process of improvement and reform. Once the Americans left, "the occupation's roads, hospitals and public works crumbled from neglect, while the economic growth foreseen in 1915 never occurred. The vast majority of ordinary Haitians continued to live in rural poverty."[8] Only the country's internal politics had changed with the controlling influence of an American security force. Revolts grew less frequent and centralized authority grew more secure, but this improvement really endured only as long as the American superstructure remained. Once the Marines left the Haitian security vacuum was slowly refilled with the domineering guard forces similar to those managed by former dictators, with one key difference: before 1915, opposition leaders had no organized, loyal, national army to fear as they marched on Port-au-Prince. The singular exception to the U.S. occupation's lack of long-term impact may in fact have been the professionalization of the Haitian Army, which emerged after the 1940s as the dominant power-broker in Haitian society. Its role was evident in the 1940s and 1950s, and although suppressed under the Duvaliers, it returned to dominance from 1986 through 1994.[9] It is a mistake to believe that U.S. Marines expanded the cultural influence of the military in Haiti, but they certainly improved ts efficiency by establishing enduring procedures and traditions within the force.

United States policy must also accept some blame for the stagnation of democratic development in Haiti during the occupation. Current U.S. nation-assistance efforts recognize the importance of involving a host-nation population in its own political development. Particularly where democratic models are already present, significant attention is paid to maintaining and strengthening their use. When no history of democracy exists, the effort is made to reveal its advantages.[10] In the 1920s, however, the importance of these actions was not well understood. Supporting democracy was a process separate from and overarching the management of the security environment. Failure to support its development in the 1920s was an antecedent for its rebuilding in the 1990s.

If the United States had devoted more effort to the democratic development of Haiti in the 1920s, the considerable challenges of conducting free and fair elections and administering government programs in the 1990s might have been eased. In fact, with a stronger democratic foundation in Haiti, the transition to a nonauthoritarian society might have been more successful when the Duvalier era ended in the 1980s, and precluded the resumption of military control in 1991. Certainly any progress the United States could have made in the maturation of an independent judiciary and the strengthening of Haitian administrative processes would have lessened the dominance of authoritarian responses when difficulties arose after 1940.

On the other hand, little use of the democratic model while under American control offered Haiti little evidence of its worth or incentive for the development of Haitian democratic institutions. Where an even-handed approach, recognizing what was best in the Haitian democratic system and fostering improvements that were in consonance with Haitian culture, might have improved the lot of the average Haitian, the techniques used by Americans during this period suffered from attempts to transplant American processes and therefore had little longevity. It should surprise few that since 1934 the most dominant event in Haiti's democratic political history has been the rule of François Duvalier, *not* the growth of democratic values. The United States simply failed to help prepare Haitians for self-rule following the occupation.[11]

THE DRIFT TOWARDS AUTHORITARIANISM

By the time the United States had extricated itself from its 19-year intervention in Haiti, the world's focus turned away from the Caribbean to confront the issues of the World War II. Relations between Haiti and the United States during the 1940s and 1950s were limited, and the Haitians were left alone to rediscover their political system. What they found was often disappointing, sometimes little better than the occupation and, in some respects, much worse. As had been the case many times in Haitian history, the freedom offered by the departure of the Americans in 1934 glimmered brightly for a while, but was soon replaced by more threatening circumstances.

Tuesday, August 21, 1934, the departure date of the Americans, was set as a second national day of independence in Haiti. Champagne balls, fireworks, and a host of personal celebrations marked the day. Port-au-Prince throbbed with "tens of thousands of humble Haitians who had been told they were free again; free of exactly what may not have been very clear to some—but 'libre' is the most intoxicating word in the Haitian vocabulary."[12] The country, upon the departure of the

American troops, was clean, with a working economy, a functioning administration, and even apolitical security forces. Just as important, the people were optimistic about the future. It seemed that the goals of independence in 1804 were finally achievable, if only the prosperity and security could be maintained.

Unfortunately, President Vincent was of the old school of Haitian leadership; he set about immediately following the departure of the Marines to ensure his long-term hold on the presidency. First, he determined to rid himself of the legislature; then using the national plebiscite tool made famous by Napoleon in France and earlier in Haiti by Dartiguenave, he would develop a new constitution and a new extension to his term of office. He took control of the national bank by plebiscite in February 1935, gained the ability to govern by decree in a second plebiscite in June, sponsored petitions supporting his extension in office (like his predecessor Dessalines), and finally obtained a new term of office beginning in May 1936. It was one of the few well-executed political plans in Haitian history, and consequently set the national democratic process back by years.

To add to the nation's woes, in the late 1930s the Great Depression began to take its toll on Haiti. Harvests in 1935 were bad and floods damaged the country during the same year. Haiti also began to run out of money after the American-management system and the investment it attracted was cast out, to be replaced by a worldwide search for short-term loans. To put a cap on his whole management technique, Vincent censored the mail, subordinated the legislature and supreme court, formed a secret police force, and curtailed freedom of the press to the point that few knew of the nation's slide back into the old ways of doing business. Aping the authoritarian trend of the day, Vincent finally decreed that Haitians were too immature for democracy and declared himself their dictator. In the words of the American minister to Haiti, Ferdinand L. Mayer, "seven years after disoccupation they have succeeded in reestablishing as venal a public administration as one could find anywhere."[13]

THE DUVALIER ERA

But even Vincent could not conceal the nation's regression for long. He ruled until he pressed for another 5-year term as president in 1941. Then the United States refused to stand by as another dictator pushed for additional power so close to its border in a year of tremendous international tension. Vincent was pressured to retire and his successor became Elie Lescot, who was a former Haitian ambassador to the United States, a virulent opponent of voodoo, and a puppet of the Dominican Republic's outspoken leader, Rafael Trujillo. Lescot's administration was not only corrupt but also obviously inept and increasingly insulting to black Haitians, who were systematically excluded from positions of power. The Lescot presidency added fuel to the négritude campaign, which was designed to place power more fully in the hands of the black Haitian majority.[14] In 1946 the campaign reached a peak, generating a student-led general strike, and resulting finally in the overthrow of Lescot. Lescot was replaced by another black, Dumarias Estimé, who was overthrown 4 years later. Both Vincent and Lescot were considered "anti black and disdainful of the peasant components of the national culture."[15] Estimé was well educated and made a concerted effort to increase access to prominent positions for more Haitian blacks, including François Duvalier. Unfortunately, Estimé too fell victim to the power of his office, and was ousted after attempting to alter the constitution to permit his own reelection. This chaotic period spawned the political growth of Duvalier.

Born in Port-au-Prince in 1907, Duvalier was the son of a black journalist, teacher, and minor government official, who was himself a leading member of the intellectual opposition to the Haitian government in the 1940s. Duvalier grew up as a member of Haiti's tiny middle class and attended secondary school at the Lycée Pétion, where he was taught by Estimé, one of the primary creators of the négritude movement.[16] Thanks to education funds provided during the American occupation, Duvalier passed from the lycée to receive medical training at the University of Haiti in Port-au-Prince.[17] During his time as a student in the capital, Duvalier circulated among the more radical and anti-American student groups feeding on the departure of the Americans. Haiti experienced great turmoil during the 1930s, incited by the repressive administration of Sténio Vincent, the departure of the Americans, and the meddling of Trujillo. During this period, Duvalier graduated from medical school, began his internship, but surprisingly focused most of his time on writing in support of négritude issues; he never developed a successful medical practice.

Duvalier then worked for the U.S. Public Health Service in Haiti in the 1940s, furthered his medical studies at the University of Michigan in 1944, and entered political life during the administration of his sponsor, Estimé, as head of the local public-health service. Duvalier had gained prominence as a member of several medical teams that brought penicillin, the cure for yaws,[18] to Haiti in 1943; this was the origin of the mythical "Papa Doc."[19] In reality, his contribution to the vaccination program was relatively small, but the program was an important factor in Duvalier's development. It was the first time he had really been exposed to the raw face of life in the Haitian countryside. He continued to focus his writing on traditional elements in Haitian culture, including voodoo and mysticism, and on the importance of Black-African pride.

Vincent's replacement in 1941 by Lescot only added fuel to the négritude campaign, generating the student-led general strike, which finally resulted in the seizure of power by a military junta, headed by Colonel (later General) Paul Magloire. The junta's search for a successor to Lescot proved difficult, but eventually resulted in the selection of Duvalier's old teacher, Dumarais Estimé. The Estimé presidency was a huge step forward in the progress of blacks in Haiti. Estimé's slogan was "a black man in power," and in his administration, government positions were opened up to blacks for the first time in years; one of these positions, Minister of Public Health and Labor, went to Duvalier. Unfortunately for all, many in Estimé's administration were as corrupt as their predecessors had been, and in 1950, when Estimé also pushed to extend his rule 2 years past his elected term, Magloire, on May 10th, 1950, led the second military coup in 4 years to topple the Haitian government. The army of Haiti had finally given up on the democratic transfer of power.

Magloire and most of his troops had been trained by the U.S. Marines during the occupation and they returned a modicum of security to the country. Magloire actually ran for the presidency in October 1950, under a system permitting the people to vote directly for candidates. But, instead of leaving the selection of the president to the legislature, Magloire and his fellow junta army officers dissolved it and directed another round of national elections for a new legislature and president. Although suffrage nominally included all Haitians over the age of 25 in the new election, there was no doubt about it's real outcome. Magloire ran for the presidency with the church, the army, the elite, and the American embassy behind him.[20] Obtaining 99 percent of the vote in the army-monitored election, he ruled with a heavy yet bountiful hand. Magloire's term of office was also marked by the return of official favoritism toward mulattos. Although the president was technically black, he was simply managed by the lighter-skinned elite, as many of his black predecessors had been. The rising tide of négritude pride and the recent access gained by the black majority would make Magloire's term the last instance for many years of light-skinned control through a black Haitian president.[21]

Magloire was bright enough to manage the best economic growth in Haiti in a century. He also sponsored increased aid from the United States and international agencies, construction and medical projects, and modernization of many Haitian institutions. Most of these improvements were made possible through the growing worldwide boom economy of the early 1950s. During 1954 the national bank of Haiti even reported a surplus of revenue![22] His administration was so secure in its prosperity that Magloire could travel outside the country on state visits, and even addressed a joint session of the U.S. Congress in January 1955. Unfortunately, rising profits also added to the temptations of power and the regime increasingly turned towards profiteering and restricting the liberties of the population. By 1956 the Magloire regime had grown too corrupt for its powerbase and the time was ripe for change, again, in Haiti. Returning to the pattern begun long before by Pétion, Magloire attempted to succeed himself, but large-scale demonstrations that included bombing incidents aimed at the government forced him to react at the end of the year. He clamped down, adroitly returned to uniform, and effectively declared martial law as his own interim successor.[23] Even that bald trick could not stem the growing tide against him. Magloire, too, failed to manage the most difficult feat of Haitian leadership: the transition of power. After martial law failed to stem the opposition, he fled the country for a quiet life in New York City. As Magloire moved to comfortable exile, the name of François Duvalier became increasingly common to the Haitian people.

Nine strange months of intermittent regimes and decaying Haitian economics followed Magloire's departure. Even the army was split into factions, and Haiti took on the aura of the pitiful years immediately preceding the 1915 invasion. This was another opportunity whereby the Haitian people could have pushed to complete a democratic revolution, if only they could have found a leader with the right agenda. Out of this stalled prosperity and internal confusion, François Duvalier emerged as the most popular candidate in a desperate, and hotly contested, national election in 1957 against Lois Déjoie, a mulatto industrialist.

Duvalier was a keen student of Haitian culture and supporter of the négritude movement. He was a prominent though less-talented member of the intellectually gifted Groupe des Griots. The Groupe des Griots was one of the most influential négritude groups in Haiti, well known for its popular journal praising African and Haitian culture. This association with culturally minded intellectuals fostered Duvalier's reputation as a wise thinker. He did publish several articles and three books, including *The Problem of Classes Throughout Haitian History,* which, significantly for the future, praised the black-African tradition and alerted Haitians that the return of blacks to real power was imminent.[24] He was strongly influenced by the authoritarian leaders of Haiti's past, notably Jean-Jacques Dessalines. This should have served as a warning of events to come.

Duvalier's entry into office during October 1957 should also have inspired hope. As a doctor, writer, and product of the middle class, he could have shown the moderation Haiti needed; instead, he quickly created one of the most repressive and tyrannical regimes of history. He began the process of eliminating any potential opposition to his rule within months of taking office. He sacked the head of the army in March 1958, shut down the opposition press, and had a state of siege declared by the legislature in May. After personally putting down an attempted coup in July, during which the army had proven itself ineffective, he created a militia as a security counterweight. Militia membership was determined only by loyalty to Duvalier.

He had rapidly developed a great fear of the army after the fall of his mentor Estimé and clearly trusted neither the mulattos nor the rich. Distant from all traditional Haitian power centers, Duvalier created his own powerbase founded upon personal loyalty to himself and hatred of other competing factions. In December 1958 Duvalier sacked his second army chief and created a new Presidential Guard that was billeted in the palace for his personal protection. He soon formed the militia and Presidential Guard into his private security force. By 1961 this force, named the Volontaires de la Securité Nationale (volunteers for national security, or VSN), was larger than the Haitian army and its members had earned the sobriquet, "Tonton Macoutes."[25] To the Macoutes he gave complete authority, and to the rule of law he gave no credence.

In October 1959 Duvalier had ousted six opposition senators, effectively silencing the legislature. He then turned his attention to other centers of power within the country, including the labor unions, the diplomatic corps, and the universities. "By 1960 Haiti's weak unions were paralyzed or moribund; by 1963 they were dead."[26] To silence foreign opposition within Haiti, Duvalier cast out more foreign chiefs of mission than had been expelled during all previous Haitian history, including those from the United States and the United Nations.[27] In September 1960 Duvalier had outspoken student leaders arrested. When other students boycotted classes in support of their leaders, Duvalier outlawed all youth groups. Eventually he held parents accountable for student actions, moved the VSN into the schools, and controlled access to the universities, only offering entries to the offspring of his supporters.

The 14-year rule of François "Papa Doc" Duvalier was characterized by increasingly arbitrary and absolute rule; as the aging president grew more infirm his policies worsened and Haiti descended to depths unknown since the civil war of Duvalier's idol, Dessalines. The only institutions remaining to oppose him were the Church and the Haitian army. The army, renamed the Forces Armées d'Haiti (armed forces of Haiti, or FAd'H) in 1958, had already been allowed to deteriorate to its lowest proficiency since 1915. Duvalier ousted all the officers who had been trained under the U.S. Marine occupation in December 1958, sacked its chief for the third time, and closed the military academy in 1961. By that time the VSN was larger than the FAd'H and had more influence. By the time the Haitian President fired his fourth army chief in 1962, the FAd'H no longer represented a force to be feared, at least as long as Duvalier was in power.

During the same period (from 1959 to 1963), priests fared no better than did the senior army officers. Duvalier began their expulsions in August 1959, coincident with a massacre and the arrest of many Catholic citizens during mass. He banished the Archbishop of Haiti in 1960, and his successor in January 1961. In the resulting backlash Duvalier was excommunicated—small punishment for a man well known as a voodoo priest. Duvalier eventually purged the entire Jesuit order from Haiti in February 1964, effectively ending the influence of the Catholic Church in the country and thereby permitting him to recast the Haitian clergy in his own image.[28] "If any regime may be said to have been fundamentally corrupt, it would be the Duvalier regime."[29]

With opposition ended, he needed only to make his rule appear legitimate to the outside world. In April 1961 Duvalier announced new elections for the National Assembly, and by the end of the month showed data to support the choice of 1,320,748 citizens for a new Duvalierist assembly and his own reelection for a second 6-year term. No votes in opposition were counted.[30] In 1964 Duvalier changed the constitution to permit himself to achieve the goal of so many Haitian heads of state before him: a life presidency.

One of Duvalier's methods of keeping control in Haiti was his very clear success in reducing the influence of nonblacks. He determined who was to have any form of power or money in Haiti, and he worked effectively to reduce the influence of the military, the Church, intellectuals, and even union leaders, but most of all mulattos. One manifestation of his intent and control was that Duvalier even changed the colors of the Haitian flag, replacing democratic blue with Duvalier black. Papa Doc's clear racism was both a reflection of the level of social disharmony in Haiti and an indicator of the ruthlessness simmering just beneath the surface of Haitian "democracy." "Estimates of the number of Haitians killed for their opposition or alleged opposition to Duvalier range from 30,000 to 60,000."[31] Duvalier's attitude concerning the governance of Haiti was well presented in one of his early proclamations, issued on August 5, 1958:

I have mastered the country. I have mastered power. I am the new Haiti. To seek to destroy me is to seek to destroy Haiti herself. . . . No earthly power can prevent me from accomplishing my historic mission because it is God and destiny who have chosen me.[32]

Some may ask why the barbarism of the Duvalier regime was tolerated by the United States, if the belief was held that democratic forms of government were the only ones to be nurtured in the Caribbean. The facts are that the United States tolerated Duvalier, and even came to support him economically, because at the time global communism was deemed to be a greater threat; Duvalier was cruel, but he was an elected leader who opposed communists. During the same period, the United States largely turned a blind eye to similar dictatorial actions by Fulgencio Batista in Cuba, Trujillo in the Dominican Republic, and the Somozas in Nicaragua. In point of fact, it was the regime of Fidel Castro in Cuba that so preoccupied the United States in the early and middle 1960s as to permit Duvalier every opportunity to expand his control over every aspect of Haitian life.

Politically astute, Duvalier lost no time in recognizing the Castro regime in 1959. In an effort to prevent any collaboration between the two strongmen and buy Duvalier's support, the United States increased economic and technical assistance to Haiti and sent the first American military-training mission since 1934 to Port-au-Prince. By 1961 U.S. aid accounted for nearly half of the Haitian government's operating budget.[33] Duvalier and the United States then played a cat-and-mouse game over U.S. aid and Haitian support of Cuba. Concerned that Haiti might deteriorate further or that Duvalier would actively support Castro, the American government first reduced aid during 1962, and then increased it again when Duvalier pawned his vote on Cuban membership in the Organization of American States. In October 1962 Duvalier offered the U.S. Navy access to his ports during the Cuban missile crisis, which clearly improved U.S. relations with Haiti.[34]

By 1965, when President Lyndon Johnson sent troops to the Dominican Republic to prevent communist gains in that country, Duvalier's excesses were also under greater scrutiny. Several historians have demonstrated that the Johnson Administration attempted a wide range of initiatives designed to bring about change in Haiti, but growing U.S. involvement in Southeast Asia soon turned U.S. attention away from Duvalier's crimes.[35] The arrival on the scene of the more forcefully engaged Nixon Administration saw Duvalier tone down his rhetoric and U.S. aid increase dramatically, but the killing and oppression did not stop.

Duvalier dominated Haiti through his program of terror, killing, and manipulation until his death in 1971, afterwhich his policies were continued, at least in part, by his son Jean-Claude. Many were concerned that the transition of power upon the elder Duvalier's death would be marked by extreme violence, as had been the case many times before throughout Haitian history. But few realized the extent of François Duvalier's dominance of Haitian life; he had effectively rid Haiti of any organized opposition. The succession of his son Jean-Claude was preferred by both the business community and the United

States over any possibility of civil disorder, which would certainly accompany any competition for succession.

Papa Doc had accomplished something no Haitian leader had been able to do since the nineteenth century: he had unified the country. His reign of terror permitted no effective alternative powerbase. Duvalier *dominated* Haiti. But in his complete control Papa Doc had unknowingly nourished the seeds of his successor's downfall. Perhaps only in the aftermath of the pressure-cooker-like atmosphere of Duvalier's Haiti could the beginnings of a popular grass-roots opposition have taken form. Jean-Claude Duvalier was no Papa Doc, and he would rule a very different Haiti.

NOTES

1. Arthur C. Millspaugh, *Haiti Under American Control, 1915–1930,* p. 2.

2. As one might expect, opinions about the true impact of the U.S. occupation vary, depending upon which side one stands. Many who observe the positive effects of American efforts of the period overlook the importance of a people's learning and improving within their own cultural perspectives. Some opponents of the U.S. intervention might even say that the professionalism of the Marines served as a standard of dedication to authority that formed a basis for modern Haitian military abuse. In truth, the answer includes some of both views.

3. The best source for the Marine intervention in Haiti is Hans R. Schmit's, *The United States Occupation of Haiti, 1915–1934.* Also of considerable value is James H. McCrocklin, *Garde d'Haiti, 1915–1934: Twenty Years of Organization and Training by the United States Marine Corps.*

4. In keeping with the French origins of Haiti and because French was the primary language of educated Haitians, many of the terms and processes of the occupation took on a French cast. For example, although officered by U.S. Marines, Garde d'Haiti became the title for the Haitian security force. The term "gendarmerie" refers to the French organization, part of the national army, which exists to provide security within French territory. Although normally used for traditional police functions, in France the gendarmerie includes mechanized and heavy weapons units as well as the best-known crowd-control forces of the state.

5. David Nicholls, *From Dessalines to Duvalier: Race, Colour and National Independence in Haiti,* p. 151.

6. Robert Debs Heinl and Nancy Gordon Heinl in *Written in Blood: The Story of the Haitian People, 1492–1971,* p. 483, note that U.S. monetary investment grew from $4 million in 1913 to over $14 million in 1930. This does not count investment through purely government-supported means such as military investment in the local economy or facilities improvements sponsored by the Marines, which would have aided businesses through the improved transportation infrastructure.

7. Only termination of debt and banking projects remained valid reasons for a continued U.S. presence in Haiti. With the withdrawal of forces, only fiscal controls were retained under Munro and his successor, Norman Armour.

8. Healy, "The U.S. Occupation of Haiti," in *Haitian Frustrations: Dilemmas for U.S. Foreign Policy,* p. 44.

9. Anthony P. Maingot noted in his "Haiti and Aristide: The Legacy of History," p. 66, that "the American occupation and creation of a 'professional' military force bequeathed a fact of extraordinary significance for the future of Haitian politics. . . . Thus

occurred the genesis of the fundamental principle of Haitian politics: whoever can control the army in the city controls uncontested state power."

10. The current Partnership for Peace (PfP) initiative of the North Atlantic Treaty Organization with the states of the former Soviet Union places a high value on the demonstration of civilian control of the military and the importance of democratic freedoms. It is by design an effort that cannot deliver prosperity to new states except through their own full participation in reform.

11. Robert I. Rotberg, *Haiti: The Politics of Squalor,* p. 145.

12. Heinl, p. 515.

13. Heinl, p. 533.

14. The "négritude" movement was based upon the proud African heritage of the Haitian people. Négritude and noirisme, a term with similar emphasis on heritage and the traditional strengths of the Haitian people, both espoused self-sufficiency and progress for the Haiti.

15. Brian Weinstein and Adam Segal, *Haiti: The Failure of Politics,* p. 36.

16. Duvalier was privileged to learn from two of Haiti's finest teachers, Estimé and Dr. Jean Price Mars. Both men were inspirational to the rising Haitian nationalist sentiment. The year Duvalier graduated, Price Mars published one of the classics of Haitian literature, *Ainsi Parla L'Oncle* (Port-au-Prince, 1928). For the background on Duvalier's early years, see Bernard Diederich and Al Burt, *Papa Doc: The Truth About Haiti Today,* pp. 29–39.

17. Elizabeth Abbott notes that Duvalier attended the School of Medicine while the tuition was free due to U.S. subsidy, with instructors provided by a Rockefeller grant. See her *Haiti: The Duvaliers and Their Legacy,* p. 45.

18. Yaws is a highly contagious tropical disease that chiefly affects children and is caused by infection and characterized by sores, especially on the hands, feet, and face. Ultimately ulcers form that can erode the body down to and including the bone. Yaws had spread in Haiti since the first part of the century, until one-third of all Haitians had the disease. "By 1954, nearly 90 percent of the population had been treated" by roving teams armed with penicillin. Rotberg, p. 265.

19. Abbott, p. 57, notes that Duvalier spent much of his time traveling from one mobile clinic to another, sharing for the first, and only time, the lives of the rural masses.

20. Heinl, p. 563. Magloire was famous for a telling quote of the period. When confronted by an opponent calling out for the will of the people, he replied, "What people are you talking about? In this country there're only two forces that count, the Army and the elite!"

21. Nicholls, p. 191, and Weinstein, p. 37, both identify the Magloire years as the first modern turning-point in the long competition between the two cultural subgroups (black and mulatto) in Haiti.

22. Heinl, p. 569.

23. Heinl, p. 573.

24. Lorimer Denis and François Duvalier, *The Problem of Classes Throughout Haitian History* (Port-au-Prince, 1948). His other books include *Les Tendances d'une Génération* (Port-au-Prince, 1933), and two volumes of *Oeuvres Essentielles* (Port-au-Prince, 1968).

25. The name Tonton Macoute, "Uncle Knapsack" in Creole, comes from the traditional opposite of "Tonton Noel," or Uncle Christmas. Where Uncle Christmas gave toys to good boys and girls, Uncle Knapsack would swoop down and steal away those who had been bad. Heinl, p. 596.

26. Heinl, p. 603.

27. Heinl, p. 605.

28. Heinl, p. 611.

29. James C. Scott, *Comparative Political Corruption,* p. 86.

30. Heinl, p. 614, quotes the *New York Times* on May 13, stating, "Latin America has seen many rigged elections in its history, but none more outrageous than the proceedings of May 7 [*sic*] in Haiti."

31. Weinstein, p. 42.

32. Heinl, p. 601.

33. Georges Fauriol, "The Duvaliers and Haiti," p. 595.

34. Edwin M. Martin, "Haiti: A Case Study in Futility." Heinl concurs, p. 618.

35. Fauriol, p. 595.

CHAPTER 4

The Rise and Fall of Aristide

Upon his succession, Jean-Claude "Baby Doc" Duvalier permitted some political and economic liberalization and gradually, Haiti even became better accepted internationally under his rule. After too many years of extreme poverty, agricultural production now increased, tourism grew, private investment finally began to take root, and other nations even returned to sponsor improvements in the impoverished country.[1] Key among several increases in foreign aid was the contribution of the United States, which increased to $23 million by 1976. Total multinational aid, underwritten by insurance from the U.S. Overseas Private Investment Corporation, reached $119 million that year.[2]

Unfortunately, as had occurred so many times before in Haitian history, just as improvements were taking root in the country other events, among them the oil crisis of 1973, severely weakened the potential of these economic initiatives. Also, for all his liberal tolerance, Jean-Claude Duvalier did not resist the corruption that marked his father's rule, and the Duvalier family continued to profit hugely from Haiti's limited wealth. Bribes, threats, and arrests still marked the political life of Haiti, as did electoral manipulation. Finally, graft and greed at the top erased even the positive economic developments.

These negative factors were compounded when the more liberal Carter Administration took office in 1977 and reversed the rising trend of U.S. support in Haiti. The effects of this decrease, combined with the recession of the mid-1980s, caused thousands of Haitians to flee elsewhere looking for better opportunities. Many of these immigrants arrived in south Florida, precursing the migrant outflow that instigated Uphold Democracy a decade later. The rise in the numbers of Haitians fleeing oppression then, in turn, focused more negative attention on the Duvalier regime from the Carter Administration. This down-spiraling problem instigated a unique political action: the involvement of the U.S. Congressional Black Caucus (CBC) and its push for improvements in the treatment of Haitians, both in the United States and in Haiti. The CBC remained very involved in Haitian affairs and would become a major factor in the decision to deploy U.S. forces to Haiti in 1994.[3]

An important religious movement also occurred during the regime of Jean-Claude Duvalier, which focused on the liberation theology teachings within the Catholic Church. François Duvalier had been an active opponent of Catholicism most of his life because he opposed interference from outside Haiti and in his efforts to support voodoo as a négritude rite. As a consequence, the elder Duvalier strongly and successfully suppressed Catholicism. By the 1980s, however, his son was confronted by a different, more activist, Church, allied by necessity to the Francophile mulatto elite.[4] Parish priests spoke out against political abuse; bishops denounced the Duvalier dictatorship and even the Pope sanctioned religious opposition to the regime. Soon Protestants joined in the effort and by mid-decade, economics and religion brought so many common concerns to the fore that massive riots and demonstrations broke out in and around Port-au-Prince. Baby Doc did little in response. The Macoutes responded but the people continued to resist; and in January 1986, 40,000 people marched against the government in Cap-Haitien.[5]

The Reagan Administration promised more patience with Baby Doc if he would be willing to curtail the immigration problem, make economic reforms, and improve his record on human rights. In 1981 the Mica Amendment to the U.S. Foreign Assistance bill made continued U.S. support contingent upon improvements in all three areas. In April 1982 Jean-Claude Duvalier actually announced gradual "democratization," including open elections and a national human-rights commission.[6] He clearly understood that maintaining U.S. support was vital for Haiti and his retention of power. His announcement preceded important U.S. congressional visits to Haiti, including one by the CBC in June 1982. United States economic assistance increased from $30 million in 1981 to $50 million in 1984, making it just over half the total U.S. investment in Haiti, nearly $90 million.

But even with some improvements internal Haitian discontent, sown by too many years of abuse and repression, continued to grow. In December 1981 Baby Doc rebuffed his first invasion attempt by Haitian exiles; although it failed, Jean-Claude remained insecure in his power because he had never been able to completely rid the nation of opponents to his rule. He was indecisive and received conflicting counsel from his mother, his wife, and several other influential persons, which made for erratic security policies. After 1982 the AIDS epidemic wiped out Haitian tourism, which combined with weakened support from international firms, severely limited the chance for any economic improvement. And in March 1983 Pope John Paul II visited Haiti and clearly called for reform. The Church, and the community-based liberation-theology movement known as Ti Légliz that it sponsored, even supported open street protests. In this respect the Church and Ti Légliz played an important role in the mobilization of the masses and the rise to prominence of Church leaders such as Jean-Bertrand Aristide. In the United States, the National Urban League and the National Association for the Advancement of Colored People (NAACP) joined the push for reform in Haiti. Additionally, growing numbers of Haitian expatriates returned to set up opposition movements. Given Baby Doc's overall ineffective leadership, it was only a matter of time before his administration expired.

The collapse of the Duvalier era began in the summer of 1985 with increasing street violence and countering government crackdowns. In support of these popular sentiments even the United States took note and began towards removing Duvalier from office. United States aid was cut pending true reform. Yet Duvalier failed to stop further repression, which included shutting down Radio Soliel, the primary source of free information in the nation. Street protests escalated throughout the fall and winter. United States firms withdrew from Haiti, causing the loss of thousands of important jobs. When Secretary of State George Shultz announced the delay of 1986 assistance to Haiti in late January, the clock started on the departure of Baby Doc.

With few options available, anti-Duvalier sentiment turned once again to the traditional arbiter of Haitian politics, the army. Even as emasculated and nearly ignored as it had become under the Duvaliers, the military represented the only group that could succeed Jean-Claude without a breakdown of internal security. With the support of the United States and the asylum granted by France, Baby Doc and his family were ushered out of Port-au-Prince in early February 1986 and replaced by a civil–military council known as the Conseil National de Gouvernment, or CNG. The council was headed by army Lieutenant General Henri Namphy, the choice of both Jean-Claude Duvalier and the United States.[7] Since the civilian members of the CNG were largely marginalized, it was the army that really ruled Haiti.

The army had ruled Haiti several times in its history, the last being in 1957, immediately prior to Papa Doc Duvalier's electoral victory to replace General Magloire. The Duvaliers had done everything in their power to negate the power of the military, but when they and their sycophants in the VSN departed, only the army remained as a source of security. Namphy ruled first as a member of a military committee, which included Major General Williams Regala, Brigadier General Prosper Avril, and Colonel Jean-Claude Paul. Because it claimed to be a transitional government preceding a return to democracy, the United States supported the military committee.

As with previous changes of political control in Haiti, Namphy's government first had to reestablish the fundamental structures of democracy before elections could take place to form an enduring administration. Throughout 1986 and early 1987 Namphy slowly accomplished several major changes: he had a new constitution drafted, held a referendum to show its acceptance by the people, restored the judiciary and the legislature through municipal and rural elections, established an impartial election commission to usher in a successor government, and even restored the Haitian flag to its traditional red and blue. But much of this reform merely veiled the discontent still felt within Haiti. Rick Marshall revealed the problems of the legislative elections of October 1986 when he wrote, "The number voting was probably below 10 percent. Because of the high level of illiteracy, voters chose from among colored ballots representing the candidates. Typically, sources report, this was done in the full view of the Army officers present."[8]

More unfortunately, even as these actions were taking place, General Namphy grew to distrust the success of popular rule. In June 1987 the army tried to take control of the election process from the electoral commission. "Massive protests forced them to back down, but they dealt harshly with their opponents. Two candidates were killed, and on the morning of November 29, election day, the army participated in the massacre of at least 34 people before it broke up polling and called off the elections."[9] In response, Canada, France, and the United States stopped all humanitarian assistance, which had been the mainstay of Haitian economics since Namphy took control.[10] Namphy simply rescheduled the elections.

It may have appeared that Namphy and his government were intent on reform and a rejection of Duvalierism, but in reality they simply had moved into power and maintained its style while transferring its benefits into their own pockets. Under Namphy, military officers had simply replaced the civilians who had dominated Haiti as the Duvaliers' VSN. "The same Duvalierist groups continued to hold influential and dominant positions within the various government agencies and private enterprises."[11] Although he tolerated certain liberties such as freedom of the press and the ability to form political organizations (made obligatory by the scope of the opposition forces in Haiti at the end of the Duvalier era), Namphy could not stem the tide of opposition. When he permitted elections in 1988, he knew his government would not survive them.

By 1987 the dark unanimity of oppression that had been forged by François Duvalier had shattered into a rainbow of different opposition groups, each with a different focus, but all moving towards more liberal approaches to government in Haiti. Several of these left-of-center political groups formed a single coalition called the National Committee of the Congress of Democratic Organizations, or KONAKOM. The coalition became both the most active opponent of Namphy's CNG and an effective motive force for reform agendas. It was largely due to the influence of the KONAKOM that a Haitian referendum held in March 1987 endorsed a new constitution, the most progressive in Haitian history.[12] This constitution of 1987 came to stand as a symbol of the political progress possible in Haiti, and time and again provided the rallying cry for future reformers. Among other provisions, the constitution gave the first democratically elected president of Haiti far-reaching reform powers to rid the nation of corruption.[13] Under the aegis of the coalition and its ability to counter Namphy's rightist controls, a number of new organizations created by the new constitution slowly broke the national government's monopoly on power and fostered something of a rebirth of democracy. For the first time in years, the elites, the Left, the bourgeoisie, the military, the religious, the poor, and the educated were all searching among different political venues in Haiti.

KONAKOM and other organizations aligned with it succeeded in bringing about some electoral reform in Haiti. It was this reform that had driven Namphy to intervene in the election process. Duvalierists in general and Namphy's CNG in particular rightly saw in the new constitution and electoral reform a threat to their continued political dominance. When all the named presidential candidates agreed to supervision by the Permanent Electoral Council (CEP), Namphy lost control and in response unleashed a terror campaign and canceled the election. Initially, the United States protested these acts but continued to support the Namphy regime as the best guarantor of security. But after all the major presidential candidates agreed to form a single opposition front and condemn the CNG, even the United States cut off all assistance to the Namphy government. All other foreign donors soon followed suit. Elections were rescheduled for January 1988, but Namphy still rejected the CEP and managed the election with an appointed council.

The winner in this rigged January election was the CNG candidate, Leslie F. Manigat, a former Duvalier cabinet minister and later Duvalier opponent who had run on a Marxist–democratic platform. Manigat ruled uneventfully until June, when he made the mistake of trying to wrest control of the import revenues from the army. He then attempted to remove Namphy from leadership of the army and quickly found himself on his way to exile in Europe following an army-organized coup. Although the United States publicly decried the coup, it was also the first to recognize the return of General Namphy to power. Namphy dissolved the constitution of 1987 and resumed full control of the country. To counter the ongoing opposition movements he ordered another terror campaign. Haiti had reached again for democracy and found only dictatorship.

Nonetheless, Namphy resumed his rule without clear mastery over the people. The poverty brought back by the extravagance of Baby Doc's regime, combined with 2 years of uncertain political control, fostered growing resentment among a variety of Haitian groups. Namphy attempted to crack down on all opposition. Abuse was prevalent, and on September 11th, 1988 violence left thirteen dead and seventy injured among the congregation of a young and very outspoken priest of the people named Jean-Bertrand Aristide.

Namphy had pushed too far with the September wave of killings; in addition, it was clear that he was moving former members of the VSN to positions of power in order to form a dominant Duvalierist block and regain control of the whole country. Since these actions were too extreme even for the army, they resulted in another coup and the fall of the Namphy government the following week, on September 17th. Through this third coup in the 2 years since Baby Doc Duvalier had been deposed, General Prosper Avril was brought to power and given a mandate to implement real reform, which included a return to the liberal 1987 constitution and an end to corruption in the government.

Namphy also had failed to accomplish the signal challenge of Haitian culture: the management of political change. From Toussaint L'Ouverture and Dessalines to Boyer, from Dartiguenave to the Duvaliers, Haiti had proven to be consistently resistant to orderly transition between leaders. This same difficulty still plagued the nation in the years following the departure of Jean-Claude Duvalier. Nothing short of the force of arms seemed to take hold for longer than a few months in Port-au-Prince. Namphy fell due to the same lack of capability to transition the government of Haiti. As Robert Rotberg wrote prophetically in 1988:

Namphy's successors, whoever they may be, have a hard and, frankly, almost impossible task. Without the backing of a robust national democratic-value system and given inherited traditions of cynical misrule, it is unlikely that the transition from authoritarianism to good government can be either easy or quick. Haitians have long endured a zero-sum existence: either one is on top or on the bottom; no group or clique shares with others. . . . No remolding of Haiti can be predicted with confidence.[14]

Following Namphy, Avril was judged by the U.S. State Department as "offering the best, and perhaps last real chance for democratic reform in Haiti for the foreseeable future."[15] But he too was a clear Duvalierist with little desire to yield to the needs of the Haitian people. Avril continued the practices of the dictators who preceded him, using graft, favoritism, and theft to benefit his supporters. The Haitian-government budget deficit increased by $60 million in his first year of rule.[16] Avril also failed to consolidate control of the downward spiraling Haitian political system and alienated the U.S. Congress by his refusal to reinstate the constitution of 1987 and hold free elections. His administration also drew opposition from the Catholic Church and almost all social organizations due to its human-rights abuses. Avril was soon overthrown by a fourth coup in early 1990, led by General Hérard Abraham and supported by the United States.[17]

Avril's successor became not Abraham, but former Supreme Court Justice Ertha Pascal-Trouillot, who agreed to serve as president and share power with a council of state until real elections could be held later in the year. But the turbulent wake of the Duvaliers was too much for even an interim government to handle. Even as the CEP was resurrected to manage the election process and the U.S. government agreed to take responsibility for financing the process, she also was soon forced to resign, admitting fiscal ineptness, and was jailed. Finally, by 1990 the elites had had enough. The military was warned that interference would not be tolerated, and the United Nations and the Organization of American States agreed to send observers to monitor the next election. That election, held on December 16, 1990, was conducted in a state of near-anarchy and with a bankrupt government; but it was permitted to proceed fairly, at least by Haitian standards. It resulted an overwhelming victory for a late entry in the election, Father Jean-Bertrand Aristide, and for the poor of Haiti whom only he represented.[18]

Robert Rotberg summed up the nation's problems after Namphy's 1988 return to power by focusing on the primary reasons why Haiti has always been unique, "a place apart."[19] For Rotberg and many others, Haiti has been marked by peculiar diplomatic isolation, poor internal communications, rural resistance to change, and poor economic development.

Isolation came to Haiti when it was ostracized by Europe and America after its terrible and bloody revolution. As a pariah nation, its relations with other countries were limited to those occasions when they could profit from Haiti's limited resources or geographic position. The United States, Canada, and France have been and remain the primary players in Haiti's international affairs. As discussed above, their participation has been comically erratic, often invasive, and occasionally even bellicose. This has produced a Haitian lack of trust in other nations that most would agree is well warranted.

Poor communications have resulted from three dominant factors: Haiti's mountainous terrain, the schism between an "educated" language (French) and a "common" language (Creole), and a functional illiteracy rate of over 70 percent. Building roads has done little to overcome what is really a significant cultural problem. Rotberg noted:

Neither the heritage of slavery and war in the eighteenth, nor the oppression of the nineteenth and twentieth centuries encouraged peasants to seek their security elsewhere other than in their isolated mountain and valley retreats. Freedom and independence were more important to ex-slaves than higher levels of prosperity. Cut off as they were—and most still are—from communications media that might have inculcated a sense of relative deprivation, and uninfluenced by missionaries (of which there were few until the mid-twentieth century), or immigrants from other cultures (of which there were none), or the towns, self-preservation has dictated an overwhelming apathy to the course of Haitian politics.[20]

The rural population resists change in Haiti for several reasons, but all of them are overwhelmed by the impact of poverty. When most citizens outside the larger cities spend the bulk of their time simply meeting their basic needs, little interest in other activity is possible. Add to this factor a basic distrust of initiatives born of the urban elite and the lack of reliable communications within Haiti, one sees little cause for rural skepticism to change in the future.

Finally, poor economic development gives little hope that the overwhelming weight of poverty will be soon eased. Lack of hope inhibits support for new ideas and makes drumming up support for most initiatives a significant challenge. All of these factors reinforce the negative impacts of apathy and make democratic development difficult.

The political history of Haiti prior to 1990 relates only a story of constant turmoil and ruthless competition for the nation's few assets, and of being progressively denuded of its natural treasure. Yet this depressing tale provides only the cover for an array of internal problems that comprise the true nemesis of Haitian progress. Before any future strides can be made, some improvement must occur within the underlying difficulties of Haitian society. These difficulties are both the root and engine of the political distress that marks Haitian history. As Aristide took office in 1991 he faced challenges beyond his imagination.

THE FIRST ARISTIDE ADMINISTRATION

This political story of Haiti clearly follows the consistent theme of dictators overthrown by assassination or exile. The election of Jean-Bertrand Aristide in December 1990 was one of the notable exceptions to that rarely broken cycle. His election appeared to offer the promise of reform in Haiti for the first time in many years. Aristide called for more than simple reform; his ascendancy in fact signaled a complete overhaul of Haitian political reality, symbolized by the name his support organization took: Lavalas, Creole for "we will wash away." It energized both the poor of Haiti and the nation's elite. Unfortunately, his presidency was rapidly cut short by the traditional Haitian response to reform: a conservative coup, again led by the military. This coup renewed American involvement in Haiti and set the immediate stage for operation Uphold Democracy.

When Aristide took office in 1991, he did so as the first head of state in Haitian history to be democratically elected by universal suffrage, having garnered 67 percent of the popular vote in an election attracting 85 percent of the electorate. The election was even monitored, not by the Haitian army but by former President Jimmy Carter.[21] Just as his election was a Haitian rarity, the new president was also a unique figure.

Aristide was born on July 15, 1953 in the small southern town of Port-Salut. His father moved to Port-au-Prince when the boy was 3 years old and eventually enrolled him in a school run by the Salesian order of the Catholic Church. Aristide graduated from college in 1979 and then left Haiti to study theology abroad; while there, he became fluent in five languages besides French and Creole. He also became preoccupied with the welfare of Haiti's poor. When ordained in 1982, Aristide had already become an outspoken critic of the Duvalier regime.

In sermon after sermon Aristide enthralled his parishioners, calling out for them to demand a better life for themselves. Given the repressive Duvalier government's dependence on fear and ignorance, Aristide quickly became a political target. He was exiled to Canada after less than 1 year in the pulpit. Aristide returned to Haiti in 1985 to play an important role in mobilizing the people to bring down Jean-Claude Duvalier. Even so, the pressure on the Church exerted by Duvalier's successor, General Namphy, resulted in the Catholic hierarchy's putting a ban on Aristide's inflammatory preaching. The slender priest appealed the decision by the Church, and won. Nonetheless, his continued outspokenness slowly alienated him from the Church and made him a target for the government in power. By 1987 Aristide's only real support lay in the Haitian poor—the Haitian majority.

In July 1987 the Catholic hierarchy reassigned Aristide to serve in a church attended by Namphy and other powerful figures; even this did not deter him. The particularly brutal series of attacks by the Tonton Macoutes in the precarious summer of 1987 included an assassination attempt on Aristide. When on September 11th Aristide was attacked again, this time at Mass, the murderous raid not only destroyed Aristide's church but also the Namphy government. The massacre was so brutal that it caused Aristide to suffer a nervous breakdown. Even so, Aristide recovered to continue his attacks on Namphy's successor, General Avril. Again the Church ordered Aristide out of Haiti, but thousands of protesters blocked his path to the airport.

Aristide soon assumed a truly mystical aura in Haiti, reinforced by his ability to speak out and still survive the attacks of the government. He preached against the evils of all previous Haitian oppressors. He linked the United States to a succession of autocratic Haitian leaders, and even took the Catholic Church to task for acquiescing to the human-rights violations of several Haitian dictators. For Aristide, any opposition to the brutality and corruption of the powers in Haiti could be justified. And as he continually took the side of the disenfranchised poor and urban homeless, he soon became *the* major threat to the system that kept the affluent and powerful of Haiti in control. Branded as an extremist, he would not stop his opposition, but finally fell ill from his constant efforts to promote reform. For preaching violence and class struggle in his relentless attacks, Aristide finally was expelled from the Salesian Order by the Church in 1988.[22] Still, he did not stop.

Aristide was too popular for even his expulsion from the Church in one of the most Catholic of countries to cause him harm. As Amy Wilentz aptly points out:

> One might have thought that, abandoned, discarded, marginalized, silenced, and kicked out, he would have lost the sway he once had over the Haitian people. The Church had publicly reviled him, as had the rest of the Haitian establishment. By all rights, he should have been at the nadir of his powers. But just as no one can prop up for very long the strongman who has no popular base, neither can anyone take away the power of those whose legitimacy is based on true popular support.[23]

Through 1989 and 1990 Aristide moved frequently from place to place and continued a radio campaign against the administration in his sharp, biting, and impassioned Creole.

Aristide did not announce his candidacy in the presidential race until October 18, 1990. Before then, he had denied any desire to seek public office, but it appears that he came to view his candidacy as the only effective opposition to the well-known Duvalierist candidates for president, Roger Lafontant and Claude Raymond. Also, in Aristide's view, he had incurred a moral responsibility to run as a representative of the people and opponent of the system that had allowed so many oppressors to hold power in Haiti. What had once been an election like so many previous ones in Haiti changed radically when the fiery priest entered the contest as the people's candidate. It is a fact that voter registration surged after Aristide's announcement of his candidacy and when the successor to the KONAKOM coalition, the National Front for Democracy and Change, offered its banner to him.[24] The result of the election held on December 16, 1990 was an overwhelming victory for Aristide, but it also represented a significant break with the Haitian past. Never before had a man of Aristide's personality, religious fervor, and relative inexperience stole so quickly, and with so little traditional support, upon the scene of national power. "The news of his victory sent tens of thousands into the streets of Port-au-Prince in perhaps the largest demonstration in the nation's history, with people honking car horns, singing hymns, and dancing."[25]

Aristide's administration was sure to require true wonders from "Mr. Miracles"[26] if it was to successfully navigate all the pitfalls inherent in governing Haiti. But what did he really have to offer? Without political experience and with no base of support among the traditional managers of Haitian affairs, Aristide had a very steep road to climb to develop political stability. He did not even have the support of a true political party. The KONAKOM coalition had always been loose, and his Lavalas support had no structure before or after the election. Lavalas was more a movement than an organization; although its broad appeal came from the inclusion of grass-roots organizations and provincial cadres, it was first and foremost an ideal of the marginalized poor and urban youth in Port-au-Prince.[27] Lavalas would not provide Aristide with a structure to begin an administration.

Hugely popular with the masses, Aristide also had enemies. Before he took office on February 7, 1991 Aristide suffered through two attempted coups; one, instigated by Roger Lafontant, almost killed him.[28] The people of Port-au-Prince rioted for 2 days in rage over the attack, and the United States pushed the Haitian army to intervene and jail Lafontant. Aristide's adminstration survived, but only for a short period. Less than 8 months later, Aristide was overthrown in yet another bloody military coup. He escaped first to Venezuela and then to the United States, where he established himself as a government-in-exile. Why was such a popular figure ousted so quickly?

The reasons behind the coup are as intertwined as its leadership. Clearly, Aristide assumed office promising to reform both the military and the economic basis of Haitian society, efforts that alienated many of the elites whose security was bound up in maintaining these two traditional Haitian power centers. Aristide and his personally chosen prime minister, René Préval,[29] established a minimum wage, instituted a war against government corruption and drugs, sought to reform the civil service, started a literacy campaign, and, in one sense, did even preach class warfare.[30] Aristide was the worst nightmare of the powerful elites in Haiti, for he did not espouse an equal democracy: he wanted what was best for the Haitian masses. Although his intended reforms were moderate in the context of other Caribbean leaders, like Michael Manley in Jamaica and Maurice Bishop in Grenada, in Haiti they were truly radical.[31]

Aristide and Préval clearly also wanted to reduce the power of the military in Haiti and separate the police and the army. Yet their only powerbase was with the powerless majority: the poor. Aristide was said to be a communist by many who had heard his sermons and read his speeches, and his economic reforms clearly sought a more even distribution of wealth. His slogan for economic reform, "move from misery to poverty with dignity," did not take into account the dignity of those who would be giving up financial power as Aristide's masses gained it. He certainly attempted to rapidly implement significant changes to Haitian society, and with little consultation with his legislature, but he did so fully empowered by the Constitution of 1987. To some, his administration did appear to be leaning towards a leftist autocracy. Still, his efforts did result in increased political openness and newly found freedoms for the press. Aristide's program was disturbing to many and his management style appeared to be erratic, but he had little time to explain and refine them.

Overall, the results of Aristide's administration through September 1991 were hard to judge. He had introduced measures to improve revenues, counter smuggling, promote tourism, and create tax incentives to encourage investment in the private sector, but had not completed enough of his program to assure the elites that he posed no real threat to them, in view of his commitment to the masses.[32] He had also failed to demonstrate to outsiders that he was committed to the democratic process. His administration had condemned Roger Lafontant to life in prison without a fair trial, and he had been known to acknowledge the usefulness of the Père Lebrun.[33] Many of his shortcomings can be blamed on his political inexperience and his arrogant belief in the messianic nature of his role in Haiti. Also, part of this failure to make known his reforms was simply due to lack of time: Haiti's culture clearly had demonstrated now, as in the past, its resistance to rapid political reform.

Yet Aristide must take much of the blame. As Anthony Maignot has argued:

Aristide's political problem had been evident from the start. Surrounded by ideologues and idealists, all political amateurs, Aristide never seemed able to distinguish friend from foe. Worse, he never seemed interested in the profane art of political maneuvering. In fact, he seemed to excel at turning allies into opponents.[34]

Aristide did not speak out against mob violence, he did not prevent the arrest of his opponents on vague charges, and perhaps most fatal to his chances for success, he antagonized both the military and the rich. Equally as damning, he failed to build any form of political rapport with his legislature, including alienating members of his own Lavalas support group.[35]

There is even some doubt concerning the origin of the anti-Aristide coup. Most think that it was engineered by the head of the Forces Armées d'Haiti (FAd'H), Lieutenant General Raoul Cedras. But, it is important to note that Aristide had retired most of the generals in the Haitian armed forces upon taking office and had personally selected Cedras, then a Lieutenant Colonel, for assignment as the new army chief of staff. Aristide and Cedras had a solid working relationship during the short period of his administration; in fact, Aristide felt quite confident in their association.[36] Roland Perusse contends that the coup was actually engineered by Michel François, the head of the Haitian police.[37] Others consider that wealthy Haitians raised money to support Aristide's ouster.[38] Regardless of the ideological credit for the overthrow of Aristide, Cedras and Michel François, the chief of police, share responsibility for the act; they were both critical to its success and shared in the additional power and money it brought them. But no one can deny that it was Haiti itself, and its chronic inability to develop an enduring government, that must take ultimate responsibility.

Aristide was a critical part of this lack of overall leadership. The enigma of Aristide is hard to penetrate. From his management of Haitian affairs one sees a lack of consistency and a degree of counterproductive emotionalism. In his personality, one can perceive everything from pious dedication to neo-communist disregard for established political institutions. Perhaps the most insightful view of Aristide can be gained by understanding his 1990 book, *In the Parish of the Poor: Writings from Haiti.* There one can see the origins of Aristide's distrust of Americans and the Catholic hierarchy, regarding them as the supporters of so many previous hated regimes; his affinity with the poor; and his infectious, if naive optimism. Aristide's complete lack of political training and his inexperience in management would have made him an unlikely success in any country so stricken as Haiti with internal problems. Faced with Haiti's past inequities and crushing economic dilemmas, Aristide's lack of demonstrable progress in 1991 should have been expected. But Haiti has never been forgiving: if the coup was accomplished by the military, it was supported by a host of others, for a host of reasons, to the detriment of all.

What was abundantly clear in the outcome of the September 1991 coup was that Haiti had once again returned to the autocratic rule that had so clearly marked its history. The Organization of American States (OAS) and the United States were drawn to Aristide's defense because of their support for democratically elected leaders, regardless of their political records. Both immediately pledged to return Aristide from exile.[39] The OAS was particularly supportive in the early days following the coup. It met in emergency session on October 5th in Washington, DC; it sent a delegation to Port-au-Prince for 2 days of meetings; it officially condemned the coup; and it finally voted on October 7th for an embargo to punish the military regime. A second OAS mission, led by Colombian Augusto Ocampo, visited Haiti later, in November, and met with a variety of Haitian groups in order to find a solution to the political dissension in the country. In December the OAS actually proposed its own solution to the crisis, which involved the naming of a new Haitian prime minister, the creation of a new government, and the use of a transition team of 500 to prepare for Aristide's return. This OAS model sowed important seeds for the eventual transition process, but never developed sufficient support to be implemented on its own.

Ocampo remained a key mediator for months after the coup, returning many times to Port-au-Prince to identify and negotiate with potential transition prime ministers and to develop an OAS civilian-observer team to monitor activities in Haiti. At one point, the head of the Haitian communist party, René Théodore, became a potential transition prime minister through the work of Ocampo, with the concurrence of both Aristide and the Haitian legislature. Théodore attempted to form a party of "national consensus," but this opportunity fell apart over difficulties in fixing a date for Aristide's return and easing the embargo of goods entering Haiti. (President Bush had approved the OAS embargo of all nonhumanitarian commercial traffic on November 5, 1991 and directed its enforcement by the U.S. Navy.)

Increased United Nations involvement in Haiti also grew following Cedras's coup, first with General Assembly condemnation of the coup, then concurrence in the OAS embargo, and finally with a full agenda of techniques to aid the return of President Aristide. This level of effort was increased after Aristide met with Secretary-General Boutros Boutros-Ghali in May 1992. This increased effort included a Security Council Resolution in November affirming support for Aristide, and the appointment of Argentine diplomat Dante Caputo as the special representative to Haiti of the Secretary-General. Caputo arrived in Port-au-Prince on February 1st, 1993 and quickly became as influential as Ocampo had been in the early months following the coup.

Another key United Nations action was the arrival of observers assigned to monitor human-rights violations in the country as part of a group named the International Civilian Mission (ICM). The ICM would eventually number about 200 personnel before two other components were added. These new components included: (1) a group of International Police Monitors (IPM) consisting of Royal Canadian Mounted Police, French Gendarmes, and police from other nations; and (2) a U.S.-led, foreign internal-defense mission named the Haiti Assistance Group (HAG).[40] These latter two groups would be retained as key components of the U.S.-led multinational intervention.

As a member nation, the United States was involved with all OAS and United Nations deliberations and also conducted its own aggressive mediation activities in the Haitian capital, at first working primarily through Ambassador Alvin P. Adams. The U.S. Coast Guard began the repatriation of Haitians who had fled the country in the wake of the coup on November 15th, in accordance with Bush Administration policy that did not view Haitians as refugees of oppression. Although the "forcible" repatriation was fought by several organizations through the U.S. judicial system for many months, it remained a focal point of the Bush Administration's policy on Haiti. Although his views conflicted at times with official Washington policies, Ambassador Adams continued to play a visible and important role in Haitian affairs through the development of the "Washington Accord" in February 1992, which called for amnesty for the army as one precondition for the return of Aristide.[41] This opportunity also failed to materialize for a variety of reasons, including the refusal of the Haitian legislature to approve the accord and the Haitian Supreme Court's declaration that it was unconstitutional.

The U.S. military was not inactive during this period. Within days following the coup against Aristide, U.S. Navy ships and Coast Guard cutters began rescuing Haitians fleeing the chaos in their homeland by boat. The United States also planned and deployed a small noncombatant evacuation force towards Haiti in October 1991.[42] By November, the flow of migrants had increased so significantly that the United States began operation Safe Harbor, in and around Guantanamo Bay, Cuba, to provide humanitarian assistance to Haitians. In addition, the U.S. military was active in efforts to convince Cedras to cooperate in Aristide's return. Major General John Sheehan, USMC, among others, conducted several visits to Haiti, assisting the State Department in making the situation clear from a military perspective.

One significant change in the approach of the United States occurred when presidential candidate Bill Clinton announced a platform that appeared to open the shores of the United States to "oppressed" peoples worldwide. Although the official American position had always been supportive of refugees, Clinton's platform raised the hopes of many Haitians for a better life in America, particularly following the defeat of President Bush in the election of November 1992. When President Clinton took the oath of office in January 1993 many Haitians had already fled towards south Florida and thousands more were posed to follow. Over the next several months the rising number of Haitian migrants seeking to enter the United States would relentlessly add pressure to the efforts to resolve the Haitian crisis.

From January to mid-July 1993 many groups within and without Haiti continued work to develop some solution to Aristide's ouster. Many of these efforts came close to being accepted, but were always thwarted in the end by the refusal of one group or another to cooperate. Aristide, the Haitian legislature, the coup leaders, the United States, and the international bodies all share in the blame. Key sticking points became intractable over time because no clean break with the past could be identified. Aristide and his followers never ceded any authority or credit to the government in place, and the Haitian legislature grew increasingly hostile to the influence of "foreign" powers in what they believed to be an internal affair. Since Aristide branded Cedras a criminal, Cedras rejected every accord. Organization of American States commissions came and went. Strikes, political murders, and internal chaos grew with each passing month, until finally the United Nations-brokered Governors Island Accord was signed by both President Aristide and General Cedras on July 3, 1993.[43] (See Appendix C for the text of the Accord.)

The Accord was designed to return Haiti to democracy through the cooperation of both parties. On September 23, 1993 the United Nations passed Resolution 867, authorizing an expanded mission to support the transition from the Cedras regime to the legitimate Aristide government. A mere 12 days later, an advance party of American military personnel from the HAG was prepared to land in Port-au-Prince to support the United Nations initiatives, with other national troops soon ready to join the force. This was over 2 weeks prior to the date that Cedras had agreed upon to step down (October 30th). The attention of almost everyone in Washington, DC was then riveted on events in Somalia, where the United States was hunting Somali chieftain Mohammed Aideed with strategic special operations forces for the United Nations.[44] The HAG mission seemed simple enough, but that simplicity proved painfully deceptive.

It is difficult to determine why the arrival of the HAG needed to be accomplished so quickly. After so many months the United Nations was anxious to see a solution to the Aristide–Cedras conflict, and the United States also sought increased stability in the region, but devoting another month to ensure a smooth transition would not have been a significant price for any party to pay. Unfortunately, in its haste to finally see an end to the Haitian crisis and with much attention focused on east Africa and Aideed, the United States and the United Nations acted prematurely, or at least acted in a manner that forced too many proud Haitians to demur. The use of troops in Haiti proved to be too explosive for the fragile basis of the Accord, and the unintended result of the push to return Aristide as rapidly as possible was a further escalation of the crisis.

Unfortunately, by October 14th, when the main body of the HAG arrived in Port-au-Prince harbor aboard the USS *Harlan County,* Cedras had already decided to repudiate the Governors Island Accord and dropped any pretense of negotiating for the return of Aristide. As the ship moved towards the dock to disembark its military force, its captain observed that another vessel had been moored in the only position large enough to accommodate the *Harlan County* and that two small motor boats, with machines guns displayed openly, were circling nearby. Unseen from the American ship, an angry crowd had formed in the port area. This crowd was filled with Cedras supporters–militant attachés bent on disrupting the arrival of the HAG. Clearly, the potential existed for conflict when the HAG came ashore. By agreement, the Americans and Canadians on board were armed only with sidearms, their rifles secured in lockers below decks; their mission depended on an environment of cooperation and acceptance by the Haitian people. Any conflict, or injuries to either side, would seriously harm the ability of the HAG to carry out its tasks. The ship's captain radioed for instructions.

On shore, the U.S. chargé d'affaires, Vicki Huddleston, planning to welcome the United Nations contingent at the dock, was prevented from entering the pier area by the angry crowd. Her limousine was then shook and pelted by the mob as Haitian police looked on. She too radioed for more guidance. Shots were fired into the air as she and other diplomats soon left the area.[45] In the United States, analyses and decisions were made rapidly by key members of several federal agencies. After the flurry of communications and with the recent deaths of 19 Americans in Somalia on his mind, President Clinton decided to recall the *Harlan County* and her underarmed U.S. and Canadian troops. The ship turned and left in full view of the crowd on shore.

To the Haitian people the turnaround of the *Harlan County* appeared to be a victory against the "invading superpower." The status of Cedras and the other coup leaders rose with their seeming ability to deter the United States. Once the ship had entered the port area of the Haitian capital the die had been cast. The conditions for permissive entry of United Nations forces were not right. The decision to abort would remain controversial, but there was really no other option at the time.[46] Clearly, after so many months of effort and the involvement of a host of mediators, something else had to be planned if the Aristide government was to return to power.

Within the U.S. government there were several schools of thought concerning the correct course in Haiti. Actions taken in Washington included the naming of a U.S. special representative, first Lawrence Pezzullo, a former U.S. ambassador to Nicaragua, and later, former Pennsylvania congressman William Gray. The U.S. Congress also remained apprised of the fray by continuing a series of hearings on Haiti, which had begun in 1992 and did not end until the decision was made to send American forces into the Haitian crisis. At the United Nations in New York few were sure where else to turn to restore democracy in Haiti. Actions in Norfolk, Virginia, where U.S. Atlantic Command—the headquarters responsible for military operations in the Caribbean—was located, included the creation of a special planning cell to develop potential military responses to the deepening crisis. Public opinion was mixed at best; few Americans had any understanding of Haiti or its problems. In an era of small interventions around the world, Haiti's problems seemed to pale in comparison to events in Somalia and the Middle East.

Whenever such diverse schools of thought form around a central issue and solutions are discussed that include the use of military force, uniformed planners throughout the armed forces take note. In particular, members of the unified commanders' staffs, those who will ultimately become involved with any use of Department of Defense assets in their region, immediately begin the development of a range of contingency plans. A range of plans is developed because, at least initially, American policy may be unclear or undeveloped and in all cases situations change over time, so such planning adds flexibility, expedites the process of military operations, and increases the odds of success in the future. The concepts that molded Uphold Democracy grew from the disappointing repulse of the *Harlan County,* compounded by the growing exodus of Haitians fleeing their chaotic nation.

NOTES

1. Brian Weinstein and Aaron Segal in their *Haiti: The Failure of Politics,* p. 43, list French, Canadian, West German, Israeli, and American projects starting in the mid-1970s. By the end of the decade over 200 factories had opened in the Port-au-Prince region.

2. Georges A. Fauriol (Ed.), *Haitian Frustrations: Dilemmas for U.S. Policy,* p. 596.

3. Georges A. Fauriol, p. 606, makes the point that the arrival of Haitians on U.S. shores in 1980 marked the significant turning point in recent history: the first time that Haiti had been perceived as a threat to the United States. It was not the first instance of massive Haitian immigration; Robert I. Rotberg noted in his "Haiti's Past Mortgages its Future," p. 107, that "at least half a million Haitians left their country for the Dominican Republic, the United States and Canada between 1964 and 1969." But these were years when Americans focused more on Southwest Asia than the Caribbean.

4. David Nicholls, "Haiti: The Rise and Fall of Duvalierism," p. 1244.

5. Weinstein, pp. 45–46.

6. Fauriol, p. 598.

7. Fauriol, p. 603.

8. Rick Marshall, "Haiti: Evolution or Revolution?," p. 40. The illiteracy problem would continue to plague succeeding administrations, including Aristide's, because modern democracy is dependent upon the people's ability to independently gauge facts and the characters of candidates, largely through print media and television.

9. Rotberg, p. 94.

10. The United States had provided $8 million of the $10 million cost of the 1987 elections. Fauriol, p. 605.

11. Alex Dupuy, *Haiti in the New World Order: The Limits of the Democratic Revolution,* p. 53.

12. Dupuy, p. 54.

13. In 1991 Aristide would be the first president to use these extensive powers; they were so far-reaching that his later reforms were viewed as threats to the elites and added fuel to accusations that he was inclined to become a communist dictator.

14. Rotberg, p. 108.

15. Anthony P. Maingot, "Haiti and Aristide: The Legacy of History," p. 66, quoting Deputy Assistant Secretary of State Richard Melton.

16. Dupuy, p. 61.

17. Dupuy, p. 65, notes that U.S. Ambassador Alvin Adams went to Avril's residence to tell him to leave Haiti. By this time the "call of the U.S. ambassador" had become a euphemism for the White House decision to oust a Haitian dictator. Dupuy, p. 69.

18. Maingot notes on p. 67: "So sudden and unexpected was Aristide's entry into the 1990 electoral campaign that he was not listed in the May 29, 1990, election handbook."

19. Rotberg, pp. 97–101.

20. Ibid, p. 100.

21. Technically, Duvalier was elected to the presidency in 1957, but that election was plagued by government influence and polling irregularities; more important, Duvalier's

legacy of personal power cast him back as a reflection of "traditional" Haitian democracy: control by the elites. See David Nicholls, *From Dessalines to Duvalier: Race, Colour and National Independence in Haiti,* pp. 208–210. See also Maignot, p. 67.

22. Jean-Bertrand Aristide, *In the Parish of the Poor: Writings from Haiti,* p. XV.

23. Ibid, p. xviii.

24. Dupuy, p. 68.

25. *1991 Current Biography Yearbook,* p. 33.

26. "Mr. Miracles" was the nickname given Aristide after so many brushes with death. Among his several nicknames, he has most commonly been referred to as "Titide." See Maingot, p. 67.

27. Dupuy, pp. 86–87.

28. Ibid, pp. 107–108.

29. René Préval was a militant anti-Duvalierist who also served as minister of the interior and national defense minister in Aristide's cabinet. One other member of the cabinet was Smark Michel, who served early in the administration as the economics minister and would return to be Aristide's prime minister after 1994.

30. Roland I. Perusse, *Haitian Democracy Restored, 1991–1995,* p. 15.

31. Dupuy, p. 101.

32. Anthony P. Bryan, "Haiti: Kick Starting the Economy," p. 65.

33. In a speech in July 1991, Aristide had endorsed the threat of placing a burning tire around the neck of certain opponents of the people. The fatal burning tire was a well-known and widely available Haitian murder weapon known as the Pére Lebrun.

34. Maignot, pp. 67–68.

35. Ibid, p. 68.

36. Perusse, p. 17.

37. Ibid, p. 19.

38. Aristide felt that he had been removed through the influence of the Haitian elite. He maintained that wealthy Haitians raised some $40 million to buy the support of Cedras and the FAd'H in order to overthrow him. See William R. McClintock and Alexander G. Monroe, *Operation GTMO, 1 October 1991–1 July 1993,* p. 9.

39. The OAS had developed the Santiago Agreement on June 5, 1991, binding its members to act upon any "sudden or irregular interruption of the democratic institutional process" within any member state. The United States was an OAS member well-attuned to democratic continuity in the region, and James Baker, as U.S. Secretary of State, supported a call for a peacekeeping force for Haiti.

40. Foreign internal defense includes the deployment of specialized American troops to train the host-nation forces in techniques crucial to their national security. Normally, these troops are provided by the U.S. Special Operations Command, under control of the regional commander; in this case, the Commander in Chief, Atlantic.

41. Later, Adams would be recalled, and because Aristide was considered to be the legitimate Haitian president, no new ambassador was accredited to the Cedras regime.

42. This operation, still classified, was named Victor Squared. It was managed by the Norfolk-based Atlantic Command primarily using Marines. William R. McClintock and Alexander G. Monroe, *Operation GTMO, 1 October 1991–1 July 1993,* p. 13.

43. The Governors Island Accord, named for the site in New York City where Cedras and his party met with Aristide, was signed July 16th, 1993. The accord included ten points: first, it stipulated that a new legislature was to be formed and a new prime minister, acceptable to the legislature, be named by Aristide. Following those actions, the sanctions on Haiti were to be suspended pending the granting of amnesty to members of the

interim government and the retirement of Cedras. All of this was scheduled to occur prior to the return of Aristide on October 30th, 1993. U.S. Congress. *Haiti: the Agreement of Governors Island and its Implementation. Hearing before the Subcommittee on Western Hemisphere Affairs of the Committee on Foreign Affairs, House of Representatives. July 21, 1993.* See Appendix C.

44. In the afternoon of October 3, U.S. special operations forces known as Task Force Ranger were caught in a firefight in Mogadishu, Somalia while searching for Aideed. The fight resulted in countless Somali casualties, the death of 19 Americans and one Malaysian soldier, and a reversal of U.S. policy in Somalia. The "Ranger Raid" dominated all actions in the Pentagon during the month.

45. Perusse, p. 55.

46. There is no doubt that the *Harlan County* incident galvanized military-planning efforts. Admiral Paul David Miller, USN, then the commander-in-chief of U.S. forces in the region characterized the incident in 1995 as "one of the dismal days of recent naval history." (William R. McClintock interview, January 19, 1995, p. 7). Captain Timothy Prendergast, USN, dated the beginning of Haiti planning to the very day the *Harlan County* left Port-au-Prince harbor. (William R. McClintock and Ralph J. Passarelli interview with Captain Timothy E. "Spike" Prendergast, USN, Norfolk, Virginia, November 23, 1994, p. 1). Lieutenant Colonel Gordon Bonham, USA, one of the chief planners for Uphold Democracy would later say, "Over and over I heard planners say 'we don't want 2380 (one of the Haiti plans) to be another *Harlan County*'" (Cynthia L. Hayden, ed., *JTF-180 Oral History Interviews,* p. 14.)

PART II

CONTINGENCY PLANNING

Appropriate planning develops options and flexibility for future actions. Perhaps more than any other profession, the modern U.S. military depends on effective planning to remain prepared for the very wide range of potential tasks that it may be assigned. In fact, since the end of the Cold War, the military-planning process has matured considerably, achieving such sophistication and developing such synergy among forces that it is considered a combat power multiplier. The situation in Haiti following the departure of the *Harlan County* presented the United States with a host of difficult choices. Faced with such complexity, the U.S. military responded with real planning prowess, demonstrated in multiple locations, by a variety of military services and defense agencies, all linked by a unifying joint-planning system, with General Shelton and Admiral Miller as focal points. This planning effort contributed significantly to the success of Uphold Democracy and deserves detailed analysis so that its lessons can assist in future contingencies and be extended to other civilian- and military-planning efforts.

Significant cooperation among the U.S. military services began in earnest during World War II. Prior to that time, the Army and Navy Departments had worked together when and where necessary, but principally just during wartime and only when it was in their mutual best interest to do so. The Department of War was established for the Army in 1789, and the Department of the Navy followed in 1798 for the Navy and Marines. The services had very different missions: the Army's was largely territorial within the United States, and the Navy's and Marine's were normally global and outside American borders. Only with the Civil War did large-scale and long-term operations requiring both services arise. And, in the Civil War, either the Army or the Navy was normally the primary agent during any particular battle, with the other service performing a supporting role. Although exceptions such as the campaigns for Vicksburg and Charleston occurred, few examples of full cooperation among the military services marked America's first 150 years.

The coordination problems that surfaced during the Spanish-American War of 1898 caused the U.S. military some embarrassment, and in 1903 a Joint Board of the Army and Navy was formed to improve the working relationships among the services. The Board had no directive authority and its initiatives did not bear much fruit. By the time of America's entry into World War I in 1917, little had been done to improve the way in which the services worked together; and because the war in Europe was so focused on ground combat by that time, no additional progress was made. The interwar years actually witnessed the three services growing further apart as each worked to specialize in the new technologies of the twentieth century: aircraft, artillery, and specialized vehicles that were enhanced by new concepts of speed, accuracy, and communications.

With the declaration of world war in 1941, the two distinct military departments were forced for the first time to work in concert to defeat the global threat of the Axis powers. The U.S. Joint Chiefs of Staff was formed for the first time in 1942, largely in response to the precedent established by the British. By 1943 the lessons of multiservice cooperation were clear to men like Eisenhower and Nimitz, who had directed campaigns comprised of forces from several military services. Doctrine for air support of land campaigns and amphibious operations improved significantly. At the war's end vast progress had been made towards fostering teamwork and mutual understanding among the services, including the newly formed U.S. Air Force. Still, strong service parochialisms simmered near the surface of the American military establishment following the war, threatening to drive the services back towards competition, particularly when funding was a concern because the military was being reduced in size.

Multiservice educational facilities were established, and collaboration among the four services, though not continual, gradually improved after the establishment of the Department of Defense (DOD) and a permanent Joint Chiefs of Staff in 1947. The military organizations involved in the Korean conflict of the early 1950s inherited a strong sense of service cooperation from their men, most of whom had served during World War II. But with the changes resulting from the advent of nuclear weapons, this cooperation began to weaken due to the competition for scarce resources and preeminence in nuclear missions. The DOD was reorganized in 1949 and again in 1958 to: (1) give better control of the department to the civilian Secretary; (2) give the Chairman of the Joint Chiefs a staff to assist him full time; and (3) give more authority to the regional commanders-in-chief. Even so, by the era of the Vietnam conflict in the mid-1960s service parochialisms had returned to prominence and the conduct of that conflict suffered from a lack of teamwork among senior commanders.[1]

After Vietnam, DOD was hindered by an era of American alienation from military affairs and the services maintained an insular perspective as they grappled with issues of race and reform throughout the 1970s. That decade saw many mid-level officers call for and participate in changes that sought to remedy the difficult problems of the post-Vietnam era. During the 1980s, significant coordination shortfalls in the rescue operations in Iran (Operation Eagle Claw) and Grenada (Operation Urgent Fury) reinforced the need for institutional change. This insufficiency was even understood by the U.S. Congress, which determined that new legislation was required to foster greater teamwork. Looking back over the period from 1941, Congressional studies clearly identified a necessary refocusing of military efforts. This change was mandated by the Goldwater–Nichols Department of Defense Reorganization Act of 1986, which for the first time required service cooperation and the preeminence of "joint" perspectives and organizations.[2]

The return of freedom to Kuwait in 1991 (Operations Desert Shield and Desert Storm) provided initial evidence of the advantages of mandated joint reform within DOD. Later operations in Northern Iraq (Provide Comfort) and Somalia (Provide Hope) showed clear progress in these military objectives, but also revealed the other types of government coordination required for lasting success. Lessons learned from peace operations supporting the United Nations in Somalia were particularly striking. In several ways, the improvements mandated by the U.S. Congress were first fully realized in Haiti during Uphold Democracy. A high level of joint cooperation was most evident in the planning and force-posturing phases of the operation, both of which demonstrated the value of a single, unified commander charged with warfighting responsibilities and empowered with sufficient authority to gain support when and as required. The Haitian operation also confirmed the need for greater interagency coordination within the U.S. government and more effective procedures between the United States and the United Nations.

NOTES

1. The position of General William Westmoreland as the commander of the Military Assistance Command, Vietnam (MACV) was perhaps more complicated than any in American history. In fact, Westmoreland was subordinate to Admiral U. S. Grant Sharp, USN, the Commander-in-Chief Pacific, yet he received much of his guidance directly from the White House and the Office of the Secretary of Defense. Within Vietnam, Westmoreland had none of the authority of a combatant commander today; he was hard pressed to exact close support from the senior Air Force and Navy commanders in the region and had running disagreements with the senior Marine commanders serving in the northern (I Corps) sector of the country.

2. Joint organizations are those composed of two or more services from different military departments. For example, the Joint Staff, which serves the Chairman of the Joint Chiefs of Staff and the headquarters of the unified commanders-in-chief (CINCs), is composed of a representative mix of personnel from all services. Interestingly, it was General David C. Jones, USAF, while serving as the Chairman of the Joint Chiefs of Staff, who first called for the reforms directed by the Goldwater–Nichols Act.

CHAPTER 5

Military Plan Development: The "Jade Green" Cell

The organization that had the responsibility of the planning for the Haitian operation was the U.S. Atlantic Command (USACOM), headquartered in Norfolk, Virginia. USACOM had been one of the original unified commands created in 1947.[1] At that time, it was known by the acronym LANTCOM and had a very distinct naval orientation, which grew from the primary mission of the command: the protection of the Atlantic and Caribbean waterways and the support of U.S. force deployments to Europe.[2] The commander of LANTCOM had also been the commander of the U.S. Atlantic Fleet and Supreme Allied Commander, Atlantic (SACLANT), one of the two major NATO commands within the military structure of the Atlantic Alliance.[3]

This naval focus was fundamentally changed in October 1993, when the composition of LANTCOM grew to include the majority of Army and Air Force forces within the continental United States, and its mission was enlarged to include planning for the land defense of North America.[4] The title-acronym was also changed to USACOM, reflecting the important additional responsibilities it received in the new Unified Command Plan published during 1993.[5] In addition to the increase in the number and types of forces he commanded, the commander of USACOM gained responsibility for the joint training of all assigned forces and the development of joint force "packages" for employment by the U.S. commanders-in-chief (CINCs) worldwide.[6] These joint force packages were then envisioned to be tailored groups of forces, formed specifically for a given crisis by a joint commander who understood the inherent strengths of all service forces and designed in coordination with the CINC who would employ them. This new concept in the organization of American military forces fundamentally altered the perspectives of planners at the new USACOM and presented a new range of options to commanders elsewhere. Much of this innovation was sponsored by the commander in Norfolk at the time, Admiral Paul David Miller, a naval officer of significant political savvy and vision, and was implemented by the Chairman of the Joint Chiefs of Staff, first General Colin Powell, USA, and then by his successor, General John Shalikashvili, USA.[7]

As LANTCOM, the headquarters in Norfolk had planned and coordinated the aborted *Harlan County* mission. That effort had ended in October, just after the creation of USACOM on the first of the month; yet there was no doubt in Norfolk at the time that the Haiti situation was not going to be resolved without U.S. involvement, including the likely use of military forces. Any military action in Haiti was the responsibility of the USACOM commander and Admiral Miller had a full measure of options in preparation, should the use of force be required. Because President Clinton had promised more open access to America for oppressed peoples as a part of his election platform, the number of Haitian migrants attempting to flee Haiti had been consistently rising during 1993. In fact, the staff in Norfolk had been standing special-duty watches on and off since Clinton's inauguration the previous January in anticipation of a massive flood of migrants. By October, the Atlantic Command included some of the most dedicated Haiti specialists found anywhere in the United States.

The new challenges and perspective of USACOM boosted morale and stimulated renewed planning for a likely follow-up effort in Port-au-Prince. The fact that the key assumptions and objectives of Uphold Democracy began to meld during the fall of 1993, when USACOM was created, contributed to the progressive development of greater joint perspectives for the operation. Also of value during this period was the presence at USACOM of three key senior officers. The first was Lieutenant General William W. Hartzog, USA, the deputy commander-in-chief of the command and the initial focal point of staff coordination for Haiti.[8] Hartzog, who had been the J3, Operations Officer, for the U.S. Southern Command during operation Just Cause in Panama, provided much early guidance that helped frame the development of the planning process.[9] The second key figure was the command's senior planner and prime architect of the posture on Haiti for the 2 years preceding the *Harlan County* incident, Major General John J. Sheehan, USMC.[10] General Sheehan had a strong personal interest in Haiti and had developed an effective working relationship with Cedras over several visits to the country.[11] Although Sheehan departed from Norfolk in October to become the Director of Operations (J3) at the Joint Staff in the Pentagon, he had already made a large impact on Haitian issues. As the Pentagon J3 he retained great influence over the planning because of his position on the staff of the Chairman of the Joint Chiefs of Staff. Equally influential was Sheehan's replacement as chief planner at USACOM—another Marine, Major General Michael C. Byron.[12] General Byron brought valuable expertise as a former planner for operation Urgent Fury in Grenada, and recent experience with the interagency coordination required for modern military operations.[13] He was exactly suited for the complex task in Norfolk.[14] These three officers would prove invaluable as Shalikashvili and Miller managed the strategy for military actions in Haiti.

United States military doctrine had provided the basic parameters for military actions since World War II, but had undergone a tremendous renaissance since operations in Grenada in 1983 revealed significant weaknesses in interservice cooperation. In 1992 General Colin Powell had published a new joint operations doctrine manual, *Joint Pub 1,* entitled "Joint Warfare of the Armed Forces of the United States," and gave a copy to every officer on active duty. The manual outlined the purpose, values, and fundamentals of joint operations and provided a primer on joint campaigns. For many, *Joint Pub 1* formally instituted a revolution in American military affairs; its focus on joint interoperability certainly had a large impact on the planning for and execution of operations in Haiti.[15]

Joint doctrine calls for the development of "deliberate plans" for use against specific, identified threats to U.S. national interests, and the construction of "crisis action plans" when an unanticipated situation arises that may require the employment of U.S. forces. The stressful situation in Haiti fell in-between these two categories. Haiti had not been identified formally as a threat at the national level, but most strategists at the time clearly acknowledged that it was the type of problem that was likely to require a military response, particularly as diplomatic and economic pressures seemed to be having little effect on the Cedras regime. Haiti did not directly threaten the United States in November 1993; however, the bellicose, anti-U.S. attitude of General Cedras and the rising number of people fleeing the country made military planning prudent. Discussions between the headquarters in Norfolk and the Pentagon resulted in the commencement of campaign planning for possible military action in Haiti. However, the new Chairman of the Joint Chiefs of Staff (CJCS), General Shalikashvili, specifically directed that Haiti planning remain "close hold" so that it would not be leaked to the press at a time when the United States was downplaying military action and still emphasizing diplomatic solutions.[16] This "close-hold" restriction ensured that plans could be developed without an adverse impact on the diplomatic efforts to return Aristide, but it inhibited staff coordination between units and agencies of the government.

Campaigns are composed of a series of major battles or multiple military operations over time, all linked to the same strategic or operational objective. Campaign planning involves the design and arrangement of these operations to achieve national policy objectives, normally through the development of one or more Operations Plans (OPLANs).[17] How these plans and their objectives are to be accomplished traditionally resides with the military commander responsible, who outlines specific guidance within a written "commander's intent."[18] Because war is an interactive process with skilled opponents who only rarely act and react as expected, campaign planning includes both *deliberate planning* and *crisis action planning.* Deliberate planning focuses on outlining a known requirement for military operations, based upon assigned national tasking; crisis action planning is conducted on short notice when an anticipated or unanticipated emergency situation occurs. The artistry in campaign planning is to develop a process for accurately identifying and countering threats to the campaign goal, through coordinated political–military actions, once an emergency situation occurs. It is a credit to military planners that they anticipate "friction" and "fog" in war and build flexibility into campaign plans. This flexibility would become a very important factor in the success of operation Uphold Democracy.

Campaign plans are intended to provide unified focus and clear direction for military operations, and to link those military operations to the other elements of national power: diplomacy, economic tools, and information management. Campaign planning supports the national strategic goals established by the President and is conducted with an eye to the long-term impact of the use of force in the theater of operations in which they may be focused, in this case the Caribbean basin and Central America. Campaign planning targets synchronized military forces against the enemy's centers of gravity, those "hubs of all power and influence" upon which the enemy's capability and will to fight depend.[19] Campaign plans must include details of the mission, phasing of forces, concepts of operations and logistics support, deployment requirements, and a command-and-control structure for the envisioned operation. They require intensive work by the military planning staff concerned, normally over a 6–18 month period, and coordination with other government departments.

Two fundamental elements of campaign plans are the synchronization of forces and the concept for their sustainment. These issues become the focus of staff effort once the basic elements of the mission are precisely defined. In the case of Haiti, the nexus of the campaign planning effort was the development of an operation plan (OPLAN) for synchronizing the forcible entry of U.S. units into Haiti and sustaining them while they executed operations to uphold the democratic process there. The development of the major plan then needed to be coordinated with other supporting actions so that every effort would be focused towards the common endstate goal of the strategy.

The first step in the joint planning process is *mission analysis,* the determination of the tasks needed for success of the operation as well as any restraints on flexibility. (Generals Sheehan and Hartzog had done much of this prior to the *Harlan County* affair, but their analysis was primarily focused on noncombatant evacuation actions, not forcible-entry operations.) Once these specified tasks and any implied tasks are analyzed, military planners check to determine what plans already exist to support the objectives of the operation and what the commander's intentions are as to how the operation should be carried out.

Because many military plans are designed to handle a range of potential emergencies, proactive ideas for methods of resolving crises can often be found among related plans. Each military plan is categorized to indicate its purpose: operations plans for military actions against a specific enemy; contingency plans for responses to general threats against U.S. personnel and property; and functional plans that employ forces in support of other major operations or national agency efforts such as disaster relief. Several plans were reviewed, but none met the particular criteria established for Haiti.[20]

THE JADE GREEN CELL

In late October 1993 General Byron decided to form a special planning group in Norfolk to develop an entirely new, deliberate plan specifically dealing with the situation in Haiti. This, the first of two plans eventually developed for Haiti, was conceived during the first week of November when a small but comprehensive cell was formed in the USACOM joint operations center (JOC) crisis-management room. The strategic concept for this plan was developed primarily by this cell under the daily direction of Captain Spike Prendergast, USN, and later, Colonel John Langdon, USMC, although representatives of each staff directorate and the supporting USACOM components also participated as required. The effort was considered "extremely sensitive military planning" and the cell was referred to using the codeword "Jade Green." The plan under development was code-named "Dragon's Blood" and later given the number 2370.[21]

Dedicated work on Operation Plan 2370 (OPLAN 2370), the forcible-entry option to return democracy to Haiti, began with review by the Jade Green cell of all "top–down planning guidance" from Admiral Miller, General Shalikashvili, and any other authoritative direction that applied to the situation in Haiti.[22] This included the CINC's approved mission statement, his intent, and the desired end-state: what he wanted to see as the final situation in Haiti. This analysis was completed in the third week of November and was outlined in briefings to the CINC and the Joint Staff in the Pentagon, including recently promoted Lieutenant General Sheehan. During the Pentagon briefing the USACOM planning cell recommended opening the planning to a Joint Task Force (JTF) commander[23] and his staff, designated as the potential operational commander in Haiti, but this move was denied again for security reasons.[24]

Security for the Haiti planning was so tight that only six or seven officers in Shalikashvili's Joint Staff in the Pentagon knew the details of the plan. Besides the Chairman and Sheehan, only two officers in the operations division, one in the plans division, and one in the intelligence division were active in plan development. This meant that even several key general officers, some who were intimately involved in the diplomatic and support actions for Haiti, were not informed of the work taking place in Norfolk. When the plan was finally executed, these officers were notified of the details only days before the major forces were scheduled to land.[25] Such precautions had been used before, notably for Just Cause in Panama, to ensure that operational security was maintained. However, this restriction of information would add significant burdens on those few who were informed of the details, because they could not leverage the knowledge of all their fellow staff members to accomplish their work.

Intense planning efforts continued through December, and on January 6th, 1994, the members of the cell returned to Washington with a follow-up briefing to General Sheehan, which included three broad options sanctioned by Admiral Miller. In response to these options General Sheehan, for the CJCS, provided the USACOM cell members with two charters for their continued planning: the employment of a large force centered on Port-au-Prince, and the establishment of an enclave in Haiti to return Haitian migrants. The enclave tasking was in response to piqued National Security Council interest in the numbers of Haitian migrants taking to sea, a concern intimately linked with all Uphold Democracy planning and execution. The connection between national security and Haitian migrants rested on the economic, political, social, and legal impacts of thousands of homeless migrants reaching the shores of southern Florida. As the Mariel boatlift of Cubans in 1980 demonstrated, the impact of large-scale migration into the United States could cause negative effects of long duration.[26] The stipulation of a "large force" option implicitly moved the planners towards a significant combat operation instead of a more limited action such as a noncombatant evacuation operation (NEO) or limited strike against key FAd'H targets using precision weapons. By moving towards a larger option, the U.S. military also committed to more long-term involvement in Haitian affairs.[27]

As a result of General Sheehan's endorsement, the Joint Staff provided the Jade Green cell with a planning directive and approval to conduct expanded compartmentalized planning, and it confirmed selection of the recommended JTF commander for the potential operation, Lieutenant General Hugh Shelton, USA.[28] USACOM sent a message on January 7th to General Shelton's headquarters at Fort Bragg, North Carolina, including a mission statement and his designation as the prospective JTF commander. Designation of the JTF commander was a key step in the planning process, because that officer would oversee actual operations in Haiti. The earlier that individual became an active part of the planning process, the more attuned the plan became to his or her particular capabilities and desires and thus the more easily executable.[29] Admiral Miller had no intention of becoming the operational commander; he felt strongly that he and his staff should focus on the strategic issues and form a subordinate command, a JTF, to focus on the details of operations.

Admiral Miller was responsible for conducting joint planning for a wide range of potential combat and noncombat actions in his theater of operations. As General Schwarzkopf demonstrated during the Gulf War of 1990–1991, CINCs plan and execute operations with considerable latitude based upon the unique attributes of their theaters and their personal style of command. For good reasons, Admiral Miller and his staff approached the Haiti problem very differently than had Schwarzkopf in tackling Iraq. The formation of a subordinate operational command was a part of Miller's ongoing theater strategy and was a familiar element in all planning and exercises in his area of responsibility. Annual exercises had been conducted for many years using two different JTF staffs: JTF-120 for maritime operations, and JTF-140 for primarily land-oriented operations. These training exercises developed expertise and honed techniques among the staffs which might be called upon to respond to crises in the region. They became an element so valuable to the proper execution of Haiti operations that participant after participant commented on their worth.[30] In keeping with operations security, General Shelton's command was numbered differently, becoming Joint Task Force 180 (JTF-180) for Haiti planning purposes.[31]

JTF OPERATIONAL PLANNING

The establishment of JTF-180 for planning was important for coherent plan development.[32] As the staff in Norfolk would not directly control the military actions in Haiti, General Shelton's staff needed a large planning role in order to direct the local campaign effectively. Admiral Miller and his staff would remain in Norfolk to channel assets, coordinate interagency support, maintain strategic management of the theater, and otherwise orchestrate the many collateral and multinational efforts required for success. The Joint Staff, in the Pentagon, was also to be an important part of the operation, facilitating support through the office of the Secretary of Defense and from other government agencies, although this remained very limited in the early months of planing due to the security restriction. Still, the early selection of the JTF-180 commander and his staff was a prerequisite for detailed development of the plan from both the strategic and operational levels. Shelton's staff would work in parallel with Miller and his headquarters to develop the plan, each focusing on the critical requirements from their respective levels. Admiral Miller and General Shelton kept the Pentagon involved as necessary to ensure unity of effort throughout the government.[33]

The joint task force concept had come into favor with the creation of the Rapid Deployment Joint Task Force (RDJTF) in Florida in March 1980.[34] Joint task forces are multiservice units that are task-organized to meet the requirements of a specific mission. They vary in size from small disaster-relief forces of only a few hundred, to huge organizations employing tens of thousands of personnel to win in war. The crucial component of a joint task force is the joint headquarters: the brain of the organization that must form, synchronize, and employ to best advantage the tactical units assigned to the joint force commander.

JTF-180 was formed around the headquarters of the Army's XVIII Airborne Corps, commanded by General Shelton at Fort Bragg. The XVIII Corps, which included the 82d Airborne Division, the 101st Air Assault Division, the 10th Mountain Division, and the 24th Infantry Division (Mechanized), functioned as America's contingency corps—its airborne rapid-reaction force. The Corps headquarters remains the most readily deployable and capable staff of its size in the continental United States. Even so, the task of planning the operation in Haiti was of sufficient complexity that it occupied the planners in Norfolk and Fort Bragg for many months. While the USACOM staff concentrated on the coordination of military assets at the national level and the strategic aspects of the plan, the JTF planning staff in Fort Bragg focused on the details of force deployment and utilization in Haiti.

Planning an operation is always a demanding task; planning under very restrictive classifications and with a large number of unknowns made the Haiti plan especially difficult to develop. The first official meeting that included key planners of both USACOM and the JTF took place on January 8th, 1994, when Brigadier General Frank Akers, Colonel Dan McNeill, and Major William Garrett of the XVIII Airborne Corps staff traveled to Norfolk to meet with and become part of the Jade Green cell. Key members of the planning team met frequently thereafter to update one another on their progress. They conducted the planning in addition to their normal work, traveling back and forth to Fort Bragg frequently with special communications equipment so that they could be notified immediately of any changes in the plan's status.[35] January only began months of work. Yet it was during that first meeting that all the details were first brought together in Norfolk so that later a concept linking USACOM's strategic goals to the JTF's future operational actions in Haiti could be honed, forces assigned, and decision-makers briefed.

Because the planning was then classified Secret and compartmented for security reasons, the XVIII Airborne Corps planners had to compile a limited list of who needed to be included in the planning at Fort Bragg, in addition to developing a full range of intelligence-support requirements, and having to find a new place to conduct their planning in isolation.[36] Within a month the decision was made in the Pentagon to upgrade the classification of the planning effort to Top Secret. This had a tremendous impact at Fort Bragg, for the XVIII Corps planners had little of the special equipment required for use whenever Top Secret work is conducted.[37] It was about this time that key personnel in the 82d Airborne Division were identified and included in the planning; this pushed the classified effort down to the tactical level of the actual units who would be doing the job in Haiti. All of this coordination was accomplished despite the concern in each planner's mind that the situation could deteriorate rapidly, thereby potentially causing the plan to be executed in a matter of days; this added enormous stress to the planning team's already complicated work environment.

Luckily, contingency plans developed coincidentally with the development of the HAG during September and October of 1993 had received much of General Shelton's attention, and he and his staff had already formed some critical-foundation thoughts on operations in Haiti.[38] One of these thoughts, a fundamental component of American warfighting since the mid-1980s and endorsed by the success of operation Desert Storm, was the use of overwhelming force from all dimensions to strike at the FAd'H. The use of overwhelming force would minimize both Haitian and American casualties by making resistance futile, and the use of forces from all dimensions would permit no gaps through which opposing forces could escape to threaten U.S. troops in the future. These concepts, which molded the entire operational planning effort, were guidelines included in General Shelton's unwavering intent[39] that was published to all and were maximized in the XVIII Corps: the right concepts, the right commander, and the right force for the job.

Finally, after a month of hard work, the initial draft of the campaign plan with Time Phased Force Deployment Data (TPFDD), indicating the specifications of all the forces and equipment to be deployed, was submitted by General Shelton to USACOM for review on February 17.[40] A TPFDD is a computer-generated listing of forces and cargo to be used, designed to translate the commander's concept of operations into data that can be used by transportation and support staffs to properly package, deploy, and support the forces and equipment required for an operation. Although creating a completed TPFDD is laborious and technically challenging, the value added by designing deployment- and logistics-support data in advance of an operation is so great as to make the production of these databases a hallmark of modern American military operations. Normally, nothing participates in an operation that is not entered into a TPFDD. Providing a TPFDD to USACOM enabled Admiral Miller to give all supporting agencies, including the military services and the other supporting commanders-in-chief, a graphic presentation of the sequence and employment of the major combat forces.[41] As Lieutenant Colonel Bonham, USA, one of the primary JTF planners said: "At the operational level, the real effort is getting it [the force] there. . . . The hard part is getting it there in the right configuration with the right stuff. And that is really, in my opinion, what joint planning in all about."[42] Shelton's plan and the TPFDD did just that.

Once a basic plan with the TPFDD is forwarded by the JTF commander and approved by the CINC, key-leader briefings can be conducted among the supporting commanders and then the draft plan can be placed "on the shelf," but ready for use should the immediate need for action arise. At the operational level the initial planning effort of JTF-180 culminated in a key-leader briefing at Fort Bragg. This meeting included General Shelton; Major General James Record, USAF, of the 12th Air Force, who would be the JTF joint force air component commander (JFACC); and Major General William Steele, USA, the commander of the 82d Airborne Division, the tactical-assault force. Discussion at this meeting involved detailed analysis of each unit's actions, the assumed opposing actions, and the corresponding reactions of the U.S. forces. The commanders made adjustments to improve integration among the joint force components and, at that point, units from all over the United States began to train for the tasks outlined in the Haiti plan. Following that meeting, a second briefing was conducted for General Sheehan and his key assistants in the USACOM joint operations center in Norfolk to ensure that the concept and support requirements were in line with national objectives. Knowingly or not, thousands of soldiers, sailors, airmen, and Marines took on new tasks that spring because those assignments were integral to success in Haiti.

REFINEMENTS AND TRAINING

Essentially, the early spring of 1994 was a waiting period for Haiti operations. The national lens was then focused on events taking place halfway around the world in Somalia, where the United States was turning over control of operations in that conflict-scarred country to the United Nations. During December, 1993 Les Aspin, then serving as Secretary of Defense (SECDEF), had undergone significant scrutiny over relations between the U.S. military and the Clinton Administration. Both of these issues, Somalia and relations between President Clinton and his military, served as watershed events in the progression towards the Haitian operation. Lessons learned during the Somalia operations, including the need for a specific date to drive the completion of operations and specific completion criteria to reduce the chance of "mission creep,"[43] were applied to improve preparations for Haiti. The often prickly relationship between the President, his advisors, and the senior uniformed officers in the DOD had been smoothed over after Aspin's resignation as SECDEF on December 15th.[44] From January through March new SECDEF William Perry worked hard and brought improved vision and focus to his department just when Haiti planning was most receptive to new ideas.

During April and early May, key units conducted additional rehearsals, including a major joint exercise at Camp Lejeune, North Carolina, named Agile Provider 94. This exercise simulated the combined amphibious and airborne assault of a Caribbean island in order to rescue stranded American citizens and destroy an opposing force threatening the government in power. Agile Provider 94 was a key event for several reasons: First, it brought Admiral Miller, General Shelton, General Record, and Admiral Jay Johnson, USN, together for several weeks, permitting them to rehearse the same roles they would play in Uphold Democracy. (Admiral Johnson was then enroute to take command of the Second Fleet and was to become the deputy JTF commander and naval-component commander of Shelton's JTF-180.) Second, the exercise permitted JTF-180 staff members to conduct a changeover of command between JTFs. In the exercise, Marine Lieutenant General William Keys originally began the operation, controlling the amphibious and airborne assaults; he then turned over control of the remainder of the exercise to General Shelton. This "turnover" allowed the XVIII Corps staff to see the effects of changing over command in the middle of an operation, something they would have to do later in Haiti. Third, because Agile Provider 94 employed many of the same forces as would the Haiti operation, a number of the logistic and transportation details for Uphold Democracy were analyzed during the exercise at Fort Bragg, Pope Air Force Base, and Camp Lejeune. Finally, the exercise enabled the CINC to meet with all of his key subordinate commanders simultaneously, with excellent operations security, to discuss the Haiti planning to date and identify any shortfalls.

Also during May, several important personal briefings of the plan were conducted to develop coordination among the major supporting players within the DOD. General Shelton briefed the Chief of Staff of the Army, and afterwards, General Hartzog briefed all the members of the Joint Chiefs of Staff in the Pentagon and, separately, the new Secretary of Defense. These briefings were a result of the lessons learned during operation Just Cause, which demonstrated the dependence of any operational commander on the supporting-agency chiefs back in Washington, particularly after an operation is executed and the friction of war requires that changes be made. A second benefit of these briefings was that a growing number of very experienced military officers and DOD civilians had the advantage of learning the details and appreciating the critical actions that had to be taken to fully execute the JTF commander's concept of operations. However, security precautions still prevented many staffers from learning the details of the plan at this early stage.

As a result of these activities and the downward spiral of conditions in Haiti, on May 25th JTF-180 was reactivated for additional planning. The reasons were twofold: to incorporate the lessons of Agile Provider 94 and to respond to a change in the availability of units.[45] One of the difficult challenges of joint operations planning is that the world situation shifts over time. United States military units are all normally assigned to a specific crisis requirement. Consequently, the availability of various U.S. military units changes in response to the fluid global situation. This can have the consequence of changing both the units and the planners involved in any developing crisis. In the case of Haiti the involvement of the Marines shifted several times, based upon the global commitments of Marine units. Through March, the JTF planners had envisioned using Marine forces in the north of Haiti to establish a secure environment around the port and airfield of Cap-Haitien. By May the situation had changed so that the Marines were assigned only a supporting role as the JTF-180 reserve force, and an additional army infantry brigade was added to the Haiti planning. This altered not only the force structure of the JTF but also the TPFDD requirement (because the Army brigade had to arrive by air, whereas the Marines could have arrived from the sea). The command-and-control structure changed as well so that required communications could be established directly linking Port-au-Prince to Cap-Haitien. Such seemingly small changes had large repercussions on the planning staff and kept them in a 7-days-a-week work environment for months.[46]

In late May a critical decision was made by the commanders to design the plan around a 10-day warning window. All plans have to be based upon certain assumptions, which normally include estimates of enemy-force actions and the time required for friendly-force counteractions. In the case of Haiti, the "enemy," usually generalized as the FAd'H and its supporters, was unlikely to threaten the United States militarily, but could threaten U.S. citizens and interests. Until May, planning had been based upon the assumption that military operations could commence with an evacuation of FAd'H-threatened American citizens and designated third-country nationals friendly to the United States. Due to aircraft-staging requirements such an operation required approximately 4 days of preparation, so the forces assigned to execute an NEO were placed on a 96-hour alert. The problem was that 96 hours was insufficient notice in order to marshal maximum U.S. combat power in the event of a crisis. The identification and loading of transport ships, the sea travel to Haiti, and the on-board rehearsals necessary to ensure safety, took much longer than 4 days. Additionally, many planners felt that the compartmentalization of the planning effort meant that more time would be needed to inform key decision-makers and coordinate details outside the military before the operation could be executed within an acceptable level of risk. With a timely and ultimately crucial decision, Admiral Miller directed that the plan incorporate, and the staffs rehearse for, a 10-day notification sequence.[47] Ten days permitted the transportation assets to be marshaled, vital coordination to be accomplished, and the full force to be poised for execution.

During early June OPLAN 2370, as the Haiti plan had been labeled once it had been approved by Admiral Miller, was updated to include a contingency plan for the use of the United Nations Mission in Haiti (UNMIH) as a follow-on force. This was in response to agreements reached with key members of the United Nations staff concerning the international importance of the Haiti mission. As Somalia had demonstrated to the U.S. military, supranational support was both an asset and a challenge. Integrating the United Nations mission into the plan from the beginning would not only better define the end result required for mission completion, it would also reduce difficulties in transition from the U.S.-led force to that of the United Nations.

After a communications exercise and a final leaders' rehearsal, the plan was submitted to Admiral Miller for his renewed approval on June 20th. Once approved in concept by the CINC, the plan was presented again to key members of the Joint Staff and to the service chiefs. It was then refined a third and final time, after a July 21st update to the Chairman of the Joint Chiefs. (This succession of briefings was driven by the fear that the plan might need to be executed on short notice, so each modification needed to be formally approved and coordinated.) On August 7th the plan was turned over to a new staff section in USACOM, labeled J35, Current Plans, under the direction of Colonel Keith Holcomb, USMC. J35 developed the final execution matrix for 2370, conducted a USACOM communications exercise during August 15–19, and transformed the plan into the operations-order format required for execution.[48] The development of OPLAN 2370 had taken 10 months from initial concept development in November to final CJCS approval and its transformation into a completed document with supporting TPFDD, ready for execution. Several headquarters had collaborated—under tight constraints to minimize risk—in the plan and to build in as much flexibility as possible. The only remaining question was: when would it be used?

Two of the most valuable lessons of this phase of 2370's development were the importance of the (1) planning relationship between the supervisory headquarters in Norfolk and the execution staff at Fort Bragg, and (2) the capability to adequately plan under heavy operations security. A current tenet of American warfighting obliges senior commanders to ensure that their subordinates are given both sufficient authority and adequate flexibility to conduct operations. General Shelton's staff was a full partner in the development of 2370 because the staff at USACOM firmly believed that the input and desires of the JTF commander had to be reflected in any plan that he and his staff would execute. Without the input of the executing staff early in the plan development, too many details would be fixed, limiting operational flexibility by those who would execute the plan once it was put into action as an operations order. In the same way, other major participants in the planning effort, including the service headquarters of the Army, Navy, Air Force, and Marine Corps, and the supporting commands that would provide forces and equipment to any operation in Haiti, were briefed and their input was factored into the plan.[49] All of this was done under the most stringent classification restraints. Although some analysts later charged that the planning for Uphold Democracy was conducted in an overly restrained manner, in reality all the *key* participants at the unified command and joint task force level were effectively and repeatedly involved with the details of the forcible entry plan, while very effective operations security was maintained.[50]

But even as 2370 was nearing completion, one of its major assumptions was coming under increased scrutiny. OPLAN 2370 was a combat plan; combat was assumed because Cedras had indicated no willingness to step down voluntarily. But the Clinton Administration had not yet admitted that combat planning was underway. Thus 2370 remained a closely held secret within the military, developed by proactive planners just in case it might be required on short notice from the President. Clearly, however, today's military cannot and does not desire to work in isolation from the rest of the government. For maximum effectiveness and economy of action, military power must be integrated with the use of the other aspects of national power: diplomacy, economic leverage, and information management. The requirement to open up the plan to other U.S. agencies in order to clearly address the plethora of details that characterize modern politics when two nations are at odds was obvious. Already, all branches of the government were dealing with some aspect of the Haiti situation. The State Department, the Treasury, the Departments of Transportation, Commerce, Justice, and even Agriculture, the CIA, all the Defense agencies,[51] plus the state of Florida were heavily engaged in multiple issues crossing jurisdictional and bureaucratic boundaries. The coordination problem among so many players became so huge that it required an immediate method of focusing all the participant's activities. With a stroke of ingenuity, one of the methods chosen was the development of another, less-classified plan based upon the then slender assumption that Cedras would voluntarily permit the return of Aristide. This plan was eventually labeled OPLAN 2380.[52]

THE DEVELOPMENT OF A SECOND PLAN AND FINAL COORDINATION

OPLAN 2380-95 was broadly conceived in the spring of 1994 as planners encountered more and more details that needed to be coordinated outside of the DOD. But it was first directed on May 20th, coincident with the lessons of Agile Provider. Luckily, the effort to produce OPLAN 2380, which was based upon the *permissive* insertion of multinational forces into Haiti to assist the country's return to democracy, was conducted quite differently from that of the 2370 plan. OPLAN 2380 required only secret-level classification because it was based upon the premise that U.S. forces had been invited into Haiti by the coup leaders. Even though there was an implicit tie between it and 2370, most of the stringent 2370 classification issues were a result of the forces used and the objectives of combat forcible-entry; with the assumption that Cedras would cooperate, 2380 required neither. In fact, the 2380 military effort became primarily a humanitarian action, and few details of such operations are normally classified. Although some spillover from the strict classification of 2370 prevented a completely normal planning process, OPLAN 2380 was much easier to develop and coordinate.[53] An initial 2380 operations plan was issued for coordination as early as July 8th, and unlike the frequently updated 2370, no major revision was issued until September 13th. That revision was based upon USACOM staff-members' review of the text of United Nations Security Council Resolution 940, which permanently linked United Nations forces to the operation.

OPLAN 2380 did not add much military activity to the preparations to return President Aristide, yet it significantly aided the interagency planning process in Washington. The plan came with a timetable for the deployment of military forces and announced specific objectives and requirements for support of military operations, which could be used for either 2370 or 2380. In effect, 2380 permitted the State Department and other planners, working with the United Nations and foreign nations not normally privy to the highly classified elements of 2370, to coordinate with both plans based upon the 2380 timetable. For example, the State Department's International Criminal Investigation and Training Program (ICITAP), a key element to the reform of the Haitian police force, could be informed of important planning factors so that its directors could better prepare for its role in the plan. The same was true for several other organizations, including the Immigration and Naturalization Service (INS), the Bureau of Alcohol, Tobacco, and Firearms (ATF) and the United States Agency for International Development (USAID).

In fact, the USACOM staff hosted several small-scale interagency planning meetings during the months of June and July to advance coordination among the various organizations that were important to success in Haiti. Although less successful than hoped, these meetings did result in at least two organizations sending officials to Norfolk to participate in the military-planning effort. This attempt to enhance interagency coordination was the beginning of USACOM's very strong push to pull the agencies closer together as events in Haiti moved from bad to worse.[54]

Thus by July Admiral Miller had two draft plans for use in Haiti. One, 2370, appeared to be the most likely option: a forcible-entry, combat-unit-heavy operation to be conducted in a nonpermissive environment. It received the codename, "Uphold Democracy." Less likely, but still possible, was the 2380 plan to peacefully enter Haiti with the consent of General Cedras; it was code-named "Maintain Democracy." Both plans shared flexible deterrent options; these would be used to shape the situation in Haiti up to the point until military force was the only option remaining to the Clinton Administration. However, before then, diplomatic, informational, and economic means still could change the situation in Haiti; since their use could also potentially modify the elements of the two draft plans, continual refinement was anticipated up to the point at which the President ordered execution or cancellation of the plans.

CAMPAIGNING: DIPLOMATIC, ECONOMIC, AND DOMESTIC CONCERNS

Because modern military actions are supported by a broad range of national concerns, plan preparation was only an initial step towards the operations in Haiti. Many other actions were conducted simultaneously or sequentially during the spring and summer of 1994. By the time these two plans came to fruition the U.S. Coast Guard had been conducting operation Able Manner, the interdiction of Haitian migrants attempting to reach the United States for 18 months. Additionally, JTF-120, the maritime JTF striking force of USACOM, had been activated to support possible noncombatant evacuation operations (NEO) for American citizens and selected third-country nationals in March 1994. It remained in the region to assist with the enforcement of economic sanctions against Haiti directed by the United Nations. In June 1994 Admiral Miller had formed another joint task force, later named JTF-160, to conduct Haitian migrant processing at afloat and at shore locations in the Caribbean in support of Able Manner; this operation was entitled Sea Signal Phase V and was still ongoing when operation Uphold Democracy was executed. The deployment of these wide-ranging, joint military force packages meant that the Caribbean basin was already a tempest of activity while execution planning for Uphold Democracy was being completed. Admiral Miller coined the term "Caribbean Campaign" to note the complexity of these interrelated, long-term military commitments.[55]

Although the use of so many forces for months in the Caribbean helped to focus media attention on the problems in Haiti, it also caused some logistical and support difficulties. None of the armed services had budgeted for such significant involvement in the Caribbean, and the deployment of ships and personnel for long periods of time stretched the ability of the Navy and Marine Corps to support other ongoing efforts worldwide.[56] The operation in Haiti was among the first to demonstrate that the smaller, post-Cold War American military was hard-pressed to support the number of crises required by the United States' global-leadership role.

On the first of June 1994 the Chairman of the Joint Chiefs of Staff formally requested, via a planning order, that Admiral Miller and the USACOM staff conduct additional preparations for operations in Haiti. This request resulted from the understanding that the President finally viewed military action as a potential tool for solving the Haiti crisis. However, the U.S. political agenda for Haiti was still not clear to military planners. What if the United States had to act less aggressively in order to accomplish its objectives? Faced with some doubt, the military sought to add flexibility to its plans. Operational flexibility is always enhanced through development of alternate courses of action and "branches" on the primary plan that permit commanders to counter the unanticipated actions of the opposing side. When time is available, further development of any plan in order to provide greater options to the President always yields great benefits during plan execution.

As evidence of the growing likelihood of force employment in Haiti, one day later, on June 2nd, the Pentagon revealed that the United States was considering deployment of American military forces to help patrol the border between the Dominican Republic and Haiti. The Vice President's national security advisor, Leon Feurth, was coordinating the efforts of several U.S. government agencies to help seal gaps in the United Nations embargo. This operation came to be labeled the Multinational Observers Group (MOG). Also on June 2nd, President Aristide expressed doubts about the effectiveness of the embargo as a tool to topple the Cedras regime and urged other actions to force the return of democratic functions. Debate over the effectiveness of economic sanctions had been a major focus of public and congressional opinion prior to the Gulf War. In general, opinion held that embargoes were not an effective deterrent, particularly when they caused additional suffering to the civilian population, which had no recourse for obtaining the staples of life, while the elites in power could frequently avoid the effects of the embargo.[57]

On June 7th the Organization of American States (OAS), meeting in Belem, Brazil, called for the establishment of a multinational peacekeeping force to assist reform efforts in Haiti after the military junta stepped down. The United Nations Security Council planned to establish this force as the second United Nations Mission in Haiti (UNMIH).[58] The participation of other nations in U.S. military operations, and the use of coalition and multinational forces in combination with the American military have become more the norm than the exception since the Desert Storm Gulf conflict. Multinational participation offers both advantages and disadvantages during an operation. The political advantages include shared costs and the resourcing of support and therefore greater acceptability of the operation by American voters and public opinion worldwide. United States objectives, regardless of their rationale, appear to be more justified when other nations join in the effort. By contrast, the challenges of command and control for an operation involving multiple nations, with multiple national agendas and force limitations, compound an already difficult task. UNMIH would demonstrate worldwide resolve, and the involvement of the OAS would help reduce potentially negative perceptions of U.S. influence in the Caribbean, which had deteriorated after the 1985 invasion of Grenada. But putting the polyglot force together and executing an operation in a manner acceptable to a worldwide team would also prove to be a challenge.

Also on June 7th, U.S. officials established a link between Colombian drug lords and the Haitian military, which increased speculation of a U.S. intervention similar to that in Panama in 1989. The war on drugs was well supported by American voters, and any connection between the rulers of Haiti and the export of illegal drugs to the United States would highlight the criminal nature of the Haitian regime. Later the same week the United States announced that it would increase sanctions by barring commercial and financial transactions between the United States and Haiti beginning on June 25th; this U.S. action resulted in a declaration of a state of emergency in Haiti by the provisional president Emile Jonassaint.

On June 16th the State Department authorized departure of the U.S. embassy staff in Port-au-Prince, reducing the number of personnel there from 118 to 75. Authorized departure was the first of three steps traditionally taken to scale down an embassy staff prior to potential conflict. In diplomatic terms it was a clear signal to the Haitian leadership and to the planners in Washington and Norfolk that the likelihood of military action had increased.

The following week, the Pentagon announced the deployment of troops along the Haiti–Dominican Republic border to help improve the effectiveness of the embargo, and also a plan to deploy an EC-130 aircraft to begin radio broadcasts of "Radio Democracy." The Haiti–Dominican Republic border mission was arranged through a bilateral agreement and should have been an operation of mutual benefit to American and Dominican interests; unfortunately, it was plagued by employment restrictions and limitations on equipment use and turned out to be of little assistance to the sanctions enforcement. The radio broadcasts on the other hand were the first of many parts of what would become an extremely effective psychological operations (PSYOPS) campaign, linked integrally with the military operations in Haiti.[59] The goal of this PSYOPS effort was to educate the Haitian people about the goals of the American involvement and prepare them for the participation of U.S. military forces in the return of President Aristide.

By late June it was obvious to many that the Clinton Administration was becoming very serious about its commitment to return Aristide; this was made evident by President Clinton's announcement of a freeze on all U.S. assets of Haitians living in the United States, with the exception of President Aristide and his supporters. On the 24th of June, the Clinton Administration also disclosed its support for a United Nations peacekeeping force of 12,000–14,000 multinational troops, with the United States providing up to 3,000 of the total. The combination of these actions and the end of airline flights bound for the United States from Haiti resulted in a massive sea exodus of Haitians towards the nearby shores of Florida during the final days of the month.

The last week of June witnessed the largest week's total of Haitian migrants intercepted at sea for the year—over 2,000. This number was almost as many as had been intercepted in all of 1993, and brought the total number for the first half of 1994 to nearly 20,000. Such numbers forced the Clinton Administration to reopen the naval facility at Guantanamo Bay for migrant processing, an act it had worked long to prevent. This caused a variety of problems, including an adverse effect on the military use of the base and potential conflicts with Cuba. It was, however, preferred over accepting these large numbers of migrants on U.S. territory where they would immediately be eligible for certain types of government-supported aid. After another 2,000 Haitians were rescued in the days that followed, alarm bells began to ring in Florida and Washington. State and federal officials saw a clear danger in the continued attempts of hundreds of migrants to flee in unseaworthy craft. The Coast Guard worked tirelessly to publicize the danger and to help protect those who placed themselves at risk, while other government agencies perceived in the migration a threat to U.S. interests. The State Department tightened sanctions again on June 29th, and the Clinton Administration revised its policy and stopped granting asylum in the United States to Haitian migrants.

The migrant problem was tied very closely with all military planning for Haiti for several reasons: First of all, military forces had been used to control and, where necessary, provide essential lifesaving functions for the migrants in the open ocean since the exodus north had begun in response to the repression that followed Aristide's fall. This was a constant drain on ships and personnel and reduced the number of assets available to support conventional military operations in Haiti. Second, the establishment of three joint task forces in the region complicated command and control and placed great stress on the efficient management of personnel by the headquarters in Norfolk. The staff at USACOM was smaller than many of the other joint military staffs and was not sufficient in number to plan and execute three simultaneous operations easily. Finally, in a political sense the plight of the migrants was taking up a growing share of available time and resources from the planning for the return of Aristide. More Americans were concerned about the Haitian boat people and their potential impact in Florida than about the lack of democracy in Haiti, which was the root cause of the migrant problem. Where American public opinion focused, so too did the attention of the President and Congress, which in turn directed the actions of the military personnel who must carry out political policy objectives. Essentially, during this period more effort in Norfolk was expended in dealing with the flood of migrants than in addressing its root cause.

Migration finally came to be viewed as a direct threat to U.S. security interests in the Caribbean in mid-July. By that time a host of diplomatic and economic techniques had been used unsuccessfully to return Aristide to his homeland. The

United Nations was fully in support of Aristide's return, as was the Organization of American States. Still, the real catalyst was the constant flow of poor Haitians taking to the sea to look for a better life in America. Soon the impact of seeing so many small boats on the television screens of average homes in the United States became too stark for Washington to ignore.

NOTES

1. Unified commands are established by the Secretary of Defense and composed of major elements of multiple services; as organizations, they execute enduring regional or functional missions in support of U.S. military strategy. The commanders-in-chief of these unified commands are collectively known as the warfighting CINCs due to their primary responsibility of providing strategic direction for combatant forces worldwide.

2. As an interesting note, LANTCOM and USACOM areas of responsibility (AOR) included the Pacific waters immediately adjacent to the western side of South America. The only "land" areas in the AOR were Iceland, the Azores, Greenland, and the islands of the Caribbean basin. Navy and Marine personnel staffed the command almost entirely. This has since been changed, and effective in June, 1997, the U.S. Southern Command has responsibility for operations in the waters surrounding South America and in the Caribbean.

3. Under the 1993 change to the Unified Command Plan the commander-in-chief of USACOM remained dual-hatted as the Supreme Allied Commander, Atlantic.

4. For the history of USACOM see Leo P. Hirrel, *United States Atlantic Command Fiftieth Anniversary, 1947–1997.*

5. The Unified Command Plan (or UCP) is a document signed by the President that outlines the geographic and functional responsibilities of the CINCs. See Ron H. Cole and Walter S. Poole's *The History of the Unified Command Plan,* and Roger R. Trask's *The Department of Defense, 1947–1997: Organization and Leaders.*

6. The nine unified commanders-in-chief include the commanders of the U.S. Atlantic Command, the U.S. Pacific Command, the U.S. Southern Command, the U.S. European Command (also assigned as Supreme Allied Commander, Europe), the U.S. Central Command, the U.S. Special Operations Command, the U.S. Transportation Command, the U.S. Space Command, and the U.S. Strategic Command.

7. Admiral Miller saw the joint force packaging (JFP) concept as central to the value added by the new USACOM and a driving force in the planning for operations in Haiti. Miller also noted that General Powell's vision and commitment was key to success and acceptance of the USACOM reorganization. (McClintock interview with Miller, January 19, 1995, pp. 1, 5.)

8. Hartzog later received his fourth star and selection to command the Army's Training and Doctrine Center (TRADOC) at Fort Monroe, Virginia. Most of those deeply involved with the operation consider General Hartzog to be the great talent behind the scenes for the planning and execution of Uphold Democracy.

9. Operation Just Cause was the December, 1989 invasion of Panama directed by General Max Thurmond, USA, as commander in chief, U.S. Southern Command. The operational commander of Just Cause was Lieutenant General Carl Steiner, USA, then the commander of the U.S. Army's XVIII Airborne Corps. President George Bush ordered the operation to protect U.S. citizens, restore stability in Panama, and bring Manuel Noriega to trial for illegal drug activities.

10. While serving as the Operations Director for the Joint Staff in 1994, Sheehan was awarded his fourth star and returned to Norfolk in the fall of the same year to command USACOM.

11. On January 6th, 1993, General Sheehan flew to Port-au-Prince to talk pointedly with General Cedras, soldier to soldier. Sheehan made it quite clear that the United States was committed to the return of Aristide and that the Haitian armed forces had to be active participants in the process of change. See Howard W. French, "Visiting U.S. General Warns Haiti's Military Chiefs," *New York Times,* January 9, 1993, p. 5.

12. Byron was later selected to become the Deputy Director for Plans and Policy for the Joint Staff in Washington. Following that assignment, in 1997 he was promoted to lieutenant general and assigned to be the senior U.S. military representative to the North Atlantic Treaty Organization (NATO) in Belgium.

13. Operation Urgent Fury was the 1983 invasion of the island of Grenada by Army, Navy, Air Force, and Marine personnel under the command of Vice Admiral Joseph Metcalf, USN, then commander of the U.S. Navy's Second Fleet. President Reagan's goals for Urgent Fury included the evacuation of U.S. citizens and the restoration of stability in Grenada.

14. General Byron was that rare officer who had held command at high levels and had had experience as a planner, as an interagency coordinator in Washington, and as a former member of the Inter-American Defense Board, a position that gave him particular insight into the concerns of the militaries of the Caribbean.

15. The revolution began when Congress overhauled the military with the Goldwater–Nichols Department of Defense Reorganization Act of 1986. *Joint Pub 1* was a direct result of the Act's goal of improving the way the armed services worked together. The manual's greatest effect remains controversial, yet no one doubts that it brought new joint perspectives and greater acceptance of joint warfighting to every officer who read it, particularly as it ascribed the successes of the Gulf War to joint effectiveness. *Joint Pub 1* set the stage for a series of key doctrinal manuals, many of which reflect the procedures used successfully in Haiti; these manuals were used in the preparation of this book as the standard of comparison for the innovative techniques and procedures used during Uphold Democracy.

16. McClintock and Passarelli interview with Prendergast, November 23, 1994, p. 3. Even so, detailed notes concerning actions that would have to be accomplished by agencies outside the DOD, such as the State Department's coordination of staging rights in foreign ports, were kept during the planning process by Major Mike Sutton, USMC, because it was clear that even many of the most classified details would require coordination. These notes would become crucial just prior to execution, when the classification restrictions were lessened and a host of operational details needed to be accomplished within a very short timeframe. General Shalikashvili had assumed his position on October 30th, just after the *Harlan County* operation.

17. *Joint Pub 5-0,* "Doctrine for Planning Joint Operations," outlines the joint procedure for planning operations. It defines a campaign plan as "a plan for a series of related military operations aimed at accomplishing a strategic or operational objective within a given time and space" (p. GL-4).

18. The method of achieving the assigned mission is always approved by higher authority and, in the case of an operation like Uphold Democracy, was briefed to the President. The commander's intent helps to focus effort and foster a deepened understanding of the operation throughout a military force.

19. "Center of gravity" is a term derived from Carl von Clausewitz' book, *On War,* still considered a fundamental text for military planners worldwide.

20. Four different plans were considered: one addressed Haiti specifically, but was not up to date; one was designed for evacuation of American citizens from the Caribbean; and two others were scoped for small island-combat operations, which did not meet the current Haitian conditions.

21. McClintock and Passarelli interview with Prendergast, November 23, 1994, p. 1.

22. Admiral Miller believed in giving his planners maximum flexibility to ensure that they considered the full range of options before returning to him for guidance; his only specific instructions to the Jade Green team of planners was to "do right." McClintock interview with Miller, January 19, 1995, p. 5.

23. The use of a Joint Task Force command structure for the operation was in keeping with USACOM's policy of retaining strategic direction and coordination functions in Norfolk and empowering a subordinate operational commander to focus specifically on actions in Haiti.

24. McClintock and Passarelli interview with Prendergast, November 23, 1994, p. 1. The most likely reason for this decision was to limit the number of personnel who knew about the planning effort for as long as possible for security reasons. It was also directed to ensure that military plans did not interfere with the effectiveness of the diplomatic effort to return Aristide. Diplomacy was still the primary tool of the Clinton Administration, which denied any plans to invade Haiti.

25. John R. Ballard interview with Colonel Robert J. Garner, USMC, former Chief, Joint Operations Division, Joint Staff, November 4–5, 1997. Colonel Garner managed the special category-planning program for Haiti, with the assistance of Lieutenant Colonels Mike Hostage and Frank Britten.

26. Between April and September 1980 over 125,000 Cubans were released by Castro and taken in by the United States. Several agencies of the U.S. government, including the Defense Department, labored for years following the event to house and care for its participants. The impact on the state of Florida was also large and in several cases negative. In the end, many of the Cubans involved in the boatlift came to rest in Arkansas under then-Governor Bill Clinton. Rioting by these immigrants later caused Clinton damage during a subsequent race for governor, which he lost.

27. The use of a large combat force could be expected to result in more extensive damage to Haitian forces and facilities; both of these sectors of Haitian society would then need to be restored in some form prior to the exit of U.S. forces. In addition to the significant amount of rebuilding that would be required after any operation in Haiti, the large-force option implied longer stabilization time after all military objectives had been accomplished.

28. McClintock and Passarelli interview with Prendergast, November 23, 1994, p. 2. Shelton received his fourth star and became first a CINC in his own right, as the Commander-in-Chief, U.S. Special Operations Command, at MacDill Air Force Base, Florida, and was later appointed as the Chairman of the Joint Chiefs of Staff in September, 1997.

29. Fortunately, General Shelton and his staff had participated in the planning for the ill-fated *Harlan County* HAG; consequently, they had anticipated the potential requirement for operations in Haiti and had commenced a review of possible Haiti options from as early as September 1993. Cynthia L. Hayden, ed., *JTF-180 UPHOLD DEMOCRACY Oral History Interviews,* pp. 14, 43.

30. See McClintock interview with Admiral Fargo, February 10, 15, and March 22, 1995, p. 3, and Hayden, *JTF-180 UPHOLD DEMOCRACY Oral History Interviews,* comments from General Shelton, p. 62, and Colonel McNeill, p. 192, as examples.

31. Operations security has the goal of preventing information of operational value from being divulged to a potential enemy.

32. Commonly, joint task forces are created first as minimally staffed planning cells. Only after the mission has been fully developed and forces and other assets have been identified for employment is the new organization activated "for operations." This saves money and resources while providing the proactive planning advantage that is key to success.

33. This JTF concept is known as the "two-tiered system" in joint military doctrine. Some confusion always exists concerning the division of labor between strategic and operational issues. Fundamentally, the strategic commander works to identify an endstate that accomplishes the national policy objectives of a campaign; the operational commander focuses the effort of the military forces and determines the time and place of action to accomplish the mission assigned by the strategic commander. During operation Desert Storm, General Schwarzkopf acted as both the strategic and operational commander; in operation Just Cause, using the two-tiered system, General Thurman was the strategic commander and Lieutenant General Steiner was the operational commander.

34. The RDJTF was not the first joint task force organization. The command elements for the atomic-bomb test units were labeled joint task forces in the 1940s, and many other similar organizations performing a wide variety of functions have come into use as "JTFs" since that time.

35. This special communications equipment included aluminum suitcases containing satellite-capable encrypting telephones so that key members of the group were immediately accessible in case of an emergency.

36. A third-floor supply closet in the Corps headquarters building was commandeered and cleaned out to serve as the planning center for the first month in Fort Bragg. Hayden, *JTF-180 UPHOLD DEMOCRACY Oral History Interviews,* p. 43.

37. For example, Top Secret work must be conducted in a secure area and all Top Secret information must be stored in a safe inside a vault when not under the direct physical control of someone cleared to see it. Everyone who works in or directly supports such work requires an in-depth clearance based upon a special background investigation, which can take months to complete.

38. See Major Garrett's comments in Hayden, *JTF-180 UPHOLD DEMOCRACY Oral History Interviews,* p. 45.

39. The "Commander's Intent" is a precise written statement outlining the most salient goals and methods to be used by the military force to accomplish its mission. Because joint operations are based upon the philosophy of centralized control and decentralized execution, the commander's intent acts as a form of glue joining the efforts of the entire force.

40. Time Phased Force Deployment Data, or the "TPFDD," is the key element in the current Joint Operations Planning and Execution System (JOPES) used by American joint commanders to conduct operations. A result of many years of worldwide deployments of forces on short notice, the TPFDD gives the commander visibility of his forces as they move to the objective area. Building the TPFDD list with all the force-planning data allows modifications to be made to respond to the host of variables that makes war the most complex of human endeavors.

41. This was the first of several TPFDDs developed over the duration of the planning process. With any major change to the concept of operations, the TPFDD would also have to be adjusted. In this connection, much credit should be given to Mrs. Emilie Klutz of USACOM and Mr. Joe Truelove of the XVIII Airborne Corps for their contributions to the success of operations in Haiti.

42. Hayden, *JTF-180 UPHOLD DEMOCRACY Oral History Interviews,* p. 20.

43. *Mission creep* is a term used to describe the evolution of the goals of an operation after the planning has been completed. As military planners develop operations with a particular terminal objective in mind, changes to the endstate become highly problematic.

44. President Clinton's early days in office were marked by heated debate over homosexuals in the military, and some senior military officers received a less-than-warm welcome from the White House staff. Later, Aspin's decision not to send reinforcements requested by General Joseph Hoar, USMC, the commander-in-chief of U.S. Central Command and the officer responsible for the operation in Somalia, prior to the shooting-down of a U.S. helicopter and the deaths of several soldiers in Mogadishu added to a climate of uncertainty. The selection of Dr. William Perry as Aspin's successor did much to relieve this uncertainty and restore smooth relations among the top echelons of the government.

45. Some of these rehearsals, although conducted using cover stories so as to conceal their real purposes for the sake of maintaining operational security, were viewed by the press and added much to the speculation that Haiti would be invaded during June.

46. Later, the role of the Marines was changed again by Admiral Miller, returning them to the mission in the north. A discussion of the Marine assignments during planning can be found in Lieutenant Colonel Bonham's interview in Hayden, *JTF-180 UPHOLD DEMOCRACY Oral History Interviews,* pp. 16–17.

47. See Bonham's comments in Hayden, *JTF-180 UPHOLD DEMOCRACY Oral History Interviews,* p. 19: "in the planning arena, to mass this joint force, and to synchronize to achieve the shock and speed and surprise required to accomplish the mission with minimum loss of life on both sides; that was rocket science."

48. An execution matrix is a planning and coordination tool. It identifies each critical task required for execution, the time in which that task must be accomplished, and the responsibility for task accomplishment. The matrix permits the multitude of necessary events within a military operation to be accomplished in an orderly manner, and it also permits a staff to prepare alternate plans as events are inevitably not accomplished on time.

49. Some of the critically important liaison officers who made inputs for other commanders included: Lieutenant Colonel George Converse, USMC, Major Anthony Tata, USA, Lieutenant Colonel Kim Kadish, USA, and Commander Bob Porter, USCG.

50. See Ambassador James F. Dobbins comments in *Interagency and Political–Military Dimensions of Peace Operations: Haiti—A Case Study,* p. 54.

51. The Defense agencies all work for the Secretary of Defense and play key support roles in any military operation; they then included, among others, the Defense Intelligence Agency, the National Mapping and Imagery Agency, the Defense Logistics Agency, the Defense Information Systems Agency, and the Defense Communications Agency.

52. Credit for the 2380 "plan as coordination tool" idea remains difficult to place; it most likely belongs to General Byron, who was quite clearly the motivating force behind the strategic development of the plan by this stage. Whether or not the individuals who helped design 2380 believed it was intended to be executed, and was something more than a sham, is clearer: Most were quite convinced that Cedras would fight.

53. By necessity, some planners worked on both plans and a very few supporting agencies had to understand both operations to be able to adjust any potential overlaps in forces or timing. Of course, decision-makers had to understand both plans as well. Keeping both plans in the running invariably resulted in associations that endangered the classification barrier between them.

54. Admiral Miller was very displeased with the lack of involvement by key members of the other government agencies. In his words, "From every vantage point that I

observed, USAID did what they were responsible for doing, and they were linked in as tight as they could. The others—we've just got a lot of room for improvement." Miller interview with McClintock, January 19, 1995.

55. There are several annotated working chronologies that were used in preparing the official histories of the campaign. These chronologies provide a guide to the primary and secondary sources related to operations Support Democracy, Uphold Democracy, the U.N. Mission in Haiti, and operation Sea Signal in Guantanamo Bay, Cuba, covering the period from April 1, 1993 to June 1, 1997. These chronologies and collected primary and secondary sources along with abstracts of incoming and outgoing message traffic, situation reports, operations briefings, and files from JTF 180, 190, and 160 are available on-line from the Army Center for Lessons Learned (CALL), Fort Leavenworth, KS, and will also be stored in the Armed Forces Staff College library. See, for example, William R. McClintock, "Working Chronologies, Caribbean Campaign: Operations Support and Uphold Democracy and UN Mission in Haiti and Sea Signal in GTMO, 1 Apr 93–1 Jun 97."

56. During the summer of 1994 the U.S. military was still involved in Somalia, tensions in Bosnia were rising, and the threat of possible conflict in southwest Asia or Korea had resulted in increased force deployments to those regions as well.

57. Robert A. Doughty and Harold E. Raugh, Jr., in their "Embargoes in Historical Perspective," pp. 21–30, point out that historically embargoes have rarely succeeded in achieving their stated objectives and have frequently resulted in rash acts by the embargoed nations. Kathryn Casa's "Iraq Embargo Toll Now Surpasses War's Horrors," pp. 10–11, is just one of the many articles that demonstrate the terrible effect that embargoes have on the poor and the sick.

58. The military portion of the first was the ill-fated Haiti Assistance Group (HAG), which floundered with the turnaround of the *Harlan County* in October 1993.

59. Psychological operations focus on explaining the reasons for military action and often seek to portray a more complete picture of the facts in societies where the government restricts or distorts the truth. In Haiti the major theme was Aristide's legitimacy and the role of America as a supporter of Haiti, not as an invader.

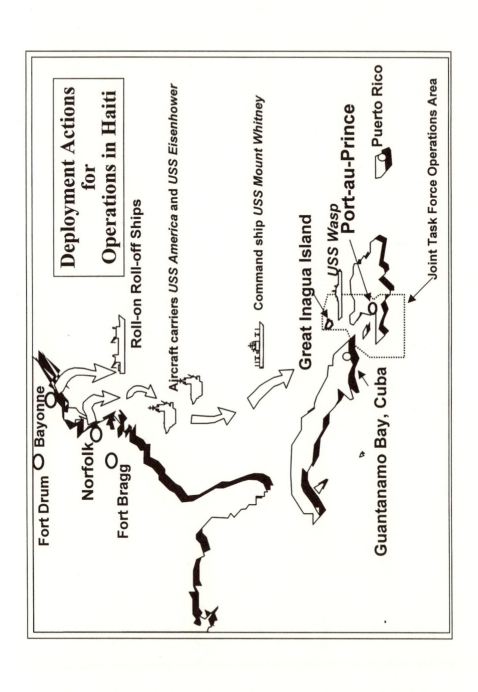

Deployment Actions for Operations in Haiti

Fort Drum
Bayonne
Norfolk
Fort Bragg

Roll-on Roll-off Ships

Aircraft carriers *USS America* and *USS Eisenhower*

Command ship *USS Mount Whitney*

Great Inagua Island

USS Wasp

Port-au-Prince

Puerto Rico

Guantanamo Bay, Cuba

Joint Task Force Operations Area

CHAPTER 6

Posturing the Force

With no apparent change in the situation in Haiti, July 1994 began a new phase in OPLAN 2380 development when CINCUSACOM selected the Commanding General, 10th Mountain Division, as Commander, JTF-190. This meant that the division commander and his staff, in concert with their as-yet unnamed component staffs, would produce a JTF-level plan to execute the strategic missions stated in OPLAN 2380, just as General Shelton and his staff had done for 2370. This development of a plan by the operational commander assigned responsibility for the campaign is a critical step. Normally, the CINC, the JTF commander, and key members of their staffs meet to ensure that the intent of the plan is fully understood by all; unfortunately, little time was available for this step when the JTF-190 staff was designated.[1] Still, by deciding to establish another joint task force, Admiral Miller sent a clear signal to his staff that operations in Haiti were growing more likely. Some even thought that the operation might be needed by the end of the month.

Still, the focus of effort in July was on the 2370 OPLAN, and few felt that the more peaceful 2380 would be executed.[2] Although Shelton's Corps staff would stay cognizant of 2380, it was not a focus of their efforts at Fort Bragg, for all indications pointed to a belligerent response by Cedras and the likelihood that 2370 would be executed within weeks. And, although events would prove otherwise in August, military planners anticipated the invasion soon. On July 6th the *Inchon* Amphibious Ready Group, including 2,000 embarked Marines, was ordered into the Caribbean to be ready to evacuate citizens from Haiti, and USACOM activated a "Haiti Response Cell" to deal with the situation 24 hours per day. Being trained to prepare for a "worst-case solution," few of the military planners felt that the advantages of the 2380 plan outweighed efforts to complete the preparations for 2370.[3]

Mid-July was the first time that both sides indicated that these detailed military preparations were underway. On the 12th of July, the Haitian Junta ordered out of the country the 100-man U.N. and OAS human-rights monitor team that had been reporting the violations of Haitian rights to the world. The same day the USS *Mount Whitney,* command ship of the Second Fleet, sailed for the Haitian area of operations (AO). This was a clear signal to military personnel that the means for conducting military operations were being placed within striking range of Port-au-Prince. The deployment of a fleet command ship is rarely required other than for large-scale naval exercises or operations. The following day, July 13th, the 24th Marine Expeditionary Unit (MEU) completed NEO rehearsals on Great Inagua Island. Such rehearsals are often a normal precursor to offensive operations.

On July 14th Madelaine Albright, the U.S. Ambassador to the United Nations, announced that eleven nations had pledged support for the multinational force (MNF) to be placed in Haiti following the removal of the junta. The following day, U.N. Secretary-General Boutros Boutros-Ghali elaborated on the Security Council's authorization of a coalition force of 15,000 to provide a peacekeeping capability in Haiti after President Aristide resumed his office. In addition he admitted that the United Nations could not organize or finance the force, acknowledging the need for U.S. leadership in the operation. Also on July 15th, Radio Democracy began broadcasting operations to prepare the Haitian people for the invasion and the return of President Aristide. These actions postured international, supranational, and U.S. national assets for operations in Haiti.

Although the Clinton Administration announced on July 19th that no invasion was possible until September due to the time required to train the peace-keeping force, it was clear that the military option was still gaining momentum. The de facto government in Haiti halted humanitarian food and fuel shipments into the country until foreign embassies in Haiti applied for a special tax on imports. In response, on July 20th Ambassador Albright then formally asked for and obtained U.N. Security Council support for an American-led multinational action against Haiti, using "all means necessary" to remove the military leaders.[4] The council authorized military intervention, over and above the sovereign rights of Haiti, for the general good of its people. The stage was set.

Thinking long-term, the United States realized that actions must be started to secure a viable future in Haiti after the potential military operation was completed. The State Department released details of a massive aid package following the restoration of President Aristide; $1 billion would be spent over 5 years. Ambassador Albright distributed her draft resolution indicating that the U.N. peacekeeping force would remain in Haiti no later than February 1996. Among the crucial details of this resolution was the reminder that the invasion force would operate under Chapter VII of the United Nations Charter; to experienced U.N. personnel, this clearly meant that Aristide might well return over the bodies of his own citizens.[5]

The last week of July was spent finalizing the details of U.N. support for the operation. On July 25th, Costa Rica, El Salvador, Guatemala, Honduras, Nicaragua, and Panama all announced support of the draft resolution. This confirmation of support from other nations in the region not only demonstrated the multinational nature of the effort, but also the commitment of OAS regional allies. On July 26th the Haitian government began to organize a November election to choose a president as well as one-third of the senate, the entire lower house, and several local officials. This would, in effect, remove the Aristide government and, when the votes were collected, presumably justify the role of the junta in power. Unwittingly, by scheduling these elections, Haitian officials set a deadline for the initiation of operations. On July 28th the junta organized a 79th anniversary observance of the 1915 occupation by the United States, including anti-U.S. demonstrations and protests against another invasion. Cedras and his followers were also using psychological tools to affect Haitian public opinion. Both sides were on the road to conflict.

GARNERING ALLIES

On July 29th CINCUSACOM specified that all planning and execution responsibility for OPLAN 2380 should devolve to the commander of JTF-190, Major General Dave Meade, USA. This order formally set the 2370 and 2380 plans apart.[6] The intent was to clarify staff coordination and to permit General Shelton to focus only on 2370, the worst-case and, at the time, most probable option. But in reality the order was more confusing than reassuring. Although it implied that General Shelton's force should concentrate only on the nonpermissive option, the order did not clearly indicate to General Meade that his JTF might be employed without the assault forces to "open the door" in Port-au-Prince. No one anticipated changing the missions of these two units at the last minute. This ambiguity would grow in importance as the time to execute grew closer.

Diplomatic and economic deterrents were *still* being employed to eliminate the necessity of having to resort to force. The last Air France flight before U.N. sanctions ended commercial air transportation left Haiti on July 30th, effectively isolating it economically. The following day the U.N. Security Council passed Resolution 940, the diplomatic signal that the world body had sufficient international agreement to authorize the United States to use force to remove Haiti's military-backed government. (See Appendix H for the text of the Resolution.) The plan was delivered, the Haitian government was isolated politically and economically, and the United Nations, acting as a world court, had authorized the use of force to bring the military rule in Haiti to an end. All that remained was the decision by the U.S. President to invade.

In the U.N. vision, the invasion was to take place in two stages: First, an American-led Multinational Force (MNF) would move in, disarm the security forces in the country, remove the military leaders who had ousted President Aristide, take control of functions essential to public security, and institute a retraining program for the Haitian army and police. Then a second, U.N.-coordinated force (UNMIH) would take over from the American contingent to maintain political stability while the Aristide government was fully reinstituted. This time sequence and phasing was later incorporated into the U.S. plans. Such a sequence of events hinged on two key achievements: replacing public security in Haiti, and producing sufficient internal stability to permit Aristide's safe return.

Meanwhile, on August 1st, the de facto Haitian president, Jonassaint, declared Haiti under a "state of siege" and officially transferred power from civilian to military leaders to "defend and protect the country." In reality, this move only reaffirmed the position then held by the Haitian military. On the same day, President Clinton's national security advisors met at the White House to review final nonmilitary options to rid Haiti of Cedras. These options included: (1) sending an envoy to warn Cedras, his chief of staff, General Biamby, and Police Chief Fran_ois of the impending invasion; (2) warning Haiti's military leaders, and providing them assistance to support their departure; and (3) sending in a U.S./U.N. military mission to ease the military leaders out of the country.

As President Clinton and his advisors were reviewing the options, the U.S. Congress was also closely monitoring the movement towards confrontation. As preparations grew increasingly obvious, Congress was becoming ever more vocal. In fact, on August 3rd, the Senate passed a nonbinding resolution stating that the President needed congressional support to invade Haiti. However, this congressional opposition never appeared to deter President Clinton from his chosen course; in fact, only days later, Clinton Administration officials revealed that even if the coup leaders should depart voluntarily, an American-led force would still be sent to restore stability in Haiti.

Five Latin American countries, including Venezuela, finally suspended their unsuccessful efforts to send a peace mission to Haiti on the 5th of August, and the following day Argentine and Colombian diplomats closed their missions in Port-au-Prince after receiving death threats. On August 11th, the USS *Wasp* Amphibious Ready Group (ARG) and Special Marine Air Ground Task Force, Caribbean (SPMAGTF Carib) arrived in the Caribbean to relieve the *Inchon* ARG, which was standing by to conduct NEO. Thus by mid-August it appeared that the United States and Haiti were ready to begin a conflict in a matter of days. Curiously, another key player in the Caribbean region, Fidel Castro, decided then to make his influence known to the United States in a way that completely altered the focus of U.S. efforts in the region.

THE CUBAN HIATUS

As discussed previously, the influx of Haitian boat-people attempting to enter the United States had already generated two Joint Task Forces: JTF-120 to conduct Maritime Intercept Operations (MIO) along with the Coast Guard, and JTF-160 to process the intercepted migrants in the Caribbean. By August the numbers of Haitians had exceeded the capacity of all the smaller processing facilities and had forced the reopening of the processing site at the naval base in Guantanamo Bay, Cuba. During late July, large numbers of Cubans began to take to the sea in boats headed for the nearby shores of southern Florida. This new Cuban threat quickly dominated the attention of the Clinton Administration, and as the numbers at Guantanamo swelled to over 15,000, the relative importance of Cuba as a threat to the United States assigned it precedence over the attention given Haiti.[7]

Castro had first threatened another Mariel boat-lift on August 8th; on the 17th nearly 500 Cubans were picked up off the Florida coast, prompting the governor, Lawton Chiles, to ready a declaration of emergency. By August 19th the Cuban flow to the sea had reached 500 persons per day, forcing President Clinton to reverse the 28-year-old policy of granting Cubans asylum in the United States and directed their collection at Guantanamo Bay—with the Haitians being already there—a move the Cuban government quickly protested. President Clinton then applied new sanctions against Cuba. On one day, August 22nd, the Coast Guard reported rescuing over 1,770 Cubans. It appeared at the time that the magnitude of the Cuban problem clearly over-shadowed the on-going planning for Haiti. In fact, some administration officials proposed that the Haiti invasion be put off until after the Cuba crisis was solved, perhaps even as late as November when the Haitian elections were scheduled. That delay would have cut the timing very close.

The migrant population at Guantanamo Bay swelled to over 25,000 on August 27th. The next day, after a variety of initiatives and talks, Castro announced that the Cuban coast guard would stop rafts and unsafe boats with children aboard. The movement of Cubans slowed, but did not stop. As the population at Guantanamo Bay swelled to over 30,000, the American and Cuban governments finally reached an agreement to increase the number of annual residence visas for Cubans to 20,000 per year, and the Cuban government promised to curb the flow of its people seeking to flee to the United States.[8]

This short but instructive two-week crisis demonstrated the *real* importance of Haiti in U.S. politics. As crucial as Haitian freedom and welfare appeared to be in the popular press, they were quickly superseded by the threat from Cuba. Cuba still posed a tangible, if limited, military threat to the United States, and the influence of Cuban-Americans was clearly greater than that of the Haitians and their supporters in the States. Just as that potential crisis was being averted, events in Haiti again grabbed the headlines. When news of the assassination of Aristide's friend, Father Jean-Marie Vincent reached the United States on August 27th, dealing with Cedras diplomatically any longer seemed pointless. At that point the pendulum of U.S. security interest priorities swung from Cuba back again to Haiti one final time.

On August 28th USACOM submitted its new 2380 plan, with the United Nations Security Council Resolution's (UNSCR) required modifications, to the Joint Staff for coordination and approval.[9] Two days later, the Caribbean Community (CARICOM) ministers voiced their support for the United Nations approved, American-led invasion of Haiti. Jamaica, Trinidad and Tobago, Barbados, and Belize even pledged troops to form a token force of 266 soldiers, to be trained at the U.S. naval base at Roosevelt Roads, Puerto Rico. Also on August 30th, the final reconciliation mission of U.N. special envoy Rolf Knuttsen proved unsuccessful. On the last day of August all dependents of American personnel were evacuated from the American military base at Guantanamo Bay, required because it was an important staging point for the operation. By that time the Pentagon estimated that the MNF troops would be ready by the 1st of October; the execution countdown for the operation had begun.

The following week, Dr. William Perry, the SECDEF, formally authorized the predeployment posturing of forces. This was the approval of the civilian leadership of the U.S. Armed Forces for preinvasion preparations and the endorsement that invasion orders would soon follow. In response, Admiral Miller activated for operations both the commander of the XVIII Airborne Corps as CJTF-180 and the commander of the 10th Mountain Division as CJTF-190.[10] This order readied two major force packages for potential operations, awaiting the decision of the National Command Authorities (NCA).[11] The CINC also directed the loading of Army forces aboard the aircraft carrier USS *Eisenhower* in Norfolk, Virginia, with a sail date of September 14th and assigned the mission in Cap-Haitien to Marine units. Admiral Miller also required the commander-in-chief of the Atlantic Fleet, the commander of the Air Force Air Combat Command, and the commander of Marine Forces Atlantic to provide supporting forces as needed by Generals Shelton and Meade. All of this activity was critical to establishing the command-and-control relationships among the key military leaders who would conduct the operation.

The American military is designed to be a flexible tool, adaptable to rapidly changing circumstances and requirements. As an example, the naval forces in the Caribbean were then conducting operations to control the flow of Haitians and Cubans attempting to enter the United States; these same forces would also be required to execute far different missions once Uphold Democracy began. Anticipating these mission changes, the staff at USACOM issued orders so that, upon change of operational control to JTF-180, Shelton's force—the naval forces already on station near Haiti, then known as JTF-120—would assume duties as JTF-185, the naval component for the forcible-entry option.[12] This change of control finished the preparations required for General Shelton to execute the invasion of Haiti. All that remained was the decision of the President to attack; the finely honed military machine designed for operation Uphold Democracy had begun to move on Port-au-Prince.

THE DEPLOYMENT PHASE

Deployment planning must first take into effect those movements that will take the longest so that they can be started early enough to bring the entire force together at the same time and place. For that reason, on September 9th, CINCUSACOM, through the Commander-in-Chief of the U.S. Transportation Command, had directed deployment of several large-vehicle-capacity transport ships with roll-on, roll-off capability (RO/ROs) under the control of the Military Sealift Command. Departing from Bayonne, New Jersey, these ships would carry most of the needed vehicle support for the divisions in Haiti. Many people fail to realize the incredible capability that the American military has to move its equipment to the conflict in a synchronized manner. Still, even with the finest planning tools, the simple yet tyrannical factors of time and distance frequently pose the most daunting challenges the military has to confront. Even with a country as close as Haiti, the details of transport for over 20,000 initial personnel and their supporting equipment required the around-the-clock dedication of hundreds of logisticians.

The following day, September 10th, Rear Admiral Thomas Fargo, USN, the USACOM Director of Operations (J3), reactivated a Crisis Action Team (CAT) to support 24-hour attention to the Haiti operational situation in the command's joint operations center. The establishment of the CAT indicated that the situation required the full attention of the CINC's staff, so additional personnel were pulled from their regular duties to man the joint operations center around the clock. In actuality, many in the USACOM staff had been working around the clock for weeks by that time; activation of the CAT more significantly signaled the need for all supporting commands to turn their attention to Haiti operations as well. This activation began a series of actions throughout the east coast of the United States, all focused around Norfolk.

General Meade alerted and deployed his 1st Brigade Combat Team and Aviation Brigade from their homebase in Fort Drum, New York, to embark on board the carrier *Eisenhower*, as the CINC had directed. The Atlantic Fleet commander, Admiral Henry Mauz, USN, directed the "chop"[13] of an additional carrier, USS America, to his warfighting subordinate, the Commander Second Fleet, Vice Admiral Jay Johnson, USN. This enabled Admiral Johnson to direct his other carrier, the *Eisenhower*, to fly off her carrier air wing of fighters and prepare to embark the Army forces. The exchange of a carrier air wing for a brigade of soldiers and their supporting rotary-wing aviation assets was not a first for an American carrier, but it was a complex task requiring great understanding and cooperation between the Armed Services.[14] This adaptation of Army and Navy assets to form a joint team based upon specific mission needs had been a personal project of Admiral Miller for 2 years. Several exercise events had been designed to overcome the training differences and remedy the adverse maintenance impacts of the arrangement. These improvements had come to fruition at just the right time.

Admiral Mauz directed the USS *Mount Whitney* to load designated JTF-180/190 forces and ordered the U.S. naval commander at Guantanamo Bay to support USACOM operations as required. As a significant sign of the seriousness of the military danger, CINCUSACOM also ordered the hospital ship USNS *Comfort* to sail in support of the joint task force.[15] The manning and deployment of one of America's two hospital ships from its reserve status show the determination of the United States and the severity of the potential casualty estimates for a given operation. On the same day, the 10th of September, the Chairman of the Joint Chiefs of Staff transmitted the approval of the NCA for a psychological-operations leaflet drop in Haiti to occur on September 11th, which was, in a real sense, the first offensive action of the operation.[16]

With all the deployment activity during the second week of September, it is important to note that although both OPLANs 2370 and 2380 had been approved and were ready to be issued, the conditions for execution of neither plan were clearly in effect. Although the C-day—deployment day—had been established by the NCA as September 10th, no D-day—the day that major operations were to begin—had been designated. The Joint Operations Planning and Execution System (JOPES), which is the foundation for all joint operations in the U.S. military, requires either a C or D day, and ideally both, so that the supporting TPFDD can be run effectively.[17] Because USACOM planners knew that 10 days were required to move the forces required by their plan, they assumed a D-day of September 21st simply to facilitate movement planning and commence the preparatory actions to match the timetable.[18]

Still, OPLAN 2370 was built based on a nonpermissive environment, and 2380 on a permissive environment. The question remained, would the President authorize an attack on a country that was no military threat to the United States? Not knowing the answer, planners continued to keep both options open by attempting a combination of the two plans and their supporting TPFDDs. If a fusion of the two could be worked out within 10 days, then the essential forces of both plans might be in position on September 21st, the date that most assumed would be the earliest the President might call for the use of force. From that point, September 21st was substituted as the D-day required for planning to continue. At such a critical juncture, with no decision by the NCA, the military had to make certain assumptions and continue to posture the entire force in such a manner that a decision by the President to execute either plan would remain supportable, when directed.

Admiral Miller understood well how critical the nonmilitary actions in Haiti were to the success of the operation. His staff had tried during various meetings to energize and incorporate interagency actions within the planning effort, but had met with little success. Few other departments of the U.S. government were resourced to conduct deliberate planning, and fewer still had sufficient staff to engage in the type of focused preparations Miller felt was necessary for the crisis in Haiti. Undeterred by the lack of interest during the summer, Generals Hartzog and Byron worked tirelessly to develop an interagency forum for Admiral Miller to pull the entire government effort together. A meeting was held at the National Defense University in Washington on Sepetember 11th, during which Miller discussed the critical tasks in Haiti in some detail with subcabinet level policymakers. The goal was to share responsibility and to exchange requirements for the postinvasion development of a secure environment in Haiti. Unfortunately, even this high-level meeting failed to generate the cooperation desired. The planning effort remained almost exclusively with the military sector.[19]

To facilitate continued planning at the operational level, General Shelton's staff developed a fusion of OPLANs 2370 and 2380, known as 2375.[20] The central element of this effort to produce a flexible 2375 force mix occurred in a TPFDD flow modification message issued on September 11th. Meanwhile, CINCUSACOM issued his operation order supporting OPLAN 2370 and stated that the SECDEF had approved 2380 for "continued planning." To military men and women, this "continued planning" stipulation indicated that no decision had been made between the two options, 2370 or 2380. However, it was clear to all that some kind of operation was imminent and the forces still required key staging and movement orders if they were to be ready. General Shelton's precautionary development of 2375 immediately began bearing fruit. CINCUSACOM completed final approval of OPLAN 2370, which next became Operations Order 2370-95, on September 12th. By mid-month there was one completed plan with a supporting operations order, 2370; another approved plan, 2380; plus, one bridging concept, 2375, still in development. But all of these efforts lacked the key date needed to synchronize operations; no execution date had been directed. Forces continued to move so that any decision by the President could be executed.

Deployment preparations at the unit level continued apace all over the United States. Soldiers completed vaccinations and executed wills; sailors loaded ammunition and supplies on ships and put to sea; airmen rigged aircraft for heavy-equipment drops and broke out ammunition; Marines rehearsed intricate amphibious load-plans and kept their field equipment prepared for immediate use. On September 12th the USS *Eisenhower* Battle Group returned to Norfolk and began embarkation of the Army ground and air elements as directed 2 days before. The following day, USS *America* got underway from Norfolk for Haiti operations with another element, the Joint Special Operations Task Force (JSOTF) battlestaff, embarked in hastily arranged crew compartments. CINCUSACOM had also directed a second leaflet drop in Haiti for September 14th. That same day, the *Eisenhower* got underway for Haiti. CINCUSACOM directed the "chop" of all of these forces to General Shelton, CJTF-180, by no later than midnight on the 13th so that he could establish communications and conduct final rehearsals. On the 14th, COMSECONDFLT and his staff were also underway on board his flagship, the USS *Mount Whitney,* for operation Uphold Democracy. In less than 7 days the JTF-180 staff had been activated for operations and had incorporated several unique and very capable joint force packages; new command lines had been established; and thousands of military personnel had been alerted—all to form the most powerful military force ever deployed from the United States to the Caribbean.

Elsewhere, in New York, an OPORD 2380 "rockdrill,"[21] or walk-through rehearsal, was conducted for the commander of JTF-190 and Admiral Miller on September 15th, D-5 (using the artificial timeline). Admiral Miller later noted that this drill supplied him with his lasting vision of JTF-190's plan for the first week's deployment. It was during this overview of the plan that the CINC confirmed the use of the Marine SPMAGTF for the operation in northern Haiti, at Cap-Haitien, instead of the 10th Mountain's Second Brigade Combat Team as had been originally planned. In comments to the assembled staff of the division the CINC stressed the importance of precise execution. He emphasized the importance of careful attention to detail and focusing all efforts to minimize the effects of uncertainty. Earlier that same day the USS *Monsoon,* a small Cyclone-class Navy ship, had run aground in the Port-au-Prince harbor, thereby showing that all was not perfect in the U.S. plan. Admiral Miller also emphasized the importance of rules of engagement (ROE) and public affairs/media (PAO) issues. Both would be critical for success at the operational level.

In his wrap-up of the CINC's personal comments upon the Admiral's departure, General Meade also focused on the rules of engagement and his concern over the delicacy of the "aggressively disarm" mission.[22] General Meade had the foresight to understand how soldiers given the task of aggressively disarming citizens might find themselves in an untenable situation: Acting with restraint in the face of armed hostiles. One of the key issues of using military personnel in operations other than war is the incongruity of using soldiers whose skills focus on destroying the nation's enemies to accomplish a very different set of tasks—making and keeping the peace.

As a final note, prior to his departure from the rockdrill, and as an added precaution against confusion, the CINC froze all encryption equipment, radio frequencies and call-signs from D-2 through D+2. This sacrificed communications security for additional clarity and communications reliability. During the Cold War the use of encryption devices became a regular part of normal training, but such devices also added to the difficulties of military communications in difficult environments. Since Haiti posed no electronic-warfare threat to local tactical communications, Admiral Miller could place his emphasis on clarity of communications, always a boon to operations. Some in the building reacted negatively to the CINC's guidance; they did not fully understand that the military paradigm had shifted from the Cold War threat to a different but just as challenging hazard.

Even as the 10th Mountain Division staff was absorbing the CINC's changes to their plan, it received even more surprising news. Based upon information from Washington, the afternoon of September 15th marked an acceleration of the 10-day execution checklist for the entire force. The 15th became D-4 instead of D-5 in the Warning Order issued by the CJCS; therefore the division was 24 hours behind its own timeline. D-4 was the critical day in the division's execution checklist and the day that the theater execute order was anticipated, which would announce the choice of OPLAN to be executed, 2370 or 2380. At 9:00 that evening, President Clinton spoke to the nation concerning Haiti; he made it clear to those listening in Fort Drum that General Cedras was an oppressive tyrant in Haiti, an enemy to freedom, and a threat to the United States. Some of the soldiers of the 10th Mountain Division anticipated being in Haiti in a matter of days. No one knew how many would really go and under what conditions they would find action there.

On the day following the President's speech (September 16th), General Meade, Colonel Miller, the JTF-190 operations officer, and members of a small advance party departed from Fort Drum for Fort Bragg and eventual embarkation aboard the USS *Mount Whitney*. The normal pace of coordination continued to accelerate, with each involved staff branching out to develop its piece of the overall scheme in ever-greater detail. The CINC's staff oriented the others on the problem of Haitian-on-Haitian violence and the mechanisms available to control it, and began developing some criteria for determining a point at which the United Nations force would be able to commence operations. The CINC declared the FAd'H hostile and cleared up any remaining doubts that the modified plan could not include lethal attacks on the Haitian security forces. This declaration was a key step in the execution of the military rules of engagement (ROE) set for Uphold Democracy. Except in self-defense, no U.S. force can fire upon another nation's until the CINC declares that the opponent is hostile. Admiral Miller was giving his commanders the authority to strike at members of the Haitian military first, without provocation, in order to ensure the protection of U.S. forces in an uncertain environment. This permitted the JTF-180 staff to hone their forcible-entry plan. In an important sign for the multinational nature of the operation, the British Commander in Chief, Fleet, directed HMS *Lancaster* to change status and come under the operational control of Admiral Johnson's naval force. The multinational naval force off Haiti then included ships from the United States and the United Kingdom, as well as Canadian, French, Argentine, and Dutch vessels.

As any operation begins, issues always surface that had not been anticipated. One of these resulted when General Shelton directed General Meade to be prepared to provide his infantry brigade on-board the *Eisenhower* as the reserve for JTF-180 operations. This caused two important discussions among staff members: (1) what was the command relationship between JTF-180 and JTF-190 before operations began, and (2) what would be the command relationships for JTF-190 forces in the Joint Operations Area (JOA) prior to the time when JTF-190 would be directed to accept operational control of forces. Fortunately, because the JTF-190 commander, Major General Meade, was the normal peacetime subordinate to Lieutenant General Shelton, because the 10th Mountain Division formed a part of his (Shelton's) XVIII Airborne Corps, the two soldiers had been working well together for some time. Still, at the time, General Meade was operating under the assumption that JTF-190 was a separate force from Shelton's JTF-180. The two staffs were planning very different operations, and any mixing of the two was bound to create a difficult coordination problem.[23]

At 7:00 P.M. on September 16th the 10th Mountain Division Chief of Staff held a meeting with the entire assault command-post (CP) group in the base chapel at Fort Drum. He stressed that he had no more accurate an idea of the deployment date or conditions than anyone else, but that the group must be prepared to move to Griffis AFB, near Rome, New York, the air base of departure for Haiti, given 2 hours' notice. He also stressed the importance of media relations, proper uniforms, self-discipline, ammunition security, and weapons safety. He revealed that even he might not know whether combat conditions would exist in the Port-au-Prince International Airport, the assault CP destination, until immediately prior to landing. The troops at Fort Drum were ready but were not-at-all certain what they would find on the ground, for some as early as the next morning.

A DIPLOMATIC PAUSE

September 17th saw the first major shake-up in operational planning: not a choice between plans, but the official merger of plans 2370 and 2380. For several weeks the USACOM staff had been working with representatives of all the commands slated to participate in the operation to develop the compromise plan, still labeled simply 2375. OPLAN 2375 appeared to be necessary because, as time grew short the different logistics requirements of 2370 and 2380 were beginning to conflict and some support concept, which could provide required assets to either option, needed to be developed. The dilemma was so pressing that modifications to the TPFDD for 2380 had been suspended to allow planners to concentrate on 2370 support, leaving 2380 idle. Unfortunately, merging the two options proved to be more difficult than anticipated due to the widely differing conditions that had to exist for the execution of either plan. On the 17th, after reviewing several possible combination ideas, the USACOM staff produced a very simple, one-page graphic, which the CINC initialed and sent to the Chairman of the Joint Chiefs as a synopsis of "the new plan." The graphic outlined for the first time a 2380(+) option, using both JTF-180 and JTF-190, with General Shelton as the senior commander over both JTFs.[24]

The 2380(+) solution did answer two very nagging questions within the headquarters at Fort Drum: First, why had the TPFDD for 2380 been frozen and the JTF 190 staff's permissions to modify that TPFDD withdrawn; and second, how could JTF-180 task JTF-190 for some of its forces? JTF-180 had directed JTF-190 to give up control of its task force on-board the *Eisenhower* so that detailed schedules and target planning could be conducted with the task force commander. This placed the commander of the 1st Brigade, 10th Mountain Division, Colonel Berdy, in the unenviable position of working for two different bosses. His personnel were required to prepare for two different plans under widely different rules of engagement. This had great potential for disaster should the usual confusion of battle exist on D-day. Enroute to Haiti, the 10th Mountain Division forces on the *Eisenhower* conducted full dress-rehearsals. Ships and aircraft all over the east coast of the United States continued to be readied for combat operations.

Also on the 17th, the Commander, U.S. Maritime Defense Zone, Atlantic, Rear Admiral James M. Loy, USCG, was designated as Commander Task Group 185.7 and as the Port-au-Prince harbor-defense commander. Cooperation between the U.S. Navy and the Coast Guard has always been close, but this use of Coast Guard assets in a combat situation was establishing new boundaries and reinforcing the value of interagency cooperation within the U.S. government.[25] The U.S. Coast Guard assets were to be used for harbor defense until D+4, when the Haitian threat was to have been destroyed. Even with all of these final preparations, the major news of the day did not focus on the military but instead centered on President Clinton's dispatching of a three-man diplomatic team in a final attempt to avert the invasion. The team was headed by former President Jimmy Carter, recently returned from his successful peacemaking mission in North Korea, and included two other men as influential as he: General Colin Powell, former Chairman of the Joint Chiefs of Staff, and Senator Sam Nunn of Georgia, head of the Senate Armed Services Committee. Carter contributed the prestige of a head of state, Powell brought a military man's rapport, and Nunn demonstrated the resolve of the U.S. Congress. This powerful team arrived in Port-au-Prince on Saturday just as the force was coming together, largely unseen, offshore.[26] They immediately went to meet with Cedras.

Everyone focused on the deliberations inside General Cedras's office in the Haitian capital, but military preparations continued. The diplomatic mission developed a rapport with Cedras, but could not form a clear agreement for the junta leaders to step down. Optimistically, they elected to remain in Haiti over Saturday night so that the discussions could continue the following day. President Clinton had prohibited the Carter mission from debating whether the invasion would occur; the only negotiable aspects involved the manner in which power would be turned over. For Cedras, the situation was deeply tied to Haitian concepts of honor and he could not conceive that his willing departure would not stain his integrity. Although President Clinton had made the limitations of the mission quite clear, Carter felt that a bloody invasion might still be averted if some compromise could be found.

While the Carter mission was still in Haiti, on September 18th the JTF-180 commander and his primary battlestaff embarked aboard the *Mount Whitney* in Guantanamo Bay. The ship was underway at 10:45 A.M. The *Eisenhower* was ordered to make best speed towards Port-au-Prince, but not to approach within 60 nautical miles of the shore. Admiral Miller turned over command and control of operations to CJTF-180 at 10:00 P.M. At the time, the Carter delegation was still meeting with Cedras. After the approval of the President was obtained, the CINC then issued the execution order (EXORD) for OPORD 2370 and confirmed H-hour for midnight of the 18th.

For the U.S. military the EXORD for an operation is the ultimate commitment. It requires the personal approval of the national command authorities, either the SECDEF or the President himself, and authorizes a military commander to conduct military operations, including the use of decisive force. Among other details, the order reminded General Shelton of the specific wording of his mission, gave him an exact time to commence the conflict, and what was perhaps unique to Uphold Democracy, included a personal guiding principle from Admiral Miller. The last words of the message were, "Do Right."[27]

The Carter mission had met late Saturday night, again inconclusively, with Cedras, but on Sunday, September 18th, the team again met with him at his home and also paid a call on President Jonassaint at the Presidential Palace. Although President Clinton wanted the team out of Haiti by noon, Cedras was preparing a counter-proposal and Powell asked the President for more time. Military planners incredulously watched the deliberations on the Cable News Network (CNN) while copies of the execute order were in their hands. For military purposes, the invasion had already begun.

At 4:00 P.M., during continued discussions with Cedras in his office, General Biamby, another of the junta leaders, burst into the room to confirm that the invasion was underway; his contacts in the United States had witnessed the 82d Airborne loading at Pope Air Force Base. This fact seemed to break the resolve of Cedras, yet he still could not agree to give up the government, stating, "This is a matter for our civilian authorities."[28] Cedras agreed to another meeting with President Jonassaint, but time had already run out on the Carter mission. Powell received word to call President Clinton, and when they spoke together, he was allowed more time but the invasion timetable would stand as designed. The negotiating team moved to the presidential palace. Less than 7 hours remained before the planned attack.

Out of site, in the dark, the U.S. military force was moving in ships and aircraft towards Haiti. Within the Haitian presidential palace the Carter mission finally found a man whose responsibility was matched with some compassion:

Emile Jonassaint. In the president's office both the ministers of defense and information refused to accept the Carter proposal and stated that they would resign before agreeing. Jonassaint's reply was curt: "We have too many ministers already; I am going to sign this proposal. I will not let my people suffer further tragedy. I choose peace." [29] Cedras pledged to accept the orders of his president, thereby salvaging his honor and perhaps his life. When received in Washington, the Carter–Jonassaint Agreement, included in Appendix D, completely upended the planning process at USACOM. Many people agreed that the accord exceeded the bounds set by President Clinton, for among other things, it permitted Cedras to stay on in Haiti. But, the agreement did facilitate Aristide's return without combat, and no one *really* wanted a shoot-out in Port-au-Prince. The forcible-entry option that everyone thought was most likely to occur was now no longer viable and had to be stopped in mid-flight. [30]

The Carter mission left downtown Port-au-Prince and headed for the airport. They shook hands on the runway, and many watching expected the U.S. Ambassador, William Swing, to go aboard the aircraft with Carter and the other members of his team to return to the States. [31] News had been sparse; only a very few senior officials knew the details of the negotiated accord. Phone calls were made back to President Clinton, and Ambassador Swing remained behind as the aircraft carrying the Carter team lifted off for the U.S. naval station at Roosevelt Roads, Puerto Rico, to return to Washington. Less than 2 hours later, the CINC ordered cessation of the H-hour countdown, and reset the entire plan for a 24-hour delay. The huge military strike-force approaching Haiti now had to be stopped at the critical moment.

The 82nd Airborne Division assault battalions were already in the air, headed for their drop zones in Haiti, when the word was sent out to stop the assault. Major General Mike Steele, USA, the division commander, actually received a warning via radio from General Shelton just as he entered his aircraft that he might have to land somewhere else other than his planned drop zone. The general boarded his flight to Haiti with his parachute on his back and wondered how he could modify his assault plan in-flight, with his force spread among over 60 C-130 Hercules troop transports and 50 C-141 Starlifter cargo aircraft. The trip soon became a bad memory for all the paratroopers involved for another reason: the weather was terrible, and turbulence off the coast of Florida soon made many sick from the buffeting of the aircraft on the long, dark flight. Around 2½ hours into the trip, General Steele was notified that his force would indeed have to abort and return to Fort Bragg. It took almost an hour simply to turn the huge formation of aircraft around in the air, and then the troopers of the All-American Division had to ride back through the same bad weather to disembark in North Carolina. [32]

The feat of turning the assault force back in time, during the middle of the night, demonstrated how well the USACOM staff, the staffs of the U.S. Transportation Command and the Air Mobility Command at Scott Air Force Base, and the hundreds of individual pilots and crew chiefs could work together amid the pressure of an operational deployment to respond to a change in the direction by the supported commander, General Shelton. Although most aircraft returned to

Pope Air Force Base, to be emptied and rerigged for support of the permissive option, perceptive analysis by transportation planners throughout the United States resulted in some aircraft being ordered to drop their cargoes in Haiti as a more expeditious option than off-loading and re-rigging the equipment in a different form back in the United States.

In the very early morning hours of September 19th, General Shalikashvili passed on the order for OPLAN 2380 as modified by the Carter–Jonassaint Accord. President Clinton agreed that the Carter mission's criteria were sufficient, that the agreement with Cedras was a good one; the invasion would not be a combat operation. Armed with the flexibility that had been developed during the planning process, CINCUSACOM immediately directed execution of OPLAN 2380, *with enhancements,* and chopped CJTF-190 and assigned forces to CJTF-180 for operations. CINCUSACOM also issued an ROE change to reflect the permissive environment. The CJTF-180, General Shelton, then issued orders to execute operation Maintain Democracy, a plan his staff had not really focused on for months.

As difficult as a military operation is to plan and set in motion, it is even more challenging to stop the forward movement of thousands of personnel and equipment in just a matter of hours. The very best capability of the U.S. command-and-control system was demonstrated as General Shelton and Admiral Miller continued to coordinate the early morning shift of plans to halt the forcible-entry operation and adjust the force-flow in order to meet the new requirements of the Carter Agreement. Turning ships and aircraft around was relatively easy compared to the picking up of combat swimmers who were already in the water approaching Haiti during the predawn hours. The overall task was immensely more complex. Hundreds of details had to be adjusted, then these new details coordinated to ensure that rerouted ships and aircraft would not conflict with one another as they changed pick-up points and drop-off times from all over the United States.

The lights in USACOM headquarters and on board the *Mount Whitney* burned throughout the night. On board the command ship Colonel Dan McNeill thought there was an almost eerie calm among the JTF-180 staff despite the fact that so much complex work was being done during the least effective hours of the day. He finally conducted a briefing for General Shelton at 3:00 A.M. to tie all the changes together for his boss, who had to begin a completely new and more unfamiliar campaign of cooperation with Cedras in less than 6 hours.

General Shelton was a leader prepared for uncertainty: he formed his personal plan for the mission that was to take place that morning, took the initiative to provide guidance for the staff in the few cases where all required answers were not available, and finally gained a few precious hours of sleep. He was inbound by helicopter to the Port-au-Prince International Airport at 9:02 A.M. to meet with Cedras. The first flight of Blackhawk helicopters from the *Eisenhower* landed at the airport shortly afterwards, at 9:40. The Haiti operation was finally underway, in a *peaceful* environment.

NOTES

1. As joint task forces are normally not organized prior to an operation, they must be formed from among a variety of organizations once their mission is formulated. A JTF "stands up" from among its component parts upon the direction of higher authority, normally the theater combatant commander or CINC.

2. General Shelton, commander of the initial phase of the operation, was also well aware of the 2380 planning effort due to his senior position in the Army chain of command, as the 10th Mountain was one of the four divisions in Shelton's XVIII Airborne Corps.

3. William R. McClintock, "Working Chronologies."

4. The key phrase "*all means necessary*" placed the U.N. action under Chapter VII of the United Nations Charter, thereby authorizing offensive military operations. This was only the fourth such authorization in U.N. history, the others having been during the Korean Conflict, the U.N. operations in the Congo, Operation Desert Storm (Kuwait), and operations UNISOM I and II (Somalia). Later, operation Joint Endeavor (Bosnia) was also authorized under Chapter VII.

5. The two sections of the U.N. Charter that specify the conditions of intervention are chapters VI and VII. Chapter VI, entitled "Pacific Settlement of Disputes," clearly involves a peaceful environment and willingness to negotiate on the part of two disagreeing states. Chapter VII deals with acts of aggression and specifically states, in Article 41, that the Security Council "may take such action by air, land and sea forces as may be necessary to maintain or restore international peace and security."

6. At the time, OPLAN 2380 was labeled "Maintain Democracy." The ongoing Noncombatant Evacuation Operation and Maritime Intercept Operation conducted at sea was named "Support Democracy." Later, all aspects of the operation assumed the codename Uphold Democracy, even when some sought to differentiate between the U.S.-led and U.N.-led portions of the operation by using different names. With a large number of simultaneous operations being conducted worldwide, the Pentagon determined that some simplicity was well worth the effort.

7. In order to maintain the lessons learned from this operation, General Sheehan ordered the development of a superb multimedia after-action report prepared by OC, Inc., in Hampton, VA. This *Migrant Camp Operations: The Guantanamo Experience,* includes a VHS videotape, a historical pamphlet, and a CD-ROM that archives the significant primary and secondary sources pertaining to the operation.

8. The scale of this migrant influx grew so large (over 10,000) that the another regional command, the U.S. Southern Command, headquartered in Panama, was asked to assist in the processing actions. This effort was known as operations Safe Passage and Safe Haven.

9. Technically, 2380 was never referred to as "Operations Plan (OPLAN) 2380"; the title "Operations Order (OPORD) 2380" was always used in official message traffic. Normally, the differences between a plan and an order are the level of detail and the number of assumptions involved—orders being more detailed, with minimal assumptions. This distinction was not true in the 2380 case.

10. Activation for planning carries no authority to direct the movement of forces or personnel; activation for operations formally begins the process of bringing all assets of a JTF together and staging them for deployment. It also removes assigned personnel and forces from other missions, thereby signaling their new priority of work.

11. In the United States, military operations require the approval of either the President, the Secretary of Defense, or their duly-deputized alternates or successors; these individuals comprise the National Command Authorities (NCA).

12. A command-and-control diagram is shown in Appendix I.

13. *Chop* is military slang for change of operational control. It indicated that the mission-tasking authority for the carrier had shifted from its peacetime commander to its wartime commander. Admiral Johnson would later, in 1996, be selected for promotion and would become the Chief of Naval Operations.

14. U.S. Army air force fighters had been transported aboard Navy carriers prior to the landings of Operation Torch in North Africa in November 1942. Before that, in April, the Dolittle raid on the Japanese home islands had been launched from the USS *Hornet.* The real issue behind this interoperability problem lies in the different procurement systems (Army aircraft are not designed for the damage caused by maritime operations) and training procedures.

15. On September 9th USACOM also ordered the activation of seven Military Sealift Command Roll-on, Roll-off (RORO) ships. These ships were necessary to transport all the vehicles and heavy equipment required by the plan. The message alerting the ROROs was a real "attention getter" for the planners at Fort Bragg, who viewed the act as the first serious indication that the operation was beginning. See William R. McClintock's interview with Brigadier General Robert D. Shadley, USA.

16. Psychological-operations forces had been used as early as mid-August to begin Radio Democracy broadcasts to ensure that the Haitian people were aware of the reasons for U.N. action in their country, but the overflight of Haitian national territory and the actual dropping of leaflets in Haiti was a much more overt and threatening act. Most nations consider these actions an act of war. Most of the leaflets in this first drop missed Haiti and floated in the waters between Haiti and Cuba for days afterwards.

17. This is due to the need to plan ahead, considering alert and movement times, so that each element of the force will arrive from its place of origin worldwide at its designated location at the time required. Given a C day or D day, planners know the movement times and can execute the details required; without either planning factor very little of the synchronization can occur.

18. Any deployment of military forces from the United States requires the approval of the Secretary of Defense; however, CINCs may position assigned forces within their areas of responsibility as required for force protection and preparation for conflict. In the USACOM case, the CINC used his proper authority to prepare for conflict in Haiti. All actions that crossed into Haitian territory prior to the execution of the plan were individually approved by the SECDEF.

19. See Admiral Miller's interview with McClintock, January 19, 1995 and Hayes and Wheatley, *Interagency and Polictial-Military Dimesions of Peace Operations: Haiti—A Case Study,* p. 16.

20. Because 2375 was more than an order and less than a plan, there was some debate about what to call it. It was about a fifty-page document that permitted the bridging of OPLAN 2370 and OPORD 2380 by identifying the key elements required by both and establishing a concept of operation should a mix be required. In fact, 2375 turned out to be the planning document closest to the real requirement established by President Clinton.

21. The term *rockdrill* comes from the U.S. Army's training experiences at the National Training Center (NTC) in California. At the NTC, unit commanders regularly create battlefield mock-ups using sand and rocks to rehearse and modify tactical actions of small units prior to conducting the training using real ammunition.

22. Reduction of the number of weapons in Haiti had always been viewed as an essential part of restoring security. The question was how should the weapons be confiscated: by force or by enticement? If the weapons were to be taken by force, many envisioned that house-to-house fighting might be necessary, and that could have been very costly.

23. For the command relationships at this time, see Appendix I.

24. This senior–subordinate relationship was maintained to ensure the best possible command-and-control relationship between the two JTFs. Although JTF commanders are not normally subordinated to one another, in the case of Haiti such close coordination was required that subordination of one JTF to the other became the best method of command and control.

25. The Coast Guard is a part of the Department of Transportation. As such, it has capabilities and authorities not held by the U.S. Navy, including the ability to stop and search vessels at sea without creating an international incident.

26. Many of the details of this mission are found in Colin Powell's book, *My American Journey*.

27. CINCUSACOM message 19001R September, 1994, paragraph 19.

28. Powell, p. 601.

29. Ibid.

30. Not only were aircraft and ships rerouted, but combat swimmers and special-operations forces were actually plucked out of the water during the night. Few military planners ever anticipate the need to stop an attack in its final minutes, yet JTF-180 staff members managed to do so without a single missing servicemember.

31. Although he could not deal directly with the coup leaders, Ambassador Swing had assumed his post in Haiti just after the *Harlan County* affair in order to accomplish the host of other tasks required of a United States mission in a crisis situation.

32. Still, the 82nd Airborne troopers were not relieved from alert posture for several days, since they became the JTF-180 reserve strike-force based in the continental United States.

PART III

MILITARY OPERATIONS IN HAITI

American soldiers, sailors, airmen, Marines, and Coast Guardsmen train daily to meet the most stringent rigors of war. As a matter of course, they use the most exacting and harsh requirements as the standards of their training. When over 10,000 of them were initially activated for military operations in Haiti, they expected full-scale combat and they were ready for that eventuality. What they encountered in Port-au-Prince and Cap-Haitien was in some ways even more difficult, for they had to venture beyond what they were normally trained to accomplish and serve as diplomats, policemen, and in some extreme cases, social workers as well.[1] It is a testament to the high level of education and discipline among American forces that they were able to execute such a mission with distinction, and with minimal casualties.

NOTE

1. This trend towards nonwarfighting tasks for the military began in ancient times but has received tremendous new emphasis since Vietnam. United States operations in Panama in 1986 first identified the differing training requirements of fighting and peacemaking. Our forces are now grappling with this divergent requirement imaginatively, with new courses of instruction and special training exercises, but have not yet mastered the challenge of training well for both combat and peace operations.

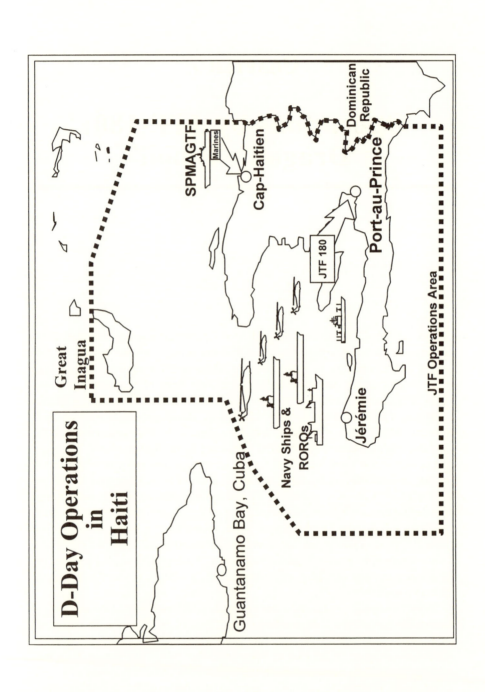

D-Day Operations in Haiti

Great Inagua

Guantanamo Bay, Cuba

Navy Ships & RORQs

SPMAGTF

Marines

Cap-Haitien

JTF 180

JTF I

Port-au-Prince

Jérémie

Dominican Republic

JTF Operations Area

CHAPTER 7

Operations by JTF-180: "Dragon's Blood"

The initial American military objectives of Uphold Democracy included conducting simultaneous airborne and amphibious assaults to take control of the airport and harborfront in Port-au-Prince, securing the main road connecting these two locations, and establishing a northern base of operations in Cap-Haitien. Mastering these objectives would give General Shelton control of the key areas of Haiti by coup de main. Meanwhile, the assault command-post and primary combat units of the joint task force were to land by strategic airlift to establish a Multinational Force (MNF) presence in the Haitian capital. The size and power of this force were designed to leave no doubt about its intention to quickly restore order and security in the key areas of Haiti.[1] Any Haitian resistance needed to be seen as both futile and counterproductive. Throughout the first day significant airborne firepower, including fighter aircraft and helicopter gunships and a large rapid-reaction force poised on the USS *America,* was immediately available should any problems be encountered with the FAd'H onshore. Meanwhile, psychological operations by loudspeaker were conducted to emphasize the peacemaking role and pacific intentions of the MNF to the Haitian population.

No detail needed to ensure a decisive and quick resolution to the entry portion of the operation had been omitted. Hundreds of combat aircraft and more than twenty ships were poised to assist. Due to the close proximity and squalid conditions of some of the Port-au-Prince suburbs, which could have been the scene of particularly violent combat, the United States had even designed a special airborne firefighting capability based in helicopters and waterbucket-laden transport planes borrowed from the national firefighting service.

Had OPLAN 2370 been executed, the sequence of events would have been very much like the following: The command ship, *Mount Whitney,* and both carriers would have moved to just within range of their rotary-wing aircraft systems as the combination heavy-drop and paratroop forces arrived over Haiti in the transports of Air Mobility Command. The Navy ships would have had all forces ready, on a time-sequenced countdown to H-hour, set for 2:00 A.M. on September 20th. The security forces at the U.S. embassy would have been at maximum alert, with as many U.S. citizens and selected third-country nationals safely in monitored areas as possible. Also closing in on Haitian airspace would have been a package of twenty-six UH-60 and thirteen CH-47 helicopters with supporting medical and observation craft, arriving from an intermediate support base on Great Inagua Island. This helicopter force was timed to back fill the *Eisenhower* after her forces were landed on Haiti, becoming the JTF reserve afloat.

The FAd'H had previously been declared hostile by Admiral Miller, so any reaction on the part of the Haitian forces as the aircraft arrived would have been met by decisive force. AC-130 Spectre machine-gun and artillery fire as well as strikes from Navy and Air Force fighter-bombers and any ships close enough to the target to engage with five-inch naval guns would have destroyed any located threat. There were two major forcible-entry operations planned: an amphibious assault by the Marine SPMAGTF at Cap-Haitien, and a combined parachute- and air-assault operation in and around Port-au-Prince. Both would have been timed for maximum effect on the FAd'H.

At H-hour, forces from the U.S. Army's Ranger Regiment would have para-chute-assaulted into two drop zones to establish local security and terminal guidance for the inbound brigades of the 82d Airborne Division arriving directly from Pope Air Force Base. One brigade of the 82d was assigned the mission of securing Port-au-Prince International Airport; the other would establish a critical heavy equipment rally point on a drop-zone north of the airport, code-named Pegasus. All the heavy-equipment of the land forces would have arrived and been air-dropped or air-landed at Pegasus. Immediately following their arrival, the two brigades of the "All-American" Division would spread out to secure twelve other key targets, among which were the American Embassy residence, the Port-au-Prince port facility, the national prison at Fort Dimanche, the national telephone exchange, the FAd'H communications center, the TV facility in the Haitian capital, and the major ammunition-storage facility.

These objectives were only half the major sites identified for immediate control by JTF-180. The area around Port-au-Prince had been divided into two assault zones. The targets of the 82d were all in the northern zone; in the south, special operations forces had seven additional target sites within the capital, one at the Haitian Naval headquarters west of the city, and if necessary, three other objectives at friendly embassies should other nationals be menaced during the immediate hours of the assault. Overall, the intent was to drop down like a thunderclap and secure all key targets in the hours before dawn. By the time the sun rose on D-day the critical units and facilities of the FAd'H would be destroyed and U.S. forces would have blanketed the region around Port-au-Prince.

The Haitian capital was definitely the center of gravity for the FAd'H and that attack was the priority of effort, with the objective of destroying all key assets under Cedras's control. Yet, the landing at Cap-Haitien, in the north, was also important to the overall success of the JTF. It provided a secondary port and airfield combination for the flow of heavy forces into Haiti, was a key bastion of Aristide support, and provided an operational reserve or safety valve for Shelton, should his forces get bogged down for some reason around the capital. The Marines were to land and seize four of the thirty critical objectives of the initial operation. These objectives included the airport at Cap-Haitien, the port facility, the local military prison, and the headquarters barracks of the FAd'H department of the north. All of these were to be under U.S. control by H+6, approximately 8:00 in the morning. The Marines' method involved landing one company of infantry over the beach in amphibious assault vehicles (AAVs), and two other companies air-landed by CH-46 and CH-53 helicopters, each company being supported by aircraft and ship firepower.

Yet, thanks to President Carter's team, none of this massive combat-power was used. On D-day, a single man went ashore from the *Mount Whitney* to meet with General Cedras: Hank Shelton. On that day General Shelton held as much real power in a foreign nation as any American general officer since MacArthur signed the peace treaty with Japan in 1945. He was backed not only by the United States, but also had the full authorization of the United Nations and was the Multinational Force commander in Haiti. Under UNSCR 940, he had the authority to use all means necessary to carry out his mission. Only days before he had heard his commander-in-chief label Cedras with every criminal name available; yet on the 20th of September Shelton landed in Port-au-Prince with orders to "coordinate and cooperate in an atmosphere of mutual respect" with the Haitian commander.[2] Because Ambassador Swing was accredited only to Aristide, and not to the de facto military regime in Haiti, Shelton was the focal point of all eyes and activity. He was the perfect man for the job.

Impressively tall, soft-spoken, yet clearly focused on his duty, General Shelton was the epitome of an American military professional. Not a West Point graduate but an alumnus of the U.S. Army's toughest schools and most demanding assignments, Shelton was a veteran combat commander who deeply understood his art and his soldiers. His intent for the Haiti mission had been the driving force in all the operational-level planning to date, and he clearly was in the best position to evaluate his approach and objectives for an initial contact with Cedras. Later, he quoted the Chinese military philosopher Sun Tzu, saying, "Know yourself and know your enemy and you might figure the outcome of a thousand battles."[3] Originally, Shelton had expected he might put Cedras under arrest and detain him as a criminal; he ended up being forced to cultivate a unique and critically important professional relationship with the Haitian commander instead.

Given less than 12 hours to prepare for his first meeting in Port-au-Prince, Shelton had determined that a reading of Haitian culture gave the best clues to the approach he should take with Cedras.[4] He knew that the use of force had been a norm in Haiti, and he also understood how fear had traditionally played an important role in keeping the Haitian people from achieving a truly equal society. Having been up until the early hours of the morning coordinating details, he had very little time to develop an approach for his all-important initial meeting with Cedras. Still, just a few hours later, Shelton used his understanding of Haitian views of force and fear to deliver a very clear message to Cedras, from his first minutes in Port-au-Prince. Knowing the Haitian general would be watching his arrival on CNN, General Shelton flew in by helicopter, without any weapon or protective equipment. Flying into the airport, Shelton could see the poverty of the nation's capital and the poor conditions under which the Haitian people had been living; he resolved to make Cedras aware from his very first meeting of the critical importance of his mission and his commitment to its success. In General Shelton's words:

It was all designed to show him [Cedras], number one, that I wasn't the least bit afraid of what the hell he had in the country and, number two, that I was an individual that was willing, basically, to take him to task at a moment's notice. I thought it was important to set the stage; that I was going to get my way come hell or high water, that the cooperation aspect of it was going to be inform versus coordinate and that he was going to cooperate with me and not the other way around. And yet, I also understood that here's a guy who has agreed now to let the United States come in and he knows he is going out . . . and that he is going to want to maintain his self-respect. And so, from the very beginning, my pitch to him was, I don't want to embarrass you, I know you're in a tough position, but you are going to have to cooperate. If you don't, you are going to be embarrassed and you are going to be humiliated and you're going to leave here as a man without your clothes on; we are going to strip you.[5]

In his initial meeting with Cedras, General Shelton outlined his position distinctly. Cedras took notes, but no one was able to predict at that time his immediate reaction to the U.S. arrival. While Cedras pondered his options, American troops and equipment poured into the airport and the port of the Haitian capital. American infantry and military-police units identified initial blocking positions at key locations and staked out a buffer zone centered on the Port-au-Prince airport, where most of the force was to enter over the following days. These arrivals and the security operations continued relentlessly throughout the afternoon and the first oppressively hot night. With Shelton's strict attitude on one hand, and the unending flow of American military-power facing him on the other, the options available to Cedras were few.

The FAd'H could have fought on the first afternoon. Cedras had several tactical options. He could have sacrificed his most loyal troops in an immediate counter-attack against the airport. That would have seriously hampered the flow of U.S. forces into the country and certainly would have created a firestorm of media attention, placing the United States in a difficult position. Such an attack also would have destroyed Cedras's entire force, as Shelton certainly would have called in General Steele's paratroopers and exercised the full capacity of fire support he had available to destroy the FAd'H. Cedras also could have fought a delaying action. Just as they had opposed the landing of the *Harlan County* by using the ambiguity of regular forces without uniforms and a mixture of local civilians pressed into service to make the action appear the result of national outrage, the FAd'H could now have begun a series of small snipe-and-run actions designed to demoralize and unsettle the entering U.S. force. This would have bought time, however, at the cost of Haitian lives, and would have exposed Cedras and the other FAd'H leaders to whatever penalty Shelton designed. As neither of these options gave Cedras any more flexibility than he already had under the Carter Agreement, the Haitian military chief decided to cooperate and wait for an opportunity to wriggle out of his predicament.

Many feared that even if Cedras were cowed, individual Haitian soldiers or rival section chiefs might decide to turn to violence for their own reasons. Yet, despite much effort devoted to countering this concern during the first 24 hours, Cedras and the FAd'H were completely compliant; no opposition was encountered and no special precautions were in evidence around the airport as dawn broke on the 20th of September, D+1.[6] Aircraft after aircraft carrying personnel and equipment had arrived throughout the night, so much so that most of the available groundspace inside the airport terminal was covered by U.S. camouflage, personnel, and equipment. Combat units and military police from the 18th Airborne Corps had established defensive positions at a variety of locations in and around Port-au-Prince. Every weapon was loaded and machine guns protruded from every appropriate vantage point.

As the sun rose, normal Haitian work habits took over as usual; the streets became busy with vehicles, security and maintenance personnel began to arrive at work, and the common people of the country began to gravitate towards the U.S. positions. When the armed FAd'H airport security guard arrived at Port-au-Prince International Airport, several soldiers uneasily watched him survey the M-60 machine-gun and barbed wire at the rear entrance to the building. He entered the terminal with little apparent concern and quietly proceeded to look for coffee, to the relief of both sides.[7]

The same benign situation existed at the port and through all the occupied areas of the city during the early morning hours. While most Haitians were just waking, civil–military operations were begun almost immediately, spearheaded by Brigadier General Dick Potter, USA, and his Task Force Black.[8] Task Force Black's objectives included capturing the key offensive weapons of the FAd'H and expanding American teams of Special Forces soldiers throughout the area around the capital. The 10th Mountain Division aviation brigade from the *Eisenhower* flew into the airport, and military-police units moved around in armed HUMVEEs[9] to establish liaison with the Haitian security forces. In the north, the JTF-180 naval forces, including the Marine Special Purpose MAGTF (SPMAGTF), conducted an amphibious landing in the area of Cap-Haitien, established a U.S. presence in the key areas of the northern port city, and began security operations in the region, known as an area of strong Aristide support.[10]

The immediate battle on D+1 was with the Haitian heat, which soared to over 90° with as much humidity. Yet, uncertainty was also on everyone's mind. The last-minute accord with Cedras gave little assurance of his *real* cooperation with the JTF, and everyone was wary of possible attacks from Haitian police, military, and even uninformed Haitian citizens.[11]

Shelton had anticipated such a period of unease in his first meeting with Cedras the day before and he wanted to use it to his advantage. The American general had taken the initiative then and kept it on D+1 by giving clear evidence of what he was capable of doing if Cedras did not cooperate fully. Shelton had long before determined that the Heavy Weapons Company of the FAd'H, located at Camp d'Application in Port-au-Prince, was the tactical center of gravity of the Haitian force; it was the only card that Cedras could play that would give him even a temporary military advantage if used directly against the Americans. Immediately and unconditionally, Shelton had demanded that the Cadillac V-150 armored vehicles and the howitzers from that company be given up to American forces. On the 20th, Shelton had passed the word so that CNN, the remainder of the press, and the Haitian people were informed of this demand. He made it possible that everyone could watch the Americans drive up and publicly tow away the best of the FAd'H equipment, while members of the Haitian army stood by helplessly. The impression of that public act on General Cedras was one of deep humiliation.

Yet due to the uncertain environment, American personnel continued to arrive with loaded weapons during the first days of the operation and wore full combat gear whenever they left the protection of the U.S.-controlled sites. Flackjackets, helmets, and full weaponry were a constant reminder that trouble could occur at any minute and were an uncomfortable but prudent precaution in the stifling heat. By D+2 the heavy forces assigned as a mobile reserve for JTF-190 (3rd Battalion, 15th Infantry [Mech] of the 24th Division) began off-loading from Military Sealift Command shipping in the port. Only then were all the airborne forces of the 82d Division, originally assigned to conduct the forcible entry, finally released to return to normal duties at Fort Bragg. The 1st Brigade Combat Team (BCT) of the 10th Mountain Division moved on to occupy Bowen Field, the former home of the Haitian Air Force just outside the capital, in order to establish secure operating areas needed for the civilûmilitary operations (CMO), which would be so very important to affecting the long-term development of Haiti. Activities designed to engender the acceptance and eventual support of the Haitian people were the focus of activity by Task Force Black all around Port-au-Prince. The JTF headquarters on land began to take shape in the light-industrial complex adjacent to the airport.[12] Inbound flights continued to off-load large numbers of personnel and vehicles. The airport began to take on the appearance of an armed camp. By the end of Day Two, over 10,700 troops were ashore.

General Shelton continued his regular dialogue with Cedras, meeting daily at first to coordinate a wide variety of issues, which ranged from local security of key locations to the management of treasury funds. Significantly, Shelton reconsidered his approach immediately after the humiliation at Camp d'Application, because Cedras appeared so very disturbed by his obvious loss of prestige. In one of the most important long-term actions of the operation, Shelton quickly understood that he had already won the competition for dominance. Cedras was not willing to oppose him. But just as important, Shelton saw that he had to be judicious in his treatment of Cedras or he would risk losing the very lever that Cedras represented to the United States: a controller of FAd'H actions. To his great credit, even in the second day of the operation Shelton perceived that his long-term goals were better served by moderating his approach to Cedras just a bit. As Shelton said later, "That was the first time that I really understood in my relationship with Cedras that if we took him down too fast he'd lose the FAd'H as an institution."[13] From that day forward General Shelton ensured that he maintained the delicate balance between dominance and cooperation. In doing so, he also ensured that Cedras and the FAd'H would remain both compliant and under control as Shelton worked to support the return of President Aristide.

Of course, relations among the key officials were one aspect of the operation, and as is common, the perception of the common people was somewhat different. The majority of the Haitian population, in general, viewed the American actions with hope, tempered with some uncertainty up to D+3, September 22nd. This uncertainty was predominantly due to the fact that the Haitian security troops did not appear to be impeded from their normal rough tactics by the presence of the U.S. forces. In fact, Haitian-on-Haitian violence rapidly became a subject of serious discussion. The majority of Haitians had been victims of the Haitian army or the Tonton Macoutes of the VSN their entire lives; they had heard of the Cayes Massacre and other stories of the U.S. military dominance in Haiti for just as long. Even Aristide had often preached about the abuse of U.S. power in Haiti. What was the average Haitian to believe about the new situation in Haiti?

It had always been anticipated that U.S. personnel might have to intervene between Haitian citizens and police, a very delicate situation for combat troops. Clearly, however, after both the U.S. ambassador and several senior military officers observed Haitian citizens nearly beaten to death (once outside the U.S. embassy and a second incident near the gates to the light-industrial complex chosen as the MNF headquarters), they realized that failure to act against Haitian-on-Haitian violence would not be acceptable to the American people or, in the long run, the troops on the ground. This issue had been hotly and repeatedly debated prior to the invasion. Admiral Miller had noted the need for a decision on the matter during his initial visit to Haiti, and immediately turned his staff to the task of coordinating an answer to the problem.

United States planners knew that the media coverage of the operation would reveal the internal problems of Haiti to many Americans for the first time. Cable News Network (CNN) and other national media were showing events in Haiti to the American public every hour. Although the U.S. troops could not tolerate illegal acts in America, conditions were quite different in Haiti; besides, an essential element of peace operations was the need to remain as neutral as possible and to abide by local law. It was finally decided that embroiling troops in internal Haitian affairs was too potentially damaging to the mission in Haiti, and so the MNF arrived with very proscribed rules of engagement. Like many planning decisions, failing to prevent Haitian-on-Haitian violence seemed a logical risk from the Pentagon's perspective, but once on the ground in Haiti a very different reality took precedence. Admiral Miller had the ROE recrafted accordingly and had the word put out that U.S. personnel would not stand by if the Haitian security forces were observed violating human rights. This decision was another of the key actions that, in the end, formed a critical part of public perception, public acceptance, and overall support for U.S. and multinational actions in Haiti.

To support this understanding of the real motives of the U.S. intervention and to reassure the Haitian people that they were not under attack, the United States continued to employ psychological operations (PSYOP) tools to get the word out. These efforts had begun before the invasion started, using leaflets and radio messages with music, to inform everyone of the U.N. objectives. In the early days after arrival, the effort was adjusted to ensure that the situation remained calm. Area specialists, intelligence officers, and even former members of the FAd'H granted entry into the United States advised U.S. military personnel working in Alexandria, Virginia and Key West, Florida concerning the mood of the Haitian population and how well the word of Aristide's return was being received. In time, this effort expanded to include daily radio messages from Aristide, and even video broadcasts of the Haitian president reassuring everyone that he was alive and well and on his way back home.[14] Some people misunderstand psychological operations and assume that they center on deception. In reality, it was the value of the truth that best aided the Haitian people to understand what was happening in their country, and truth was the message of psychological operations in Haiti. Unfortunately, in a nation so long deceived by its leaders even the truth was hard to accept.

The major goal for D+3 was the occupation of the Camp d'Application complex by U.S. forces. The camp had been the home of the heavy-weapons company of the FAd'H, the largest single military threat to U.S. forces, and the only source of working armored vehicles. (These were the ones that were quickly moved to U.S. custody at the airport.) Task Force Black assets successfully occupied the camp without incident and began to inventory the large cache of weapons inside on September 24th. Initially, the camp guards were not very cooperative, but they became much more helpful when the U.S. soldiers made it clear they were not on the scene to negotiate, but to demand compliance. The AC-130 Spectre gunship orbiting overhead served notice that the U.S. forces would fight if opposed.[15] The camp guards complied fully, and with the "Camp D" threat neutralized, the focus of U.S. operations began to shift from the threat of combat operations to a purely security role. In fact, during the evening video-tele-conference with the CINC, Admiral Miller began to propose actions to reactivate the Port-au-Prince power grid and improve city basic services with engineer units.[16] He was already thinking ahead to actions that could immediately demon-strate the willingness of the U.S. forces to aid the Haitians in everyday life.

Planners focused on the arrival of other national forces on D+4, particular-ly the Caribbean Command (CARICOM) battalion of 266 troops then in train-ing in Puerto Rico. This unit had significance greater than its size because it would represent the first visible non-U.S. unit of the MNF in Haiti. The only non-U.S. forces participating in operations thus far were naval ships, which were largely invisible to the press and Haitian population. The arrival of ground forces from other nations, particularly other countries of the Caribbean, would demonstrate that OAS support for the operation was not a sham. Caribbean sol-diers on the streets of Haiti would also help blend the disparity between the local population and the American military. The sign in front of the headquar-ters in the light-industrial complex near the airport now read Multinational Force, Haiti. Smooth integration of the CARICOM force into the U.S. order of battle was also important, because the CARICOM battalion's integration could serve as the model for the Bangladeshi, Guatemalan, and other national forces planned to arrive in the future.[17]

Also on D+4, the PSYOP campaign grew to include a special emphasis on "nonviolence" and the upcoming effort to disarm the Haitian population, known as "Guns for Cash." Because the number of incidents of Haitian-on-Haitian vio-lence was still increasing, all commanders were concerned that a total breakdown in law and order could result if the populace rose up against the FAd'H before sufficient numbers of trustworthy police were identified and put in place around the country. For the same reasons, in view of the reduced effectiveness of the national security forces during the vetting process and the limited crowd-control capability existing in Haiti, it was vitally important to reduce the number of guns within the general population. Special Forces "B" teams were inserted into the towns of Jacmel, Gonaives, and Cap-Haitien and then spread throughout the countryside to provide "eyes and ears" for the commanders and to deter violence through presence alone.[18] The insertion of additional Special Forces teams throughout the countryside, beginning on D+5, would also help ease potential problems by building a solid rapport with the people living outside the major cities, as had been amply demonstrated in a variety of conflicts since the Special Forces actions in Vietnam.

On September 24th the SECDEF, Dr. Perry, and Chairman of the Joint Chiefs of Staff, General Shalikashvili, visited Haiti. The official party toured several sites within the area of operations and were pleased to witness the scheduled arrival at Port-au-Prince International Airport of the first returning humanitarian-aid flight, carrying 16,000 tons of supplies. The flight was one more bit of evi-dence that the U.S. effort was focused on the humanitarian needs of the Haitian people as well as the reform of the FAd'H. These humanitarian activities soon came to the fore just as the "Cash for Guns" program began, and humanitarian assessments of the electrical power-generation, water distribution, waste and garbage disposal, and fire-fighting requirements in Port-au-Prince were also initiated. To the servicemen and women on the ground, humanitarian actions were clearly the priority once the physical security of people in Haiti had been addressed; the difficulty lay in convincing others that the large military force was committed to humanitarian relief.

Also on D+5, elements of the Army's 2nd Brigade Combat Team (2 BCT) began arriving in Cap-Haitien by C-130 to join with Marine forces in the area. The 2 BCT was later assigned operationally to the Marine commander, Colonel Tom Jones, another example of the military services working well together in order to meet operational objectives. During these early days of the operation naval and aviation forces of the JTF, including the ships from Great Britain, Canada, Holland, and Argentina, continued to conduct Maritime Intercept Operations (MIO) as part of the embargo as well as perform other support operations around Haiti. The U.S. Coast Guard was providing port security in addition to patrolling the nearby waters and assisting the Navy with security boarding teams onboard ships. The Coast Guard also continued the mission of intercepting Haitian migrants at sea and returning those individuals either to Haiti or to Guantanamo Bay, Cuba, for repatriation processing. The *Mount Whitney* and both aircraft carriers remained inside "the claw,"[19] providing command and control and mobile basing in support of JTF-180 operations. The U.S. Air Force provided ready strike aircraft from bases all over the United States, surveillance and intelligence-gathering aircraft, and a massive number of cargo aircraft, which airlifted all manner of equipment and personnel into Haiti. Although most observers considered Uphold Democracy to be a ground operation, conducted primarily by the U.S. Army, in reality all four military services and the Coast Guard were active members of the joint team. By this time, there were 13,816 U.S. military personnel in the country, working in the Haitian heat.

INITIAL COMBAT

Late in the morning of Saturday, September 24, 1994, word was suddenly received that a Marine patrol had exchanged fire with Cap-Haitien police; ten Haitians were reported dead and one American wounded. Following the firefight, the local population had ransacked the police headquarters in the city. Although the reaction of the local population in Cap-Haitien was a joyful celebration of the Marine action in putting down the oppression of the FAd'H, many members of the press debated the reasons for the firefight and its disproportionate results. Military commanders and the U.S. Ambassador stood by the decision to fire made by a young Marine, Lieutenant Chris Palumbo. This event broke the psychological back of the Haitian resistance and support of it was important proof of the commitment of everyone involved in Uphold Democracy.

In modern military operations, where worldwide media coverage is the norm and the acceptable level of casualties is at an absolute minimum, every initial combat action receives extreme scrutiny. In this Cap-Haitien incident the risks were many: U.S. public opinion over the deaths of Haitians and the wounding of an American could have been negative and cast a harsh light on the possible future achievements of the operation; also, the action could have resulted in a massive uprising of the FAd'H and commensurate increase in the level of combat in Haiti; and finally, perhaps most crucially, had the Marines not demonstrated their resolve, the Haitian people might not have witnessed so clearly the level of commitment and willingness to confront the illegalities of the FAd'H, which they needed to have impressed on them in order to completely support the overthrow of the military regime. Still, the incident caused everyone to hold their breath. Were the Marines justified in firing on the Haitian soldiers?

The rules of engagement in effect at the time gave U.S. forces the authority to employ lethal force, to initiate fire, if a member of the FAd'H pointed a weapon at a U.S. servicemember with intent to fire.[20] The Haitians in Cap-Haitien had clearly done this. During the incident a small Marine patrol had been stopped by armed members of the FAd'H. The Haitian group was warned off, but threatened the Marines in response. When the Haitians raised their weapons to aim at the Marines as they normally did to intimidate other Haitians, they met with a torrent of returning U.S. firepower. Commanders at all levels supported the Marines who had acted; but how would the rest of the FAd'H react—with acceptance, or with revenge in mind? Again, General Shelton, understanding the history and psychology of Haiti, acted to ensure that the incident was perceived in the right way by all concerned.

Shelton immediately took General Cedras to view the bodies of the dead Haitians. The clear American intent was to support the servicemen who fired in self-defense, once threatened. The destruction wrought by the volley of Marine-returned fire was undeniable, as were the casualty ratios: one slight Marine injury to ten Haitian dead. The Americans had shown their resolve and willingness to fire against the FAd'H. The message went throughout the countryside that the Americans *would* fight, and fight effectively; the FAd'H would pay a high price for any opposition, and there would be no cover-ups or excuses. The Haitians understood and admired strength and perceived in Shelton's visit with Cedras a clear lesson: "We, the Americans, were right to do this, and will do so again if the FAd'H is not kept under control."[21] Now that the first blood was spilled the FAd'H could not question the eventual results of confronting the Americans, and the majority of the Haitian people demonstrated their joy at the punishment exacted on the FAd'H strongmen.

The shooting was also occasion for an important reinforcement at home in the United States. When the facts of the incident were shown, the Clinton Administration did not demur and the American people understood the situation. In each case of overseas military action, the cost in potential human losses must be constantly gauged against American public support. Each incident of hostile fire poses the threat of objections by members of Congress and by the citizens, who are the ultimate support organization of the military. This early, limited combat action passed the test of home support and commitment. It served to reinforce the important understanding of military men and women that their actions were in keeping with the expectations of America's citizens.

The following day the military staffs begin looking ahead and focusing on the return of the de jure Haitian government of President Aristide, which still included officials ousted along with him. A large demonstration was expected on the third anniversary of the coup, just days away. There was some fear that this demonstration might be used by the anti-Aristide party in Haiti to oppose his return. Since this demonstration posed a serious threat to the maintenance of positive public opinion, the desire was to begin the return of key individuals coincident with the anniversary to help diffuse the impact of any anti-Aristide rallies. Planning for this potential demonstration was the cause of the decision to delay the relief of the Marine SPMAGTF in Cap-Haitien, still serving as the JTF-180 reserve force, until October 2nd, after the coup anniversary. The First Battalion, 22d Infantry, moved by helicopter to the area of the national palace, and Military Police began a security assessment of Aristide's residence. These efforts validated the understanding that public opinion in Haiti needed to be nurtured. Linking the return of individuals such as the former mayor of Port-au-Prince to the coup anniversary would help turn away any potential effort by the FAd'H to use it as an excuse to literally or even figuratively attack the MNF.

More significantly for the long term, September 26th witnessed the first repatriation of Haitian migrants from Guantanamo Bay to Port-au-Prince. The critical question was: What would be the reaction of the Haitian government to "forced" repatriation of Haitian citizens? If the government in Port-au-Prince viewed the repatriation as a violation of the rights of Haitian citizens or of Haitian national sovereignty, there could be a serious impact on the future return of others. Even in the United States the return was hotly debated among lawyers supporting the Haitian need to flee oppression, the American Civil Liberties Union with its concern about the use of camps for needy migrants, and those who opposed bringing any migrants at all to the United States for succor.

Also on September 26th, a plan was developed to expand security operations throughout Port-au-Prince, both to demonstrate the MNF presence and to dissipate possible movements of retribution against the FAd'H. The military logistics flow shifted from combat units to combat support units and service forces; shortfalls in quality-of-life support ashore, particularly toilets, water, and shower facilities, were emphasized at all levels. A major effort was begun to locate and deliver waste-removal trucks. Meanwhile, the SPMAGTF retrieved weapons from a cache in Grande Rivière du Nord, and the first U.N. observers arrived to monitor the activities of U.S. forces and begin coordinating the transition between the MNF and the United Nation's Mission in Haiti (UNMIH), slated to arrive in the spring of 1995. The U.N.'s arrival in Haiti was very important.

Although Shelton's troops were in the country under a U.N. mandate, they were not wearing the Blue Berets of the U.N. peacekeepers. Most of the world understood that the U.N. Security Council had authorized Uphold Democracy, but in Haiti that information had been distorted by the Cedras regime. Having U.N. officials on the ground therefore would be a significant demonstration of the operation's legality.

On D+8 incidents of violence and looting increased and a contingency plan for promoting civil order was briefed to the USACOM staff. More Special Forces teams were inserted throughout the countryside to gain an improved awareness of Haitian intentions. Task Force Mountain, the major ground force of the 10th Mountain Division under the command of Brigadier General George Close, USA, provided security for a variety of Haitian government facilities, including the Parliament building, city hall, and Ville d'Accueil, in order to ensure that government functions would be continued regardless of the threat to security. Other actions in Haiti began to become routine. Repatriation of Haitians from Guantanamo Bay, begun on D+4, continued with 147 Haitians returned on the U.S. Coast Guard cutter *Durable*; Marines acted to break up another Haitian-on-Haitian beating in Cap-Haitien; soldiers conducted security patrols in the capital city and Special Forces teams continued to expand their circles of influence in the countryside.

By September 28th JTF-180 had 19,479 personnel in the country, nearly 5,000 more than had been announced as the estimate of forces required after the assault phase was completed. The combination of the two plans had resulted in a bunching effect in the numbers of the force that could not be avoided. The overage was undesirable for several reasons, including the cost of the operation, the risk to individuals deployed, and the added drain on an already widely committed U.S. military-force structure. In response, the CINC directed that the JTF develop a plan to return to the level of 15,500 personnel intended for steady-state Uphold Democracy operations. The number of Americans committed to the operation was capped at that level for more than just political and economic reasons; working within that ceiling would also help prevent "mission creep," the expansion in the number and types of tasks given the military that had plagued American involvement in Somalia. At the strategic level, success was already being evaluated in terms of the numbers of troops required and the duration of the operation. Because perceptions can often be as damaging as facts, the CINC wanted to ensure that everyone kept to the initial planning figures.

At the same time, in the final days of September, International Police Monitors (IPMs) began arriving in the country as the vanguard of the movement to observe, retrain, and professionalize the security force of Haiti.[22] The IPM operation was focused on one of the most critical requirements for success of the operation—FAd'H reform—so the arrival of the IPMs was a welcome sight to the members of the JTF staff. The repatriation and Weapons Buy-Back programs also continued on course, so three critical efforts of the campaign were being implemented according to plan. United States forces also facilitated the safe opening of the Haitian Parliament, which achieved a quorum for the first time in many months.

Since Admiral Miller and General Shelton knew that any military success in Haiti would be measured in part by the longevity of President Aristide and functional democracy, the effort to develop enduring security by Haitians in Haiti was an early priority. Such Haitian security was based upon three key elements: the return of the legislative process; judicial and police reform; and reductions in threats to security. These elements were viewed as three legs on the table of Haitian security, and making progress in all three areas was very important in the early days of the operation. The U.S. military could do little to facilitate the legislative process, but at least it could ensure the safety of members of the government. Likewise, judicial and police reform were more the purview of the Department of Justice, but when possible Shelton's forces began any effort that would help provide law and order, including the matching of IPMs and military police to local jurisdictions. Finally, buying-back guns would not end crime, but was well worth the cost simply in terms of reduced violence and as a demonstration of commitment towards improving local security throughout the country.

On September 29th, as had been feared, violence that focused on the third anniversary of the coup against Aristide erupted, leaving 40 Haitian casualties (a grenade had exploded during a crowded demonstration) in Port-au-Prince. The CNN focused on the resulting brief firefight as U.S. soldiers attacked a warehouse believed to be the location of the killer. Identification of the perpetrator was immensely difficult in the bustling, fear-ridden streets of the overpopulated city. The security situation in Haiti was complex, because multiple bands—from the old Cedras regime, the old Aristide government, traditional Haitian interest groups, and new political factions—were all jockeying for a role in Haiti. Among these was Emmanual Constant's Front pour l'Avencement et le Progrès d'Haiti (FRAPH), which had been the group of attachés that initially opposed the landing of the *Harlan County* in 1993 and that still terrorized the countryside as the political arm of the FAd'H. The FRAPH instigated riots and fueled individual attacks of violence, but it was not the only group that took advantage of the shifting of power in Haiti. Even Aristide's own Lavalas support group was blamed for some violent incidents. Simply sorting out who was behind a given incident was a challenge for the security operations in Haiti.

Still, momentum was important and military actions continued to grow in scope and intent. The 2nd BCT completed movement to Cap-Haitien and the SPMAGTF prepared for relief/reembarkation. Special Forces team insertions continued in an ever-growing number of the smaller towns in the country to work as closely as possible with the rural inhabitants to aid in the transition from authoritarian to democratic government, while contributing to increased security in the interim. In advance of further demonstrations that were feared on September 30th, U.S. forces moved to secure radio and television stations in Port-au-Prince. These facilities had been controlled by pro-junta elements and had continued to voice opposition to the U.S. force's presence while not permitting the speeches of President Aristide to be aired to the people. Some rioting *did* occur on the 30th, but there was much less violence than had been feared; in fact, the crowds were small in comparison to the numbers of the previous day. Even so, several Haitians died during a fight between attachés and supporters of President Aristide. Although U.S. soldiers were near the area of the disturbance, they did not interfere; the press in the United States was highly critical of their lack of response in news reports the following day.

October 1st was a relatively quiet day. The focus of U.S. efforts returned to the humanitarian operations to restore services and provide food to the Haitian population, although soldiers of the 10th Mountain Division also conducted two raids on weapons caches. (Weapons were confiscated at both the Admiral Killick Naval Base and at the Hotel Voyager in Port-au-Prince.) Those who did not realize how closely related the resumption of basic electrical power and water services was to reducing violence did not understand why the efforts of U.S. troops seemed so divergent. In actuality, the long-term success of any assistance given to Haiti was integrally linked to and dependent upon aid to the people, who desperately lacked even the most rudimentary necessities of life. In what was to become an increasingly common procedure, U.S. soldiers worked together with aid-agency representatives and the Haitian people late in the day to stop looters from raiding food-storage areas in the capital.

This emphasis on the humanitarian needs of the Haitian people sheds much light on the real sources for success in Haiti. In the 3 years of military rule preceding the invasion the Haitian economy had suffered a significant decline. It is estimated that per capita income dropped from $390 to $240 over the period, and real gross domestic product fell 34 percent. Exports dropped from $163 million in 1991 to $72 million in 1993, while imports declined from $300 million to $173 million. The primary cause of the economic downturn was not just the military regime: the hemispheric trade embargo imposed in October 1991, the U.N. oil embargo of June 1993, and the total trade embargo imposed in May 1994 destroyed what little economic vitality was left in the country and resulted in the loss of an estimated 100,000 jobs. As a result, the national currency, the gourde, lost 60 percent of its value in 1994 alone.[23]

No democratic reform could possibly take place in an environment as insecure as Haiti's and under such dire economic conditions. Still, the MNF had to walk a fine line between restoring critical services and infrastructure and supplanting the very institutions that they were trying to resurrect. The military mandate given General Shelton did not support nation-building or long-term U.S. involvement. The restrictions of Title 10 of the U.S. Code placed specific limitations on the use and support available from U.S. forces.[24] Yet Shelton clearly understood that no democratic institutions could be nurtured in Haiti without a return of security and some degree of economic self-sufficiency. Both were significant challenges for military-force operations under a Chapter 7 directive from the United Nations.

The final obstacle to real change in Haiti was the departure of General Cedras. On the 1st of October, a U.S. congressional delegation led by Senator Christopher Dodd met with Cedras to reconfirm his intention to depart from Haiti by October 15th, in accordance with the terms of the Carter Agreement. As the 15th approached much work had to be completed in order to make a smooth transition possible, not the least of which was coordinating the departure of Cedras and the arrival of President Aristide, while also maintaining the tenuous hold on the FAd'H that Shelton had through Cedras. Unfortunately, Cedras had not yet indicated his intention to leave. This lack of commitment generated concern over the timing of his departure in relation to the return of Aristide, which was entering the final planning stage. The two events needed to be coordinated and conducted safely in order to ensure a smooth transition and thereby maintain the momentum of reform.

Sunday the 2nd of October saw continued raids on suspected arms caches by American forces. The focus on arms was a result of the need to decrease the potential for fighting in the country, not only between the Haitians and Americans but, even more likely, between Haitian groups jockeying for the remnants of power as the old military regime was eased out of the country. Still, indices of threatening activity in the Haitian capital were being reduced every day. A clear reflection of this relative calm in the city was the decision to return the hospital-ship USNS *Comfort* to its homeport in the United States. The *Comfort* represented a significant part of the medical support that might have been required to support combat operations in Haiti; her departure from the region was evidence that the commanders were satisfied that the potential for even low-intensity combat operations was finally deemed quite small.

BUILDING MOMENTUM

Even so, limited combat operations were still ongoing. In Port-au-Prince, U.S. troops surrounded the headquarters of FRAPH, which still strongly supported the Cedras regime, arrested thirty-five of its key members and confiscated numerous weapons and stocks of ammunition. During similar raids in Cap-Haitien and Grande Rivière de Nord, another seventy-five FRAPH attachés were detained in those cities. These actions were very important efforts to make it absolutely clear to antigovernment group members that their illegal opposition to the returning Haitian government was not going to be tolerated. Extinguishing the FRAPH would also greatly reduce the street violence that frequently pitted reactionary FRAPH members against Aristide supporters.

The first truly international security effort of the operation in the Haitian cities began on October 3rd. Under the direction of former New York City police commissioner Raymond Kelly, IPMs began working with and training the Haitian police. Since the early days of planning, this crucial reformation of the Haitian security force had been given a high priority. The American forces had insufficient police personnel to provide security for all of Haiti; in addition, no one wanted to repeat the mistakes of the 1920s and 1930s by replacing security functions rightly belonging to Haitians. The difficulty was in transforming the largely suspect police force in Haiti to an impartial police organization, while still allowing it to carry out its daily functions. The plan was to identify members of the FAd'H who could be trusted and retrain them to carry out proper police functions; however, good policing was already a scarce commodity. For example, on October 3rd, in Les Cayes, unknown Haitians shot and wounded a U.S. soldier, Sergeant Donald Holstead, USA, who was taken to the 28th Combat Support Hospital and treated for wounds. He recovered, but the incident showed that Haiti was still a dangerous place.

The following day brought several bits of good news. Lieutenant Colonel Michel François, chief of the Haitian police, fled Haiti for sanctuary in the Dominican Republic; his more moderate successor was Colonel Jodel Lesage. Additionally, Emmanuel Constant, the head of FRAPH, also asked fellow-Haitians to forsake violence following the U.S. troop raids on his headquarters. Opposition was lessening, either by escape or by conversion; but the situation in Haiti still hid several traditional dangers: would the elites remain neutral, or would they find their own replacements for the key coup leaders? Would the people in the countryside accept American-provided security over that of the former FAd'H? Would the most militant of the members of the FAd'H form a guerrilla movement in the hills?

The U.S. efforts in Haiti received their most significant vote of confidence later the same day, when, in an address before the United Nations, President Aristide vowed he would return to Haiti on October 15th as planned. During a news briefing General Shalikashvili related that U.S. troops in Haiti had peaked at almost 21,000 on October 2nd, still exceeding the 15,500 planning figure, but that the number would begin to decline to 16,500 within several weeks, and hover at 15,000 by the end of the month. The effort to return Haitians from the migrant center in Cuba continued with USCG cutters *Vigilant* and *Diligence* repatriating 245 and 249 voluntary Haitian migrants, respectively, to Port-au-Prince. On October 4th Admiral Miller again visited his troops in Haiti, expressing to them the high marks the entire operation was receiving.

The next day SECDEF Perry revealed that the United States was training Haitian security personnel to guard President Aristide. This issue was of great importance for several reasons, but primarily because of the very real concern for Aristide's safety. On the one hand, it was difficult to mount an extensive protective detail around Aristide without giving the appearance that he was not returning by the wish of the people; on the other, even the smallest injury to the Haitian President could have severely hampered any hope for a real return to democracy in Haiti. The degree of U.S. support for Aristide's personal safety became a hotly debated political issue. In the end, Aristide decided that he would develop his own security detail, although the U.S. forces did continue facility security missions in support of the Haitian Parliament.

President Clinton and SECDEF Perry visited Norfolk for Haiti briefings at USACOM headquarters and tours of the recently returned USS *Eisenhower* on October 6th. The President proclaimed that Admiral Miller and his staff had "imagined almost every conceivable circumstance and devised their response" for the operation. It was clear that the operation was achieving exactly the results that the Administration had desired prior to the invasion. A clear sign of this was the redeployment of Marines from Cap-Haitien on the same day. Although they remained onboard the USS *Wasp* and USS *Nashville* as a "floating reserve" for the JTF in case they should be needed during the upcoming return of President Aristide, the tide of operations had clearly turned from offensive to humanitarian actions.

Meanwhile, in Washington, the Senate passed a nonbinding resolution by a vote of 91 to 8 that criticized President Clinton for not seeking congressional approval before sending troops to Haiti. The House also passed a similar resolution and continued debate over establishing a cutoff date of March 1, 1995 for the return of troops. Congress was hostile both to the Clinton Administration and to the rising frequency of American troops deployed overseas. Although this action was purely political and had no effect on the ongoing operation in Haiti, it did cause some members of the force to wonder how well the American people supported the operation.

On October 7th, one day after the House of Deputies voted for an amnesty agreement, Haiti's Senate approved an expanded amnesty bill that would allow President Aristide to pardon military leaders for political as well as for other crimes. This agreement would permit Cedras and the other coup leaders to depart from Haiti without being tried for crimes ranging from treason to drug dealing and theft. Earlier that same day, noting the passing of the last legal hurdle to Cedras's departure, and in response to the concerns of the Congress, Pentagon officials had predicted that U.S. forces in Haiti would number less than 6,000 in 4 to 6 months. Clearly, the focus of planning was shifting towards decreasing the U.S. presence in light of the impending departure of the coup leaders. Even so, almost 5,000 pro-democracy demonstrators marched in Port-au-Prince to demand the resignation of General Cedras.

With the first successful moves to ease out the Cedras faction, the international community also began to act. Fifteen countries pledged $77 million to cover Haiti's international debts, which opened the way for assistance loans from the World Bank, the Inter-American Development Bank, and the International Monetary Fund for more than $230 million. These efforts were crucial to the long-term success of reforms in Haiti. After less than 3 weeks had passed since the arrival of U.S. forces, and still prior to Aristide's return, the driving forces within the U.S.-led operation were already changing significantly from military to other means of support.

The military had planned and prepared for multiple tactical eventualities in Haiti. However, once the coup leader's departure was arranged and the level of security in Port-au-Prince required to protect Aristide was obtained, the roles of other national agencies in Uphold Democracy began to stand equal to that of the military. Economic support was only one area where the military had little or no long-term contribution to make, unless its was to take on a nation-building mission—a task decidedly unpopular and insupportable given the lack of military nation-building success of the earlier U.S. intervention. However, the preparedness of the non-DOD agencies, including the United Nations and other national support, remained suspect: Could the other agencies step in as actively and quickly as required? Would the momentum of the military action in Haiti be lost because the other elements of U.S. and U.N. power were not prepared to act? In early October these were very serious concerns.

Accompanying international economic support were over 1,000 Bangladeshi soldiers, who arrived in Haiti as part of the MNF operations. This was clear evidence of multinational military support, and not just from another member of the OAS but a nation halfway around the world. Bangladesh's commitment, although not large in numbers of troops or in funds, sent an important global signal. Meanwhile, U.S. soldiers stationed in Gonaives arrested twenty-three Haitian soldiers in an arms raid on Saint-Marc and captured a truckload of guns in the continuing effort to remove weapons from the streets.

Defense Secretary Perry and General Shalikashvili visited Haiti again on October 8th to assess the progress made towards restoring President Aristide to power, scheduled for the following week. Overall, they saw that much headway had been made but that a good deal more remained to be completed, not the least of which was the reorganization within the Haitian government that would be required in order to permit Aristide to effect needed changes upon his return. Many of the key elected leaders of Haiti had only just returned to their legislative duties, and much of the inner workings of government had been allowed to decay during the tenure of the coup leaders. Normally, the U.S. military could do nothing to help in this effort outside of providing personal security for the newly returned Haitian leaders; the Department of Justice (DOJ) was the organization that had the bulk of the needed expertise, but the DOJ had no readily available, deployable personnel to accomplish legal-reform training. In the end, U.S. military reservists whose civilian jobs were in criminal justice and the law stepped in to form mobile training teams to assist in this effort.

On October 9th in Miragoane, forty miles east of Les Cayes, a pro-FAd'H driver crashed his bus into a crowd of pro-democracy demonstrators, killing fourteen people and injuring many others. Efforts to establish a new model police force in Cap-Haitien failed after locals rejected the former military members and their training with IPMs. The wounds were too deep for many Haitians to accept that the preinvasion police-force personnel could be reformed in such a short time. Particularly in the north, the traditional home of the Cacos, many Haitians were unwilling to entrust their security to any former member of the police or the FAd'H. Progress in redemocratization throughout the different sections of Haiti was distinctly uneven. Some villages had been spared serious abuse in the past and were more inclined to trust the assurances of the United States and the IPMs; others, more brutally served by Tonton Macoute and FAd'H treatment, were violently opposed to any of the old police remaining. Still, all efforts continued in Port-au-Prince to ensure the departure of the coup leaders by October 15th.

DEPARTURE OF THE COUP LEADERS

General Cedras finally resigned on October 10th and turned over command of Haiti's military to Major General Jean-Claude Duperval; Brigadier General Phillippe Biamby also stepped down in favor of Brigadier General Herve Valmont. These two resignations demonstrated that the operation had achieved its major objective: the end of the regime that had plagued the nation since the 1992 coup. In response, President Clinton announced confirmation that President Aristide would return to Haiti on Saturday, October 15th. Also on the 10th, regular commercial airline flights were restored to Port-au-Prince.

The day following Cedras's resignation, U.S. troops removed employees working for Haiti's military-backed government from the National Palace and other government buildings and opened the way for the return of Prime Minister Malval and the rest of President Aristide's government. Efforts to restore the working elements of the government were stepped up to facilitate Aristide's rapid return and the reinstitution of democracy. Two days later, with initial conditions for transition accomplished, Haiti's de facto provisional president, Emile Jonassaint, and his government resigned in preparation for the return of President Aristide. In the early morning hours of October 13th, Cedras and Biamby arrived in Panama with their families after being granted sanctuary there as part of an agreement between the United States and Panama, brokered by the U.S. State Department. The United States also lifted its freeze on the Haitian military's bank accounts, estimated at over $79 million.

With the departure of Cedras and Jonassaint's resignation, the government that had ousted Aristide ceased to exist. This did not mean that the anti-Aristide movement was destroyed, but it did create a dangerous period when no legitimate structures were in place to direct the internal or external affairs of the Haitian state. During this precarious period several groups felt threatened: the supporters of the coup leaders felt that they were left without any real protection and feared that their actions during the 2 previous years might result in prosecution or acts of revenge from the populace at large; the newly returned legislators felt that they might still be targets of anti-Aristide sentiment; and former security personnel felt at risk from both the populace and future Aristide-government retribution. It was an uneasy time for all. Haitian soldiers at the Belladere barracks refused to surrender to U.S. forces, not knowing what fate really awaited them, and senior Haitian officers fled to the hills, ostensibly to train followers in guerrilla tactics.

With Cedras gone, control of the remaining FAd'H members was tenuous at best. This meant that one of the few levers for managing the internal situation in Haiti was no longer available. At least Cedras had had sufficient influence to maintain control. General Shelton worked hard to ensure that Cedras's successor, General Duperval, could maintain his authority as the Haitian army commander-in-chief by treating him deferentially and ensuring that his subordinates did the same. If the FAd'H had become fragmented, the MNF would have had a much more difficult time making the transition to a new security force in addition to having to deal with the constant threat of FAd'H revenge.

During ceremonies at the White House on October 14th, President Clinton bade farewell to President Aristide, who was able to return to power after 1,111 days in exile. The next day, President Aristide, accompanied by U.S. Secretary of State Warren Christopher and more than 200 diplomats and congressional leaders, participated in welcoming ceremonies at the Presidential Palace in Port-au-Prince. The question remained: How would Aristide act towards his opponents once he returned to power? The history of Haiti included no forgiving ex-presidents, and there was a very real concern that the joyous celebrations of Aristide's return could degenerate into festivals of revenge and retribution. Fortunately, Aristide called for reconciliation among all parties and classes, but few were certain how he could make reconciliation work in a land where it had little historical precedent.

On October 16th rioting in Port-au-Prince's slums claimed the lives of two FRAPH supporters as U.S. Ambassador Swing and Senator Dodd met for the first time with President Aristide after his return. Despite Aristide's plea for reconciliation, few were sure if even he held enough influence over the population to control random acts of violence. Nevertheless, despite the ongoing unrest in the region, U.S. forces continued their phased withdrawal from the Joint Operations Area (JOA). This withdrawal was progressing apace—a strong effort to markedly decrease the number of U.S. forces involved in Haiti by November 1st—so that the size of the force could fit within the original planning guideline. As part of this effort the Pentagon announced the return of four ships deployed to the Haiti JOA: the amphibious assault ships USS *Wasp* and *Nashville,* the aircraft carrier *America,* and the dock-landing ship *Ashland.* The only ships remaining included the command ship USS *Mount Whitney,* the oiler USNS *Leroy Grumman,* and the coastal patrol crafts *Hurricane* and *Monsoon.* Had internal actions in Haiti been more volatile, this period could have been a critical weak point in the operation; luckily, the drawdown of forces was not matched by increases in Haitian violence.

INITIAL GOAL ACHIEVED

Over the first 30 days of the operation, the type of U.S. support offered in Haiti had evolved significantly. Primarily, this evolution was due to changes in the political goals established for the force. Forces designed to conduct violent combat operations were initially replaced by the peacekeepers of the 10th Mountain Division; reinforcing forces with tanks and rapid-reaction capabilities were slowly reduced in number and replaced by security and special operating forces. Supplies and logistics support grew in importance over time as the focus of operations shifted from stability operations and force protection to support of security efforts to true humanitarian activities. As a sign of this progression, on the 18th of October forces of JTF-190 began an "Adopt a School" program, with soldiers from the 10th Mountain Division devoting their off-duty time to repairing Haitian schools and distributing clothing and supplies. This was a far cry from the combat tasks assigned to the 82nd Airborne; nothing could have made the interests of the Americans more clear than soldiers volunteering their time to help the children of Haiti.

These efforts were completely consistent with the original plan to move rapidly towards an eventual transition to U.N. control. The only question had been how soon was the transition to take place and how many personnel would be required to participate in the U.N. effort? At that time, USACOM proposed a plan to the United Nations that called for a 6,000-person U.N. Mission in Haiti. The United Nations responded to USACOM's proposal on the 19th, indicating its concern that paramilitary gunmen opposed to President Aristide needed to be disarmed prior to the arrival of U.N. peace-keepers. In the U.N. definition of "secure environment" no armed threat was permitted. This requirement was more stringent than the USACOM planners had anticipated. Simply defining the level of security in Haiti had become a governor for success of the operation. The United Nations and United States had differing ideas of what constituted a secure environment and therefore some agreement had to be reached prior to the deployment of U.N. forces, but no qualitative criteria were available and no definition seemed to meet the expectations of both organizations. Essentially, this put the USACOM staff in the difficult position of attempting to satisfy the challenging requirements of the United Nations while managing a reduction of U.S. force levels. Again, lessons learned in Somalia had helped the USACOM staff to anticipate this divergence of views, and the efforts of many in Norfolk and Washington quickly combined to resolve the small but critical difference of opinion so that transition planning could continue.

At this point in the operation some of the efforts of the many agencies involved in Uphold Democracy began to be refocused. With Aristide returned, Ambassador Swing was clearly the primary U.S. spokesperson. Generals Shelton and Meade assumed a more purely military relationship within the team, focusing on relations with Duperval and the reformation of the FAd'H. Other U.S. government agencies, including the State Department, stepped up to shoulder more of the responsibility for the return of normal functioning of government in Haiti. As President Aristide pledged to make balanced cabinet appointments in his ongoing efforts to get Haiti's factions and people of all economic groups working together to remake the government and rebuild the country, U.S. support mirrored his actions by concentrating on electrical-power generation, food distribution, and the construction of roadways. As a part of this effort, Aristide signed a $15 million agreement with the U.S. Agency for International Development (USAID) that fixed the price of gasoline, a commodity in critical shortage since the inception of the embargo. This agreement was conducted simultaneously with the arrival of the first large tanker to bring fuel to Haiti since the end of the embargo. USAID had been one of the most proactive of the government agencies during the planning phase of the operation and was one of the first to really start work in Haiti.

A key change in the force mix in Haiti took place on October 20th. As the elements of the SPMAGTF that had participated in the initial invasion were returned to North Carolina, the first element, 400 members, of the Bangladeshi battalion arrived in Haiti to reinforce the CARICOM battalion in the MNF. The mission in Haiti was still overwhelmingly a U.S. effort, but the combat forces were quickly being replaced by multinational troops from the far corners of the world. Such a transition was difficult to manage, as diverse nations' forces have special needs and habits and do not necessarily arrive with the equipment nor doctrine that can be easily integrated into a single cohesive force. Still, the overwhelming political advantage of this demonstration of international support of the operation made painful integration well worth the effort.

Noting the importance of internal stability, the Haitian Senate acted strongly on October 21st, outlawing paramilitary groups in Haiti. Three days later, the training of vetted FAd'H members under the direction of the International Criminal Investigative Training Assistance Program (ICITAP) began at Camp d'Application outside Port-au-Prince—significantly, at the infamous former stronghold of Cedras support. Also on the 24th, President Aristide announced the selection of Smark Michel, who had been the key figure in the movement to bring all parties back together in Haiti, as his prime minister. Michel was a long-time ally of Aristide but also had the respect of many divergent groups within Haiti and provided an acceptable guarantee that the new Aristide government could take into account a variety of Haitian views.

With the transition of forces well underway—the plan for transition to UNMIH having been submitted to the United Nations, Cedras and Biamby were gone, and the return of President Aristide completed—the major objectives of the first phase of U.S. involvement in Haiti were already accomplished. Because he was due to retire at the end of October, Admiral Miller traveled to Haiti to pay a farewell call, with Ambassador Swing, on President Aristide on the 24th. That evening the CINC directed the redeployment of the JTF-180 staff to the United States and the assumption of operational control in Haiti by General Meade's MNF staff, still known as JTF-190. Operation Uphold Democracy had completed its initial mission of restoring Aristide to Haiti and paving the way for the introduction of U.N. forces to monitor the ensuing peace. The next test would be establishing the environment of stability required for complete transition to the U.N.'s forces according to the mandate.

JTF-180 withdrew from the Haitian operations area because its core, the XVIII Airborne Corps, was America's contingency-response command. By doctrine and choice, it was sent to accomplish a short-term but critically important mission: The neutralization of armed opposition to Aristide. Once the environment that permitted Aristide's return had been created the mission in Haiti changed. This change represented a crucial turning point in the relationship between Haiti and the United States.

Would America continue to direct the affairs of state in Haiti or would it accept a less dominant role and permit Aristide to govern as he saw fit? In the past, the United States had stayed too long and monopolized too much. In October, 1994 it decided to transition to a true support role—not nation-building, not dominance but the full return of Haitian sovereignty. Even so, much effort was still required if Haiti was to survive such a stressful transition—an effort that increasingly required the active participation of nonmilitary agents. America's next great challenge in Haiti, now that Aristide had been restored, was to manage the far-reaching support required to return the Haitian economy, legal system, and security forces to self-sufficiency.

NOTES

1. As in 1915, Port-au-Prince was the Haitian center of gravity because it remains the national focal point for political, economic, and military activity.

2. These were the words of the Carter–Jonaissant Agreement negotiated to avert the combat entry of U.S. forces. See Appendix D for the full text of that accord. General Shelton said later, "Never in my wildest imagination did I expect that I would be coming here (Haiti) with the mission of cooperating and coordinating in an atmosphere of mutual respect." Cynthia L. Hayden, *JTF-180 UPHOLD DEMOCRACY Oral History Interviews,* p. 62.

3. Ibid.

4. See Hayden, p. 63.

5. Ibid.

6. Despite popular perceptions, D-day is not the first day of a military operation. The designation of D-day most realistically relates to the day the major action of an operation commences and could mark the beginning of a defensive action or even the start of a humanitarian-relief supply-distribution effort.

7. Like most of his fellows, the guard was dressed in a khaki and green uniform resembling that of the U.S. Marines.

8. General Potter and his soldiers were members of the U.S. Army Special Operations Command provided by General Wayne Downing, the commander-in-chief, U.S. Special Operations Command. They were specifically trained in Haitian culture and language and had the major mission of establishing contact with individual hamlets all over Haiti and winning the trust of the Haitian people once the threat in Port-au-Prince was diminished.

9. HUMVEEs are wheeled, heavy-duty combat vehicles, replacing the Jeep in the U.S. military inventory.

10. Cap-Haitien had traditionally been the starting point for change in Haitian politics, as in the 1915 revolt, which resulted in Admiral Caperton's landing. And as a place of strong Aristide support, it offered an alternate support-base away from the capital region and therefore a relatively secure location to begin operations.

11. Only days before, CNN had provided coverage of Haitian citizens armed with a variety of personal weapons who vowed to repulse any "U.S. invasion" of their homeland.

12. General Shelton and his staff remained embarked onboard the USS *Mount Whitney* in Port-au-Prince harbor. The ship provided such important communications capability and convenience that it remained off-shore as the JTF command ship for several weeks. General Meade's staff set up their headquarters inland and began to accept functions as a MNF headquarters.

13. Hayden, *JTF-180 UPHOLD DEMOCRACY Oral History Interviews,* p. 64.

14. John R. Ballard interview with Lieutenant Colonel Thomas E. Barnes, USA, Norfolk, VA, February 5, 1997.

15. The AC-130 is a transport aircraft fitted with a highly accurate large-caliber cannon; the aircraft can orbit closely over a designated position and, when required, unleash a tremendous volley of supporting fire. They were used very effectively in a security role in Somalia and were frequent supporters of operations in Haiti as well. It normally only takes one demonstration of a weapon like the Spectre to convince opponents of its capability; from that point forward, it serves effectively as a deterrent.

16. The U.S. military use of video-teleconferencing (VTC) as a communications means was greatly expanded during Uphold Democracy. Admiral Miller held nightly meetings with all of his subordinate commanders and individual planning groups coordinated interagency actions, intelligence management, and logistics issues, among others, by VTC. This tool expanded the information-exchange capacity and increased situational awareness greatly among the staff members, who viewed routine exchanges of information by their leaders for the first time. Within minutes, VTC capability tied individuals onshore in Haiti to the *Mount Whitney,* and from the ship to Norfolk, Washington, Atlanta, Tampa, and other support centers.

17. Lieutenant Colonel Linton Graham, 1st Battalion, Jamaica Regiment, and commander of the CARCOM Battalion noted: "We want to be able to ensure that the people of Haiti understand that we are here to help them. We (in the Caribbean Community) are their brothers, and as a regional body, we want to adopt a regional approach because we would like to see Haiti, not as an observer within the CARICOM community, but . . . as a member in the very near future." Hayden, *JTF-180 UPHOLD DEMOCRACY Oral History Interviews,* p. 34.

18. An excellent insight into what the Special Forces soldiers encountered in Haiti can be gained by reading Tracy Kidder's "The Siege of Mirebalais." "B" teams are small groups of Green Berets assigned to establish relations with the local population and facilitate its support by the U.S. military.

19. The area between the two western peninsulas of the Haitian landmass was referred to as "the claw" due to its resemblance to a lobster's claw.

20. For a discussion of rules of engagement see Micheal L. Grumelli, "Rules of Engagement Employed in Operation Uphold Democracy, September, 1994–March, 1995."

21. Shelton's views on the incident are clear. He remembers that, "I thought it essential to help bring a bit of control and also to establish my presence up there and to show him [Cedras], that you screw with us again you are going to die; this is just the way it goes. . . . But inside, it was just another step down and he knew it and this would become the norm if he tried to resist and so he had to somehow show the FAd'H he still cared, that he was still their commander but he knew damn well he was going to have to cooperate— he didn't have a choice in that." Hayden, *JTF-180 UPHOLD DEMOCRACY Oral History Interviews,* p. 64.

22. See Forrest L. Marion's, *Development of a Haitian Public Security Force.*

23. Anthony P. Bryan, "Haiti: Kick Starting the Economy," pp. 65–66.

24. For example, "U.S. Government goods can be donated, and U.S. Government services can be provided in support of humanitarian activities"; however, "no supplies or equipment could be ordered, purchased, or contracted for the sole purpose of humanitarian support." Nancy C. Henderson, "Civil Affairs and Logistics in Haiti," p. 21.

1. General Henry H. Shelton, USA, and U.S. Ambassador William Swing, who was both a knowledgeable partner in all the major decisions and an important link in the interagency process. *U.S. Government photo, courtesy of the Joint Combat Camera Center.*

2. Admiral Paul David Miller, USN, the first commander-in-chief of the U.S. Atlantic Command, and then-Lieutenant General Henry H. Shelton, USA, the commander of JTF-180. *U.S. Government photo, courtesy of the Joint Combat Camera Center.*

3. The deployment of U.S. Army forces aboard the aircraft carrier USS *Eisenhower* was only one demonstration of this joint technique. *U.S. Government photo, courtesy of the Joint Combat Camera Center.*

4. General Shelton with General Meade at FAd'H headquarters. Early in the operation General Shelton, center, established a rapport with General Cedras that ensured that he determined the pace of events prior to the return of President Aristide. *U.S. Government photo, courtesy of the Joint Combat Camera Center.*

5. Distinguished visitors, including SECDEF Perry, pictured here in khaki accompanied by General Shalikashvili and Ambassador Swing, ensured that the actions in Haiti were well understood in Washington. *U.S. Government photo, courtesy of the Joint Combat Camera Center.*

6. Buying surplus weapons and confiscating illegal weapons was a successful contribution to security during operation Uphold Democracy. *U.S. Government photo, courtesy of the Joint Combat Camera Center.*

7. Military personnel serving in Haiti during the early days were never sure whether crowds had peaceful intentions; any situation could change radically in moments. *U.S. Government photo, courtesy of the Joint Combat Camera Center.*

8. Security was provided in many ways and in many locations for Haiti's people. Here a U.S. Marine helps Haitian migrants with food and medicine in Guantanamo Bay, Cuba. *U.S. Government photo, courtesy of the Joint Combat Camera Center.*

9. When the JTF-190 staff initially began operations in Haiti, it contracted for an abandoned warehouse just outside the airport to serve as the multinational force headquarters. *U.S. Government photo, courtesy of the Joint Combat Camera Center.*

10. The multinational force accomplished much in Haiti with the support of the Haitian people. *U.S. Government photo, courtesy of the Joint Combat Camera Center.*

11. President Aristide's return to the Presidential Palace. *U.S. Government photo, courtesy of the Joint Combat Camera Center.*

CHAPTER 8

Stabilization by JTF-190: The MNF in Haiti

On the 26th of October, 1994 President Aristide met with some 400 members of the Multinational Force (MNF) at the National Palace in Port-au-Prince to thank them for their work. Aristide clearly understood both the contribution that the military had made to his return and his dependence on its continued good work. The following day, General Meade met with President Aristide to brief him on MNF operations. With the departure of General Shelton and the JTF-180 staff the focus of events in Haiti had shifted distinctly from the projection of force designed to reduce the threat of the FAd'H and restore Aristide, to the development of a secure environment that would enable the future arrival of the United Nations Mission in Haiti (UNMIH). Development of this security was a new and very different mission from that which had faced General Shelton. It posed unique challenges for everyone who worked towards achieving it, and was a key step towards establishing real democracy in Haiti.

JTF-180 had accomplished its military task in a superb manner, but its mission to subdue the FAd'H was one that the command had trained long and hard to accomplish. Its mission was also well-bounded in time and force requirements. In fact, Admiral Miller could have pulled General Shelton out of Haiti as early as the 10th of October, when Cedras and his FAd'H had ceased to pose an organized threat, but he elected not to do so. Shelton and his staff remained because they were performing superbly and because the JTF-180 staff had developed a tempo of operations that kept the American forces continually one step ahead of all emerging requirements. In short, pulling JTF-180 out of Haiti could have resulted in an obvious and potentially damaging lull in the pacification of Haitian threats. And with several transitions of control already planned over the full term of the operation, each one progressively easing back control of security to Haiti, the added stability resulting from retaining Shelton only made good sense. Still, the XVIII Airborne Corps was not designed, nor available, for a long-term peace operations commitment outside the United States. Moreover, JTF-190 had always been planned as the transition force to U.N.-directed operations, so its staff needed to step up and take over control.[1]

General Meade and his staff had enjoyed none of the benefits of the long planning time that contributed to JTF-180's smoothly running operations. As discussed earlier, Meade had first been notified of his command's involvement in the potential Haiti operation in the last week of July.[2] Within days he had traveled to Norfolk, had met with Admiral Miller on August 3rd, and had received instructions that he needed to be ready for operations by the 1st of September, less than 30 days away. For the entire month of August Meade and his 10th Mountain troops had worked intensively to plan, train, and prepare for deployment. They had completed their own operations plan only on August 10th. They then coordinated their own time-phased force-deployment data (TPFDD), designed a loading plan for troops transported on the aircraft carrier, developed a working relationship with the Navy, conducted a reconnaissance of available intermediate-support bases, and trained their helicopter pilots to land on the deck of an aircraft carrier (by painting the outline of the ship's flight deck on the ground at the Fort Drum airfield).[3] They had also conducted full dress rehearsals on August 30th and had placed their units onboard the *Eisenhower* by September 13th. All in all, a very busy month!

However, throughout August and early September JTF-190 had been planned as the secondary, follow-on transition force. Few if any of its personnel believed that they would be called upon to land in the initial waves on D-day. Fortunately, General Meade had flown aboard the *Mount Whitney* with General Shelton on September 18th and was privy to the ongoing consultations between Shelton and Admiral Miller over the negotiating process of the Carter mission. From their perspective, at sea things were clearly not developing as planned. As the strategic situation evolved, so did the command relationship between Generals Shelton and Meade.

Eventually, the two generals formed a new type of command team that had not been envisioned during the planning process. Due in part to the great adaptability of the forces in the "bookends" plan (combat force option on one side of the potential environment in Haiti, and the noncombat option on the other), the resulting command structure had Meade and his full staff working as Shelton's ground-component command in Haiti for the weeks that Shelton and his JTF directed operations from the *Mount Whitney*. This permitted the XVIII Airborne Corps staff to focus on coordinating the overall operation, while Meade's staff got into Haiti early and concentrated only on the management of army forces and the security issues within the immediate areas of Port-au-Prince and Cap-Haitien. This arrangement provided for a fairly clean division of effort while maximizing the effectiveness of both staffs.[4] Even so, many planners, including General Meade, had underestimated the magnitude of the initial task once his force came ashore. Meade's division staff did not realize how complex setting up the MNF in Haiti would become.[5] He had no advance party, an ever-expanding staff formed from a variety of sources, insufficient communications infrastructure, and initially no headquarters facilities at all.[6]

Initial impressions are important, even in military operations. Shelton and his XVIII Airborne Corps staff had been studying Haiti for over a year prior to the invasion; Meade's division staff had soundly rooted experience in Somalia, a similar peacekeeping operation, but had not been fully engaged with Haitian culture and issues. In addition, the 10th Mountain Division had had a very different task in Somalia: it had worked as an infantry division there, its normal Army function, under another joint task force headquarters staff. When Meade's small divisional staff initially grew by over 200 percent and eventually to over 880 personnel to become the MNF staff, it lost much of its internal cohesion in the process. Meade later noted that this had had a significant impact on his ability to operate in a proactive manner.[7] Compounding the difficulty of operating with so many augmentees, his staff was sent to Haiti before it had completed its full manning, and it had to mature quickly as a command under intense international and Haitian scrutiny.

Despite these challenges, General Meade's command had performed very well in the first few days of the operation. It had established itself solidly within the Port-au-Prince harbor area and the international airport and had begun its initial expansion out into the countryside. Its initial reception by the Haitian people had been very positive, and even the FAd'H took a wait-and-see attitude. The single greatest challenge to the MNF during its first days in the country turned out to be wholly Haitian in origin. When Cedras's security forces continued to beat Haitian citizens in full view of the arriving U.S. troops, onlookers both in Haiti and through television coverage urged a more proactive U.S. military role to stop the abuse. In response, Admiral Miller had changed the rules of engagement (ROE) and directed that U.S. forces could intervene to protect Haitian lives and property. Once these modifications were made to the initial ROE, the soldiers' involvement in deterring Haitian-on-Haitian violence quickly reduced the number of incidents of abuse and the situation in Port-au-Prince began to settle down.

Even though Port-au-Prince was the center of Haitian life, it was not the only site of armed conflicts between Haitians. Although General Meade wanted to spend more time pursuing security operations in Port-au-Prince, Shelton's staff soon perceived that the U.S. forces had to make their calming presence felt widely in Haiti to keep potential abuses in check. As a consequence, Shelton directed General Meade to push his troops out more rapidly into the countryside. After JTF-180 had directed this expansion of the U.S. force presence to regions outside the capital, Meade's forces responded quickly and experienced similar positive effects, calming tensions wherever they patrolled. By October 20th the MNF had focused on the tasks at hand and assumed management of the detailed work of the operation.

In retrospect, the MNF staff had benefited in some ways from their earlier-than-planned arrival in Port-au-Prince. By mid-October it had become well supported by individual staff augmentees from many U.S. commands, and the arrival of other national forces on the ground gave the command improved leverage as a true multinational force.[8] This was facilitated by the continued presence of JTF-180. By mid-October General Meade's command was a well-rounded and truly multinational force, with nearly 30 days of experience in Haiti. Most of the initial inequities had been resolved, and the enhanced multinational-force staff had begun to function aggressively. Unfortunately, the MNF was still confronted with a very complex mission, which would have challenged any organization, military or civilian.

Establishing a secure environment in Haiti had been the cherished yet unfulfilled goal of many previous Haitian leaders. How was the MNF to manage the construction of a smooth-running, enduring civil-security environment in the country when its commander could not make Haitian policy and did not even control the critical contributions of non-DOD U.S. agencies, the private volunteer organizations (PVOs), or foreign agencies in the country? The MNF needed to tread a very fine line between the goalposts of occupation on the one side and nation assistance on the other, besides needing to accomplish a tremendous amount throughout the country in as short a time as possible if it was to achieve the goal set for it: Turning over a peaceful Haiti to the United Nations in less than 6 months.

Two years before, the 10th Mountain Division had learned significant lessons from the operation in Somalia. In 1994 it still had many officers and noncommissioned officers who were experienced and confident in managing operations requiring close involvement in a strange and somewhat threatening, closely knit community. By late October, 1994 Haiti was no longer as threatening as Somalia had often been in 1993, but the task at hand was just as daunting and the staff in Haiti was significantly smaller than the staff of the headquarters that had managed affairs in Somalia.[9] General Meade had his hands full: he had to focus on creating a relatively safe Haiti, where none had ever existed before.

Four elements stand out as cornerstones for the type of security environment that the MNF had as its goal in October 1994: (1) creation of a new, functional security force in Haiti; (2) further reduction in the incidents of Haitian-on-Haitian violence; (3) reintegration of the Haitian migrants from Guantanamo Bay, Cuba; and finally (4) creation of an electoral process to invigorate and strengthen the Haitian democratic system. Two challenges stood in its way: First, its soldiers, sailors, airmen and Marines could not make all of these things happen on their own. Accomplishing these cornerstones of security was a challenging assignment requiring the active participation of many non-DOD agencies. These agencies were the only real source of assistance for much of what ailed Haiti. The agencies had the money, tools, and experience to improve Haitian life. Their efforts required close coordination with military actions because only the MNF could provide the secure environment they needed to accomplish their tasks. Interagency working groups were already being formed to move in to coordinate actions where required, yet even with interagency help, one critical element of the solution remained out of the MNF's control.

Tied closely to the success of any of these goals was a second, critical underlying factor: Even with interagency help, Haitian participation provided the only enduring road to success. The Haitians needed to develop confidence in, or at least no opposition to, the achievement of these cornerstones if they were to become active participants in a true democratic society over the long term. No amount of improvement in Haiti would long survive without the acceptance and commitment of the Haitian people, including those returned from Guantanamo Bay. This requirement for Haitian involvement was a clear lesson of the first U.S. intervention and was an acknowledged prerequisite for mission success by the MNF. The MNF staff understood that developing this nurturing involvement first required continued progress in restoring essential human services to Haiti. As a demonstration of the operation's humanitarian intent and as a building block of national support to ensure that the other objectives could endure after the U.S. forces and their multinational partners departed, nothing beat restoring electrical power, providing fresh water and food, and making the transportation system functional. Developing Haitian involvement in Haiti's improvement needed to begin even as these primary cornerstones were being put in place. The simple fact was that the basic human needs of Haiti's people had to be met before any lasting improvements in the political and security systems could be achieved.

Of course, the MNF's challenges did not end with supplying these basic human needs. Improvements in the political administration and the security apparatus in Haiti were interrelated in a complex way. Accomplishing administrative and security improvements in Haiti often required starting some activities nearly from scratch, yet any advances in administration had to be matched by appropriate progress in security in order for them to function. For example, many local judges had no education in the law and no training in keeping records or files, and some officials had no office location to keep such supporting documents. Some government employees had received no pay for years. This lack of resources meant that local justice was often arbitrary, with only oral documentation. With no effective judicial process, arresting criminals often resulted only in a short-term delay of their criminal activities. Seeing this, few local citizens and shopkeepers had any faith in security measures, and fewer still felt capable of expanding their markets or hiring new workers. Even providing new security police would not slow criminal activity in such an environment; and without a reduction in criminal activity the local population could never improve its lot in life sufficiently to become active in any political process.

The Cedras regime had centered all administrative functions in the hands of a few select individuals, and many of them were no longer acceptable to their neighbors as political figures. In 1994 new officials were needed at administrative posts throughout the Haitian countryside just to keep the nation running, and the only effective way to bring in new officials was to conduct safe and fair elections, which required a secure environment. This was a vicious cycle of conditions that caused the MNF and the interagency organizations to spread their efforts over many different but interrelated tasks. When Meade arrived, the MNF had a plan for executing multiple improvements timed to match an anticipated MNF-to-U.N. transition scheduled for March of 1995. Unfortunately, due to delays resulting from insufficient financial and personnel resources, and lacking a guaranteed security environment, it appeared in late October that the first series of elections, planned for December, would have to be rescheduled to January, 1995. General Meade knew that his timetable for turnover of control to the

United Nations would be jeopardized by any delay in the improvements in Haiti, so he decided to do everything he could to assist in the election process.

MILITARY COMMAND TRANSITIONS AND ELECTION SUPPORT

Another significant event during this late October–early November transition period occurred outside of the region, but very much within the tight circle of the friends of Haiti. General John J. Sheehan, USMC, left the Pentagon to return to Norfolk and assume command of USACOM and SACLANT on October 31st, relieving Admiral Miller, who retired. Sheehan was the first Marine to command USACOM and was the ideal choice as the strategic commander for the Haiti operation. Not only was he an acknowledged expert on the country and the former chief of military plans in the region, but he had been the key source of military advice concerning Haiti to the Clinton Administration during the months preceding the invasion. In General Sheehan, Uphold Democracy received as its chief military architect one of the most powerful and agile minds in the U.S. Armed Forces, and an astute and decisive leader. He immediately made his mark on the operation and remained intimately involved with all aspects of Uphold Democracy until its completion.[10]

During the first week of December USACOM announced the new rotation of U.S. forces assigned to MNF. The new rotation would employ units from the 25th Infantry Division (Light), assigned then at Schofield Barracks, Hawaii, to replace the 10th Mountain Division forces beginning on December 6th. The 25th Infantry Division Commander, Major General George A. Fisher, USA, was to relieve Major General Meade as the MNF commander as well. This rotation of the core U.S. unit within the MNF would accomplish several things: First, the change would return the 10th Mountain Division to the United States to rest, cover its personnel and materiel, and restore its level of combat readiness. By 1994 it was commonly understood that months of service in peace operations did not enhance normal combat-preparedness.[11] Second, it would provide the 25th Division with much-appreciated experience in a deployment for peace operations. Finally, although the transition would create a short window of vulnerability as the two divisions switched places, the influx of personnel from the 25th would also refresh the spirit of the MNF with vigorous initiatives and approaches.

This decision to schedule the U.N. arrival in March gave General Fisher and his 25th Division 3 months to contribute to the restoration of democracy in Haiti and prepare to shift control to the United Nations. Having been advised of the plan to use the 25th Division as a transition unit in November and having received an extensive USACOM operations order, Fisher's staff did a very detailed mission-analysis of the operation in sufficient time to place all required personnel in a leave status prior to their deployment. Fisher also ensured that his advance party arrived in Haiti in enough time to acclimate to the environment and simply observe the men and women of the 10th Division executing their duties, as well as "to gain street smarts" in order to build a preparatory training plan for the division.[12]

The 25th Division, as one of the U.S. Army's light divisions, was already familiar with the type of mission called for in Haiti. It had undergone peace-operations training rotations at the Army's Joint Readiness Training Center in Fort Polk, Louisiana, and the division staff had just completed its annual "warfighter" training exercise. General Fisher asked for a special orientation package from the Center for Army Lessons Learned and another site visit by soldiers from Fort Polk to completely familiarize his soldiers with the Haitian operations environment. The division even devised 20 vignettes of potential Haitian scenarios that might try the management skills of its junior leaders once deployed. Later, nineteen out of twenty of these scenarios were actually encountered by division troops.[13]

THE HAITIAN ELECTORAL PROCESS

On December 4th Haiti's Senate agreed to President Aristide's proposals for a Provisional Electoral Council (CEP) to initiate procedures for holding elections. President Aristide immediately signed the decree and initiated a process for planning and conducting national elections. The CEP concept, which provided central management by an independent body, had been used before in Haiti with varying results. Essentially running counter to norms in the country, the concept required individuals who would not necessarily benefit from election results to design, resource, conduct, and terminate the process. It would be a difficult job with few rewards. Problems occurred at many points along the election schedule, but overall the choice of using a council to conduct the elections was probably the right one.

Demonstrating the improvements accomplished since September, Aristide played an important role in a meeting of his regional peers on December 11th. Hosted by the United States in Miami and attended by President Clinton, the Summit of the Americas was the largest such meeting since 1967. Representatives from all western hemisphere nations except Cuba attended. The meeting was an opportune time to increase cohesion among the many partners from the area who were helping to restore Haitian democracy. Boosted by the conference, back in Port-au-Prince President Aristide on the 13th called for public support to prosecute those who had been involved in human-rights violations, including the former army leaders.

At the same time, the government of Haiti was able to announce the appointment of the last of the nine members of the CEP, which opened the way for the country to begin the process of legislative, municipal, and local elections. President Aristide appointed a new head of the "Commission of Justice and Truth," designed to open up the government and its policies more to the people it assisted, and serve as a watchdog on political activities. The next day, Ambassador Swing met with President Aristide to review administration of justice projects, including training courses for judicial personnel and improvements in the national penitentiary. These administrative reforms were producing tangible results and Aristide's government was moving forward in many important areas. With events progressing well, General Sheehan directed the staffs of the MNF and the 25th Infantry Division to coordinate planning for transition to UNMIH forces.

At the end of the greatest year of change in centuries of Haitian history, Haiti's CEP announced its officers and the planned passage of an electoral law in Parliament. These announcements were followed by an explanation of the logistical preparations for national and local elections. On December 29th, after conferring with President Aristide, U.S. State Department officials advised the remaining Haitian migrants at Guantanamo Bay that they had until January 5th, 1995, to register for voluntary repatriation or else they would be repatriated involuntarily without any cash incentives. The key elements of stability in Haiti were slowly but steadily coming together.

The new year, 1995, began quietly, evidence of the improvements that the multinational force and the return of President Aristide had wrought. General Shalikashvili visited Haiti as the 10th Mountain Division began to be replaced by elements of the 25th Infantry Division from Hawaii. Not only did the morale of members of the MNF improve with the execution of a unit rotation, but tactical proficiency was also enhanced by the influx of fresh, rested organizations. Here, U.S. military lessons from Somalia again contributed to success in Haiti by ensuring that the effects of peacekeeping duty on unit readiness were managed over the long term. Plans were made before the arrival of the 25th Division to place a new focus on finding ways of maintaining the division's readiness while deployed in Haiti. The long-term goal was a balancing of both the benefits of peacekeeping experience and the toll of such operations. The arrival of the division from Hawaii demonstrated that U.S. Pacific Command units could easily execute missions in the Atlantic as well. This movement of units was also a boon for the Army, which wanted to spread the experience and burden of peacekeeping duties through several of its divisions. As the 10th Mountain Division had gained important experience in Somalia, the 25th Infantry would obtain valuable experience in Haiti for use in future crises in the Pacific.

On January 4th, at the opening of the 104th Congress, Senator Robert Dole, then the Senate Majority Leader, proposed a Post-Cold War Powers Act that would prohibit U.S. troops from serving under U.N. command and cut U.S. funding for any future U.N. peacekeeping missions. As with his earlier opposition to keeping troops in Haiti beyond the year's end, Dole's announcement had little real effect on troop performance, but it caused some concern about the level of support in Congress for the completion of the mission in Haiti. Many tasks frequently suffer from loss of interest by supporters over time, but Haiti was at a critical stage in development and could not reap the benefits of work already accomplished without additional time to complete the whole reform effort; therefore the friends of Haiti viewed these statements by Dole with alarm. Fortunately for them, as time passed his remarks appeared to have been largely political in design, and did not indicate a lack of resolve to complete the work necessary. Significantly, the MNF commander, at the time still General Meade, chose the same day to make the historic declaration that a "secure and safe environment" existed in Haiti. This determination was one of the principal requirements needed to transition the force from U.S. to U.N. control. General Sheehan concurred with the estimate, and the timetable for transition remained fixed for March 31st.

Unfortunately, just as so much progress was being made and a new, hopeful year was dawning for Haiti, tragedy struck the MNF. The first death of a U.S. soldier by hostile fire in Haiti occurred on January 12th at a checkpoint in Gonaives. Sergeant 1st Class Gregory Cardott, USA, was killed in action, and a second Special Operations Forces (SOF) soldier, Staff Sergeant Tommy Davis, USA, was also wounded. Although the protection of the military personnel in Haiti had always been the primary concern of the commanders involved in Uphold Democracy, the level of risk in the operation had finally surmounted even the best of sound precautions. By all accounts the operation thus far had exceeded safety expectations, particularly considering the number of personnel and vehicles and the poor conditions of work in Haiti; but nothing could overcome the sense of loss and the renewed commitment to protect the force that followed Sergeant Cardott's death.

Two days later General Fisher assumed command of the MNF from General Meade, and the 25th Infantry Division formally replaced the 10th Mountain Division. The MNF staff, which supported both Meade and Fisher, was by January quite robust and effective in its control of the wide range of activities ongoing in Haiti. The staff had reached a personnel strength averaging over 400 men and women, all working in the same abandoned warehouse selected by General Meade's advanced party during the first week of the operation.

By the time General Fisher arrived, the decision had been made to focus all the logistics aspects of the operation under one Logistics Support Command. Using this concept, General Fisher had a single clearinghouse for all logistics coordination and one manager to ensure that the various needs of all portions of the MNF were met fairly and efficiently.[14] The magnitude of this logistics-coordination challenge was considerable. Not only did the lack of local infrastructure make resupply and transportation difficult, but the international composition of the MNF also increased the complexity of the task. Some units arriving in Haiti needed uniforms and equipment; materiel sent from one nation was not always compatible with that of the other national contingents; and even food and water usage was different among the various elements of the force. As religious, cultural, and economic differences marked the individual member units of the force, it was the MNF staff's job to ensure that these unique aspects of national character were brought together to produce the best overall effect for the entire force. The importance of maintaining cohesion within the MNF was never lost on General Fisher. As he later pointed out:

One of the things that was absolutely critical to success of the MNF effort was the way the coalition partners were handled and treated. . . . Many of them have very special needs, most of those driven by cultural or religious practices. In order for there to be a good team approach and operational cooperation, all of these factors have to be taken into account. The challenge is to manage the religious requirements such as food, preparation of food, and the times and days of the week that are religiously sensitive to certain countries. All of these factors had to be worked and coordinated by the MNF headquarters.[15]

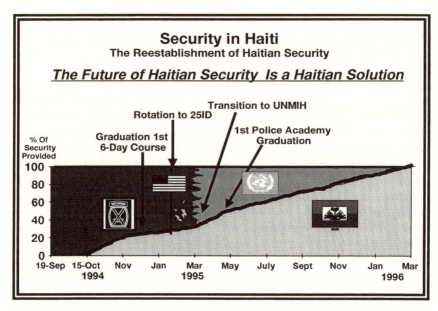

Figure 8.1 Security transition from the invasion to the end of the U.N. mandate. *U.S. Government, courtesy of the Training and Audiovisual Support Center, Fort Eustis, Virginia.*

The MNF had accomplished a great deal in the early months of its tour in Haiti. In large part these successes were based upon a thoughtful understanding of the real issues that needed to be solved if the Haitian people were to make their democracy work. Each of these areas deserves analysis to show how the adverse effects of the Cedras regime were corrected over time. The most fundamental of these issues was the development of a secure environment.

THE DEVELOPMENT OF A SECURE ENVIRONMENT

Among the interwoven fundamental goals of the MNF, the development of a reliable and professional Haitian security force was an early priority for JTF-190.[16] In October the reality was that the MNF was providing the great bulk of security in Haiti. As shown in figure 8.1, by March, 1995, when the United Nations was scheduled to arrive, that equation had to be completely reversed. The availability of a Haitian security force also impacted on the election process, because the force was intended to provide a safe environment for voting and thus demonstrate to Haitians that they were profitably involved in improving the nation's future. The development design for the new force had been started within the USACOM staff in mid-July, and by October it had been coordinated with a wide range of supporting agencies, including the U.S. Departments of State and Justice, the United Nations, and many contributor nations. But it was not until the first weeks after JTF-190 assumed control that Haitians witnessed the first shifts back to normal life.

The development of a new Haitian security force was designed in three phases: First, Interim Police Security Force (IPSF) personnel would be designated immediately from among former members of the FAd'H who had been "vetted" and appeared to have potential for service in the new Haitian National Police (HNP). Second, the international police monitors (IPMs) would be integrated into the patrols of the IPSF to ensure impartiality and advise and mentor the IPSF personnel. Third, training classes would be conducted for new security personnel—those with no FAd'H background—to increase the number of police, reduce unemployment, and expand the involvement of the population in its own security. Of importance to each phase of this plan, elements of the MNF would be integrated into the process to add another degree of impartiality and to coordinate all security operations through the MNF staff.

During October, 353 former members of the Haitian military were already in training as prospective members of the new HNP. This training was conducted by members of the U.S. State Department's International Criminal Investigation and Training Assistance Program (ICITAP) under the supervision of U.S. and Canadian forces at the former FAd'H strongpoint of Camp d'Application. But this was a vastly inadequate number of police for a nation such as Haiti. The next class of the new police training was scheduled to begin on October 31st, and maximum participation was desired to facilitate the rapid development of an "untainted" police force.[17] In addition to U.S. and Canadian trainers, Ray Kelly, former chief of police of New York City and a U.S. Marine veteran, had arrived in mid-October with a staff of IPMs, effectively beginning phase two of the new Haitian police force's development. Kelly managed his own program to ensure that his monitors could remain strictly impartial, assigned liaison officers to the MNF headquarters, and provided his personnel to combined teams of IPSF personnel, MNF soldiers, and IPMs, under the tactical direction of the MNF. This security-team concept very quickly provided the MNF commander with a method for improving security, while beginning the changeover to Haitian management of the security problem.

Eventually, Kelly's IPMs numbered over 1170 personnel from 24 nations, including large contingents from Jordan, Bolivia, Israel, Argentina, Bangladesh, and even fifty-nine members from the former Soviet-bloc nation of Poland. Although the U.S. contribution of thirty-five police and Australia's contribution of twenty-nine to Kelly's force added a sizable thread of English-speaking continuity, these two important national contingents were small in comparison with those arriving from the local nations of the Caribbean. As Haiti's neighbors the island nations of the region had much to gain from its return to stability, and thereby showed their support through the commitment of a significant percentage of their own security forces to the IPM contingent. Grenada's force of ten, the Barbados team of nine, St. Kitts and St. Lucia's ten each, added to Dominica's four and St. Vincent's twelve members represented not only strong geographical support, but also an important example of regional team-building. This Caribbean involvement was the fruit of a long-term regional-engagement policy on the part of USACOM to develop interoperability and cohesion among these Caribbean security forces, which came together just as it was hoped.[18]

Once acclimated to the terrain and their duties, the IPMs conducted 24-hour patrols in nine separate locations in Haiti, including Les Cayes, Jacmel, Port de Paix, and Jérémie. They also brought 351 interpreters to Haiti, a capability which, given the tremendous linguistic challenge presented by a contingent of 20 nations, was very welcome. Unfortunately, even as phase two of the development program for Haiti's new police was beginning in earnest, other events occurred that were temporarily counterproductive to increased security. As an example, in early November President Aristide ordered the dismissal of all the Haitian section chiefs—the local civilian police leaders in Haiti's provinces. He did so in order to further diminish the influence of the FAd'H and increase national control of the police function. This occurred just as the first 100 recruits for the new police force arrived in Regina, Saskatchewan, Canada, to begin a 3-month course led by members of the Canadian Mounted Police. The net result was a short-term decrease of nearly 200 police on the streets of Haiti. Similar examples of temporary setbacks exist in other areas of the national government as Aristide slowly wrought reform by replacing coup supporters and antidemocratic processes. As happened during the difficult process of governing Germany after the Nazi defeat in World War II, for every step of progress made, it seemed that all too often other requirements arose to cancel the gain. However, Aristide's reforms were needed eventually to reestablish national control, and he *was* the Haitian President. Accordingly, the MNF commander, Kelly, and Berkow, the chief member of the ICITAP training team, adjusted as required, their sights set on the long-term goal.

After all, the international goal was Haitian democratic control of the country and the national police. Multinational force maintenance of local security was required while the future police force was in training, but this could only be a temporary measure while longer-term solutions were put in place. The key was to provide a minimum of MNF support and place as much burden as possible on Haitian institutions so that the fragile local security and administrative structures would strengthen, and not be replaced by, outside assistance. This process had to be carefully crafted and monitored on a regular basis. It was normally accomplished in the series of weekly meetings held between Ambassador Swing, the MNF commander, the other agency chiefs in Haiti, and the various Haitian ministers. This process of helping to develop national institutions while at the same time providing security had little precedent.[19] Working generally towards a common goal, all the key leaders played a role and contributed based upon the strengths of their organizations to slowly and effectively transition control from the MNF back to the Haitians themselves. Still, in the short term, the MNF was very much the dominant player.

The reform of the Cité Soleil slum in Port-au-Prince offers an illustration of the rapid impact of the MNF presence on Haitian security in the early days of the operation. The Cité Soleil region was characterized by high unemployment and high crime; violence was so prevalent there that even the FAd'H had stayed away in the months prior to the invasion. Initially, the area was off limits to the MNF and was designated a danger zone due to a complete lack of information about the activities occurring there. As congested and dangerous as the area was, however, it was too centrally located in the city to be effectively ignored and would have created a natural haven for disaffected and combative elements if it were not made more accessible and safe. General Meade and his staff quickly viewed reform of the area as a necessary challenge and good test case for security operations elsewhere.

Initial patrols began in Cité Soleil as early as October 20th, when for the first time soldiers entered to conduct assessments. At that time the streets were deserted, residents were reluctant to talk to anyone in authority, and crime rates were constantly rising. Cité Soleil was a sort of Wild West town or urban "combat zone." Nevertheless, within 5 days of the start of U.S. patrols illegal activity began to decrease, some businesses started to reopen, and some of the less fearful residents became more willing to work together to improve their situation. The MNF assessment of the area determined that the once-sprawling slum could be improved, with the proper mix of foot patrols and citizen engagement, once MNF units were prepared and rehearsed. In late October the decision was made to expand the MNF activity to include security sweeps to clean out the worst areas.

By November 15th regular U.S. patrols had been augmented with teams of the IPSF and IPMs. Military police units and psychological operations forces were then employed in building up the citizens' confidence that the area could be made livable. Eventually, a community watch was established that took on its own part in the policing function. The dangerous slum became tolerable for average Haitians for the first time in years. Patrols were expanded again in late November as the livable portion of the slum grew larger. By December 5th a new police substation had been established, the crime rate had dipped, and many businesses were operating normally. Effective civilian–police cooperation had been restored and the area was no longer so threatening to its inhabitants. This experiment clearly showed that team security operations composed of the MNF, IPSF, and IPMs, employed with the tools needed to restore civilian confidence, could develop a positive community attitude where none had existed before. Although Cité Soleil was an extreme case in which the inhabitants were expected to more willingly cooperate to improve the neighborhood, the integrated approach of all security tools seemed to work well if combined with effective assessment and measured and enduring confidence-building approaches.

As this balancing act in Cité Soleil was being conducted, Meade and his MNF forces were confronting several related issues. While MNF Special Forces operations continued to keep Haitian paramilitary groups on the run, other problems were discovered in the security environment. On October 28th U.S. forces uncovered a large cache of weapons in a tunnel in Port-au-Prince, which underscored the ongoing concerns over the capability of the MNF to disarm the paramilitary groups still active in the country. Soon thereafter more than a hundred prisoners at the National Penitentiary escaped, largely through the ineffectiveness of the prison-guard force; the IPMs and U.S. troops could recapture only eight, but these included only two of the most dangerous. This clearly added to the suspected threat of resentful Cedras supporters in the countryside and certainly did not enhance the reputation of the growing MNF security effort. Even though the MNF commander, Kelly, and others involved in Haiti's new security structure had no real responsibility for these actions, that fact made little difference. In Haiti, where word-of-mouth information was the norm, perceptions were just as important as facts. What few Haitian police there were in place appeared to be less competent to the population in light of these incidents. Multinational force military police and international observers were already spread thinly, but still would have to do more in order to retain public confidence.

In reaction to these incidents and in view of the vast workload of and progress made by the MNF, U.S. embassy officials stepped up their activity. The embassy staff in Port-au-Prince expressed concern over getting the public-security trainees in Guantanamo Bay transferred back to the Haitian capital to function as police on the streets. The Chief of Mission in the U.S. embassy also accepted greater control of the Army's Civil Affairs Ministerial Advisor Detachment from the MNF, and the State Department took a more leading role in the improvement of administrative functioning within the upper levels of the Haitian government. Thus the ties between the diplomatic and military functions of the effort in Haiti continued to grow in response to the requirements of the mission. This was one more important step away from dependence on military action and helped shift the interagency responsibility within the U.S. government from the Department of Defense back to normal operations in a foreign nation under full State Department leadership.

On the surface most of these issues were invisible, given the hectic pace of events throughout the country. On November 2nd, MNF troops provided protection for President Aristide during wreath-laying ceremonies in Port-au-Prince. The following day Lieutenant Colonel Claudel Josephat, former commander of Haiti's northern district, surrendered to U.S. forces in the Haitian capital. (He had resigned after U.S. Marines had killed the 10 Haitian soldiers in Cap-Haitien on September 24th, and since he was allegedly connected with a resistance movement against U.S. troops, his surrender greatly reduced concerns in northern Haiti.)[20] By November 4th small teams of IPSF, MNF, and IPM personnel pushed into areas near St. Marc and Gonaives to provide security where little or no effective law had existed before. Special operations forces continued to patrol the Haitian countryside and businesses were beginning to reopen in the more devastated parts of Port-au-Prince. In early November, for the first time since the invasion, reported incidents of FAd'H violence against the population dropped drastically. Things were improving.

President Aristide also recognized the importance of garnering support for his administration among the Haitian people. On November 8th MNF troops provided security for the address he made to the first two classes of FAd'H graduates to become trained members of the IPSF at the former heavy-weapons company barracks at Camp d'Application. On November 9th accompanied by Ambassador Swing and the MNF commander, President Aristide also visited Cap-Haitien, under heavy MNF security, to deliver a personal message of reconciliation to the people. These were all-important steps forward.

However, some sporadic incidents of violence continued to occur that set progress back in certain areas. Two Haitian employees of the U.S. embassy in

Port-au-Prince were killed in a payroll robbery and car hijacking on the 10th of November. If this criminal activity associated with the U.S. embassy was not damning enough, it soon became clear that a bodyguard for Ambassador Swing was suspected in the killings. How could *real* progress in Haitian security be continuing if Haitians in the employ of the United States were committing criminal acts? Perceptions that the United States was maintaining a double standard for the Haitians it supported could have severely damaged the working relationship between the governments. This robbery was only one of several incidents that would eventually result in charges that U.S. policies were unevenly applied in Haiti.[21] Nothing was ever proven that demonstrated that the United States used a double standard, but as noted earlier, perceptions were important to continued close relations between the United States and Haitian governments; therefore any such accusations were destabilizing and potentially harmful to mission accomplishment.

It seemed that events in Haiti always included unanticipated twists. For example, on the 17th of November President Aristide nominated Brigadier General Bernardin Poisson to become the new FAd'H CINC, replacing the interim commander, Major General Jean-Claude Duperval. This act made the future of the Haitian army appear bright. Haiti celebrated Armed Forces Day on November 18th, but even as the holiday and the new commander were being observed several members of the Haitian government questioned the need for a standing army. Considering the historic role of the army as a power broker and the number of coups that had been executed by Haitian generals, there was much evidence to support at least the partial demobilization of the FAd'H. Particularly in view of the limited threat to Haiti posed by her neighbors, serious consideration was given to a reorganization of the military. Three days later, Brigadier General Poisson began reorganizing the General Staff, the high command of the Haitian army.

In late November President Aristide referred to the Haitian army as "a cancer" that he wanted to cure rather than cut out, a choice of words that indicated continued efforts to reform instead of abolishing the army, but this feeling did not last long. This reference was only the first of several acts that did eventually lead to the demobilization of the FAd'H under Aristide. Although he could not constitutionally rid Haiti of its army, Aristide realized that he could so fiscally undermine the force that it would eventually cease to exist as a Haitian base of power. Eventually, he ceased to fund the FAd'H and it did just that.

At the end of November there were still valid security concerns throughout the country. Any nation undergoing reform that required the imposition of foreign troops was bound to suffer internal violence; predictably, Haiti was never immune from a variety of subversive acts. On the 17th a pipebomb exploded in a house in Cap-Haitien, killing a mother and child. Elsewhere in the same city a mob attacked Haitian soldiers, who were then rescued by U.S. troops. By then, President Aristide had already taped a message to the Haitian migrants and security-force trainees in Guantanamo Bay that Haiti was "ready to receive them." What he needed most was calm. Too much needed to be done very quickly and Aristide wanted to do it all, even when the internal situation remained far from stable.

Although Haiti's image had improved internationally, domestic problems continued. On December 21st almost 1,000 former FAd'H members protested at the Port-au-Prince national army headquarters, demanding pension refunds after the Haitian government reduced the army's strength to 1,500. This was a sizable and serious protest, which alarmed the Haitian government and the MNF. Reducing the size of the army too quickly could lead to greater tension as unemployment increased and the number of discontented persons, many still possessing weapons, rose as well. This demonstration was a warning signal to many that reform could be pushed too far and could quickly become counterproductive. Tensions remained high throughout the holiday season.

After the Christmas holiday, demonstrations erupted again at the FAd'H headquarters in Port-au-Prince. These continued for several days and resulted in the deaths of several discharged Haitian soldiers who were simply demanding back pay. Multinational force troops moved in during this period to restore order. Again, the demonstration resulted in another assessment of the unanticipated effects of reducing the FAd'H. President Aristide had initially pushed to rid the country of what he perceived as a threat, but the demonstrations caused many to urge a more cautious pace. Still, when President Aristide again urged reconciliation following the demonstrations at the FAd'H headquarters, many of his other supporters marched in Port-au-Prince to demand the abolition of the Haitian army. The long history of militarism in Haiti ensured that the fate of the FAd'H would remain a divisive and impassioned issue for weeks.

On the 7th of January President Aristide issued a decree on military and police issues, which included the promotion of Brigadier General Pierre Cherubin, the establishment of three commissions for restructuring the new armed forces, and the relocation of the FAd'H headquarters, which was to be vacated for the newly created Ministry of Women's Affairs. Aristide's intent for the FAd'H remained clear, even if the pace of its demise had slowed. It was particularly poignant that the former military headquarters should become the launching point of the new Haiti's desire to see women better cared for and better integrated into society. On January 13th President Aristide formally announced his long-held plan to reduce the FAd'H to a small corps of 1,500. Just 4 days later, the last class of vetted FAd'H members graduated from the 6-day course taught by police instructors at Camp d'Application. This graduation class increased the total to 2,960 police on the streets. The transition from the FAd'H to a professional Haitian security force was proceeding, but slowly.

President Aristide officially dismissed the remainder of Haiti's army on the 17th of January and created a border patrol of 1,500 former FAd'H members in its place. He then met with General Fisher and agreed to add 400 former FAd'H personnel as police, following completion of the 6-day IPSF course, for an end strength of almost 3,400 members of the IPSF. These actions demonstrated the progress that had been made to replace the threatening elements of the old Cedras regime with the democratic vision of Aristide, the United States, and the United Nations. They also demonstrated that Aristide's administration was capable of meeting the domestic obligations implied by the international mandate that deposed Cedras.

On the last day of January the first 4-month police-training course began at the Police Academy, Camp d'Application, for 262 of the 375 applicants. While MNF troops increased street patrols, President Aristide asked Haitians on February 26th to observe Mardi Gras with peaceful celebrations—the first since his return from exile and another sign of the progress towards peace. In fact, at the end of Haiti's carnival celebrations on March 1st, only minimal violence had occurred. Slowly, the internal improvements in Haiti began to bear noticeable fruit.

Still, problems remained. On the 10th of February U.S. Immigration and Naturalization Service officials reported that Emmanuel Constant, founder of the FRAPH and a supporter of the deposed military, had entered the United States on a 6-month tourist visa, but then disappeared. Constant's entry into the United States made it appear that he had indeed been on the payroll of a U.S. intelligence agency, as had been alleged in the American media. This inflamed anti-U.S. sentiment among those who still harbored resentment of the past U.S. involvement in Haiti. Armed Haitians attacked the police station in Limbe on February 11th after U.S. troops had pulled out of the area. Three Haitian IPSF members were later missing, and authorities confirmed the IPSF commander's death. An Argentine IPM in Petionville was shot on February 15th—the first time an IPM had been injured since the arrival of the MNF. These acts of violence demonstrated to all that dangerous undercurrents still existed in Haiti that could jeopardize the progress made to date if not kept in check. Discipline and safety were reemphasized: Personnel throughout the country applied just a bit more caution to each act and everyone focused on the final goal of a secure environment.

Just as everything appeared to be progressing well, on March 28th Port-au-Prince gunmen assassinated Mireille Durocher Bertin, a well-known opposition leader who had supported Haiti's deposed military junta and served as spokeswoman for General Cedras. This was potentially a severe setback to pacific relations among the various political groups in Haiti. Desiring very much to ensure that the resulting investigation be judged fair and impartial, the next day President Aristide requested assistance from the FBI to investigate the assassination of Durocher Bertin. The incident had occurred only 3 days before President Clinton's scheduled visit to witness the transition to UNMIH, an event that would officially confirm that a safe and secure environment had been achieved in Haiti.

Everyone understood that security was a condition that required constant vigilance and needed time to become the normal environment in a land torn apart by strife for so many years. As time passed the IPSF and the MNF worked hard to ensure peace; security improved, but Haiti was prone to acts of violence for some time to come. Still, given Haiti's history of oppression and the state of terror that existed prior to the invasion, the MNF and the Haitian government had achieved much in only a few short months. Colonel James Campbell, the MNF chief of staff, put it well: "Stop and think what has happened, and it almost overwhelms you. . . . This country has gone from chaos to order. . . . Parliament has been reinstated and is now functioning. The President of this country, who had been oust-ed in a violent coup, has returned and is governing his country. . . . All of this has been accomplished and there is a safe and secure environment."[22]

THE WEAPONS BUY-BACK PROGRAM

Another of the operation's success stories was the Weapons Buy-Back pro-gram. Beginning in late September the MNF had commenced a program of pay-ing cash for weapons and munitions as an incentive to encourage the voluntary disarmament of the population. This effort was designed to remove weapons and munitions that were a threat to the security of both the MNF and the citizens of Haiti. The Weapons Buy-Back (WBB) program was a relatively inexpensive way to reduce the number of armaments in the country, which otherwise could have proven very difficult by any means short of house-to-house searches. General Meade and his staff, in addition to many other agency planners who had antici-pated this issue, had determined early on that house-to-house searches were too hazardous and inefficient to be practical given the MNF mission. Still, Haiti was full of weapons, and the number had to be reduced before any realistic assertion of a secure environment could be made. As this determination was an important part of the preconditions for U.N. entry in March, the WBB was high on the MNF priority list from the beginning of the operation.

The basic procedures for weapons buy-back allowed any Haitian to turn in an operational weapon at specified locations and be reimbursed with a set fee. A published list showed the purchase price for each weapon. For example, a pistol was initially priced at $50, and a grenade, $100. The Haitian turning in the weapon was paid in cash in Haitian currency. Multinational force units operated static WBB sites regularly in Port-au-Prince and for short periods in outlying areas of the country. Beginning on October 2nd a chit system was introduced so that units could accept weapons at any time and issue chits as receipts; the Haitian who turned in the weapon could redeem the chit at any WBB site for cash.[23]

As progress was being made in military-supported actions within Haiti, one pressing issue with political implications needed to be resolved early: disarming opponents of the Aristide government. Aristide, many of his supporters, and some planners in the United Nations believed disarmament was a necessary pre-cursor to the development of a completely secure Haitian environment. In the United States, where the memory of weapons-recovery operations conducted in Somalia against a much more potent force had proved to be complex and politi-cally explosive, many were opposed to any forcible collection of weapons. Legally, the Haitian constitution, like that of the United States, supported weapons ownership; therefore any form of confiscation would have judicial implications. Simply devoting the time and resources that would be required to search out the millions of weapons believed to be in Haiti implied an effort did not fit the scale of operations the United States wanted to conduct. Accordingly, SECDEF Perry rejected President Aristide's request for aid in forcibly disarming

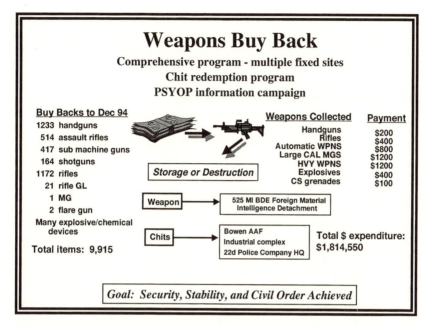

Figure 8.2 The results of early MNF weapons buy-back operations. *U.S. Government, courtesy of the Training and Audiovisual Support Center, Fort Eustis, Virginia.*

Haitian terrorists and disloyal soldiers on November 27th. Thus the WBB program remained the only method for reducing arms in the country, short of confiscation during apprehension for a crime.

The WBB program was planned in three phases: Phase I extended from September 27th to October 24th; Phase II, from November 1st through the 24th; and Phase III, from January 3rd to February 15th, 1995. Each phase incorporated the lessons learned during earlier phases, so that by early 1995 the system was a well-accepted and smoothly run process. Among the lessons learned during the program were the facts that (1) unit continuity in the program eased administrative difficulties, (2) keeping program consistency through the use of fixed sites and rotating site-operating hours to meet demand improved results, and (3) tight local security was mandatory based on the large amounts of cash and weapons at each site.[24] Multinational force units often had to escort Haitian participants to safe, remote locations after they received their payment, because cash made them lucrative targets for muggings. Psychological operations support also proved indispensable for publicizing the program and making site locations well known.

The WBB program was constantly monitored to ensure that the concept remained attractive. As participation in the program declined, due in many cases to a lack of armament "excess," price hikes revitalized participation. Prices were doubled twice so that in phase III a pistol was worth $200; therefore incentives to turn in weapons remained high. As shown in figure 8.2, WBB operations produced substantial successes: at its end, a total of over 13,500 items, including over

4300 weapons, was purchased at a cost of $2.3 million.[25] The average price per weapon was approximately $256.[26] This was a small price to pay for the added security resulting from a decrease in the availability of weapons, and was minuscule when compared to what the cost associated with house-to-house searches would have been. No dollar cost could be associated with the risk to individual members of the MNF if they had been required to search from house to house, but it certainly reinforced the fact that the WBB program was an effective way of directly reducing the threats to Haitian security. The fact that the program had its precedents in Admiral Caperton's pacification program of 1915 might not have been as well known, but the effectiveness of the WBB concept was obvious enough so that it was even soon tried in local areas of the United States where citizens were also confronted by alarming numbers of weapons on their streets.

Throughout 1994, MNF personnel supported the WBB all over the country, with very good results. On January 2nd Aristide continued to push for the return of weapons in his Founding Father's Day speech to the nation. Up to that point over 15,000 firearms had been retrieved by the WBB program or street-sweep operations conducted by the MNF. Although resource intensive, it was a program that clearly showed measurable results. The WBB remained an important part of the MNF's security operations through the spring, until USACOM approved plans to transfer the program, effective on the last day of March, to U.N. supervision. The number of weapons turned in indicated that the program had succeeded in significantly reducing the excess of firearms, yet its stabilizing effects also appeared well worth the program's continuation under UNMIH.

HAITIAN DOMESTIC IMPROVEMENTS

As security and weapons concerns were lessened, progress was also made on the legislative front. On November 5th Haiti's Parliament approved President Aristide's choice for prime minister, Smarck Michel, who had selected his cabinet for approval by the Haitian lower house. After the vote of confidence from Parliament, on November 8th Prime Minister Michel and his seventeen new cabinet members took office at the National Palace. The formation of this new administration was a very positive step, for it represented cooperation and forward movement by both the executive and legislative branches of the government. Unfortunately, improved administrative functioning was at this point only a very thin veneer.

In Haiti, although huge numbers of personnel were often listed among the work force of a government agency, in most cases very few people ever did any of the work required. Most government posts were simply sources of graft and nepotism. Becoming a cabinet member before Aristide's return implied more monetary reward than work required, and many government agencies had woefully inadequate administrative offices and procedures. Most kept no accurate records. In short, much improvement was required in 1994 to enable the newly appointed members of Aristide's administration to effectively run their offices and the programs for which they were responsible. This requisite improvement was clearly in the best interest of the MNF as well, for it contributed to stability in Haiti. To assist in this effort U.S. Army civil-affairs personnel were formed into small groups known as Ministerial Advisory Teams or MATs and assigned as advisors to numerous Haitian agencies.

Ministerial Advisory Teams were formed to advise Haitian leaders in almost every government function. In the early months these teams included the commander of the 358th Civil Affairs Brigade, Brigadier General Bruce Bingham, USA Reserve, who was assigned specifically to the prime minister, and groups of advisors working with the Haitian ministers of Commerce, Interior, Justice, Defense, and Foreign Affairs, among others. Later, other MATs were provided to improve information coordination and cultural development, national education, public works, women's affairs, and even the central bank. Planning and public administration were also important processes that benefited from MATs. Eventually, seven different rotations of personnel would serve as MAT members, keeping the improvement going through the entire period of U.S. military involvement.[27]

Ministerial Advisory Team members first completed an assessment to clearly identify what was required to improve the functions they were assigned to assist. After the assessment was evaluated, each MAT identified what improvements were achievable during the time period allocated to the team members. It is important to remember that many of the civil-affairs team members sent to Haiti were Army reservists, with full-time occupations back in the United States. They had invaluable expertise in their fields; many were professional advisors, teachers, lawyers, doctors, and engineers. But they were also limited in the amount of time they could spend in Haiti. Each project had to include specific objectives that could be completed within the period of duty allowed. In some cases these duty periods were no longer than 14 days; others were extended up to 29 days; and in some cases teams were combined with active-duty personnel to extend a project over a 60-to-90-day period. In all cases, little time was available to complete massive and important amounts of work.

The real value of this MAT effort is impossible to quantify, but it was recognized by General Meade and several others as one of the key elements of improvement in Haiti and one of the operation's most significant success stories.[28] The MATs were the best way for the MNF to help with structural and procedural changes, which were needed to increase the effectiveness and efficiency of the Haitian government. The improvements would in turn make advances in the security situation more enduring and would provide additional reasons for the Haitian people to appreciate and support their government.

HUMANITARIAN ASSISTANCE IN HAITI

The MNF understood that its mission included providing a very significant proportion of humanitarian aid in Haiti. Although the U.S. forces were prohibited from supplying more aid than was mission-essential or required for immediate humanitarian requirements like medical support and water purification, any humanitarian gesture was welcomed by the Haitians and contributed much to improving the relationship between the U.S. forces and the Haitians.[29] The single most significant demonstration of the humanitarian dedication of the MNF occurred during the response to hurricane damage in November, 1994. Tropical Storm Gordon hit Haiti and the migrant camps at Guantanamo Bay and although there were no serious injuries to those in Cuba or to MNF troops in Haiti, the Haitian population's death toll from the storm rose to over a hundred, principally near the town of Jacmel on the southern claw of the country.

The storm produced over fifteen inches of rain in less than 12 hours, which resulted in eight-foot-deep flooding in places around Jacmel. Nearly 1500 Haitians were rendered homeless, crops were ruined, food supplies were contaminated, and bridges were washed out. Although most of these deaths occurred in the river valleys between Jacmel and Leogane, the devastation was extreme in many places. It immediately overwhelmed the Haitian disaster- response capability. Noting the severity of the storm and its devastation, the MNF immediately provided rescue operations and began planning for disaster relief in the worst-affected areas.

Following the storm, engineer and civil-affairs teams were deployed to the Jacmel area to assess the damage. While the assessment was being conducted, heavy equipment was already being moved to Jacmel from Port-au-Prince using a military landing-ship vehicle (LSV). Simultaneously, the MNF was reestablishing critical services in many of the affected portions of the country outside the most devastated area. Military aircraft and ships provided support to non-governmental and private volunteer organizations, which could supply immediate aid, and moved equipment, personnel, and supplies to the areas most seriously damaged. Multinational-force military engineers constructed bypasses to a severely damaged road-network and reopened ground transportation to the southern claw of Haiti, which had become impassable during the storm, so that Haitian assistance efforts could proceed. Engineers worked to clear mud slides and construct fords where key bridges had collapsed under the force of the downpour. The entire effort to assess the problem, provide immediate relief, reopen the roads, and distribute essential aid was accomplished in 7 days. No one could doubt the humanitarian dedication or professionalism of the MNF after Tropical Storm Gordon.

Other important actions at all levels continued through late November, particularly in the realm of civil–military affairs. The MNF Civil Military Operations Center (CMOC) in the force headquarters had been active since the first days of the operation coordinating support requirements and capabilities all over the capital region. By the late autumn, a second CMOC had been established in the northern part of the country to respond to the needs of local citizens in the Cap-Haitien area. That city's poor infrastructure created a host of problems. As in the capital, electric power-generation capability was restored and sanitation was improved, while a particular effort was made to prevent the spread of disease. Just as important to the building of a stable environment, soldiers helped Haitians to settle claims, to report and process human-rights violations, and to even interact with the media.

In Haiti, civil-affairs work reached new levels of achievement in the coordination and improvement of services. While many soldiers worked with individual Haitians and nongovernmental relief and support organizations to improve basic living conditions, others continued to work on improvements in the internal functioning of the Haitian national government and a host of provincial and local administrative offices. The civil-affairs MATs continued to provide support to the various Haitian ministries, thereby improving their ability to handle the huge load of pending actions needed within the country—actions that had been ignored during the Cedras regime. The civil-affairs effort in Haiti was extensive, successful, and critically important; the people who accomplished it truly fulfilled the hope of the old Creole motto: "Do every good that you can, all the times that you can, every way that you can, every place that you can, for everybody that you can until you can't continue."[30]

MIGRANT-PROCESSING ISSUES

Returning Haiti's security to Haitian control had to be accomplished simultaneously with the return of Haitian migrants from the U.S. naval base in Cuba. The flow of migrants had always posed the main threat to regional stability, beginning back during the Bush Administration in 1992. By the fall of 1994 it was still an ongoing mission requiring hundreds of troops, aircraft, and ships and the cooperation of multiple agencies.[31] Just caring for the thousands of Haitians in the Guantanamo Bay camp was a costly and potentially dangerous mission. Because few Haitians could justify entry into the United States, the vast majority needed to be repatriated to Haiti, and returning those citizens who had fled the country posed its own unique security threat. Returning migrants added to the huge jobless pool and many faced threats of reprisal when they attempted to rejoin local communities and reclaim any property remaining at their former homesteads. As if this situation were not complex enough, some American legal officials decided to make the repatriation process a matter for the U.S. courts, thereby restricting the flexibility of those attempting to process the migrants as effectively as possible.

On the 1st of November a U.S. district court judge extended his temporary restraining order against involuntary repatriations of Cuban migrants from Guantanamo Bay, and that action was extended to include Haitian migrants detained at the base. The Cuban migrants at Guantanamo Bay started demonstrations protesting U.S. efforts to return them to Cuba. Overturning portable latrines and throwing rocks to show their frustration, fifteen of them even attempted to swim to sovereign Cuba. Although all the Cubans were recovered, such violence certainly did not ease concerns in the Haitian areas of Guantanamo Bay; the situation there grew quite tense as legal and emotional pressures increased throughout November.

In response to rising pressures in the naval base, the commander of JTF-160 in Guantanamo Bay planned to upgrade facilities and living conditions in the camps. He was clearly caught among various considerations: the military necessity of processing the migrants as quickly and safely as possible; the human concern for their welfare while housed in Guantanamo Bay; and the efforts of others to provide the migrants U.S. versions of legal counsel. Meanwhile, an International Organization for Migration (IOM) charter flight did carry 180 Haitian migrants seeking asylum to Miami. This flight somewhat reduced the level of anxiety by illustrating that some migrants in Guantanamo Bay could still at least hope to be admitted to the United States. Two days later, the 11th U.S. Circuit Court of Appeals in Atlanta overturned the U.S. district court's order banning involuntary repatriations of both Haitians and Cubans, but it did allow the migrants access to legal counsel. The CINC directed the JTF-160 commander to begin screening Haitian migrants at Guantanamo Bay again for voluntary repatriation after the district court's temporary restraining order expired. Hereafter, the flow of migrants back to their home countries slowly increased, even as the pace of individual processing was slowed by ensuring that appropriate counsel was available.

Meanwhile, the U.S. Coast Guard cutter *Mohawk* and her sister ships continued to steam from the naval base in Cuba and other sites around Haiti to interdict and return migrants. These efforts were not just simple transport missions: Coast Guard cutters and Navy ships were not intended as transports, and having large numbers of migrants on board reduced their operational effectiveness. As an example, the *Mohawk* made a run in early November, returning thirty-eight noninfectious tuberculosis patients from Guantanamo Bay to Port-au-Prince, while ensuring that their medical needs were met along the way, a tough job for a small crew. By that time, under the U.S. Coast Guard's migrant-interdiction program, nearly 70,000 Haitians had been repatriated to their homeland in similar small groups, by ship and by plane.

In mid-November the U.S. Military Sealift Command announced the charter of a Greek cruise ship, SS *Britanis,* to replace the two other charter ships used in Guantanamo Bay for troop berthing. For some time the United States had found it necessary to contract for the additional berthing spaces required and had resorted to renting cruise ships as the most readily available source of mobile hotel facilities. The use of the Guantanamo Bay base as a processing facility was clearly less than desirable given its small size and the tenuous relationship between the governments of Cuba and the United States, yet it was very close to Haiti and was the only site outside the United States where space, however insufficient, was available to accomplish the mission. Other nations had been asked for support, but no other site offered could really provide what the Americans needed.

On November 14th Clinton Administration officials indicated for the first time that the United States was planning to allow Cuban migrant families with children in Guantanamo Bay to enter the country for humanitarian reasons, thus providing another humanitarian safety valve for the pressure in the camps. The return of Haitian migrants could have been viewed as one of the less important requirements of the fall rebuilding period. However, for internal political reasons in both the United States and Haiti repatriation was an important but contentious issue. Judge C. Clyde Atkins of the Miami Federal District Court ruled on November 22nd that the 231 unaccompanied Haitian minors in Guantanamo Bay should be allowed to enter the United States in the same way as Cuban children. On the following day the IOM assisted 185 Haitians seeking asylum in the United

States to depart directly from Port-au-Prince for Miami after they had been cleared by embassy officials. Permitting Haitian migrants to come to the United States had long been acknowledged as a potentially destabilizing signal to send to both Americans and Haitians. But as conditions in Haiti were returning to normal, the situation in Guantanamo Bay and the psychological climate in Haiti were deemed sufficient to support continued acceptance of Haitians. The governments in Washington and Port-au-Prince still had to work out a solution to the very real due-process needs of Haitians who would never be admitted to the United States and who were still fleeing or being processed in Guantanamo Bay.

By late November all the signs pointed to the fact that the migrant-processing mission was meeting its objectives. The flow at sea had decreased, processing in Guantanamo Bay was exceeding the influx in numbers, and involuntary repatriation, the original position held by the Bush Administration in 1992, was still working effectively. Perhaps most importantly, in the 45 days since the return of President Aristide in mid-October a total of 15,199 Haitians had been repatriated to Port-au-Prince. Because of such success, the U.S. Coast Guard finally terminated operation Able Manner, which had officially begun on January 13, 1993 to rescue Haitian migrants seeking asylum in the United States. On December 2nd the Coast Guard cutter *Bear* repatriated 250 more Haitian migrants who had been trained in law enforcement at Guantanamo Bay as future members of the IPSF, along with twenty-five of their family members, all of whom were welcomed back by Haiti's defense minister. By December 12th, although JTF-160 was still requesting assistance from USACOM in order to promote interest among the remaining Haitian migrants in seeking voluntary repatriation, the toughest part of the mission had been accomplished and the migration threat to the United States was effectively over.

Two days prior to Christmas, the U.S. Coast Guard repatriated the last 215 voluntary Haitian migrants from Guantanamo Bay to Port-au-Prince, and the Bahamian government requested U.S. assistance in repatriating some 700 Haitian migrants who had arrived aboard the motor vessel *Shantel* in Matthew Town, Great Inagua, Bahamas. These repatriations signaled the end of the voluntary processing effort for Haitian migrants. Just as the Coast Guard had been able to stop full-scale interdiction operations once the processing of the migrants had been established in November, the U.S. government effort shifted after Christmas to a focused program designed to decrease migrant camp levels, to continue direct repatriations of all intercepted migrants, and eventually to close the Guantanamo Bay processing facility.

At the end of December 294 Haitians had accepted the U.S. offers and were voluntarily returned to Port-au-Prince aboard the Coast Guard cutter Thetis; this was another indication of the improvements in security taking place in Haiti. On January 3rd the U.S. Defense Department announced plans to send almost 2,000 troops from the 9th Infantry Regiment in Fort Lewis, Washington to Guantanamo Bay. This move was designed to augment security forces at the U.S. base in Cuba in anticipation of repatriating the remaining 4,500 Haitian migrants and transferring the nearly 8,400 Cuban migrants from the operation Safe Haven villages in Panama to join the 21,600 other Cubans already at Guantanamo Bay.[32] Maintaining security for thousands of migrants had become a very costly burden on America's defense establishment.[33] With small numbers of military police in the active force, many regular infantry units and even reserve battalions were eventually used to ensure that the camps remained secure.

Efficient transition in Haiti depended upon resolution of several remaining issues, among which the migrant-repatriation problem figured significantly. It was clear that all Haitian migrants would not return voluntarily; the Haitian government was not very accepting of forced repatriation of its citizens, and courts in the United States were still hearing attempts to change the migrant-processing efforts that were underway at Guantanamo Bay. Even so, the commander of JTF-160 began processing Haitian migrants on January 5th in Guantanamo Bay for both voluntary and involuntary repatriation to Port-au-Prince aboard U.S. Coast Guard cutters. The *Valiant* repatriated 139 voluntary Haitian migrants. Following the denial of an appeal in the Miami federal district court to stop Haitian repatriations, U.S. forces repatriated 54 involuntary Haitian migrants on the next day. On January 7th the *Valiant* repatriated another 110 voluntary Haitian migrants, and the *Boutwell* repatriated 289 involuntary ones to Port-au-Prince.

In the United States the 11th U.S. Circuit Court of Appeals finally ruled in mid-January that Cuban and Haitian migrants at Guantanamo Bay did not have the same constitutional rights as U.S. citizens and could be repatriated to their respective countries. This ruling was helpful to the resolution of the migrant problem because it greatly reduced the legal barriers to the U.S. government's policy of repatriation. Although some human-rights advocates continued to complain about the process, the implication to the military was that the "green light" was given for returning migrants in increasing numbers.

This remained a far-flung effort requiring large numbers of assets. As examples, USACOM had directed the MNF to provide rations for 442 Haitian migrants at Matthew Town, Great Inagua, Bahamas, prior to their repatriation to Port-au-Prince; the Dominican Republic continued to repatriate Haitian migrants across its border; and several cutters remained at sea to intercept the latest migrants who for whatever reasons did not appreciate that things had begun to change in Haiti. Although continued upgrades were accomplished within the infrastructure of the processing facility at Guantanamo Bay and although migrants continued to flee Haiti, repatriation could finally be viewed as a complete solution with an identifiable ending date for the processing action. Finally, in mid-January a delegation of U.S. and Haitian officials met with the remaining Haitian migrants at Guantanamo Bay to obtain their consent for voluntarily returning to Haiti. Because it finally had a judicial process in place, Haiti accepted back its problems and began to sort out possible solutions for those who did not want to live within Haitian law.

Multiple sites and multiple issues made migrant processing a difficult effort to coordinate among the various agencies. Personnel from the U.S. Departments of Defense, State, Justice, Immigration and Naturalization, IOM, the Coast Guard, medical services, and the government of Haiti, among many others, all cooperated to safely process and transport the migrants. While not easy, the processing effort was a superb example of interagency cooperation and one of the true success stories of Uphold Democracy.

All four of these interrelated programs—the security improvements, the WBB process, the humanitarian-assistance efforts, and migrant-processing and repatriation—were significant steps forward. With each, the MNF tread a fine line between providing too much nation-assistance and failing to provide support where Haitian resources were insufficient to the task, judging with each act the potential long-term effects on Haitian–U.S. relations. These programs were successful because they were managed carefully and focused well; they offer very important examples for future use in similar operations. Used effectively by the MNF, they were critical to achieving level of security required for the all-important arrival of the United Nation's Mission in Haiti.

NOTES

1. As long as the commander and staff of the XVIII Airborne Corps were deployed overseas, the United States had no readily available strategic-reaction force for a contingency elsewhere in the world.

2. The decision that the 10th Mountain Division and General Meade were to be responsible for the second stage of the Haiti operation was made by the commander of the U.S. Army Forces Command, located in Fort MacPherson, Georgia, in consultation with General Shelton. On the 29th of July General Meade went to Fort Bragg to meet with Shelton and receive a briefing from Major General Mike Byron, the USACOM J5, Director of Plans. The major reason for the assignment was the 10th Mountain Division's experience in Somalia and its availability for long-term—perhaps 6 months—commitment.

3. David C. Meade interview with Dennis P. Mroczkowski, Port-au-Prince, October 27, 1994, pp. 1–3.

4. Meade's staff was considered the Army service-component of Shelton's JTF even though it had personnel assigned from all five uniformed services. This was a function that the 10th Mountain Division had already performed in Somalia. The ability of JTF-190 to manage other service concerns grew over time.

5. These are Meade's own words in summarizing the initial difficulties. See Meade's interview with Mroczkowski, Port-au-Prince, October 27, 1994, p. 4. Had JTF-190 been able to form and operate for a time at Fort Drum, some of the early problems could have been sorted out more effectively, yet no amount of preparation could have altered the fact that Haiti was an inhospitable and uncertain environment and JTF-190 did not have the luxury of operating from the USS *Mount Whitney*.

6. This lack of basic support is uncommon for U.S. Army divisions, which are designed to work as part of an Army Corps. The Corps includes all the special staff officers and units that establish support bases and facilities for its subordinate divisions.

7. 10th Mountain Division, *10th Mountain Division "Operation Uphold Democracy" After Action Report, Operations in Haiti August 1994 through January 1995*, p. 24.

8. It is perhaps unfair to say that such an early arrival was an advantage. At first the accelerated deployment found JTF-190 slightly unprepared, and the command appeared to bog down in the city; however, once they expanded into the countryside and became active in Haitian society, the personnel of the command learned quickly and began to develop highly effective working relationships with a host of important officials and agencies and the Haitian people. These relationships served them well once JTF-180 departed.

9. Lieutenant General Robert Johnston, USMC, and his staff from the 1st Marine Expeditionary Force had directed operation Restore Hope in Somalia from January, 1992 until the mission's transition to the United Nations.

10. Two years after his assumption of command, General Sheehan would be one of the few military men invited to attend President Aristide's wedding. This personal gesture of esteem was only one small indication of the debt Haiti owed Sheehan for his leadership during the period from 1990 to 1997.

11. General Meade and his officers had always been concerned about this tendency for troops to lose combat skills while serving within a peace-operations environment. Consequently, they constructed a live-fire combat range for unit training in Haiti and conducted a wide range of combat patrols, twenty-nine separate company-level operations, and seven emergency-deployment readiness exercises, to maintain their combat proficiency. At the conclusion of the division's service in Haiti, the 10th Mountain was still certified as being "highly ready," with strong marks in most areas.

12. J. Burton Thompson interview with Major General George A. Fisher, USA, Schofield Barracks, HI, May 8, 1995, p. 1.

13. Ibid, p. 3.

14. Fisher noted that this organizational change was "an excellent decision. It brought plenty of experts and the right degree of command to the [logistics] effort." He also recommended that a general officer's leadership within the Logistics Support Command was key to the success of such a concept. Thompson interview with Fisher, p. 3.

15. Ibid, p. 4.

16. The best short study on this subject remains Forrest L. Marion's *Development of a Haitian Public Security Force, September 1994–March 1995.*

17. Many people, both inside and outside Haiti, doubted whether the former members of the FAd'H could be so easily retrained. The central issue focused on the moral commitment of Haitians to provide unbiased police functions and resist returning to long-established habits of graft and corruption. Although some never met the challenge and failed to become reliable public servants, most *did* provide an acceptable level of professional conduct, particularly once their salaries provided an effective deterrent to temptation.

18. For years, the USACOM staff had supported a series of month-long exercises designed to bring these national police forces together for enhanced training and discussions of mutual benefit. Known as "Tradewinds," this exercise resulted directly in the active participation of both the CARICOM battalion and these national IPMs in Uphold Democracy.

19. The progress made in reforming certain aspects of Japan and Germany during the occupations following World War II shares certain similarities with the 1994 situation in Haiti, but the cultures were strikingly different and the political situations were also dissimilar.

20. See William R. McClintock, "Working Chronologies."

21. One damning accusation concerned assistance given members of the Haitian paramilitary groups by the CIA after the invasion in return for information they had provided to the United States during the Cedras regime. Another involved a supposed cover-up by the United States of documents seized during the invasion that indicated that it knew about and condoned illegal practices in Haiti. None of these accusations was accompanied by any real proof or resulted in any convictions of U.S. personnel.

22. Hayden, *JTF-180 Operation Uphold Democracy Oral Interviews,* p. 52.

23. 10th Mountain Division, pp. 42–43.

24. Ibid.

25. Forrest L. Marion, *Captured Weapons and the Weapons Buy-Back Program in Haiti, September 1994–March 1995,* p. 17.

26. Ibid.

27. John R. Ballard interview with Lieutenant Colonel Edgar C. Seely, III, USA Reserve, Norfolk, VA, March 13, 1997.

28. Ibid, p. 44. The importance of the MATs was also stressed in 10th Mountain Division's after-action report on operations in Haiti. *10th Mountain Division,* p. 84.

29. Despite restrictions on the use of military funds for developmental programs, a wide variety of services was provided to Haiti during the operation. Just one example was Operation "Light Switch," which provided the fuel and technical expertise to repair and restart sixteen power plants throughout the country. Some of the affected locations had not had electrical service for over 3 years. Providing this electrical power is estimated to have benefited over three million Haitians. See *10th Mountain Division,* p. 86.

30. Hayden, *JTF-180 Operation Uphold Democracy Oral Interviews,* p. 141. This saying was given to Lieutenant Colonel Eric I. Mitchell, USA Reserve, the JTF-190 Public Health Officer by a Haitian doctor during the operation.

31. The best presentation of this topic is found in USACOM's after-action review, *Migrant Camp Operations.*

32. Operation Safe Haven was a support operation for both Uphold Democracy and Sea Signal. In Safe Haven, the U.S. Southern Command sponsored camps in South America for the processing of Cuban migrants, thus reducing the population and pressure at Guantanamo Bay.

33. President Clinton's Report on Haiti reflected a total cost in 1994 of $750 million, including $346.9 million on troops; $173.2 million for interdicting and housing Haitian migrants; $116.2 million for reconstruction aid; and $68.6 million to enforce economic sanctions.

CHAPTER 9

The U.N. Mission in Haiti: Toward a New Democracy

At the same time that Generals Meade and Fisher were changing command, U.N. officials announced the nomination of Major General Joseph W. Kinzer, USA, then Deputy Commanding General, Fifth U.S. Army, to command the U.N. Mission in Haiti (UNMIH). (Kinzer would move into Haiti once Fisher had completed the development of the United Nation's preconditions for deployment.) By that point in December, several important decisions concerning the UNMIH deployment had been made. The U.N. Security Council had generated sufficient consensus by then to assure the passing of the resolution announcing that Haiti had achieved a "stable and secure environment." To add to this degree of confidence, Secretary of Defense Perry also pronounced Haiti to be "safe and secure" for turnover to the UNMIH forces.

Coincidentally, unlike during the harried first days of Uphold Democracy when the United States had had to develop its own coalition to compose the Multinational Force (MNF), the U.N. staff had been at work to actually form the international coalition contributing forces to UNMIH. United Nations Secretary-General Boutros-Ghali notified the Security Council in mid-January that the United States and eighteen other nations had volunteered military components for the UNMIH. United States Ambassador Albright then proposed the formal Security Council Resolution that would allow UNMIH forces to assume peacekeeping operations in Haiti from the MNF by the end of March, and General Kinzer made his first visit to MNF troops in Haiti in preparation for his role in the operation. The Resolution began the 60-day process of turning the operation over from the MNF to UNMIH, but no guarantee of UNMIH's arrival existed unless the social and political situation in Haiti remained calm. The onus for the maintenance of that security fell on both General Fisher and the Aristide government; its continuance was easy for neither party.

On January 30th the U.N. Security Council passed UNSCR 975 to transfer the Haitian peacekeeping mission from the United States to the UNMIH effective March 31st. This left very little time for the United Nations to address the myriad of details required to field and establish supporting structures for UNMIH. In some cases this lack of preparation time resulted in the failure to achieve all the prerequisites desired by General Kinzer prior to his assumption of control in Haiti. Having studied earlier U.N. military missions, he understood the importance of thorough preparation, and even though he was unable to achieve all of his requirements prior to assuming control, his prior planning greatly assisted the transition process.

As actions in the United States prepared for the end of U.S. military operations in Haiti, events elsewhere also indicated that progress continued to be made. In Port-au-Prince Haiti's Chamber of Deputies passed the electoral law and sent it to the Senate, but added requirements that all candidates have a high- school diploma and excluded the clergy from public office unless a candidate had been retired from the Church for at least 1 year. The Bahamas also repatriated 625 Haitian migrants to Port-au-Prince. At a meeting in Paris, the World Bank and international agencies from twenty donor nations pledged a $660 million reconstruction package and another $240 million in military assistance for Haiti's economic recovery over the following 15 months. By far the most significant of these actions was the endorsement of the World Bank, which for the first time indicated that the major contributions required to put the Haitian economy back on its feet would be forthcoming. Haitian Prime Minister Michel announced on February 1st that parliamentary elections would be held beginning in April, provided that all the procedures were approved in parliament. Three days later, after modifying amendments inserted by the lower house, the Haitian Senate sent the Electoral Law for President Aristide's approval before all elected officials' terms expired on that day, the 4th. It was a very close call. Had the electoral details not been confirmed prior to the end of the legislators' terms, Aristide's government might have been unable to legally proceed in replacing echelons of the government. In a very real sense the government and all the progress it had made since September might have expired before it could ensure its own legal continuation. On February 10th Haitian election officials announced that legislative and local elections would be held in late May or early June.

Support for the United Nations was growing in importance, but the United States still had very real concerns about the world body's management effectiveness during a crisis and hesitated in committing large numbers of U.S. troops without an assurance of U.S. command. As a consequence, the U.S. Secretary of State sent a draft letter of assurances concerning the assignment of General Kinzer as commanding general of UNMIH forces to the U.N. Secretary-General. Kinzer was nominated to serve as the U.N. commander only until February 29, 1996. The United States was committed to Haiti, but felt that U.N. missions had a tendency to linger for too long in certain situations. After all, U.N. forces had remained in Cyprus and the Golan Heights for decades; the intent was to keep the U.S. presence in Haiti limited in duration and scope.

As the MNF's tenure in Haiti was drawing to a close, the security situation remained despite some problems. The MNF reported assisting in restoring order on February 18th at Haiti's National Prison. Fifteen prisoners had escaped in protest of the lack of due process concerning their cases. To continue in efforts to correct these problems, General Shalikashvili directed continued support of the Haitian Judicial Mentors Program, using military civil-affairs personnel, until the end of April. On the 21st, Haiti's Defense Minister announced the dismissal of forty-three high-ranking IPSF officers, including the commanding general, General Bernard Poisson, and Brigadier General Cherubin, top aide to President Aristide, which further weakened Haiti's shrinking border patrol force. The restoration of the democratic process was at least progressing well. Haiti's Electoral Council set legislative elections for June 4th, followed by runoffs on June 25th. Key events included voter registration from March 26th to April 17th, campaigning from April 24th to June 2nd, and distribution of voting materials from May 26th until June 3rd.

On the 23rd of February former President Carter, accompanied by General Powell and Senator Nunn, began a 3-day visit in Haiti. The three-man team that had prevented bloodshed in September received a mixed reception by Haitians only 5 months later. At the end of his visit Carter asked President Aristide to maintain his neutrality during the legislative and municipal elections. Some Aristide supporters misconstrued Carter's advice as U.S. meddling in Haitian politics and protecting "old U.S. allies." Much had changed in Haiti, but fears and misperceptions continued.

During a luncheon on March 4th President Aristide reiterated his intent to maintain political neutrality during the upcoming elections. Three days later he hosted Deputy Secretary of State Strobe Talbot and U.S. business leaders who would back economic assistance in Haiti. On the same day, USACOM issued the execute order (EXORD) for transition from the MNF to UNMIH, with U.S. forces capped at 2,400. General Sheehan would remain as the U.S. strategic-level commander—the U.S. "supported CINC" for UNMIH operations. This ensured continuity at the strategic level and maintained USACOM as a coordinating body for U.S. interagency support of the operation. In all U.N. operations, it is important to maintain established national command chains, so this continuing role of USACOM was not at all unusual.

Later in the first week of March Radio Metropole in Port-au-Prince announced that President Clinton would attend the MNF-to-UNMIH transition ceremonies on March 31st. United States forces in Haiti also offered to provide support for the incoming CARICOM III contingent of soldiers, including housing, food, transportation, and vehicle maintenance. These support services were critical to the effective operations of the unit but were in short supply in the CARICOM nations, so it made good sense for the United States to support its allies in these areas.

Mid-March witnessed a flurry of activity as the transition to UNMIH grew closer and President Aristide pushed several initiatives in Haiti. Pakistan deployed the first 180 of 850 troops pledged for the UNMIH forces on March 14th. The next day, President Aristide requested U.S. extradition of Emmanuel Constant, former head of FRAPH, alleged to be in hiding in the United States. Aristide and others wanted to ensure that Haiti solve its own problems and that suspect Haitians anywhere be judged by Haitian law. President Aristide also pushed to keep due process inside the country; he reiterated that the "vigilance brigades" were not to take justice into their own hands because "reconciliation and violence are not compatible." A second tripartite meeting was held in Port-au-Prince to discuss the transition of the MNF to UNMIH forces. General Sheehan arrived in Port-au-Prince to review transition plans and progress. Haiti and the United Nations signed the status of forces agreement for UNMIH that outlined the mission's rights and duties while in Haiti. Within the country, the communal electoral offices (BECs) and departmental electoral offices (DECs) began operations under the overall control of the CEP. In his report to Congress under the War Powers Act, President Clinton reiterated that Haiti "remained calm and relatively incident-free."

USACOM announced on the 27th of March that the U.S. portion of the MNF in Haiti would revert to the designation "JTF-190" on March 31st and again, transition to a third commander. The JTF was to be placed under the command of Brigadier General James T. "Tom" Hill, USA, who would replace Major General Fisher upon his redeployment.[1] Hill was chosen for his demonstrated understanding of logistics requirements, which was the single greatest contribution his force was to make to ongoing MNF actions. Because he was a member of Fisher's staff, the choice of Hill also would ensure an easy transition of control of U.S. forces in Haiti. Again, the primary goal during the transition to UNMIH, as during the earlier turnover between the 10th Mountain and 25th Infantry Divisions, was to maintain progress and ensure continuity of command.

On the 30th, General Sheehan and many other dignitaries arrived in Port-au-Prince to participate in ceremonies for the MNF transition to UNMIH. At the ceremony, President Aristide affirmed that Haiti was secure enough for transferring command from the U.S.-led MNF to the United Nations. The most significant military phase of the campaign to uphold democracy was complete.

UNMIH TAKES CONTROL

On March 31st President Clinton, U.N. Secretary-General Boutros-Ghali, and General Sheehan along with other dignitaries attended ceremonies in Port-au-Prince that transferred operational control of the military forces in Haiti from the MNF commander to the commander of the UNMIH. With this act, Major General Kinzer assumed command of both the U.S. forces in Haiti (USFORHAITI) and the UNMIH forces.[2] The choice of Kinzer, a well-respected combat veteran familiar with coordination of civil–military actions within

Washington to hold both positions was well designed. United States troops made up about 40 percent of UNMIH's 6,000-person force, and as the U.S. and U.N. commander, Kinzer would be best placed to effect all the required coordination in both the United Nations in New York and USACOM in Norfolk. As the U.N. commander Kinzer reported through his civilian U.N. boss, former Algerian foreign minister Lakhdar Brahimi, to the Secretary-General, and as the senior U.S. commander he reported to General Sheehan.

Kinzer would hold operational control of the other national contingents of the U.N. force and, as the U.S. commander, ensured that the command of U.S. forces remained totally within a U.S. chain.[3] The MNF to UNMIH transition had been preceded by a 1-week staff-training program in early March. This program gave the key personnel in the UNMIH headquarters an opportunity to develop a common understanding of the mission and area of operations as well as the rules of engagement and staff procedures to be used there. It proved to be very advantageous and was adopted as a permanent part of future operations by the U.N. Department of Peacekeeping Operations staff in New York.[4] Kinzer later noted that this short training session helped set the right tone and quickly established important working relationships within his staff that were key to a smooth transition and effective work from the outset in Haiti.[5]

UNMIH's mission included several specific goals: (1) sustaining the secure and stable environment in Haiti, (2) establishing an environment conducive to free and fair elections, (3) professionalizing Haiti's security forces, and (4) protecting international personnel and key installations (required to achieve the first three objectives). These goals flowed well from the preceding missions of the MNF and were in keeping with the long-term plan of USACOM, which always anticipated the eventual control of operations in Haiti transitioning to a U.N. headquarters. The most basic mission of UNMIH was assisting in the elections for a new president to succeed Aristide, the only act that would really signal that sufficient political progress had been achieved. A successful election was viewed as proof that Haiti was able to manage its own affairs without a foreign presence.

Thus the contingency operations portion of Uphold Democracy came to a close with the successful installation of U.N. forces within a peaceful Haitian environment. Although the United States military continued to support Haiti, other nations and agencies took on increasingly important roles. In particular, the United Nations became much more active and began to establish the tone and style of operations in Haiti. The composition of the U.S. military contingent in Haiti also shifted from combat forces in a security role, as had been the case within the MNF, to support forces providing the logistics for other national contingents. For these reasons the primary U.S. military role in Haiti, as it had been established in the summer of 1994, ended with General Kinzer's assumption of command.

The MNF had been assigned the missions of facilitating the return and proper functioning of the government of Haiti, improving Haitian security, establishing a secure environment, and efficiently transferring responsibility to the United Nations. It had served as the focal point for a host of actions that assisted in the recovery of most Haitian government functions, including provision of basic services, transportation and fuel, maintenance, judicial process, and even limited medical care. The Haitian security force had been rehabilitated and refocused by a process that included vetting, which identified the members that could be trusted to execute their duties in a professional manner, and retraining before its members were returned to the streets under joint MNF and IPM observation.

The stable and secure Haitian environment was to be a direct outgrowth of renewed government processes and a restored sense of security. These improvements did demonstrate very quickly that increased stability and security were the keys to returning Haiti's viability as a democratic state. Yet, experienced Haitian observers understood that the appearance of calm and even the achievement of a period of greatly reduced instability could not counter-balance the years of cultural and societal abuse that had been the Haitian standard for most of the preceding century. The only real solution for Haiti would be a healing process that took time and the recovery of a sense of identity that engendered trust among Haitians in all walks of life. The question of how much time foreign forces were needed to ensure this long-term recovery in Haiti remained open to speculation.

By the end of 1994 most observable factors did point to a level of security sufficient to transition control to the United Nations. But one element largely outside the control of the MNF still posed a threat: the Haitian economy was improving too slowly to support the changes required in Haiti.[6] In parallel with improvements made in the security situation, it was assumed that the economic deprivation in Haiti would be eased through a large influx of foreign monetary support and private investment. This flood of economic aid really did not occur as envisioned.[7] Even by March, 1995 the funds provided had fallen far short of the levels required to return the Haitian economy to a sufficiently productive status. This posed a challenging dilemma for the MNF and the United States as its lead nation. The easy solution would have been to fall back into the trap of providing Haiti with a robust nation-building program, letting the United States rebuild the country as it had in the 1920s. But the lesson of nation building had been well learned by 1995[8]: along with nation building invariably came an increase in the duration of military operations and concomitant growth in the dependence of the assisted nation upon the aiding nation. No one wanted this to happen in Haiti; the country needed to stand on its own if it was ever to remain independent of foreign assistance.

The United States made a strategic decision to avoid the mission expansion that nation-building entailed. The tough judgment was to settle for more enduring, but much slower, growth in Haiti's economy instead of a more rapid, more costly, and less stable influx of U.S. aid. The MNF's support was limited to only that assistance that served a military purpose; Generals Meade and Fisher were prohibited from contributing directly to the Haitian economy. Yet, with the economic aspects of the mission outside the military's span of control, no other organization stepped in to provide the assistance needed to fully restore the financial foundation and economic productivity that real, enduring stability required. This was the one significant weakness in the program of stability and security in Haiti; its impact was minor in 1995, but it posed the potential of desta- bilizing Haiti's continued progress.

By March, 1995 operation Uphold Democracy had met every task assigned to it. Over the preceding 18 months, U.S. military forces had accomplished a wide variety of tasks to support the return of Aristide and the establishment of a secure Haitian environment. These included the collection of thousands of weapons, the creation of an Interim Police Security Force, the demobilization of the FAd'H, and the conducting of municipal and local elections. Thousands of troops from all the military services had contributed skills ranging from water purification and road-building to supply distribution, medical support, and the enhancement of law and order so the average Haitian could lead a more normal life. Completing the transition to real democratic functioning in Haiti would be the mission of UNMIH, but the most fundamental—and most important— improvements had been established as planned by the dedicated men and women of Uphold Democracy: Theirs were significant achievements accomplished under difficult conditions. President Clinton met them at Warrior Base outside Port-au-Prince and summed up their achievements in a few simple words:

Today, because of you, the Haitian people know why we call the United States "land of the free and home of the brave." You have allowed freedom to triumph over fear here. You have helped to remind the world that democracy is still on the march, even though it still has enemies. And you have stood up for a principle upon which our country was found- ed, that liberty is everyone's birthright. Thank you, each and every one of you, and God bless America.[9]

ACTIONS UNDER THE UNITED NATIONS

Operation Uphold Democracy effectively ended with the transition of control to the United Nations and UNMIH, but the story of democracy's return to Haiti is incomplete without an understanding of the actions implemented under U.N. control leading up to the Haitian presidential election of December 17, 1995.[10] It was this election that was the true endstate goal of the campaign in Haiti. The great lesson of the first U.S. intervention (1915) was the requirement to foster democratic foundations so that the country could continue to develop and pros- per on its own once the military forces departed. Therefore from an American point of view fostering democratic stability became the essential mission of UNMIH and its best test of success. As follow-on reinforcements of the impor- tant actions of Uphold Democracy, the efforts to improve the security apparatus and recover the basis of Haitian politics and economic viability rightfully remained the priority of operations in 1995.

Early April witnessed a variety of transition concerns that could have endan- gered the success of UNMIH's mission at its inception. The redeployment to their home nations of MNF forces from all over Haiti had to be managed so that power and security vacuums were not created to give rise to antigovernment or criminal activity. With the new Haitian security force not fully fielded, the redeployment-induced reduction in military strength in the countryside could have created a lapse in public confidence or indeed a resurgence in antigovernment activities. The WBB Program, then in its fifth phase, also transitioned to U.N. control at the same time. Continuing this effort to rid the nation of illegal weapons remained critical if Haiti was to maintain momentum in the effort to develop a viable national-security environment. Various hostile factions within the country still required continual monitoring so as to alert MNF forces against any attack on Aristide or his key supporters. This monitoring effort was also needed to transition smoothly to U.N. and UNMIH control. The danger during any transitional phase is that reductions in emphasis and slight changes in technique can allow even very successful programs to diminish in effectiveness. The United States learned during the transition to U.N. control of its forces deployed in Somalia that even small changes in approach could produce costly consequences when formerly cooperative Mohammed Farah Aideed became an opponent and eventual target of the U.N. mission. No one doubted that similar problems could have resulted in Haiti.

Concurrent with all these efforts to restore security and stability, the United States continued to reduce its overall military presence in the country and hand-off active involvement in Haitian affairs to other national and nongovernmental bodies. Throughout April, final plans for the phased departure of U.S.-controlled forces had progressed, and on April 24th, USACOM directed the creation of the U.S. Support Group Haiti (USSPTGPHAITI). This organization was designed as the military-caretaker command for American forces as the transition made the United States a minority partner in the international force. The USSPTGPHAITI became effective on the last day of April and assumed responsibility for operational control of all non-UNMIH U.S. forces in Haiti. The next day, JTF-190 was inactivated with the arrival of USSPTGPHAITI advance elements in the country.[11]

During this time of transition other elements of stability in Haiti also remained precarious. Perhaps most threatening to mission success, the Aristide government itself remained suspect in light of the country's tradition of political revenge by plotting to destroy its opponents.[12] Some people feared that key members of the Aristide government were willing to use illegal or disreputable methods to ensure full implementation of Aristide's major initiatives. Furthermore, the economic support of other nations still lagged behind expectations, which resulted in fewer measurable improvements in the livelihood of the average Haitian. Judicial reform also had proven to take more time than anticipated, as judges and local administrators had to be trained and procedures redesigned before major efforts could start to reduce the backlog of court cases that stretched back for years.

In this hazy environment of uncertainty UNMIH forces had to step in and continue to tread the very fine line of impartiality required by peace operations, while staying focused on the continued development of the long-term stability of the elected government. When General Kinzer originally analyzed this task he came to the immediate conclusion that he could not command UNMIH under the mandate originally designed for it by the United Nations. Envisioned initially as a Chapter 6 peace operation, without the ROE that permitted the MNF to stop Haitian-on-Haitian violence, UNMIH would have been limited to the tasks of observing and reporting on events in Haiti. General Kinzer realized that such powers were too limited for him to maintain order and despite the objections of some, he was finally authorized to intervene as required. This put UNMIH's mandate in-between those traditionally granted to Chapter 6 and Chapter 7 operations.[13]

With his authorities appropriately strengthened, General Kinzer and his force focused immediately on maintaining the momentum of reform in Haiti. The first significant stepping-stone was near: more elections. Elections were an important UNMIH opportunity because the successful completion of presidential elections was the acknowledged endstate goal of UNMIH, and because the exercise of conducting local elections provided a valuable opportunity for learning and training prior to the national-level event. In addition, the successful completion of local elections could provide the best indicator of Haitian support of the national government and Aristide's programs. It was anticipated that their outcomes would show mass support for the President's Lavalas support group, reinforcing Aristide's position almost as much as a presidential election would have. Finally, the local elections could serve as an excellent vehicle for teaching the fundamental concepts of democracy that had been frequently ignored in the years since Papa Doc Duvalier took control.

Due to their importance and the need to minimize any chance of irregularity, on April 10th Haiti's CEP delayed the elections for three weeks, from June 4th to June 25th, and the runoffs from June 25th to July 16th. In part, the decision was also the result of President Aristide's meeting with leaders of 26 political parties, who determined that the extra time would allow more candidates to file for office and more voters to register.[14] By May 17th the CEP was able to publish a list of candidates authorized to campaign for the June 25 elections, which included 133 for the Senate, 650 for the Chamber of Deputies, and 650 for local elections. Clearly, the elections would mark a significant turnover in government positions at all levels and could help set the stage for the establishment of effective democracy in Haiti.

Although it was not normally a military task, UNMIH military forces did have something to contribute to this important electoral process. On June 11th SECDEF Perry approved sending a UH-1 helicopter detachment to Haiti to support U.S. operations associated with Haitian elections. Three days later, after receiving a formal request from the U.N. Secretary-General via the Department of State, the SECDEF also approved the airlift of 215,000 pounds of printed Haitian election ballots from Travis Air Force Base in California to Port-au-Prince. The election effort had garnered such military attention that General Shalikashvili visited troops in Haiti for briefings on the election preparations. Following the Chairman's visit, USACOM provided a C-130 airlift to move election materials from Port-au-Prince to Cap-Haitien. On June 20th the CEP began distributing ballots to 10,031 polling stations throughout Haiti for the 3.5 million registered voters, while SECDEF Perry approved an additional airlift of 30,000 pounds of printed election ballots from Travis Air Force Base to the Haitian capital. The same day, General Kinzer publicly reported that UNMIH forces were ready to support the Haitian government in the upcoming elections—a statement that revealed as much about security roles required during the election as it did about the psychological support offered to democratic institutions.

As promised, on Sunday the 25th of June UNMIH forces provided logistics support and security for Haiti's first round of national elections. In the end, more than 50 percent of the population had registered to vote for some 10,000 candidates for office, which was a significant demonstration of the people's faith in the democratic process. Unfortunately, immediately following the elections Aristide's political rivals accused his Lavalas party of voting fraud and irregularities, even noting the involvement of the United Nations. The lack of planning and training for election personnel was cited as the primary cause of electoral problems and much of the blame fell on the CEP. Voting continued through Monday to accommodate voting bureaus that did not open or were open for only a short time during the previous day. And on July 5th the CEP postponed the runoff elections from the 23rd of July to August 13th after many of the political parties had protested the irregularities of the first round of voting.

Overall, the voting process was certainly flawed but had met the most important objectives set for it; an orderly process for change of government leaders had been conducted. Election irregularities had become almost commonplace in Haiti and protests were bound to occur even if there was in fact little evidence of wrongdoing. As with so many nations in the lesser-developed areas of the world, elections presented significant problems to Haitians. One fundamental problem was illiteracy. Ballots had to be color-coded because the vast majority of registered voters could not read the names on the ballots. This presented challenges to confidentiality as well, which in turn exposed the election process to charges of undue influence by the government in power. To further magnify the scope of the election task, poor transportation made access to polling more difficult and insufficient experience among election administrators at all levels complicated efficiency. Moreover, the sheer magnitude of distributing the election materials throughout the entire country and the large number of positions and candidates on the ballot made this first national election much more difficult than any comparable process in more experienced nations.

Despite the charges of wrongdoing and inefficiency, the election provided one inestimable contribution. Just as important as the choice of new members of government at all levels was the creation of a new administration committed to completing the reforms, and the return of active civil participation in democracy and renewed support for the democratic process was an advantage that impressed each and every voter. As with the long-term improvement in the Haitian economy, any real renaissance in democratic participation would clearly require additional time: Only time could bring about true healing to a democratic freedom requiring trust and free exchange among Haitians in all walks of life. But even this first election in June demonstrated that the country was well on its way towards democratic health.

Another key effort in returning popular support and internal security was the continued training of the new Haitian security force. On May 15th the U.S. National Security Council in Washington had approved the choice of Fort Leonard Wood, Missouri, as the site of the national police training for Haitians within the United States. The graduates of this program would be the first to assume full duties as members of the new Haitian National Police Force, which would replace the IPSF then on duty in Haiti's streets. The Fort Leonard Wood site increased markedly the number of trainees and the quality of the training provided to the new Haitian police force. It also eased the logistical burden on UNMIH in Haiti by moving people to the site instead of creating and maintaining the training school in Haiti. The first class of this U.S. Department of Justice International Criminal Investigative Training Assistance Program (ICI-TAP) training program, which included 375 Haitian National Police cadets, began on June 28th.

Even as the availability of security training greatly improved, indicators of the present security situation in Haiti remained unimpressive in relation to the high hopes of many in the United Nations. On June 22nd the U.N. Civilian Mission in Haiti issued its Human Rights Report for May, 1995, which listed a number of issues and specific concerns over the upcoming elections, crime statistics, and the lethargy of Haitian legal proceedings. As just one example of the small but menacing number of politically linked crimes in Haiti, on June 27th the former Haitian army Colonel Dumarsais Romulus was shot near his home by unidentified gunmen in Port-au-Prince. It was all too convenient to classify such cases under a general heading of attempted robbery or revenge killings; the most troubling aspect of such crimes was the suspicion that the Aristide government might be linked to or even supportive of such attacks on former members of the elite under the Cedras regime.

As work progressed on internal improvements, the flow of migrants from its shores toward the United States also continued, albeit at a much reduced rate, and efforts to control and react to these dangerous attempts still took up much time and many resources. Haitians continued to flee poverty and uncertainty in small boats; on April 16th the U.S. Coast Guard apprehended 115 people packed aboard a small motor vessel off Miami Beach. Haiti still rejected any plans of renegotiating an Alien Migrant Interdiction Operation (AMIO) agreement with the United States, which would have allowed the rescue and direct repatriation of Haitian migrants at sea. On May 3rd the U.S. Coast Guard cutter *Northland* had repatriated 27 Haitian migrants, including 14 unaccompanied minors, to

Port-au-Prince without incident. Three days later the cutter *Forward* repatriated another 21 unaccompanied minors to the Haitian capital. The flow of migrants out of the country had not ceased. On June 27th the cutter *Vigorous* rescued 41 Haitian migrants 25 miles northwest of Haiti's northern claw and returned them to Port-au-Prince. As of the end of that month, the Coast Guard had repatriated 75,523 Haitian migrants since the beginning of the AMIO program.

As these incidents show, although security concerns had decreased significantly since the arrival of the MNF in the previous September, they in no way had disappeared. While the Haitian police were still being trained and reformed, normal police functions had to be shared by UNMIH. On April 13th prisoners at Haiti's National Penitentiary had rioted over their treatment under the inefficient judicial system. While quelling this riot, UNMIH forces wounded two prisoners. Four days later in Cap-Haitien a gang fight left ten people wounded after being brought under control by UNMIH forces and local police. On April 25th eleven prisoners, including a security guard who had been arrested for killing two U.S. embassy employees, escaped from a Port-au-Prince police station. Early in May students in the capital began protesting in support of teachers' raises; UNMIH forces restored order over a period of 3 days, and, as a consequence, President Aristide announced a 100 percent pay raise for the teachers. On May 22nd a 61-year-old Haitian businessman, Michel Gonzales, was killed by unknown gunmen very near to President Aristide's home in Tabarre. Part of the solution to these criminal acts had to wait for the arrival of the new, better-trained members of the Haitian Police Force, but the United States also deployed a number of civil-affairs officers under the control of Major General (Judge) Donald F. Campbell, U.S. Army Reserve, who focused on improving the efficiency of Haiti's legal processes. For months, legal advisors continued to assist and train lower-level members of the Haitian judiciary, penal system, and courts.

On June 4th President Aristide and U.S. Secretary of State Warren Christopher addressed the first 357 graduates of the Haitian National Police training program and announced that the number of cadets would nearly double, rising to 600 by February, 1996. The following week, due to a misunderstanding in the IPSF chain of command, some IPSF personnel left their posts in the northern department under the mistaken belief that they were being replaced summarily by the Haitian National Police. In Port-au-Prince, the transfer from IPSF to HNP went more smoothly. This at least was demonstrable progress in an area that many believed would take years to achieve: the institution of a new national police force within 8 months of Aristide's return.

At mid-month, USACOM issued a deployment order for engineering assets to conduct "Fairwinds" operations in Haiti in support of both infrastructure improvements and humanitarian civic-assistance projects. This was another effort to target long-term projects supporting a Haitian return to prosperity after the embargo, but it was also linked with an actual training benefit to the military engineer units involved, similar to other security-assistance efforts conducted worldwide by the United States. "Fairwinds" was another innovation: clearly contributing to the renewal of the Haitian economy, the exercise also provided another controlled venue for the United States to make legal military contributions towards the rebuilding of the country. Additionally, the exercise rotated servicemembers through Haiti on a manageable scale, providing them with solid skill-training in exchange for their engineering contributions. Of course, these men and women in uniform also enhanced the security environment merely by their presence in Haiti.

In Norfolk, at the USACOM theater staff level, Haiti remained only one of several crises requiring attention during the summer of 1995. The Cuban-migrant problem was rising in importance during the early spring in anticipation of riots, which threatened to occur in the crowded camps during the hot summer months. General Sheehan pushed for early action, and thorough coordination with other agencies of the government, critical to the solution in Guantanamo Bay. On May 9th USACOM had hosted a Cuban Interagency Working Group in Guantanamo Bay to discuss draw-down plans and Cuban-migrant policy with key officials in all other affected government agencies. This was another in the series of highly effective interagency coordination meetings pioneered by USACOM in its efforts to ensure that all aspects of Caribbean operations were properly linked and mutually supporting for a coherent theater policy. This was one area where clear progress had been made, largely due to the support produced for Uphold Democracy.

Another signal event in the return of Haiti to the international community was the hosting in Port-au-Prince of a meeting of the OAS General Assembly, scheduled for June 5th. Planning for the meeting intensified during the first days of June in Port-au-Prince to ensure that the meeting opened on time, even under tight security. On June 8th the host nation benefited significantly from its efforts as the OAS General Assembly passed Resolution 824, granting Haiti $500,000 for judicial and administrative reforms. Haiti looked forward to rebuilding its tourism industry from the security foundation these reforms would create. The former pariah nation could finally point to normal cooperative relations with its neighbors and to increased optimism for economic growth.

The following week, the United Nations voted to extend its human-rights monitoring mission in Haiti until February, 1996, linking the monitoring function to the duration of the UNMIH mission. July 28th saw the military and security forces in Haiti placed in a high state of readiness by the Haitian government and the UNMIH commander, in anticipation of the 80th anniversary of the 1915 U.S. occupation. Fortunately, no major demonstrations were reported. Since the situation in Haiti still contained the potential for violence, each possible occasion for demonstrations was countered by security precautions, but fewer and fewer of these occasions occurred.

On August 12th Prime Minister Michel appointed four new cabinet ministers to oversee the new developments in Haitian society since the stabilization wrought by the MNF. These new offices included ministries of administration and public service, social affairs, environment, and commerce and industry. More than just tokens that the government had been reorganized since the departure of Cedras, these new ministries demonstrated Haiti's commitment to sectors of society long trampled over in favor of raw power and profit. Thanks to the work of the ministerial advisory teams, these new organizations even had the advantage of some basic operating procedures and policies, raising hope that in time they could make a real difference in Haiti.

At the end of the twelfth month following the arrival of the MNF, the cost of U.S. involvement in Haiti since the invasion began was estimated at $596 million. The value of that commitment was justified by the results of the second round of national elections, scheduled at the same time. Run-off election support, including 68 national races in the Chamber of Deputies and the Senate, was provided by UNMIH beginning on September 17th. This time the process was deemed violence free and well organized, although voter turnout was very low (less than 10 percent). Results again supported Aristide's Lavalas group, which won forty-two of forty-six congressional seats and all four senate seats. The decrease in voter participation could have been due to several factors, including the fact that the majority of running candidates had already been successfully seated and that this election only finalized a limited number of contested seats. Equally important to remember was the normal decrease in voting levels that frequently accompanies subsequent elections in a nation undergoing rapid change; complacency seems to result from economic and social progress.

Small crowds demonstrated in Port-au-Prince against the privatization of certain large corporations in the interest of economic growth on the anniversary of the MNF invasion, September 19th. Three days later, key members of the Clinton Administration, including National Security Advisor Anthony Lake and the USACOM Director of Plans, Major General John Sams, USAF, visited President Aristide to assess progress since the invasion and discuss plans for the future. Overall, much had been accomplished, but much remained to be done as well. On September 28th President Aristide declared a 2-week period of national mourning to commemorate the coup against him, which had occurred on September 29th, 4 years earlier, and his restoration on October 15th of the year before. It was clear from these events that Haiti had changed a great deal since the coup of 1991.

Then, in what many viewed as a setback to Haiti's continued political progress, Prime Minister Michel resigned on October 11th after the Haitian cabinet rejected the privatization provisions required by the World Bank and the International Monetary Fund for increased monetary support. Privatization had become a politically sensitive issue—one that would take many months to solve. As late as November 8th even the Clinton Administration announced it was withholding $4.6 million in aid pending reform of the economy through privatization,[15] but many of the economic elite in Haiti refused to embrace privatization on the grounds that it went too far. Michel had been the ideal transitional prime minister. He was an influential arbiter during the period of Aristide's exile and had served well as a bridge between Aristide's most loyal supporters and those who had kept the government functioning under Cedras. But over time, with growth in Aristide's support and the electoral conversion of most of the government to Lavalas control, Michel had lost many of his unique contributions towards political stability. By October, in reality, it was time for Aristide to designate his own Lavalas prime minister. Haiti's Foreign Minister, Claudette Werliegh, was later named by Aristide on October 23rd to replace Michel.[16]

On October 13, 1995 the CEP announced its plans for the long-awaited December presidential election, and 2 days later U.N. Secretary-General Boutros Boutros-Ghali and U.S. Vice President Al Gore attended ceremonies commemorating the first anniversary of the return of President Aristide to Haiti. Everything appeared to be on track for the election, but plans for any contingency were still required. Concern about the pace of preparations for December elections in relation to the U.N.'s planned withdrawal date from Haiti of February, 1996 soon became an issue. It was clear that there was little margin for error if the presidential elections became delayed or were contested. This placed even more pressure on UNMIH to ensure that preparations, which were largely outside its control, were supported to the maximum possible extent.

The 1st of November became a historic day when the last of the 21,783 Haitian migrants processed at Guantanamo Bay finally returned to Haiti.[17] Over the course of the processing operation fewer than 1,000 Haitians had been admitted to the United States. This meant that over 40,000 transits to or from Guantanamo Bay and locations in Haiti had been accomplished by the U.S. military since the United States began Operation Sea Signal in June, 1994. Although rarely in the forefront of news coverage and unknown to many in the United States, the migrant-processing activity had involved thousands of U.S. civilian and military personnel and had maintained a critical venting capability for the success of operations in Haiti. Just as one of the announced reasons for the intervention had been the threat to U.S. national security posed by the flow of migrants to south Florida, the successful completion of the processing operation was an important step in the resolution of operations in Haiti. Lesser known and in too many cases lesser rewarded, the efforts of the people who made operation Sea Signal a success must rank with all the others who participated in operation Uphold Democracy.

Very late in the process leading up to the national elections, on November 9th President Aristide's cousin, Feuille, was killed in an apparent robbery attempt in Port-au-Prince. Here again, a single crime threatened the progress of Haitian reform because of its history of social division and the prevalence of retribution. Aristide reacted strongly to the attack on his family at a critical time in his administration. His words showed that the level of trust in Haiti had not yet overcome the burden of the past inequities and that he would turn against anyone when threatened. During the same week the CEP announced the presidential election schedule, listing the election itself on December 17th, and setting the inauguration for February 7, 1996. Aristide's tirade was too close to the election and too explosive—it nearly stalled the process of reform.

His speech at the November 11th funeral of his cousin led to several days of riots. In it, Aristide accused UNMIH of providing insufficient security in the country, virtually blaming the U.N. force for the death of his cousin. By that time, both the United States and United Nations were solidly committed to the established date for the withdrawal of UNMIH. Both entities conducted discussions for transition planning with the government of Haiti despite the furor caused by Aristide's remarks. The following week, the CEP officially opened the Haitian presidential campaign by accepting all fourteen registered candidates. No country envisioned turning its back on Haiti after UNMIH's departure. The United States in particular understood that the first months of the new president's administration would be plagued by the difficulties that accompany any national change of government. Therefore plans for a continued U.S. security presence were firmed up even as the withdrawal of UNMIH was the top agenda item on most lists. The USACOM-sponsored exercise "Fairwinds," the public vehicle for engineer and humanitarian assistance to Haiti by the United States, continued also.

The real menace during the final month preceding the election came from Aristide himself. Always mercurial and independent, he mentioned publicly the possibility of his staying on for 3 more years, largely because he had been deprived of his full elected term of office by the coup. The idea was popular among many Aristide and Lavalas supporters; in fact, he remained the preferred popular candidate during the electoral process until he named the successor-candidate of his choice. Aristide understood the political sensitivity of his possible term-extension. Most observers believed he mentioned the idea in order to retain control of the process and remind everyone of his own popularity, thus giving his choice of successor a tremendous boost in the polls. Later, Aristide announced that he would indeed leave on schedule.

During the last days of November Aristide introduced a flurry of actions designed to leave his stamp on several of the dominant institutions in Haitian society. First, he again protested the direct repatriations of Haitian migrants by the United States (the U.S. Coast Guard repatriated 557 Haitians to the capital on November 29th). In doing so he retained to the end of his administration a vocal emphasis on support of the Haitian people in need, regardless of the choices they made. Second, he announced his plans to marry.[18] The Catholic Church and Aristide had long been at odds, but since he had been ejected from his order and defrocked, he certainly had the right to marry. The symbolism of Father Titide taking a new wife when giving up his official duties was not lost on the Haitian people. He also fired his Police Director, General Rameau, and replaced him with Lieutenant Colonel Jean-Marie Celestin, the head of his own presidential security force.[19] Finally, Aristide also ordered the demobilization of thirty-seven naval personnel to phase-out the Haitian Navy and form a Haitian Coast Guard. This was done in much the same way as the FAd'H had been demobilized and converted to a civilian-controlled national-security force. To complete the picture of a revamped Haitian security apparatus, the

IPSF was demobilized on December 6th and officially integrated into the new Haitian National Police by Aristide.

On December 8th presidential candidate René Préval, already known as a front runner in the presidential race, indicated that he would ask the United Natons to stay on in Haiti after its specified mandate had expired "in the interests of the Haitian people." Finally, on December 15th Aristide nipped speculation completely and endorsed his former best ally, Préval, as his choice for the next president of Haiti. This action not only cemented Lavalas support for Préval, but also swung many uncommitted votes of those awaiting Aristide's last-minute decision to run. It was clear to most that Préval would be very hard to beat after receiving Aristide's endorsement, though most also conceded that Préval had the background and temperament needed to function effectively as Aristide's successor.

The long-awaited presidential elections were held on December 17th; there was only a small turnout, but also there were few disturbances. Préval had been expected to win, and the expectation was fulfilled. Of the 25–30 percent of the registered Haitians who voted, 80 percent lent their support to Préval. During the following week, on December 23rd, the CEP officially announced Préval as next president of Haiti. Officially, he had received a total of 87.9 percent of the vote, with only 27.9 percent of Haiti's 3.7 million registered voters participating. Although the turnout was less than expected, Préval's popularity was clear. Most understood that the small turnout was the result of his clear advantage over his opponents and the likelihood that the Lavalas candidate would win. However, it was also a disturbing sign that so many Haitians seemed to take their democratic responsibilities less seriously as conditions in the country improved.

Préval lost no time in acting on his victory. On the 26th of December he met with President Clinton's National Security Advisor, Anthony Lake, and with General Shalikashvili to formally discuss extension of the U.N.'s mandate with as the policymakers of UNMIH's largest contingent. There was little doubt that some continued military presence was desirable. The only questions were the size and composition of the force and its relationship to the government in Port-au-Prince.

As promised, Préval officially requested an extension of the U.N.'s mandate for 6 months after its scheduled February departure. On January 10th the United Nations and the government of Haiti agreed to the retention of a small force of 1,000 to 1,500 civilian and military personnel in Haiti after the February departure date. Three weeks later the United Nations announced that Canada had agreed to lead the military force in Haiti following UNMIH's scheduled withdrawal. The U.S. redeployments began on January 5, 1996, but 2,200 U.S. military members remained in Haiti after UNMIH had transitioned to Canadian leadership at the end of February, 1996. The USACOM redeployment order initially set a April 15th target date for the return of all U.S. forces. Fittingly, on February 6th the Haitian Senate voted to officially abolish the crippled post-FAd'H Border Patrol, thereby ridding Haiti of the last traces of its traditional source of state-sponsored authoritarianism. On the following day, René Préval was inaugurated in the first democratic transition between two presidents elected by universal suffrage since 1804. Madeleine Albright, Ambassador Bill Swing, and General Sheehan were in attendance to watch the ultimate goal of Uphold Democracy take place.

Just after the inauguration U.N. Secretary-General Boutros-Ghali recommended that some 2,500 U.N. personnel be extended in Haiti for 6 months in support of President Préval's request. The U.S. support group of approximately 300 personnel was immediately extended until April. On February 29th the U.N. Security Council approved a 4-month extension of the U.N. mission, and on March 1st Brigadier General J. R. P. Daigle of Canada assumed command of UNMIH from General Kinzer, who returned to the United States. The UNMIH continued its mission under Canadian control and with important U.S. support until the end of the 4-month extension. In June, 1996 another U.N. effort, known as the U.N. Support Mission in Haiti (UNSMIH), was recommended to provide assistance to Haiti as it continued through the process of internal reform.

The UNMIH was the intended successor to the multinational force that returned democracy to Haiti. As such it provided international technical and logistical support to the election effort, assisted in the training of the Haitian National Police, and helped restore the infrastructure that was vital to the economic requirements of the new Haiti. Just as the MNF met all objectives assigned to it, UNMIH completed its tasks in superb fashion prior to its planned mission-end date. Although U.N. efforts continued in Haiti on into 1998, there is no doubt that the application of multinational and U.N. military and civilian support accomplished the tasks assigned. The effects of the anti-Aristide coup of 1991 were corrected, and Haiti was returned to the path of democratic advancement.

FINAL U. S. ACTIVITIES IN HAITI UNDER THE UNITED NATIONS

The last active-duty commander of USSPTGPHAITI, Colonel Jon Stull, USMC, arrived in Port-au-Prince on the 1st of October, 1996. His mission was to continue conducting civil–military operations in the Republic of Haiti and exercise command and control over all U.S. forces as they executed humanitarian civic-assistance, security operations, and contingency exercises (exercise "Fairwinds" was still in progress). During his tour of duty he directed the activities of a joint staff of approximately 580 uniformed personnel still under General Sheehan's overall authority. His U.N. counterpart was General Pierre Daigle when he arrived, but the U.N. commander changed over time and later became another Canadian, General Gagnon. Stull's staff was separate from that of the United Nations, although his headquarters was located adjacent to the U.N. compound; as had previous U.S. commanders, Stull worked closely with the U.N. mission in all of his efforts. He also remained a key member of Ambassador Swing's "country team" in the Haitian capital.

When Stull arrived in Haiti, like all others new to the country, he was struck by the poverty and deprivation visible at every turn.[20] Garbage was piled up to a height of ten feet in many areas and human waste ran commonly in the same streets where children played. The Haitian National Police (HNP) were rarely in sight, even at traffic intersections. Over the period of his year-long stay, this situation changed visibly. The garbage was cleaned up in some areas and slowly, almost imperceptibly, the HNP presence improved. First, some police actually assumed positions at busy intersections; later, they began to appear in uniform. By the end of the year the HNP openly wore side-arms and their uniforms improved in appearance. The question remained—did these HNPs ever actually catch any criminals and were the guilty ever incarcerated?

For their part, the HNPs still faced a difficult conundrum: they had been trained in the methods of regular police and did not resort to the type of brutality that was so prevalent during the years of the FAd'H. Unfortunately, because the bulk of the population had known no other "security" experience other than the nightsticks of the former Haitian Army, the "professionalized" HNP appeared weak and dubious at best. For a member of the HNP to prosecute a criminal at any length was to incur risk, with little assurance of help and no real reward. Even job self-satisfaction was difficult to cultivate when the Haitian government was constantly at odds over the role of the police. The average HNP's best interests lay in the direction of looking good, doing only what was required, and trying to stay sufficiently neutral so that he could easily shift to whatever side might eventually win out in the future Haiti. Few HNPs stood up to big crime or confronted the violations of important people: too much fear and not enough trust existed to significantly change the old ways of Haiti. No one was willing to bet fully on the Préval agenda.

Colonel Stull remained engaged in a wide range of local activities as well. Inspections of HNP precinct offices showed that logbooks, once rare, had begun to be kept so that prisoners could at least be accounted for. In one trip to Hinche, the jail in the old barracks constructed for Marines in the 1920s was the only large government building still in good repair. Unfortunately, it was discovered in that inspection visit that, as occurred all too often, no lengths of prisoners' sentences were included in the logs that *were* kept.[21] Few knew how long someone placed behind bars had been there or when they were to be released. The records of the local court were as spotty as those of the jail or even more so. Still, the required effort was clear. Judicial-system reform remains one of the three critical areas where improvements shall ensure a better future for Haiti. The work of ICITAP and the MATs was very beneficial, but continued improvement is essential in law enforcement, including additional vehicles, and improved procedures for the judiciary and the penal system.

President Préval had reached an impasse during Stull's assignment: he had no effective government with which to continue a long-term campaign of improvements. The Lavalas support of Aristide's term was no more, split into two factions that fought among themselves over all the important issues. As Préval had called for an extension to the U.N. presence, his own legislature passed instead a measure designed to end the foreign presence in the country. The results of that bill remain uncertain. The majority of the USSPTGPHAITI staff will probably leave during 1998, in the tracks of the United Nations. Some coordination cell for continued "Fairwinds" activities, later renamed "New Horizon—Haiti," will most certainly remain, but its capability will likely shrink.

The population in Port-au-Prince still demonstrated a wait-and-see attitude during 1997. The rest of the country was too focused on the basics of everyday life to debate the "big issues," most of which involved improvements in the capital anyway. The average Haitian had probably lost faith in any real progress being made until economic improvements are accomplished. President Préval sincerely wanted to pursue reform and complete the programs of importance to the country, but he was not a rousing speaker nor a committed liberal and deep inside may even have harbored the realization that he was simply holding the presidency until his good friend Aristide could return in the year 2000. He appeared to be very frustrated—yet he must endure until that year.

Préval's agenda still includes economic improvement, the second of the pillars supporting the country, but his efforts have borne little fruit. There is little sense of economic "opportunity" in Haiti. Two-thirds of the budget still comes from foreign aid. As many often quipped, Haiti is "millimetering along." United States support has accomplished much; twelve kilometers of road paved, seventeen wells drilled, and over thirty schools built or significantly improved seems meager until one understands that such figures represent a significant percentage of all that is available in Haiti. More clearly evident is the benefit of having over 40,000 Haitians seen for medical treatment by the U.S. military. All of this was accomplished in a single year.

The United States did well to "intervene with delicacy" in Haiti. Although some Haitians felt that not enough was done by the autumn of 1997, it was clearly time to withdraw. The allusions to another occupation were occurring too frequently. The United States and United Nations demonstrated that they were willing and able to provide humanitarian assistance. Average Haitians in the streets observed the professionalism of the U.S. military. They were struck by its compassion when it intervened to help after the terrible ferry accident of September, 1997, just as it had after the storm of 1995. ICITAP remains—so do the many nongovernmental and private volunteer agencies that have always done so much for Haiti.

Yes, there was more stability. Crime rates had been reduced, to lower levels in fact that several U.S. cities. Education, President Aristide's great focus, had perhaps made the greatest strides and has become "the strength of Haiti." The improvements were most noticeable in Port-au-Prince, but were slowly spreading to other locations in the country. Significantly, the number of Haitians leaving in small boats for futures elsewhere had been reduced to a mere 30 per year: Haitian democracy was not very responsive, but the people now could sleep safely at night. As long as change remained possible they would stay at home. Haiti was still "the busiest poor place on earth."[22] The Haitian people were constantly working—if they could only begin to move the huge crushing weight of their own history.

NOTES

1. The largest subcomponent of the joint task force transitioned upon the departure of the 25th Division to the 2nd Armored Cavalry Regiment, from Fort Polk, Louisiana, commanded by Colonel Walter Sharpe, USA.

2. It is interesting to note that General Kinzer was the first U.S. officer to hold both U.N. and U.S. senior commands in a nation since General MacArthur during the Korean War. As commander of U.S. forces in Haiti, General Kinzer was also General Hill's supervisor during the period that Hill commanded JTF-190.

3. The U.S. Congress had only recently passed a law requiring that American troops not be placed under foreign command.

4. Robert B. Killebrew and David H. Petraeus, "Winning the Peace: Haiti, the U.S., and the U.N.," pp. 40–41.

5. William Neale, interview with Major General Joesph Kinzer, USA, December 4, 1995.

6. Essentially, even the most credible improvements in this society still required funding. Someone had to pay the new security forces and the judges and administrators who would maintain security. Roads and other infrastructure improvements required money. The embargo had decimated the Haitian economy, and very little capital could be generated from internal sources.

7. J. Burton Thompson interview with Major General George A. Fisher, USA, May 8, 1995, p. 4.

8. This lesson that nation building could bring with it much greater long-term negative effects than anticipated was more a result of the weaknesses in U.S. efforts in Somalia during operation Provide Relief and even in Panama after operation Just Cause than from Haiti in the 1920s, but the point was very much the same. Reform can only rarely take root in an effective manner when it is instituted from afar.

9. *Public Papers of the Presidents of the United States: William J. Clinton, 1995, Book I—January to June 30, 1995,* p. 436. The full text of the White House press release is included in Appendix G.

10. For consistency, U.S. actions in Haiti retained the name Uphold Democracy even after the change to U.N. control.

11. On May 11th the United States and the government of Haiti approved a Status of Forces Agreement (SOFA) for non-UNMIH U.S. forces remaining in Haiti, which ensured the legal responsibilities of both nations for any military activities outside of UNMIH.

12. On April 6th the Pentagon warned the American embassy that over two-dozen political opponents of President Aristide were on a "hit list"—marked for assassination.

13. William Neale interview with Major General Joseph Kinzer, USA, December 4, 1995.

14. Later, General Kinzer reported that over 1.1 million, or 67 percent, of Haiti's eligible voters had registered for the elections. Any election of such a size would be demanding; in Haiti, where the democratic process had been fractured over time, it was an even more daunting task.

15. Even so, the U.S. government did release $1.3 million to pay for the national elections held in December. Economic support came more conditionally than aid, even though it would assist UNMIH in completing its mission.

16. Werliegh formed her new cabinet on November 6th and was soon sworn in by Aristide as the first female prime minister in Haitian history.

17. See USACOM's *Migrant Camp Operations*.

18. Aristide married his legal advisor, Mildred Trouillot, on January 20, 1996 with General Sheehan and Anthony Lake in attendance.

19. This action required legislative approval and was indeed rejected in due course by the Haitian Senate.

20. John R. Ballard interview with Colonel Jon Stull, USMC, Norfolk, VA, November 19, 1997.

21. Ibid.

22. Ibid.

PART IV

INNOVATION AND PROGRESS

Operation Uphold Democracy has set a new standard for the degree of peace and civic order that has been kept in a peacekeeping operation. From the moment the armed services began planning, they demonstrated an extraordinary capacity to adapt and change, to identify and understand the problems, and to solve them effectively. When Haitian military dictators agreed to step down, within minutes we were able to recall our assault forces and within hours they had shifted to a deployment posture suitable for intervention in a permissive environment. In the months that have passed, our military's accomplishments—which have ranged from quelling initial outbreaks of Haitian-on-Haitian violence to disarming the paramilitary gangs to, literally, turning the lights back on in Haitian cities—have been truly outstanding.[1]

Deputy Secretary of State Strobe Talbot
March 9, 1995

Uphold Democracy was only one of several operations conducted by the United States during the 1990s. Operations Desert Storm and Provide Comfort in Iraq, Eastern Exit and Provide Hope in Somalia, Sea Angel in Bangladesh, and Deny Flight and Joint Endeavor in Bosnia-Herzegovina all contributed improvements in the tactics, techniques, and procedures of the U.S. Armed Forces. However, none of these operations accomplished their objectives with greater success or with more innovation than did Uphold Democracy.

Although the Haitian experience owed much to its particular circumstances of being near the continental United States and of being rather short in duration, its achievements merit close study for possible incorporation into future events of its kind. In particular, the flexible planning, command-and-control agility, joint interoperability, media relations, management of transitions, theater strategic-coordination, effective joint training, and interagency coordination were noteworthy in their success. Conditions always change from one military operation to another, but these demonstrated accomplishments are sufficiently central to the new way in which the United States carries out the military component of its national power in the post-Cold War period that they should be studied for future use in other crises.

NOTE

1. Strobe Talbot, "Promoting Democracy and Economic Growth in Haiti," pp. 185–186.

CHAPTER 10

The Distinctions of Uphold Democracy

Operation Uphold Democracy demonstrated several aspects of the considerable progress that has been made by the United States in joint warfighting during the 1990s. Interoperability of multiservice forces reached a new plateau during the operation, and the successful transition from the huge, Cold War military force to the downsized and optimized joint force packages of today was proven in crisis. The campaign that returned President Aristide to power was not the type of operation that U.S. military forces had anticipated during the 1980s: it was much less focused on combat, and much more dependent upon the interagency cooperation of all agents of the U.S. government. The operation's development was overly isolated due to its political sensitivity, and its execution was marked by tremendous last-minute changes in force structure and rules of engagement (ROE). Uphold Democracy's success despite these difficulties was proof of concept to reorient future military planning. Lessons from Uphold Democracy contributed directly to making operation Joint Endeavor in the former Yugoslavia more effective and secure and should also aid other operations in the future.

Uphold Democracy confirmed that a new security paradigm now dominates the world, bringing with it a new set of challenges to military and political leaders. In many ways, the operation also showed the great strides made in U.S. military training and organization over the past 25 years. The features of Uphold Democracy deserve review so that their value and future implications can be more fully recognized.

FLEXIBLE PLANNING

Uphold Democracy was unique because it was developed using two separate but parallel plans, respectively numbered 2370 and 2380. Planning for

2370, the combat option to return democracy to Haiti, was begun during early November 1993 and was classified Top Secret. Due to the plan's classification and political sensitivity, 2370 lacked detailed coordination with supporting government agencies. Fortunately, OPLAN 2380, the noncombatant insertion of multinational forces under a U.N. mandate, was developed quite differently. Because it was based on Haitian acceptance of a transition force, 2380 was classified at only the Secret level. All U.S. military and civilian interagency planners could work openly on the details of 2380 with their U.N. counterparts, thus ensuring better coordination and unity of effort. This less-restricted development of the 2380 plan clearly facilitated the cooperation that would be crucial to the success of either one, 2380 or 2370.

Simply having two plans to choose from, each with a different emphasis and force mixture, added flexibility during execution. Admiral Miller essentially had a joint task force and a plan for either a hostile or a permissive situation in Haiti. What made Uphold Democracy noteworthy was the effort to fuse the two plans and view them as "bookends" that enclosed a variety of options. This was General Byron's greatest contribution to the operation and a lesson that, given the time required, should be considered for similar operations in the future. Having a "bookends" framework, developing a series of time-phased force-deployment data lists to support multiple employment options, and developing a checklist of execution actions and key decision points prior to the operation gave both Admiral Miller and General Shelton more strategic flexibility, and therefore greater initiative, than any previous commanders of multinational operations.

Inside and supporting this overall strategic agility was a high degree of operational flexibility developed within the JTF-180 staff. When confronted with the probability that President Carter's negotiating team might achieve a degree of success immediately prior to the invasion, Colonel McNeill and Lieutenant Colonel Bonham were able to present General Shelton with additional options within hours because they had developed a series of branch plans and sequels to the main plan. Branch plans gave Shelton the ability to tailor the force already en route to Haiti in order to develop just the right mix of combat power and security in the initial hours of the operation. In the event they were required, sequels had been developed in case the entire mission was ordered to be changed or even scrubbed due to other national priorities.

Planning flexibility has been a goal of the United States since at least the Civil War; it is taught in all high-level military schools and is constantly reinforced in training. Unfortunately, due to time and resource constraints, few commanders have made the effort to build significant flexibility into real operations plans. It was not luck that made the Uphold Democracy force capable of rapidly reorganizing itself once Haiti's leaders accepted President Carter's terms; it was the flexibility bred into the plan at all levels, the deep understanding and confidence that the senior commanders had in the plan, and the professionalism of support staffs spread throughout America that made such significant changes possible.

COMMAND-AND-CONTROL AGILITY DURING EXECUTION

In the end it was a slightly modified 2380 plan that was used by the assault forces to enter Haiti. As the decision to execute the noncombatant plan had been made only hours before the initial entry of forces, the capability of shifting from one plan to another, even after the majority of forces had begun deployment, was one of the significant successes of Uphold Democracy. Flexibility of this kind of extreme nature may never be required again, but its capability of changing the flow of forces in reaction to evolving political circumstances adds so much to operational effectiveness that it should become a recognized part of every operational plan.

This ability to change was a result of three primary factors: effective command structures, very thorough preparation, and the efficient use of the joint operations planning and execution system and its time-phased force-deployment data list. The effectiveness of the command structure was directly attributable to the high degree of team building and focused nature of the rehearsals that preceded the operation. Admiral Miller and his key staff members had met with and discussed the important elements of the operation with all the major force commanders. Exercise Agile Provider 94 and other conferences had developed a strong relationship of trust among the key decisionmakers, principally Admiral Miller, General Sheehan, Admiral Fargo, General Byron, General Shelton, Admiral Johnson, and General Record. Adding to the strength of these relationships were the professional ties forged between Generals Shelton, Meade, and Steele within the XVIII Airborne Corps at Fort Bragg. The shared vision among all these officers spread over critical locations on the 19th of September kept the decisionmaking process ahead of the actions required to change the force-flow: they were able to be proactive and to anticipate rather than be reactive and victimized by events.

Thorough preparation contributed more than the experience gained in exercises and planning conferences prior to the intervention. Preparations included a range of branch plans developed by the JTF-180 staff, which had already identified the essential decisions and support required to accomplish tasks outside the basic framework of the 2370 and 2380 plans. For example, the staff was able to inform General Shelton about how quickly the 10th Mountain Division forces could be substituted for elements of the 82d Airborne Division in the initial assault and what types of equipment reconfigurations would be required. Having done the work prior to the event permitted the staff to remain proactive and thereby concentrate on the secondary effects and implications of the change and not on the change mechanism itself. This is the essence of command-and-control flexibility: the capability to make decisions ahead of event requirements.

This thorough preparation was largely the result of the JOPES/TPFDD process that required the planners to manage all their personnel and logistics requirements in a systematic fashion. The amount of time and effort required to construct TPFDDs for just the 2370 and 2380 plans was large; the added requirement to develop bridging TPFDDs, which would support multiple variations on these two plans, was immense. Thanks to the diligence of people like Emilie Klutz, Joe Truelove, and their associates, seven TPFDDs were eventually built to give General Shelton the flexibility he wanted prior to the assault. This altered the time required to change the force-flow from days to minutes. Although largely unnoticed on September 20th, as command and control is often invisible unless it fails, this powerful capability certainly saved lives and made a direct and lasting contribution to the success of the operation by ensuring that the first impressions made by U.S. forces in Haiti were positive and that their actions were effective.

JOINT INTEROPERABILITY

On September 10th soldiers of the 10th Mountain Division were embarked on board the aircraft carrier USS *Eisenhower* in Norfolk. The Eisenhower was directed to fly off her aircraft and embark the Army forces while a second carrier, the USS *America,* was assigned to transport a joint special operations task force to Haiti. This exchange of carrier aircraft for non-Navy personnel and their supporting equipment was a first for a supercarrier. This adaptation of Army, Navy, and special operations assets to form a joint team based on specific mission needs had been in development for 2 years, coming to fruition at just the right time. Although this utilization of aircraft carriers is cited often as a primary example of interoperability during operation Uphold Democracy, what fails to be realized is that this example was only one among a host of new interoperability techniques that have come to distinguish current operations of U.S. military forces.

The aircraft carrier innovation is really an illustrative case in one sense only: the degree of advanced training and preparation accomplished. Like so many other events that occurred in Haiti, the introduction of Army and special operations assets to a Navy vessel was successful because it had been well researched and rehearsed, well coordinated and well accepted by those who made it work. Army units had operated off of ships before Uphold Democracy and continue to do so today; but to make the sizable arrangement required for the Haiti operation work still took many months of thorough preparation. First, soldiers had to familiarize themselves with the differences between shore-based Army facilities and the type of environment that existed at sea. This included coordination meetings on-board various ships with the ships' crews to determine just what techniques were required and what restrictions would have to be placed on the use of Army equipment to make their cohabitation work. Then the soldiers rehearsed some aspects of the transition at home stations; for example, when the helicopter pilots of the 10th Mountain Division painted a carrier deck on their own airfield to practice maneuvering with limited space. But a host of other coordination efforts were needed at bases and stations throughout the United States.

Once initial coordination and rehearsals were begun, additional details concerning communications requirements, equipment and ammunition storage, and financial-reimbursement agreements were settled so that the movement onto ships would be as rapid and efficient as possible. Once the soldiers were embarked they received additional orientation briefings and tours, so to ensure that they could effectively react to hostile conditions and fulfill all safety requirements on-board the vessels. This still left days of intense training that were required to develop the marshaling, embarkation, and launch techniques needed to quickly project the combat power of the Army units off the carriers during the invasion process. In all these efforts, the teamwork and true cooperation exhibited by the men and women of all the services exceeded anyone's expectations. As General Meade noted, "The success of the operation is certainly an endorsement of jointness . . . and an endorsement for the quality of (the) soldiers and sailors and airmen and Marines and Coast Guard that we have. . . ."[1]

More important, this level of teamwork was demonstrated in many other areas that were just as important to the operation's success but that have received much less publicity. For example, the effort previously cited in preparing the overall plans for the operation included members of every armed service and several non-Department of Defense agencies. All of these people had to give up parochial loyalties to their own organizations in order to develop plans in which all agencies and units had important roles and in which unity of effort was paramount. The staffs of both JTF-180 and JTF-190 included significant percentages of officers and enlisted personnel from all services so that actions in every dimension—air, land, and sea—could be monitored, coordinated, and synchronized. Several units involved in the operation were "joint" in composition, including permanently assigned members from several services.[2] Finally, a number of special-purpose joint boards and cells were created within the Uphold Democracy force to coordinate the actions of units from multiple services. These included, among others, a joint combat search-and-rescue center on-board the USS *Mount Whitney,* a joint movement-control center and joint information bureau located inside the Port-au-Prince International Airport, and joint medical-support organizations in several locations.

The contributions of these organizations and the superb working relationships among the military services in general during the operation were testaments to the efforts of many officials inside the U.S. Congress and the Department of Defense who had labored to bring about this improved interoperability and true spirit of joint cooperation within the military. Traditional competition and even interservice rivalry were suppressed for the overall good of the force. Marines and soldiers commanded subunits of both services; Air Force transports supported everyone equally; air support and air-control capabilities were extended to the entire force; ships transported, fed, resupplied, and even sheltered people from every service and even nondefense agencies. This same spirit extended overall to elements of the multinational force as the operation progressed so that other nations learned the benefits of interservice cooperation. These actions were not new to Uphold Democracy, but during the operation they were expanded into new areas and, perhaps for the first time, were genuinely accepted as the norm for the future.[3]

MEDIA RELATIONS

The coordination of media efforts also demonstrated an important degree of improvement during operations in Haiti. Over the years of Aristide's exile, and particularly in the months immediately preceding the invasion, hundreds of print articles and radio and television segments concerning Haiti were produced.[4] When the operation began, the media relentlessly followed the events of the early days. The American public and the world television audience probably knew more about how Uphold Democracy would unfold than they ever knew about any previous American use of force.[5] The basics of the invasion plans had even been printed in *U.S. News & World Report* and *Time* magazines.[6] This coordination with national and local media by all levels of the federal government resulted in one of the most complete and satisfying media efforts of any recent campaign. Uphold Democracy was executed with a planned media-exposure program that had been designed to let the operation tell its own story.

The plan was developed in mid-July as soon as the elements of 2380 were refined, enabling people outside the military to have access to the planning effort. The brainchild of Lieutenant Colonel Tim Vane, USA, the public-affairs officer on the XVIII Airborne Corps staff, and supported wholeheartedly by the chief public-affairs officer on the USACOM staff, Colonel John "Terry" Tyrrell, USAF, the idea was to educate commanders at all levels about the media and to actually sponsor a proactive media-coordination effort supporting access by the media to all facets of the campaign. Thus, the military changed its approach to the media from one of distrustful or begrudging acceptance to one of active support.

On September 8th, with General Shelton's concurrence, Lieutenant Colonel Vane briefed the key commanders on "Fighting the Information War."[7] This briefing was designed to increase the commanders' understanding of the number of journalists to be expected and their technical sophistication. It also sought to provide clues that would enable commanders to let the facts tell their units' story in Haiti. Efforts like this helped to change attitudes and eventually make the press a valuable part of the overall effort. Still, even more was required if the complexity of the Haitian situation was to be understood by the American public.

Vane and Tyrrell decided to aggressively pursue the involvement of the national media pool. Not only were reporters to be involved during the preinvasion period, they were supported with transportation and helped with ideas for producing stories.[8] Although the Pentagon initially was cool to the idea, the office of the Assistant to the Secretary of Defense for Public Affairs soon perceived the wisdom of this more proactive approach. The real question was whether such an approach would prove to be too risky to security of the operation: Could the journalists really be trusted with full disclosure at the unit level?

During September, individual journalists were briefed before the operation and were blended into teams to accompany many front-line units, even in the initial airborne invasion. These media information briefings and media team formations were designed to ensure that visual, print, and sound media were integrated and focused on likely areas of action so that all were sure to be in the right place at the appropriate time.[9] At D-5, Admiral Peese, the Navy's Chief of Information, proposed adding fifty extra independent-media representatives to the national media pool to increase the exposure of supporting-service functions in the operation.[10] At D-1, at Andrews Air Force Base near Washington, the twenty-six members of the DOD media pool were personally briefed by the USACOM deputy commander, General Hartzog, on the specific objectives to be accomplished, including the actual locations of the operation. This group was flown directly to Guantanamo Bay, Cuba, en-route to Port-au-Prince on D-day. The independent-media representatives plus several other members of the local media from the Norfolk, Fort Drum, Fort Bragg, and Camp Lejeune areas, were divided into five- and six-person teams and sent down to the individual unit level to go inside ships and aircraft to Haiti. Vane and Tyrell even included a media team on the airborne command-and-control center aircraft.

Media preparations for the operation were not limited to individual journalists. In fact, as the situation in Haiti unfolded during September, all elements of the U.S. government began to become active in the media realm. Given the power and influence of the national networks and the awesome potential they have to cover breaking-stories worldwide, certain ground rules were hammered out with the help of David Gergen of President Clinton's personal staff to ensure that operations security was maintained and no U.S. force was inadvertently placed at risk.[11] These rules included: withholding visibility of the departure of the assault aircraft from Pope Air Force Base in North Carolina; no lights on the drop zones during the initial parachute insertion; and limitations on the coverage of certain forces employed in Port-au-Prince. These agreements were honored throughout the operation.

The media plan was designed to ensure that military operations and media coverage coexisted and were mutually supporting. Such instances included helping the media with added transmission capability, including International Maritime Satellite and video teleconferencing, and providing lodging during the initial period of instability after the media entered Haiti with the assault troops. Of course, when the plan was changed at the last minute due to the diplomatic settlement achieved by the Carter mission, many of the journalists that had embarked with the assault-force units were returned to Fort Bragg and were then unable to rejoin the operation in Haiti for several days.[12] Even so, this unprecedented level of access and accommodation reaped great benefits as the operation proceeded.

One other contribution of the Haiti operation was the creation of a new-style joint-information bureau, or JIB, which integrated support for all media functions. This Haiti JIB was composed of 28–30 people at its peak, including military public-affairs specialists, drivers, supply clerks, and other support personnel assigned from all four military services to coordinate between the military units and the members of the media who wanted to cover units' stories. The JIB provided a forum for military public-affairs specialists to discuss journalists' desires, inform the journalists about unit functions and unit locations, and coordinate travel for the journalists to join the selected unit. When required, the public-affairs specialists could also accompany the journalists and help with the development of the story, but most journalists really wanted unaccompanied access and were so numerous that, by mutual agreement, the JIB evolved into an extremely effective coordination center.

Thus the level of integration, the degree of access, and the nature of the support provided to the media during the operation in Haiti represented a significant advancement over previous operations. For these reasons, media portrayals of the operation were well developed, fair, and timely. The fact that the U.S. military actions in Haiti were overwhelmingly positive was nothing new, but the improved opportunity of the American people to judge that fact for themselves was beneficial to all. Uphold Democracy was an operation intended to help Haiti, and by permitting it to tell its own story, was a tremendously successful idea, with many positive implications for the future of military–media relations.

MANAGING TRANSITIONS BETWEEN FORCES AND BETWEEN THE UNITED STATES AND THE UNITED NATIONS

Few outside the military understand the risk associated with the transition period that occurs between two different commanders. At its best such a period represents a time of uncertainty and adjustment, which parallels similar change within a civilian institution. In such a situation, no one is certain what policies or procedures—indeed what people will even remain—and which will be replaced by new, less familiar entities. Often the pace of progress in both the military and civilian domains diminishes during this period of uncertainty. At its worst a transition period can destroy trust and productivity and lead to corporate failure within the civilian work force. During military operations, when thousands of personnel are at physical risk of injury or death, transition periods take on an even more perilous aspect. As a campaign, Uphold Democracy was designed to have two transition periods: from General Shelton's JTF-180 to General Meade's JTF-190, and then from Meade's command to General Kinzer's U.N. Mission. In execution, three other transitions were added: one within JTF-190, between General Meade's 10th Mountain Division and General Fisher's 25th Infantry Division, one between the 25th Division and the 2nd Armored Cavalry Regiment, and a final transition from Kinzer's UNMIH to the U.N. Support Mission in Haiti follow-on force that remained after President Préval's election.

Each of these transitions represented a potential weak point in decision-making as commanders changed, and in execution as staffs succeeded one another. Knowing this, military planners put special emphasis on transition supports, which would minimize any potential risk. Invariably, visits and exchanges of information among the participants preceded each transition. Also, layers of the force were shifted in phases to reduce the negative effects of transition. Usually, this meant some overlap, as in the several weeks that JTF-190 worked subordinate to JTF-180, and the shorter period when General Fisher's troops worked alongside those of General Meade. In several instances the multinational contingents from certain nations transitioned from Meade to

Fisher and even into General Kinzer's UNMIH. This was true of the Bangladeshi, Nepalese, and CARICOM forces. Each of these techniques shored-up the overall effectiveness of the force during the changeovers.

Training also played an important role during transition. Most noticeable was General Kinzer's decision to hold training sessions for his UNMIH staff in Port-au-Prince during February, prior to his assumption of command.[13] But General Fisher also ensured that his staff spent time with their counterparts within the 10th Mountain Division before he took command of the MNF, and some training for the men and women of General Meade's division was provided by the USACOM staff immediately prior to their quick departure for Haiti.

Although the effort spent on ensuring uneventful changes within the command structure of the forces in Haiti will go largely unnoticed because it was successful, it remains one of the clear strengths of the operation. One has only to observe the problems associated with the transition to U.N. control in Somalia and to a lesser degree the fitful origins of command and control in Bosnia-Herzegovina to understand the value of planned and well-phased transitions within an operation.

THEATER STRATEGIC COORDINATION

There are many reasons for the success of Uphold Democracy; the most fundamental of these was the fine spirit and thorough training of the thousands of soldiers, sailors, airmen, Marines, and Coast Guardsmen who served in and around Haiti during the operation. Their fine, dedicated service there, as during Desert Storm in Kuwait, Provide Comfort in Iraq, Provide Hope in Somalia, and Joint Endeavor in Bosnia-Herzegovina provided a foundation of competence and performance that could have compensated for inefficiencies elsewhere. But in Haiti, individual performance was also maximized by an important strategic-level process that integrated sound leadership with long-term vision to produce the best, most lasting success for the Haitian people. Unlike so many past efforts, in Haiti and in other places around the world where military action has been used for immediate yet quite ephemeral effect, Uphold Democracy was designed and executed through a much improved national-security process that produced more unified and enduring advantages.

This improved process originated in the frustrations of the post-Vietnam period, when military and civilian defense personnel began to improve weaknesses in defense procedures that were made apparent during the failed 1980 Iranian hostage rescue operation, code-named Eagle Claw, and also in the inefficiencies noted during the effort to return the *Mayaguez* in 1975, and in those of operation Urgent Fury in Grenada in 1983. New concepts resulting from this period included the creation of the U.S. Readiness Command in 1985, which spawned both the Rapid Deployment Agency, a forerunner of the U.S. Transportation Command, and the U.S. Central Command, which prosecuted Desert Shield and Desert Storm under the command of General Schwarzkopf. Another step forward was the creation of the World-Wide Military Command and Control System (WWMCCS) in the 1980s to meet the need for more rapid, reliable, secure communication from points around the globe. (WWMCCS has since been replaced by the Global Command and Control System, used operationally for the first time in Haiti.)

The reforms resulting from the Goldwater–Nichols Department of Defense Reorganization Act of 1986 were important and far-reaching. Progress was made in the coordination of all elements of U.S. national power to focus control, enhance the quality of advice given to the President, and synchronize the efforts of the many elements of the Department of Defense in order to meet the critical requirements set by the National Command Authorities. These improvements resulted in a shortened, clearer chain of command from the President and the Secretary of Defense directly to the theater commanders-in-chief, and placed the Chairman of the Joint Chiefs of Staff in a position to offer the best possible advice on military matters, regardless of service parochialism. It gave appropriate power to the Chairman to direct cooperation, doctrinal development, and shared support for all DOD functions among the services. The Goldwater–Nichols Act clarified the relationships among the nation's senior military leaders and left no doubt that the service chiefs were executing a supporting role to the theater commanders in the prosecution of any operational campaign. All these improvements placed the real onus of operational success on the theater commander and staff.

As a result, the theater strategy, which was unique to the region concerned and focused on long-term stability in support of U.S. interests rather than on short-term requirements, became a key unifying theme for all actions in the regions of the world where the United States has national interests. For Haiti, the theater strategy established by USACOM formed the foundation for the planning, prioritization, and sequencing of operations. It followed that all operational requirements should also be set by the theater commanders, for if they had no justified requirement for a unit or resource, it was unlikely to be worth the efforts of procurement, training, and maintenance. On the other hand, when USACOM's Admiral Miller began to speak of a requirement to integrate Army helicopters and Navy ship capabilities, he now had the power to make it possible.

Admiral Miller and his staff also established the framework for planning and the endstates desired in Haiti. Although they did not intrude much upon General Shelton's desire to retain flexibility by developing his own operational plans, the USACOM staff did establish the hard boundaries for execution and facilitated the required coordination among outside and multinational agencies. Most importantly, the strategic level of command permitted General Shelton to concentrate his efforts, once in Haiti, on the direct threat—Cedras and the FAd'H—while USACOM shifted into a direct support role. With USACOM providing rules-of-engagement coordination, increased interagency support, and coordination of all the actions external to Haiti that would indirectly affect Shelton's mission, the JTF commander could concentrate on actions in Haiti itself. Efforts such as the training of the CARICOM Battalion, the ongoing migrant-processing effort, building coalition support, coordinating for transition conditions with the United Nations, and managing the support provided by other theaters, such as the insertion of the 25th Division following the 10th

Mountain's departure, were accomplished by USACOM, with General Shelton's input as desired.

It must also be stressed that having General Sheehan perform three critical assignments in direct support of the Haiti mission provided an immeasurable aspect of continuity to the operation. His insight into Haitian culture and the personal relationships he was able to develop with a variety of key decisionmakers added much to reduce risk during the operation. Finally, his repeated visits to Haiti, beginning in the early 1990s while assigned as director of plans for Admiral Miller and continuing while director of operations of the Joint Staff and later as CINCUSACOM, ensured that the truth about operations in Haiti were well understood by the entire military community. Sheehan also understood well the tough role that must be played as a strategic U.S. commander in support of other operational commanders in a U.N. operation. Generals Shelton and Kinzer spoke frequently of his value as a strategic coordinator. These qualities are a testament to the effectiveness of the U.S. command-and-control organization at the strategic level, which seeks to mine such valuable perspective.

This effectiveness at the strategic command level will always be difficult to establish. During operation Desert Storm, General Schwarzkopf's theater staff had to manage both the operational employment and the strategic oversight of the campaign. This forced a Janus-like schism in the Central Command staff that was masked and managed only through the superb leadership ability of the commanders involved. The separation of the operational and strategic levels of command in Panama, Somalia, and Haiti helped make those (albeit much smaller campaigns) more flexible and adaptable to changing circumstances. This paradigm remains a valuable concept that should grow in importance during future campaigns.

EFFECTIVE JOINT TRAINING

One of the recurring themes of the participants in Uphold Democracy was the contribution of effective joint training to the success of the operation. In part, this was due to the fact that true joint training was a fairly new concept when the operation was planned. Furthermore, this essential contribution reveals how challenging operating in a multiservice environment had become and the extent to which joint operations had effected change in the way individual service forces had been operating prior to 1994. Most important, the operation took place during one of the watershed periods in U.S. military history, when techniques of war were changing to keep pace with new threats and the ever-expanding types of crisis environments. For all these reasons joint training grew in importance, and the servicemembers who participated in Uphold Democracy recognized its significance in time to better prepare through more effective joint training.

Joint training was certainly not new in the 1990s, but the reforms, which followed the Goldwater–Nichols Act of 1986, changed the scope and importance of joint training to such an extent that it appeared to have a new focus. The Desert Storm operation in Kuwait had also demonstrated certain shortfalls in the effective execution of a joint campaign, which appeared to lend themselves to an increased emphasis on joint training: First, then Chairman of the Joint Chiefs of Staff General Colin Powell saw the need for improvements and the advantage of assigning a single manager for the training of joint forces in the continental United States; then Admiral Miller stepped up as an avid supporter of the idea as Commander of a new Atlantic Command with joint training-management responsibilities.

The world perspective of the U.S. military, having changed following the fall of the Berlin Wall and the end of the Soviet Union, was in flux in the early 1990s. Without a single large global threat, it found itself too sluggish in reacting to a host of smaller, less-well-defined crises. The desire to become more responsive, while still withdrawing from forward bases worldwide that were less justifiable without a Soviet threat, caused an increase in support for joint cooperation just as the facilities to support that goal were being created. Joint action rapidly became less an ideal and more a reality.

Still, definitions of joint training, the identification of joint requirements, and even consensus on joint terminology were not immediately forthcoming. Admiral Miller and other senior officers attempting to change old paradigms in training met vocal resistance from military members at all levels of command.[14] Yet, adjustments were made. Before 1990, joint training was centered in a few very large-scale field exercises conducted by the theater commanders, largely for reasons other than joint training benefit. Exercises with names like "Solid Shield," "Display Determination," and "Team Spirit" provided some joint experience with large numbers of personnel to commanders of all four military services, but they did so with very scripted scenarios and limited operational flexibility. In one sense they served more as political demonstrations than training events aimed at improving joint combat-readiness. Such exercises were often too large and unwieldy; they were also inefficient because most of the personnel involved received little personal benefit from the training. Many individuals found themselves being used more as aids to provide experience to fledgling joint staffs and new commanders then as the beneficiaries of field training.

This large-scale, joint exercise-training paradigm changed slowly after 1992. First, computer simulations, which could replace large numbers of troops, became generally available and methods of integrating air simulations with ground and sea simulations made a "joint" replication of battle possible. This was the case when parts of the JTF-180 staff were able to practice some of the Haiti requirements during exercise "Agile Provider 94." Then, with troops finally separated from the staff training requirement, much greater flexibility and realism were introduced. For the first time new joint commanders and their staffs could really test themselves against realistic situations, and even try each situation a second or third time if they were not satisfied with the results. Additionally, an idea taken from the U.S. Army's Battle Command Training Program added selected retired senior officers to exercises specifically to mentor commanders. General Shelton's staff was able to reap these benefits during exercise "Purple Dragon" in the summer of 1994.

These improvements were directly tied to an increase in awareness of joint command-and-control concerns on the part of the XVIII Airborne Corps staff. They also developed important benefits within all the other headquarters that supported the exercise programs. In Admiral Miller's theater, the Marine, Navy, and Air Force component staff members who exercised with the XVIII Airborne Corps staff in the summer of 1994 expanded professional relationships and developed an ever-greater understanding of important joint issues simply by working more frequently together. This increased frequency of exercising joint issues and professional growth also benefited the USACOM staff, which improved its operational procedures and command-and-control capability continually over the months preceding the September 1994 invasion of Haiti.

Many express doubts regarding this training advantage, saying that good commanders do not gain much from joint training. General Shelton felt otherwise. As he pointed out, "the biggest lesson learned out of this is that you can talk all you want about forming a JTF . . . but you have got to put it together, you have got to train it, interpersonal relationships have got to be established, and then you can do it, and you can do it fairly quickly."[15] Admiral Miller noted that his biggest challenge as the theater commander was to "instill the spirit of joint operations, the crying need to ensure that we have the mechanisms in place to train and exercise jointly to be ready to be employed in a true, joint operation."[16] The Haiti operation clearly showed that these two factors did come together just when required, due in part to the contribution of improved joint training.

INTERAGENCY COORDINATION

The interagency process's goal is to leverage the core competencies of the myriad agencies to achieve common objectives.[17]

As the United States adapted itself to an age of specialization, capitalizing on the flow of information, so too did the U.S. military. Few people envisioned that this new paradigm would take the military out of the realm of the self-contained and into an era of agency integration. One of newest challenges for the U.S. military is interagency coordination during joint operations. It began simply enough: during the Cold War the military services identified the opposition, the Soviet bloc, and marshaled the resources to counter that threat. Tank for tank, ship for ship, the force ratio required to generate sufficient odds was always the goal. Each service developed the capability to counter its rival Soviet service, but what also gained the attention of the American public and its congressmen was the rivalry between the military services for procurement dollars. When the Soviet Union finally fell apart, internal military rivalries became less acceptable. The Goldwater–Nichols Act had an important impact when Congress demanded the interoperability of service forces for efficiency, even before fiscal constraints dictated improved service cooperation. As the DOD budget stabilized, force-structure cuts trimmed redundancies in service capabilities and the numbers of personnel in both the active and reserve components of the services. The term "total force" took on new relevance, as we see in Haiti. To their credit the services, active and reserve, meshed capabilities, but even this was not enough for the task that neared nation-building. The core competencies of other nongovernment organizations and private volunteer organizations were needed in order to meet the numerous nonmilitary requirements found in modern peace operations. These other organizations brought the critical societal and cultural remedies, which were not present within the U.S. military arsenal.

The new challenge resulting from this closer civil–military involvement was the development of an appropriate organizational culture and methods of dealing with extreme differences in decisionmaking. The military services were somewhat prepared for this change in a cultural sense due to the recent push for total quality management, which addressed greater member participation and a willingness to accept new ideas. But never before was it so obvious that the military mission would fail without consensus building.

Culture, diplomacy, technology, and a host of allied issues have always affected the nature of armed conflict. In the post-Cold War period of the 1990s conflict diversified and adapted to a range of methods unknown during the era of U.S.–Soviet hegemony, including new emphasis on terrorism, economic sanctions, unconventional warfare, and other means. These new applications of the tools of conflict expanded the traditional American response so that now military agencies are much more dependent on and tied to other agencies of the federal and state governments. This new relationship resulted in an increased reliance on coordination among the government agencies to attempt synchronization and unified effort. Known as "interagency coordination," this phenomenon required much painful development with each advantage it produced.

The critical need for interagency coordination in Uphold Democracy did not surface with any degree of emphasis until relatively late in the plan-development period. Although the principal planners at USACOM and within the XVIII Airborne Corps realized early on that important aspects of the plan's execution would need to be synchronized with the requirements from other U.S. government agencies, they had little time or technique for accomplishing it. The multinational and U.N. aspects of the operation, which were certainly to be driven by the State Department, were also quite clear from the spring of 1993, yet no real tool to develop such coordination within the American government or with the United Nations or allied countries could be implemented as long as the plan itself was highly classified and politically sensitive. In any case, in the winter and spring of 1994 the planners were so concerned that the operation would be executed before the plan was complete that they had little time to develop interagency-supporting requirements until later in the summer. The simple facts were that the planners were never convinced that they would have sufficient warning to execute the operation without a high degree of risk until the Chairman approved the plan and issued his planning order in June. Even then, the focus of effort remained primarily on completing military coordination and rehearsals.

In June, 1994 the Pentagon approved requests from USACOM to begin detailed coordination with other government agencies. Captain Spike Prendergast and his USACOM J5 crew had realized in May that the involvement, at a minimum, of other western hemisphere nations in the multinational force should be considered and that the follow-on U.N. portion of the operation would require significant dialogue within the organization itself. This realization was initially not well supported by the Pentagon, because relations with Aristide and his supporters within the Washington, DC area were then in significant turmoil.[18] But the reality of the situation was undeniable; official U.S. policy endorsed a coalition approach to the problem, and coalitions always required a high level of interagency dialogue.

Some people believe that soldiers and civilians in government are at opposite ends of the ideological spectrum when it comes to worldviews and solutions to world problems. Certainly, many military members look to peace through strength and to hierarchical controls for unity of command; many civilians on the other hand seek to develop peace through nonaggression and through horizontal exchange in order to develop consensus. In reality, the tools and approaches of the soldier and civilian have many important similarities, including altruism, broad perspectives on world concerns, dedication to service, and professional self-reliance. These similarities mean that coordination of individual tasks is not as difficult as some think. Problems in coordination are due to conflicting or at least differing objectives and approaches at the agency level. Thus the real focus of coordination is among the various agencies that may be involved in a conflict.

Most commonly, the Department of Defense has early warning of a potential crisis but does not control the management of the decisionmaking process, which results in an American government response. The National Security Council provides this national security policy-development and implementation through a system of committees involving all affected agencies. In order to highlight the innovations of Uphold Democracy, one must explore what the military had to do in order to accomplish national objectives, as well as the activities of those organizations who would assist, or compete with, the military effort. The difference between "assist" and "compete" may well be due to the level of understanding that the military members and their civilian-agency counterparts have of the interagency process.

One aspect of the civil–military framework in the United States bases effective action on consensus developed among a variety of organizations, which provide checks and balances for one another. Another key aspect is civilian control of the military. These two fundamentals combine in any military operation to require close coordination of civil–military actions. Civil–military actions are conducted on the basis of the framework created originally by the National Security Act of 1947 (NSA 47). Civil–military action is not the same as the interagency process; however, this term has been developed to symbolize the complex but workable relationships developed by each successive administration to execute the concepts of NSA 47. It is important to view the role of the military as only one of several elements of national power generated within the U.S. government. Other elements include diplomatic actions, economic actions, and the use of information to shape events. From flexible deterrent options through initial armed contact, conflict termination, and redeployment, other governmental agencies will be working closely with the military to integrate and execute all functions of national power.

Within the overall civil–military framework there exists an all-important linkage—interagency coordination—that makes things work. This linkage rests largely on the actions of staff members in all departments of the government. Decisionmakers at all levels should be aware of the importance of the interagency process, and planners must understand its strengths and weaknesses. The interagency process is centered in Washington; formalized by NSA 47, the National Security Council (NSC) provides the principal forum for consideration of national security issues requiring Presidential decisions. The NSC is involved in all aspects of security policy: domestic, foreign, intelligence, economic, and, increasingly, informational. The Secretary of Defense is a voting member of the NSC and with the President, is one of the two members constituted as National Command Authorities (NCA), empowered to authorize military activity.

Two acknowledged keys to working with the NSC staff and the interagency process it manages are *coordination* and *consensus. Coordination* is critical because the process does not decide as much as it manages. Each national agency has its own core values and vision, which do not always coincide with those of others working on the same issue. Domestic politics and the personal agendas of decisionmakers cannot be ignored in the process. Few understood the impact of Haitian migration better than President Clinton, who as governor of Arkansas inherited the end-product of the Mariel Boatlift of 1980, and Democratic Governor Lawton Chiles of Florida, whose local domestic interests in Cuban- and Haitian-migrant issues were equaled only by his access to the President. Coordination was absolutely necessary if the widely focused departments of the government were to come together to act with one voice in the immigration matter.[19] (This has recently been reinforced by Presidential Decision Directive 56 [PDD-56], which directs that political–military plans be developed with greater focus on interagency coordination.)

Unity of effort comes from the development of *consensus* at the lowest levels of coordination. This is one purpose of the interagency working groups (IWGs), which provide the foundation for the entire system. Interagency working groups aid in the development of policy as issues work their way to the President. Interagency working groups identify and assess the interests of the various departments and agencies, and disseminate positions and information to key participants. Interagency working groups can be formed as the result of a crisis situation or when an issue is referred to them by the White House, but they most commonly are formed for development of long-term strategy perspectives. For Haiti, a standing Haiti Working Group was formed with membership from all involved organs of government early in 1994. It was this group, particularly under the direction of former Congressman William Gray, that coordinated the U.S. government's positions on Haiti and developed consensus throughout the government on the right path to follow.

When issues addressed by the Haiti IWG became significant enough to warrant referral to the President they became the subject of a Deputies Committee (DC) meeting. The DC focuses on policy implementation and makes known the importance of a given issue to all relevant government agencies. These committees may meet via video-teleconference (VTC) in the first hours of a crisis situation to authorize the initial preparations for a national response. The DC meeting can serve as a critical signal of impending national response, and it includes the key assistants in each agency to ensure that high-level coordination has been initiated.

An Executive Committee (EXCON) is often formed once a situation requires a crisis response, and normally includes high-level membership of all agencies involved. The EXCON membership focuses at the Assistant Secretary level—appointees who have the power to get things done within an agency, regardless of precedent, and who are most faithful not to agency procedure but to the Administration and its immediate goals in a crisis. EXCONs manage the details of complex interagency-crisis response towards the envisioned endstate goal.

The Principals Committee (PC), composed of all the key members of the NSC with the exception of the President, endorses decisions to the President once consensus or the impact of a crisis requires a possible executive decision. In the preparatory stages of Uphold Democracy many different PC meetings were held to direct execution of the many separate actions that collectively moved towards the decision to use military force. Not only was each meeting critical in and of itself, but the cumulative effects of all the decisions concerning Haiti had to be monitored and assessed. The impact of the *Harlan County* turn-around is only one example of the type of action that affects future events in a variety of ways.

The interagency process is developmental, fluid, and adaptable—it can also be frustrating to those who do not understand how it works. Although it is easily and commonly modified to suit the desires of the administration, it remains the single process that integrates all elements of national power within the Washington arena to provide policy recommendations to the President. For the military, most national security policy-implementation is accomplished by the theater commanders, but they are not directly involved in most of the interagency process. The Joint Staff of the Chairman of the Joint Chiefs, residing in Washington where the huge majority of these committees meet, provides the input to and output from the committee process to the theater staffs.

Outside of Washington interagency coordination is even more challenging. The relative authorities existing among the ambassador, who as a presidential appointee has not only real authority but very real influence through direct access to the President, the military commander of the area, and special envoys from supranational organizations like the OAS and United Nations are always less than clear, as are the authorities of other U.S. agency chief representatives. Admiral Miller understood this difficulty so well that he traveled to Washington to brief interagency key persons twice before the operation began, once in July, and again on September 11th, just as the force was beginning deployment. Although neither of these meetings developed the degree of interagency cooperation desired, they were landmarks in the development of the current interagency process. The planning effort and execution coordination of Uphold Democracy made such a positive impact within the Washington arena that succeeding operations in Bosnia and the Middle East were accomplished with much greater coordination. In many ways, PDD-56, was a direct result of the Haiti planning effort.[20]

On the operational level, one of the most significant actions taken by General Shelton in the early days of the operation in Haiti was his decision to integrate his activities with those of Ambassador Swing and the U.S. embassy in Port-au-Prince. As a multinational military commander exercising Chapter 7 authority provided by the United Nations,[21] Shelton was not required to confer with the U.S. ambassador. However, Shelton clearly understood that the situation in Haiti required long-term political solutions, which exceeded the mandate he held. Therefore he sought out Ambassador Swing, used his own military authority to return Swing to a position of knowledge and influence,[22] and thus began a process of close cooperation between the Departments of State and Defense in Haiti that was elemental to the success of Uphold Democracy.[23] While some ambassadors are decidedly pro-military and understand military points of view, others are less familiar and less inclined to share and integrate their efforts with those of the DOD; but as the senior U.S. government representative in a foreign nation, the ambassador is a key to any long-term effort. Although the ambassador never has command of military forces, neither does a CINC have authority to act, short of war or self-defense, without coordination with the State Department and the ambassador's country team. This establishes a healthy interdependence between the military and State Department. In practice, this also means that the CINC's position as a resource manager becomes a valuable asset for all other government agencies, which lack the capability inherent in his uniquely powerful position.

One method of facilitating interagency coordination, which was successfully executed by USACOM, was the creation of an interagency planning cell (IPC) within the staff. This cell, sourced primarily from the J5 Plans and Policy Directorate and including key members of the entire staff, provided the same function for the CINC as the IWGs did for the President (communications, research, and coordination among interagency participants). USACOM IPC members, primarily Colonel John Langdon, USMC, Major Mike Sutton, USAF, Lieutenant Colonel Phil Idiart, USA, Lieutenant Colonel Lee Cochran, USA, and Major Joe Doyle, USMC, worked around the clock in the early days to ensure that the myriad of interagency details required to support General Shelton and his staff were accomplished in a timely manner. These included ongoing development and unit procurement for the multinational force, development of training plans and International Police Monitors for the new Haitian security force, migrant-repatriation policies, and coordination for efforts such as the Weapons Buy-Back program, which required the active involvement of assets from non-DOD agencies. This IPC concept has since been adopted by other staffs for use during crises in Bosnia and Africa.

Admiral Miller, General Shelton and General Meade were all assigned political advisors (POLAD) by the State Department to help the flow of information between the military and State.[24] This relationship aided coordination between Norfolk and Washington, but the ties between Norfolk and the individual national capitals in the USACOM theater of operations also needed consistent attention. Normally, ambassadors also have Defense Attaché Offices (DAO) that facilitate U.S. military actions in foreign nations and coordinate activities between the CINC's staff and the ambassador's country team. As the peacetime focal point for military coordination in his/her country, the DAO always has a challenging job in working to balance a multitude of activities for several agencies. The working relationship that the DAO has with the ambassador and the senior local military officials will be a dominating influence on any operation within a foreign nation. Operation Uphold Democracy did not have the advantage of a working DAO in Haiti because of the strained relations between the two countries; however, a few key officers were present in Port-au-Prince prior to the invasion who made significant contributions to the operation's success. Among them was Major General Charles Bates, USA, who was assigned as a special representative of the Joint Staff in Haiti, working for General Sheehan in the Pentagon.[25]

With the current growth in types of other military operations, the number and extent of interagency involvement continues to expand. Critically important to the implementation of the interagency process are groups of organizations known as Private Volunteer Organizations (PVOs) and Non-Governmental Organizations (NGOs). Many of these bodies normally have long-standing relationships in foreign nations and considerable stakes in the outcome of any military operation in the region. They have invaluable knowledge of the cultural habits, key persons, and underlying problems of an area of the world, all of which are valuable contributions to success in a military operation. As the ties between the strategic decisionmakers were reinforced by an exchange of personnel—POLADs and DAOs, for example, with the State Department—so too the ties between the U.S. government and the PVOs and NGOs in a nation were reinforced through constant contacts. The problem in Haiti was that these contacts had been frayed considerably over the years after the Cedras coup, and reinforcement of these ties was considered critical to the success of the operation. The tool chosen by the military to reinforce these ties and integrate civil–military cooperation on the ground in Haiti was known as the Civil–Military Operations Center or CMOC.

The CMOC concept was an outgrowth of many other techniques that had proven successful in Vietnam and other previous conflicts. In particular, the CMOC was employed very effectively by Marine Lieutenant General Robert Johnston and Ambassador Robert Oakley in Somalia, where it was used to bring together the multitude of conflicting requirements of the Somali people during relief operation Provide Hope. The Somalia model was observed by members of the 10th Mountain Division, who had served in Somalia, and taken with them when they arrived in Haiti. It was used very effectively there from the earliest days of the operation to match local needs (transportation, clean water, food, and shelter) with U.S. government resources (trucks, water-purification units, PVO food stocks, and engineering capabilities). The CMOC also served as a site for the creation of a forum of all involved agencies in both the United States and Haitian governments and the PVOs and NGOs in Haiti. Thus in one important respect, the CMOC formed the key bottom-link in the interagency coordination chain.

If any one aspect of Uphold Democracy can be identified as critical to mission success, it must be the level of interagency coordination that was achieved at all levels and among so many agencies. Even the most admirable performance by the military members of the multinational force could not have treated the real ills of Haiti: These were altogether the product of Haitian history and the schisms of Haitian society; they could not be mended by force. Only the concerted effort of nonmilitary agencies could have turned the tide of social injustice and the absence of law and order in Haiti.

MISSION SUCCESS IN HAITI

These successes would have been noteworthy in any military operation. They are particularly noteworthy in Uphold Democracy because of the restrictions that surrounded the planning and impacted the execution of the operation. Restrictions of compartmentalization, insufficient early coordination, lack of response time, lingering inconsistencies in the U.S. national position on Haiti, and simple unknowns made the superb execution of the operation even more notable. First among these restrictions must be listed the stringent conditions under which the operation was planned. Top Secret classifications are troublesome, yet not uncommon in the military, and are dealt with on a regular basis. What made the Jade Green compartmentalized-planning restrictive was the limited-access requirement, which placed the entire planning burden during the critical early months on a group of fewer than fifty individuals. Not only did they work long hours under pressure, but they also had to do so along with all their normal duties to maintain security. They had to develop creative ways of seeking information and support when they could not reveal the real nature of their requirements.

Coordination among different military organizations was difficult early in the planning as priorities were still not clear and ongoing efforts in Somalia and elsewhere vied for precious time. The feeling among military planners that they lacked critical information, even though they were dealing with a bubbling cauldron that might overflow at any minute, compounded this. A few key persons worked almost in isolation for months with the terrible feeling that their work might be overcome by an immediate requirement to evacuate citizens from Haiti and begin combat operations because of some mistake by Cedras. Doubt concerning the priority of U.S. interests in Haiti also complicated matters. The Clinton Administration rightfully tried every other available means before resorting to the use of military power to return President Aristide, but in doing so, it made the military planning effort more demanding and uncertain. Finally, the "unknown" plagued operational execution until the very day of execution: Would the Haitian people accept the U.S. military as helpers and peace-makers or would they fight? Would Cedras keep his word, or would he repudiate the Carter Accord in the same way he did the Haiti Advisory and Assistance Group's effort when he opposed the *Harlan County*? Would President Clinton continue to see the justification for U.S. involvement in Haiti or would he seek a less compassionate but safer route? These issues were influential, and the fact that they were overcome through dedication and professionalism remains a testament to the quality of the people involved in Uphold Democracy.

Any assessment of the level of success attained by Uphold Democracy must take into consideration the mission assigned and the restrictions placed on the operation. By any traditional measure of military assessment, the operation was a remarkable success because minimal casualties were incurred (on both sides) and the timelines established for completion were met or exceeded. However, this level of assessment does not do justice to the professional accomplishments of the thousands of people who made the operation run. Viewed in light of the difficulty of the mission and the severe restrictions placed upon key decision-makers, the success of the operation becomes even more noteworthy.

The initial mission assigned to Admiral Miller in January 1994 was to plan for "forcible entry into Haiti" and "the creation of an enclave for the return of Haitian migrants." After study by the Jade Green planning cell and coordination with the Joint Staff in Washington, the strategic mission statement became:

When directed by the national command authorities, CINCUSACOM conducts military operations centered in Port-au-Prince, Haiti, to protect U.S. citizens and interests, designated Haitians and third-country nationals, neutralize armed opposition and create a secure environment for the restoration of the legitimate government of Haiti; forces will conduct operations as required to preserve or restore essential civil order in Port-au-Prince (at a minimum) and elsewhere as required by emerging events. Provide technical military assistance to the government of Haiti. On order, pass responsibility for military operations to the United Nations Mission in Haiti (UNMIH).[26]

Later, after the Carter Agreement, the phrase "neutralize armed opposition" would be struck from the mission, and the guidance from Admiral Miller to "gain the respect and support of Haitians and the international community" would be added.[27] Over the months of planning, significant study of the Haitian environment, both historical and current, and the international perspective had caused notable developments in the details of the mission.

The requirement to "conduct military operations centered in Port-au-Prince" was testimony to the historic importance of the Haitian capital as the source of power in the country. True to Clausewitz, Port-au-Prince was the center of gravity, the hub of all power, in Haiti. General Meade noted: "The countryside is much, much more disconnnected from Port-au-Prince than one might imagine; it's only in Port-au-Prince that all the various military, economic, and political pieces are plugged up into a national level grid where they have national importance."[28] Although controlling Port-au-Prince would not pacify the countryside, failure to establish a dominant presence there would have been fatal to the mission. Just as Admiral Caperton saw in 1915, any successful military action in Haiti must ensure that the legislature, the elites, and the army, all located in Port-au-Prince, are involved.

Simply controlling the Haitian capital would also not establish all the conditions necessary for success. In order to "restore the legitimate government of Haiti" (Aristide), the use of military force had to "create a secure environment."

Aristide could not return to any situation in Haiti where his safety and the safety of his key officials were not guaranteed. Without such guarantees the entire goal could have been lost through the actions of a single assassin. Aristide's death would have resulted in massive internal strife and might have prevented any retention of democratic forms. He would certainly not have been the first Haitian head of state to be assassinated.

However, establishing a secure environment is a very challenging military mission. Short of creating a military-controlled government like those established in Germany and Japan immediately following the Allied victory, the American military has few assets to establish and maintain civil order.[29] Civil order, short of an occupation, is now an interagency task requiring the active participation of several government departments. The fact that this was realized and acted upon by the USACOM staff prior to commencement of operations was noteworthy. The staff's efforts in conducting interagency-planning meetings in July and September, 1994 and ongoing teleconferences during the operation were major contributors to success.

Even more important in a real sense was the manner in which these tasks were accomplished in Haiti. Given Admiral Miller's guidance to "gain respect and support of Haitians," General Shelton, General Meade, the other commanders, and the individual soldiers, sailors, airmen, Marines, and Coast Guardsmen who participated in the operation far exceeded the limits of normal military training. They delivered a degree of compassion and care to the Haitians that remains laudable. They established a solid working relationship with the population in a nation where any uniform had come to mean cruelty and where American uniforms still held the memory of oppression during the 1930s. In doing so, the U.S. military did not push aside the members of the PVOs and NGOs working in Haiti: It fully incorporated the capabilities and requirements of their multinational partners. General Richard Potter said, "this is neither peace nor war; it's neither peacekeeping or peacemaking; it's neither nation-building or occupation. It's kind of a combination of it all, and with the soldiers, many times working on their own initiative in isolated pockets, ninety-nine percent of the time they continually make the right decisions."[30] They kept the use of force to the absolute minimum required; formed an effective team from a variety of dissimilar elements; gained the cooperation and even respect of the Haitian people; and steadily improved the security situation in Haiti until it met the requirements of the United Nations. They even supported a complete round of elections to form a new Haitian administration. These accomplishments required techniques quite different from those used to expel Saddam Hussein from Kuwait by firepower and maneuver. Even so, the men and women of Uphold Democracy achieved all goals established for them and departed from Haiti on time. They had followed Admiral Miller's guidance by *doing right.*

NOTES

1. Hayden, *JTF-190 Oral History Interviews,* p. 11.

2. Among these units were the USACOM staff, the Joint Communications Support Element, the Joint Special Operations Command, and liaison teams from all the other supporting unified commands.

3. Joint cooperation among the individual services had been well demonstrated in Panama, Somalia, and Kuwait, but each of these operations also saw vestiges of the old rivalries as well. The operation in Haiti seemed to be taking place at a time when many of these problems had been put to rest and when the positive lessons of the earlier operations had become better accepted among all elements of the force.

4. The number of print-media articles during the period averaged thirty per month until October 1993, when the *Harlan County* incident spiked coverage to 230 articles. The numbers returned to the thirty-per-month average rate again until April, 1994, when the word of a possible U.S. invasion, mixed with the UNSCR, pushed numbers above sixty per month for each of the following months. The number of print articles for September, 1994 reached 600, and these were accompanied by at least that number of radio and television broadcasts.

5. The 1989 operation in Panama was as much a surprise to Americans as it was to the Panamanians. Operation Desert Shield in Kuwait began so quickly that it took both the media and the military by surprise; its follow-on, Desert Storm, was a superbly organized media-event combining good operations security with some use of the media to reinforce deception activities. The initial amphibious landing in Somalia was in some ways a response to worldwide media attention and was met with a glare of television lights, which disturbed military planners. The operation continued to attract media attention throughout its duration. In all four operations, there was a feeling that the goals of the media and the military were somewhat in opposition.

6. See *U.S News & World Report,* "Caribbean Cruise," July 18, 1994, pp. 33–35; *Time,* "Invasion Target: Haiti," July 18, 1994, pp. 22–23.

7. Hayden, *JTF-180 Operation Uphold Democracy Oral Interviews,* p. 156.

8. John R. Ballard interview with Colonel John Tyrell, USAF, Norfolk, VA, June 23, 1995.

9. Hayden, *JTF-180 Operation Uphold Democracy Oral Interviews,* p. 156.

10. John R. Ballard interview with Colonel John Tyrell, USAF, Norfolk, VA, June 23, 1995. These journalists were known as unilaterals and were intended to act as additional conduits for major media organizations that could not be included due to space restrictions. As a boon to the national media representatives, who were to have a priority due to their membership in the pool, the unilaterals were asked to delay stories for 10 hours.

11. Ibid.

12. Even this could become a great advantage; for example, there is the telling story produced by a radio reporter who was able to overhear the conversation between the pilot and loadmaster of one of the assault-wave aircraft transporting the 82d Airborne Division. He was able to observe the complex emotional reactions of the soldiers when their combat jump was aborted after the long uncomfortable ride from Fort Bragg and then relate the story of their professionalism, even in relief and disappointment.

13. Kinzer pointed to this training session as one of the keys to success for the UNMIH staff in a briefing presented in March 1994.

14. Perhaps Admiral Miller's most famous trial balloon was the substitution of a Marine special-purpose force for carrier aviation assets on one deployment of the aircraft

carrier USS *Theodore Roosevelt.* While based on sound principles, the idea was roundly criticized and eventually rejected. It was, however, an essential antecedent for the placement of the U.S. Army helicopter force on the USS *Eisenhower* in 1994.

15. Hayden, *JTF-180 Operation Uphold Democracy Oral Interviews,* p. 72.

16. William R. McClintock interview with Admiral Paul David Miller, USN, January 19, 1995, p. 17.

17. *Doctrine for Interagency Coordination, Joint Pub 3-08,* I-2.

18. Aristide had repudiated the Repatriation Agreement in the spring of 1994, at a time when the numbers of Haitian migrants were becoming a significant problem. Within the United States, many were also scrutinizing Aristide's fitness for power, and he was not universally supported inside or outside the U.S. government.

19. In this example, the Department of Justice was waging a long battle over the legal implications of repatriation, the Department of Transportation, as the normal controlling agency of the U.S. Coast Guard, was managing the interception and transportation of migrants, the Departments of Commerce and Treasury were advising the Administration on the utility of the embargo and its affect on U.S. markets, the Department of State was negotiating for locations outside the United States where processing could be accomplished without having to grant certain rights to the migrants, which they would have obtained by touching U.S. soil, and the Department of Defense was planning for military action. This excludes coordination with congressional committees, the OAS, the United Nations, nongovernmental agencies, or fluctuating organizations like the Congressional Black Caucus that have significant influence over the acceptance of any policy on the American legislature and electorate.

20. PDD-56, "Handling Complex Contingencies," is a Clinton Administration directive that provides a systematic approach to interagency coordination, under the direction of the National Security Council. It even includes a generic political–military plan format that assigns planning requirements among the various agencies involved in contingency operations. It has already demonstrated its value during crises in Bosnia and Iraq.

21. Chapter 7 of the United Nations charter addresses those instances when the Security Council may authorize the use of force, even when such actions are not supported by the government where the action will take place. Chapter 7 authorization has been granted rarely and normally implies that combat operations may be coincident with the deployment of U.N. forces.

22. As Ambassador Swing was accredited only to the Aristide government, he was forbidden by the U.S. State Department to interact with the Cedras regime and thus was not as fully informed or integrated into Haitian affairs as would have been normal for a U.S. ambassador with full access to his host nation's government.

23. Some ambassadors, such as Robert Oakley in Somalia and William Swing in Haiti, were tremendous aids to the military commander, often using their personal influence and bravery to accomplish military objectives. Little exists that specifically outlines the complex relationships existing between ambassadors and military commanders in their host countries during peacetime; each team must be built based upon personality, situation, and endstate desired.

24. See William R. McClintock interview with Robert M. Maxim, Political Advisor to USACOM, July 7, 1995 for Maxim's views of interagency coordination.

25. There is now a military liaison officer assigned to the embassy in Port-au-Prince.

26. From USACOM's execute order for operation Uphold Democracy, dated 18 September, 1994.

27. From USACOM's second execute order for operation Uphold Democracy, dated 19 September, 1994.

28. Hayden, *JTF-180 Operation Uphold Democracy Oral Interviews,* p. 11.

29. This is not to denigrate the superb capability of the civil-affairs groups, military-police battalions, and psychological-operations battalions and squadrons of the U.S. military. On the contrary, their performance has been superb, both in Haiti and in Somalia and Bosnia. But these units are relatively few in number for the huge requirements currently placed on them. For a different approach, with its own disadvantages, one should observe the role of the Gendarmerie in France, which is a true civil-security military force.

30. Hayden, *JTF-180 Operation Uphold Democracy Oral Interviews,* p. 19.

CHAPTER 11

Epilogue: Haiti Today

"Today, Haiti stands at a crossroads in history."[1]

Jean-Bertrand Aristide

Operation Uphold Democracy gave Haiti critical breathing space. The operation facilitated the return of the legal Haitian government and provided the initial security required for that government to find its roots and regain managerial control of the state. Like Admiral Caperton's 1915 expedition to Haiti, the operation clearly was not intended to remake Haitian national institutions, but instead to permit Haitians to return themselves to democratic governance. That responsibility still lies with the Haitian people. The world should assess whether the operation changed things for the better and whether Haitians can now have the future they deserve.

Proper assessment of Uphold Democracy must ask two questions: What has changed in Haiti since September, 1994, and is the future now brighter for the Haitian people? Some might also ask: Has the Haitian revolution, which started nearly 200 years ago, finally entered its terminal stage? Although these important questions are only now beginning to be addressed, they must be answered fully before the international presence in Haiti is brought to an effective close. The world should judge whether the multinational intervention was worthwhile, and also should analyze whether Uphold Democracy helped Haiti. Americans should ask whether the operation will fall among those military interventions of the past that were costly in blood, national resources, or both, yet did not improve the lot of those they were designed to aid. Though the future of Haiti is not yet clear, every indication is that Uphold Democracy may well be regarded as an operation that accomplished its mandates and made the critical difference, at just the right time.

Several issues must be considered in order to frame an analysis of the operation's effectiveness because modern U.S. military operations are conducted for a variety of reasons and with a broad range of missions in mind. The deployment of over 20,000 U.S. servicemen and women during Uphold Democracy was not conducted merely for training nor for an international demonstration of power projection: these may have been valid reasons in the past, but they did not fit the situation in 1994.[2] Uphold Democracy was conducted too close to the United States, accomplished over too long a period, and executed in too complex a manner to have produced meaningful increases in training or readiness. The deterrence operations by JTF-120, known now as operation Support Democracy, had already been executed prior to the landings in September, 1994. And although the deployment of the 82nd Airborne Division certainly affected decisionmaking in Port-au-Prince once it became known to Cedras, Biamby, and François, deterrence had long before been supplanted as an intended effect of the operation. Uphold Democracy was executed because all other elements of U.S. national power, including the embargo, nearly 3 years of diplomatic initiatives by several countries and the United Nations, and a strong information campaign designed to convince Cedras to step down had been tried and had failed to achieve the objective of restoring a calm Haitian environment. Those deficiencies left military force as the only remaining option to achieve that goal.

Even so, the use of military force in Haiti was not intended to be an isolated action. It was designed to propel and complete the other interagency and international actions then in use in order to force a rapid resolution of the crisis through ongoing efforts, but not to provide a solution in its own right. Because diplomatic and economic initiatives had failed over a 2-year period to restore Aristide, military power was employed to force the issue. The military mission was to restore Aristide and create a stable environment in which other agencies could effectively treat the ills that plagued Haiti. Thus military power became the largest and most capable but not necessarily the dominant arm for the resolution of the crisis. The military was really a supporting agent designed to assist reform in Haiti. Though the military objectives originally included the destruction of the FAd'H, mission accomplishment in Haiti did not require combat. As it turned out, lethal force was used in only a limited number of isolated incidents.

This did not mean that the FAd'H posed no threat to the U.N. and U.S. goals in Haiti. However, simply put, the military threat to all but other Haitians was insignificant. Certainly the Cedras regime's anti-U.S. rhetoric and posturing were viewed by some as a cause for alarm, particularly after the *Harlan County* incident; but no force in Haiti posed a direct military threat to the United States, and a Haitian alliance with Fidel Castro's Cuba, the only other anti-U.S. force in the region, was highly unlikely in the 1990s.[3] Furthermore, if the United States had really desired to end an identified Haitian military threat, it simply could have executed the operation as originally designed in Plan 2370 and blotted out the FAd'H in a matter of hours—all legally done within the mandate provided by the United Nations. Instead, the United States took a more difficult and costly route, with a deeper objective in mind. The United States employed its military, under U.N. auspices, as a vehicle to facilitate political change in Haiti.

Few nations outside the hemisphere cared at all about Haiti or its problems. Haiti's was not the type of crisis in which television coverage of human deprivation, like that made famous in Somalia and Central Africa, would stimulate the world to act. Nor was the situation in Haiti likely to produce the degree of international response that was generated in reaction to the genocide in Rwanda or Bosnia-Herzegovina. Haiti was simply not a nation that was cared for or supported by many other countries. Although some large states, particularly the Francophile nations of France and Canada, and closer neighbors, such as Colombia and Venezuela, *did* care about events in Haiti, there was very little likelihood that any of them would have acted in any significant way without the initiative and leadership of the United States. In one respect, Uphold Democracy demonstrated that the reverse of the Roosevelt Corollary does remain true: After the demise of the Soviet Union, no other nation will intervene in the Caribbean without U.S. sanction.

But why did the United States take the risk of acting, with military force, in such an unsettled situation? Drug trafficking was mentioned as a reason. After the trial of Panama's Manuel Noriega, dealing in drugs was a common way for American statesmen to show reason to confront foreign officials. But drugs do not appear to be a significant factor in this decision to intervene.[4] Although many in Haiti were narco-culpable, their negative impact was very minor in the big scheme of international narco-crime; and had drugs been the root cause or even a meaningful reason for the intervention, the U.S. response clearly would have resulted in calls for extradition and trials in the United States for drug kingpins. In fact, quite the reverse has occurred; Americans have been more willing to harbor participants in the Cedras regime than have the Haitians themselves.[5] Drug trafficking in this case was not sufficient reason to act militarily.

Many have presumed that stopping the migrant flow was the reason behind the deployment of U.S. troops.[6] Although this explanation appears viable, the primary reason for the invasion could not have been *only* the requirement to stop the flow of migrants towards the shores of the United States: President Bush had demonstrated quite convincingly that simply intercepting and returning those people using Coast Guard assets had worked in the past to reduce the flow of people from Haiti and discourage future waves of migrants. In fact, since 1995 the number of migrants leaving Haiti has increased again and the United States has quietly returned to forceful repatriation, with little or no press coverage nor national concern for any violations of human rights. Counter-migration efforts were costly: Deputy Secretary of State Strobe Talbot estimated that the United States paid "nearly $300 million to deal with Haitian migrants, sanctions enforcements, and humanitarian relief" in 1994.[7] But they did not of themselves constitute sufficient reason to intervene with U.S. military forces.

Other authors have reasoned that President Clinton backed himself into the deployment in response to concerns over his presidential image prior to the congressional elections of November, 1994.[8] Most of these opinions cite the effectiveness of Aristide inside Washington circles of influence, the missteps of the

State Department in the diplomatic effort to reduce the oppression of the Cedras regime, the potent messages of concern sent to Washington by Florida Governor Chiles, and the strong influence of the Congressional Black Caucus in general and William Gray in particular in the development of U.S.–Haitian policy as evidence that the Clinton Administration was being managed by special interests during the Spring, 1994 interagency campaign for calm in Haiti.[9] Certainly these influences all had some effect on the decision to intervene, but to oversimplify the decision in such a manner fails to recognize the overall consistency in the Administration's condemnation of abuse in Haiti from the beginning of President Clinton's election campaign through the election of President Préval. The Clinton Administration may have modified its message to attempt differing approaches, and it may not have always felt comfortable in the Aristide camp, but it never ceased to work for a restoration of legal democratic government in Haiti. Perhaps unknowingly, once President Clinton had accepted the plight of the Haitian people as a U.S. strategic interest and continued harboring President Aristide, he accepted a major role in the stabilization of the crisis in Haiti. With historical perspective it is just as valid to state that the United States has indeed only maintained such interest in Haitian affairs since the early 1900s, and that the commitment of U.S. power in Haiti in 1994 will most likely be viewed as a natural part of the political interaction between the two nations throughout the twentieth century.

With superpower-force demonstration, military and economic threats, international pressure, drugs, migration, and domestic pressure all excluded as primary reasons to intervene, one is left with a single major motive in undertaking Uphold Democracy.[10] The fundamental reason left for the operation was the desire to eliminate the underlying cause of the migration and the systematic abuse of Haitians on Haitians by helping end the long-standing and undeniable internal instability of the Haitian government. It was this distress that allowed a succession of authoritarian regimes to plague the country and that forced Haiti's people to take to the sea in small boats.[11] It was this instability that was the real threat to security in the Caribbean. No military, economic, or diplomatic force could completely cure such chronic distress, for only the Haitians themselves could complete the revolution began 200 years before and create a functioning republic that recognized the value of all its citizens. But military interventions have helped develop conditions for such reforms in the past, and it appeared likely in 1994 that only military force could achieve the goal in the short term. In retrospect, the military intervention does appear to have stabilized the internal crisis in Haiti, thereby providing the opportunity for the elections needed to reinforce democratic functioning and thus permitting the limited influx of international aid that is requisite for improvements in the Haitian economy.[12]

The U.S. and international agencies had pushed their agenda with ever-increasing pressure over a period of nearly 3 years. After all the international diplomatic-maneuvering, the people controlling Haiti, principally Cedras, Biamby, and François, began to realize that they were playing a game for their very survival in a superpower league. They could not back down, for the rising tide of discontent in Haiti would clearly cast them out if they gave up any of their hold on power; they could only trust in a bluff and hope that their problems really were too insignificant for the United States to act upon. The timing, in September, 1994, was such that the intervention served as the final step after all other means had been largely exhausted to permit the Haitian political revolution to continue down the path of democratic reform.

The end of internal abuse and instability comes out clearly as a theme in the U.N. Security Council Resolutions, in President Clinton's speech prior to the invasion, and in the mission statements developed for the military commanders. They are echoed by Aristide and by most Haiti analysts. All the primary goals of the operation—the return of Aristide, the holding of new elections, and the development of a secure and stable environment—are acceptable reasons for intervention. Assuming this, one important issue remains: How well were these goals achieved and what has been the effect on Haiti today? Is Haiti more stable and secure and therefore less a threat to its own people and to other states after the completion of Uphold Democracy?

Before an answer to this question can be developed, one should also frame the possibilities: Whether any external action, particularly any action of less than 3 years' duration, can have a stabilizing effect on a society that has been in turmoil since its origin remains to be debated. Can the Haiti of Sonthonax, Dessalines and Ogé, of Boyer and Duvalier, of Namphy and Cedras be reformed by outsiders? Can the situation possibly be ameliorated in the short term? Many political scientists would claim that nothing short of decades must pass before any long-term stability can be achieved in a nation with such a limited tradition of law and democratic process.[13] Haiti's history, particularly the more recent administrations of Lescot and Pascal-Trouillot, shows that enlightened leaders cannot stand alone in the face of what appears to be a Haitian predilection for authority figures and despotic rule.

However, taking a longer view of Haitian history, one can see that the nation's march towards real democracy has been ongoing, albeit at a slow pace, since the nineteenth century.[14] Republican spirit started strong in Haiti in the early 1800s, sputtered during the mid-century years of debt and confused government, and then was further weakened by extranational involvement in the late 1890s and early 1900s. Still, five important events stand out in this century as markers along an ambling course set towards democratic reform: (1) the "second independence" in 1934; (2) the noiriste movement of the 1940s; (3) the cooperative fall of Baby Doc Duvalier; (4) the development of the Constitution of 1987; and (5) Aristide's own election in 1990. Each of these events helped nurture the original sentiment of the republic's founding concepts, and more importantly, assisted in the development of ideas and a culture that could sustain democracy, even in a nation as poor as Haiti. Given that the majority of the population still seems today to strongly support democratic reform, one could answer with a qualified "yes," Haiti desires democracy. "Yes," if the meaningful progress democracy promises can be made in the economic and social fabric of its society. This then is the real test of Uphold Democracy: The support and establishment of a viable foundation for economic and social reconstruction that can permit a stable government to pass efficiently from administration to administration and thus endure.

PROGRESS IN HAITI

One insightful view of the Haitian progress made to date comes from former President Aristide. In the spring of 1996, after the succession of President Préval, Aristide wrote a short article outlining the reforms that had been made since his return to Haiti. In "Passing Milestones: Political and Economic Renewal in Haiti," Aristide optimistically outlined the progress made towards many of the same goals that had been the objectives of Uphold Democracy. He noted at the start of his appraisal that "democracy is measured not only by elections but also by the degree to which a democratic government responds to the needs of its people."[15] With this assertion he demonstrated the understanding that the transition to Préval was not an end in itself, but a single crucial step towards the greater objective. And later in the article he identified the keys to success as improvements in the state of law, justice, jobs, food, literacy, education, health care, and an end to corruption within the state. For Aristide, progress in Haiti, to really be effective, "must move beyond political and legal reform, [it] must also remove economic and social barriers which keep the majority of Haitians in abject poverty."[16] Not only did he illustrate how complex the task in Haiti had become, but, more importantly, he also demonstrated great optimism for the future—he spoke as if the key turning point for democracy in Haiti had already been reached. With his unique perspective, Aristide saw that the failure of the coup regime to consolidate its power during 1994 demonstrated that a new crisis had occurred within Haitian society: the society that had historically accepted being controlled through force had finally become unwilling to condone its use. Therefore, Aristide believed, the road was finally open to the progress Haiti so desperately required.

Aristide listed several successes up to 1996. His first challenge was the dismantling of the FAd'H, which he accomplished in three steps: First, he retired the majority of the officers, and following that, he demobilized most of the soldiers. Those few that remained were integrated into the Interim Police Security Force, under civilian leadership. Then, in a third step, he let the parliament dissolve the Haitian army by using budgeting tools. With no effective budget the FAd'H quickly disappeared. Aristide proudly noted that the former army headquarters is now the Ministry of Women; force of arms as an element of Haitian power had been replaced by an increased recognition of the importance of women in a democratic society.

Aristide's early focus on the FAd'H as the source of instability in Haiti was simplistic, for the Haitian army rarely acted without at least the tacit support of the elites of the nation, and these, the elites, have not yet effectively embraced the power structures of Aristide and Préval. Aristide's goal of placing the control of Haiti back into the hands of the majority of its citizens has yet to be achieved. Responsibility and power-sharing remain to be reflected in their greater acceptance of all citizens as equal partners—elite, poor, black, or nonblack. Still, the end of the military's role as a powerbroker in Haiti was one of the significant steps that has been taken since the invasion.[17]

It was a well-known fact that "in Haiti, justice was bought and sold by those with power and money."[18] This would have remained true as long as no independent judicial process existed. Now also this absence has been rectified with the help of the MNF and the supporting nations of the world. Haiti has opened a new training institute for police, has significantly raised judges' salaries, and has created new courts in jurisdictions that needed them. The MNF first created an interim police security force (IPSF), and with international help then trained over 5,000 new police officers. Now Haiti has a civilian police force under civilian control. Although some members of the FAd'H were brought in as members of the IPSF, and some remain today, so far they have presented few problems. The longer-term issue will be the maintaining of the new Haitian National Police (HNP) force and the rather expensive, at least in Haitian terms, judicial structure required to process the criminals that the HNP identifies, as well as the equally expensive penal system needed to punish and reform those convicted of crimes. These challenges are large, given Haiti's limited fiscal resources.

Disarmament is also still a key issue for long-term stability in Haiti. Although the U.N. Security Council resolution of June, 1994 provided for the disarmament of paramilitary groups, this has not been completed largely because, as in the United States, gun ownership remains legal in Haiti. Thanks to the success of the Weapons Buy-Back program the threat now is not based in individual weapons ownership but in the numerous criminal gangs and private security organizations that have sprung up in the wake of the departure of international military forces.[19] The criminal gangs proliferated following the demobilization of the FAd'H as former soldiers in search of employment with their only marketable skill found lucrative positions among the criminals they once were assigned to police. These gang members now pose a significant problem in certain areas of the country where they outnumber and out-earn the HNPs. Although the various gangs do not cooperate with one another and are not well-organized internally, they have carved out limited control in some areas, thereby placing citizens at risk. On the other hand, numerous security organizations now exist that provide a valid function by protecting their employers from gang violence and providing security in the areas where the HNP may be weak. These security organizations were particularly useful in the early stages of the HNP's development, when security around the country was still inadequate. But the continued existence of these organizations, operating independently from government control, is a destabilizing influence. The simple visibility of numerous armed, private security personnel in the streets of Haiti runs counter to a stable environment.

As discussed previously, security is only one aspect of the reforms in Haiti. Aristide's goal was "to move from misery to poverty with dignity."[20] Such progress requires economic revitalization, improvements in education, and patience. Few jobs have been created in Haiti, while the cost of living continues to rise. Although Haiti has been able to reduce the rate of inflation by 50 percent, much remains to be done.[21] Real economic change must come from agricultural revitalization, which requires land reform, more effective utilization of whatever arable land remains, and, in the long term, the recovery of natural resources—an end to the ecological disaster that has left the country with an ever-decreasing level of agricultural productivity. As would be true with any people, there is some reluctance on the part of the rural population to change the ways of the last five decades and support the reform initiatives of the administration in Port-au-Prince.

Economic revitalization requires more than land reform; changes in the management of business and industry in Haiti to better benefit the whole of the nation must accompany it. For most, this change in management style calls for increased privatization of state-supported and -run businesses. Privatization was specifically listed by the potential contributor nations as a natural prerequisite for many types of aid. But privatization remains "an extremely divisive process," because it will certainly result in at least the temporary loss of jobs in a time of unemployment distress and may indeed only shift the profits of major businesses from one elite group to another.[22] Economic growth still poses a very severe challenge.[23] The flour plant was privatized in September, 1997, and it appears that the cement plant may also soon transition to a profitable position under private control; perhaps the telephone exchange and the hydroelectric plant may follow and actually provide reliable service to the people in the near future. At that point the Haitian economy will have made solid progress.

Literacy is another fundamental problem. Aristide sought to reduce levels from 85 percent illiteracy to 85 percent literacy in 3 years! "Literacy brigades" were created to do the work in a decentralized manner. Democracy depends in many ways on an informed citizenry and an ability to make issues visible to the public. Without increases in literacy, democracy in Haiti will be forced to operate on the very precarious foundation of a word-of-mouth communications system. In addition, the major difficulties that confronted the elections held since the return of Aristide have been rooted in the need to make the voting process visual. Until the majority of the Haitian population can at least read the names on a ballot and be capable of using the ballot without assistance, democracy will face troublesome difficulties.

Fundamentally, Haiti also has to overcome a problem rooted in its colonial past: It must somehow develop the trust within its citizenry that is required to sustain a democratic institution. As Aristide said, "our leaders must now maintain the faith and confidence of the Haitian people by continually listening to their voices, meeting their social and economic needs, and guaranteeing their participation in the life of the nation."[24] But this is only part of the answer. The Haitian people must not only be well represented, but they must become active in the democratic process and must accept the underlying assumption that the majority should speak for the nation. This is a concept that runs counter to 200 years of the smallest minority making decisions for all of the country, and is a large step in cultural liberalism that may take a very long time to become effective.

Still, with all these issues left to be resolved, the fabric of Haitian society has been changed since Uphold Democracy. The level of security, the effectiveness of public administration, the economic outlook, and the foundations of democratic process have all made large strides. The question remains: How long will it take for Haiti to pass the danger point and be capable of progressing on its own? Certainly, until the end of President Préval's term of office, significant international monetary and technical support will remain necessary. Following another series of national elections, sufficient time may have passed to improve the economic situation at least enough to reduce the jobless rate and transition many of the government-controlled businesses to private management. Even then, the problems will not be solved. It is the degree of cultural change required that presents the greatest obstacle for the Haitian people. That significant change will certainly require the growth to adulthood of a new generation to adequately address.

Uphold Democracy was support, not reform. Haiti must make all the further steps, and for any amount of change similar to that required in Haiti, only time can really provide the healing force.[25] Still, Haiti's neighbors have done as much as possible to assist in the process and should be proud of the effort and results thus far. Regardless of what the future brings to Haiti, it is no longer under the rule of force, no longer a pariah state, no longer a threat to the region, and the Haitian people have sufficient faith in their nation's future to remain at home and work to make it a reality. The international effort known as Uphold Democracy was more than just one step in a long procession of Haitian–American activities—it was most likely also the best. "We intervened because it was in our national interest, we intervened after every alternative had been exhausted, and we intervened because it was the right thing to do."[26]

AFTERWORD: 1998

The streets of Port-au-Prince bustle with commerce, but remain blighted by poverty and neglect. People in rural areas still suffer from malnutrition; the poor still flee hunger, including some few who remain convinced that they must leave Haiti to survive. However, the international community remains committed and involved. Although the U.N. military mission in Haiti officially ended on the last day of November 1997, its sponsor-nations remain committed. A U.N. police training force remains; CARE continues to feed thousands of Haitians every day, and U.S. military men and women remain in Port-au-Prince to assist in making democracy succeed. The hopes of the world remain with Haiti, but the onus is now clearly on the Haitian people.

President Préval has achieved much since his election, including new construction and an increase in agricultural productivity. But Haiti had a long way to go to achieve self-sufficiency after the 1994 ousting of the Cedras regime, and much remains to be done. This new construction is evident not just in the cities but also in some areas of the countryside. Although the roads that never were improved during the high tide of U.S. engineering projects are still rutted and almost impassable, those that *did* experience improvements have been maintained and commerce does manage to increase, albeit slowly. Some of the democratic functions of the government continue to push into the smaller hamlets, but Port-au-Prince, as always, remains the main bastion of wealth, privilege, and security.

Unfortunately, Préval's government still suffers from serious problems. The Prime Minister, Rosny Smith, resigned in June, 1997, and political infighting has hobbled the government and resulted in reduced aid and foreign investments. Nearly 70 percent of the population remains out of work; gangs still out-gun the Haitian National Police; disease and lack of food remain critical problems. Much more remains to be done.

The architects of Uphold Democracy understood that success in Haiti depended upon helping average men and women lead more secure and productive lives. Haiti has always been an agriculturally based country, and the great majority of the Haitian people still look to the land for support. Although coffee and some other fruit and vegetables have again begun to be exported, the country is far from reaching self-sufficiency in food. Although self-sufficiency is a lofty goal, which many developed nations in the world will never reach, Haiti knows that it must work to achieve it alone, for it cannot continue to depend upon the assistance of so many other countries in order to meet the basic nutritional needs of its people.

The UNMIH was renamed the U.N. Support Mission in Haiti in 1997, and its leadership was assumed by the Canadians while its roughly 600 personnel still provided much that was essential in Haiti. Indeed, some believe that the pressure exerted by the U.N. military mission was the major reason behind the continued agricultural and economic improvements. Certainly the international military presence served as a watchdog, ensuring that no breakdown in Haitian national-security occurred unnoticed. Most Haitians wanted the U.N. troops to stay—that fact is telling enough. In response to the needs of the Haitian National Police and to maintain a presence, the United Nations authorized a 300-member international police-training force to stay until November, 1998. But the fact remains that the final departure of the U.N. military force still left Haiti with much to accomplish for lasting security. For these and other reasons, U.S. forces still work in the Haitian heat to help its people meet their objectives.

Haiti has made some progress. The world has given the Haitian people a chance to start afresh, or least a breathing spell to determine how they should proceed. If the past is any indication of the future, then Haiti will certainly suffer more threats to democracy. Of course, that is the nature of freedom; and as the oldest republic in the Caribbean, Haiti knows well what it takes to maintain the essential elements of democracy. The U.S. military was chosen in 1994 to spearhead a U.N. operation that provided the opportunity of renewal to the people of a neighboring nation in distress. The United States and the United Nations did well to provide such help, and Haiti will determine its own path.

NOTES

1. Jean-Bertrand Aristide, "Passing Milestones: Political and Economic Renewal in Haiti," p. 78.

2. Demonstrating commitment and training improvements were the major reasons behind the Cold War exercises known as the "Reforger" series, and, more recently, U.S. deterrence against possible Iraqi aggression was the impetus behind the operation known as Vigilant Warrior. But neither of these useful, historic reasons for force deployments was appropriate for the situation in Haiti.

3. For a different type of economic threat, Strobe Talbot testified before Congress on March 9, 1995 that the cost of nonintervention during the period that the Cedras regime was in power amounted to $300 million each year, whereas the cost of Uphold Democracy over its first 18 months was only $700 million. Strobe Talbot, "Promoting Democracy and Economic Growth in Haiti," p. 189.

4. Although President Clinton did not include drugs among the reasons he cited for authorizing the operation in his speech to the nation on September 15, 1994, William Gray had listed drug trafficking as the fourth of six U.S. interests in Haiti in his June 8, 1994 testimony to the House Foreign Affairs Committee. "Establishing the Basis for a Successful Conclusion to the Crisis in Haiti," p. 425.

5. In March, 1997 former Port-au-Prince police chief Michael François was charged with helping to smuggle thirty-three tons of cocaine and heroin into the United States. The Associated Press revealed at that time that there had been a confidential Justice Department memo revealing concerns that U.S. intelligence agencies may have cooperated with Haitian drug-smugglers. In 1994 the U.S. Drug Enforcement Agency estimated that one ton of cocaine reaching the United States per month had passed through Haiti. See *The Virginian-Pilot,* March 8, 1997, p. A5.

6. Here President Clinton did point to a major security threat to the United States, stating that if the Cedras regime stayed in power the United States "would continue to face the threat of a mass exodus of refugees and its constant threat to stability in our region and control of our borders." "The Possible Invasion of Haiti." *Vital Speeches of the Day,* October 1, 1994, pp. 738–740.

7. Strobe Talbot, "Promoting Democracy and Economic Growth in Haiti," p. 185.

8. See Alex Dupuy, *Haiti in the New World Order: The Limits of the Democratic Revolution,* pp. 156–159; Gaddis Smith, "Haiti: From Intervention to Intervasion," p. 58; and Robert I. Rotberg and John Sweeney, "Was Intervening in Haiti a Mistake?," p. 146, for interpretations that President Clinton was pressured to intervene.

9. See Roland Perusse's *Haitian Democracy Restored, 1991–1995.*

10. It could be argued that the sum of these separate influences was sufficient to cause President Clinton to intervene. Placed in the context of the Somalia campaign that preceded Haiti and the concern "not to let that happen again," any speculation that the decision was forced by events should be severely discounted.

11. Robert I. Rotberg and John Sweeney have suggested that President Clinton's reasons for ordering the invasion were due, at least in part, to purely domestic political influences: the Congressional Black Caucus and Governor Chiles's reelection campaign, and a public-relations move seeking to paint Clinton as a tough and decisive leader. These reasons cannot explain years of military planning that started before Clinton's election and gained momentum before Clinton was briefed on military capabilities against Haiti. See Rotberg and Sweeney, p. 150.

12. Past foreign military interventions that have helped nations to resolve or at least contain internal political crises include the U.N. operations in Cyprus and the Belgian Congo/Zaire, and the 1964 U.S. intervention in the Dominican Republic. Related actions include the provision of relief supplies to starving Somalis by the United States in operation Provide Relief, and the sheltering of the Kurds from Saddam Hussein during operation Provide Comfort.

13. Donald E. Schulz, *Whither Haiti?,* chap. VI. Schultz also proposes that the United States continue aid for at least 5 more years to make the improvements viable. The idea that reform must take significant time in Haiti in order to grow effective roots is echoed by Anthony P. Bryan, "Haiti: Kick Starting the Economy," pp. 68–69, and Andrew Reding, "Exorcising Haiti's Ghosts," p. 15.

14. Rick Marshall wrote of the evolutionary potential of change in Haiti after the fall of Baby Doc Duvalier in "Haiti: Evolution or Revolution?," p. 40.

15. Jean-Bertrand Aristide, "Passing Milestones: Political and Economic Renewal in Haiti," p. 42.

16. Ibid.

17. Schultz, *Whither Haiti?* particularly emphasizes this improvement in the Haitian power structure (chap. V, p. 1).

18. Aristide, "Passing Milestones: Political and Economic Renewal in Haiti," p. 43.

19. Donald E. Schultz, *Haiti Update* (Strategic Studies Institute Special Report), pp. 8–9.

20. Aristide, "Passing Milestones: Political and Economic Renewal in Haiti," p. 77.

21. Pamela Constable, "A Fresh Start for Haiti?," p. 66.

22. Aristide, "Passing Milestones: Political and Economic Renewal in Haiti," p. 78.

23. Talbot: "Bringing the economy to life will be Haiti's most difficult task." Strobe Talbot, "Promoting Democracy and Economic Growth in Haiti," p. 188.

24. Aristide, "Passing Milestones: Political and Economic Renewal in Haiti," p. 78.

25. The length of time required for Haiti to stand independent is very difficult to anticipate. As Strobe Talbot writes, "before the coup of September, 1991, Haiti was the poorest country in the hemisphere. It may take until the end of the decade for its people to work their way back even to that level." Talbot, "Promoting Democracy and Economic Growth in Haiti," p. 188.

26. Talbot, "Promoting Democracy and Economic Growth in Haiti," p. 189.

Appendix A

Haiti's Rulers

Name	Dates	Fate
Jean-Jacques Dessalines	1804–1806	Assassinated
Henri Christophe	1807–1820	Suicide
Alexandre Pétion	1807–1818	Died in office
Jean-Pierre Boyer	1818–1843	Removed from office
Charles Herard	1843–1844	Fled
Philippe Guerrier	1844–1845	Died in office
Jean-Louis Pierrot	1845–1846	Overthrown
Jean-Baptiste Riche	1846–1847	Died in office
Faustin Soulouque	1847–1859	Forced from power
Fabre Geffrard	1859–1867	Forced from power
Sylvain Salnave	1867–1869	Executed
Nissage Saget	1870–1874	Retired
Michel Domingue	1874–1876	Fled to Jamaica
Boisrond Canal	1876–1879	Fled to Jamaica
Louis Felicite Salomon	1879–1888	Fled to France
F. Florvil Hyppolite	1889–1896	Died in office
Tiresias Simon Sam	1896–1902	Fled
Nord Alexis	1902–1908	Fled to Jamaica
Antoine Simon	1908–1911	Fled to Jamaica
Cincinnatus Leconte	1911–1912	Blown up
Tancrede Auguste	1912–1913	Poisoned
Michel Oreste	1913–1914	Fled to Jamaica
Oreste Zamor	1914	Murdered

continued

Name	Dates	Fate
J. Davilar Theodore	1914–1915	Fled
J. Vilbrun Guilaume Sam	1915	Dismembered
Philippe Dartigueneve	1915–1922	Forced from office
Louis Borno	1922–1930	Forced to resign
Stenio Vincent	1930–1941	Pressured to retire
Elie Lescot	1941–1946	Ousted
Dumarsias Estime	1946–1950	Fled to U.S.
Paul Magloire	1950–1956	Overthrown
Joseph N. Pierre-Louis	1956–1957	Forced to resign
François Sylvain	1957	Overthrown
Daniel Fignole	1957	Overthrown
François Duvalier	1957–1971	Died in office
Jean-Claude Duvalier	1971–1986	Fled to France
Henri Namphy	1986–1988	Stepped down
Leslie Manigat	1988	Overthrown
Henri Namphy	1988	Overthrown
Prosper Avril	1988–1990	Fled to U.S.
Ertha Pascal-Trouillot	1990	Forced to resign, jailed
Jean-Bertrand Aristide	1991	Fled to U.S.
Emile Jonassaint	1991–1994	Stepped down
Jean-Bertrand Aristide	1994–1996	Completed term
René Préval	1996–	Serving

Admiral Caperton's Operations Order, July 28, 1915

Cruiser Squadron
U.S. Atlantic Fleet

U.S.S. WASHINGTON, Flagship

PORT-AU-PRINCE, HAITI
Twenty-eight July, fifteen, four P.M.

Campaign Order Number Four.

FORCES:

(a) <u>Landing Force</u>
Captain George Van Order
Washington:
Two companies marines.
Three companies seamen.

(b) Support
Washington 10″-6″-3″ guns
Armed launches.

1. French and Dominican legations entered by mobs yesterday and this forenoon and General Oscar and President Guillaume forcibly removed and killed.
No government authority in PORT-AU-PRINCE
French cruiser Descartes expected PORT-AU-PRINCE tonight.

2. This force will occupy PORT-AU-PRINCE for the purpose of protecting life and property and preserving order.

3. (a) <u>Landing force</u> land at once on beach near BIZOTON. Begin advance to occupy PORT-AU-PRINCE as soon as landed.
   (b) <u>Support</u> support landing operations.

Washington cover landing of Landing force and support advance to PORT-AU-PRINCE. Be prepared shift berth promptly to position of FORT ISLET.

Armed launches in command Lieutenant Rhodes support left flank Landing Force and cover Water Front of town.

(x) Anticipate resistance. Avoid injury to non-combatants and their property.

4. Lieutenant Rhodes. Washington. take charge transportation of Landing Force to beach: assume duties of beachmaster: return boats, less armed launches to ship when landing is completed. Washington provides maintenance and subsistence for Landing Force.

5. Squadron Commander on Washington. Use flagship time.

Washington, armed launches, and Landing Force maintains signal communications.

> [Signed]
> W. B. Caperton
> Rear Admiral
> Commanding Cruiser Squadron

Appendix C

Agreement of Governors Island

United Nations
July 3, 1993

The President of the Republic of Haiti, Jean-Bertrand Aristide, and the Commander-in-Chief of the Armed Forces of Haiti, Lieutenant General Raoul Cedras, have agreed that the following arrangements should be made in order to resolve the Haitian crisis. Each of them has agreed to take, within the scope of his powers, all the necessary measures for this implementation of these arrangements. Furthermore, they both, in any case, express their support for the implementation of these arrangements and pledge to cooperate in implementing them.

1. Organization, under the auspices of the United Nations and the Organization of American States (OAS), of a political dialogue between representatives of the political parties represented in the Parliament, with the participation of representatives of the Presidential Commission, in order to: a) agree to a political truce and promote a social pact to create the conditions necessary to ensure a peaceful transition; b) reach an agreement on the procedure for enabling the Haitian Parliament to resume its normal functioning; c) reach an agreement enabling the Parliament to confirm the Prime Minister as speedily as possible; and d) reach an agreement permitting the adoption of the laws necessary for ensuring the transition.

2. Nomination of a Prime Minister by the President of the Republic.

3. Confirmation of the Prime Minister by the legally reconstituted Parliament and his assumption of office in Haiti.

4. Suspension on the initiative of the United Nations Secretary-General, of the sanctions adopted under Security Council Resolution 241 (1993) and sus-

pension, on the initiative of the Secretary-General of OAS, of the other measures adopted at the OAS Ad Hoc Meeting of Ministers of Foreign Affairs, immediately after the Prime Minister is confirmed and assumes office in Haiti.

Appendix D

The Carter/Jonassaint Agreement

1. The purpose of this agreement is to foster peace in Haiti, to avoid violence and bloodshed, to promote freedom and democracy, and to forge a mutually beneficial relationship between the governments, people, and institutions of Haiti and the United States.

2. To implement this agreement, the Haitian military and police forces will work in close cooperation with the U.S. Military Mission. This cooperation, conducted with mutual respect, will last during the transitional period required for insuring vital institutions of the country.

3. In order to personally contribute to the success of this agreement, certain military officers of the Haitian armed forces are willing to consent to an early and honorable retirement in accordance with U.N. Resolutions 917 and 940 when a general amnesty will be voted into law by the Haitian Parliament, or October 15, 1994, whichever is earlier. The parties to this agreement pledge to work with the Haitian Parliament to expedite this action. Their successors will be named according to the Haitian Constitution and existing military law.

4. The military activities of the U.S. Military Mission will be coordinated with the Haitian military high-command.

5. The economic embargo and economic sanctions will be lifted without delay in accordance with relevant U.N. Resolutions and the need of the Haitian people will be met as quickly as possible.

6. The forthcoming legislative elections will be held in a free and democratic manner.

7. It is understood that the above agreement is conditioned on the approval of the civilian governments of the United States and Haiti.

APPENDIX E

U.S. Government Agencies Involved in Haiti

Department of Commerce

Department of Defense
    Department of the Army
    Department of the Navy
    Department of the Air Force

Department of Energy

Department of State
    U.S. Agency for International Development
    Office of US Foreign Disaster Assistance
    U.S. Information Agency
    Immigration and Naturalization Service

Department of Transportation
    U.S. Coast Guard

Department of the Treasury
    Bureau of Alcohol, Tobacco, and Firearms

Central Intelligence Agency

Federal Emergency Management Agency

National Security Council

Peace Corps

APPENDIX F

Nongovernmental and Private Voluntary Organizations in Haiti

Adventist Development & Relief Agency
America's Development Foundation
American Council for Nationalities
    Service
American Friends Service Committee
Action International Contre la Faim/USA
American Jewish World Service
AmeriCares Foundation
Ananda Marga Universal Relief Team
Baptist World Alliance
Brother's Brother Foundation
Cooperative for Assistance and Relief
    Everywhere (CARE)
Childreach
Children's Survival Fund, Inc.
Church World Service
Coordination in Development, Inc.
Direct Relief International
Doctors of the World
Grassroots International
Foundation for International Community
    Assistance
Hebrew Immigrant Aid Society
Heifer Project International
Interchurch Medical Assistance, Inc.
International Center for Research on
    Women

International Medical Services for
    Health
Laubach Literacy International
MAP International
Medecins Sans Frontieres USA
Medical Care Development
Operation USA
Outreach International
Oxfam America
Pan American Development Foundation
Partners of the Americas
Planning Assistance
Salvation Army World Service Office
Save the Children
Systèmes d'Approvisionnement et
    Distribution Alimentaires
Trickle Up Program
Unitarian Universalist Service
    Committee
United Methodist committee on Relief
United Way International
U.S. Committee for Refugees
World Concern
World Learning
World Neighbors
World Vision
World Wildlife Fund

APPENDIX G

Fact Sheet on Haiti:
The Road from Dictatorship
to Democracy

THE WHITE HOUSE
Office of the Press Secretary

For Immediate Release   March 21, 1996

FACT SHEET ON HAITI
THE ROAD FROM DICTATORSHIP TO DEMOCRACY

AMERICAN LEADERSHIP and the perseverance of the Haitian people has helped restore democracy to Haiti and provided concrete hope for a better future. The inauguration of René Préval as Haiti's new President on February 7, succeeding President Jean-Bertrand Aristide, represented the first peaceful transfer of power from one democratically elected President to another in Haiti's almost 200-year history. The United States is proud to have helped return democracy to Haiti and given it a chance to take hold.

America's decisive action helped to:

—Restore the legitimate, democratically elected government of Haiti.
—Dramatically improve the human rights situation in Haiti.
—Reverse the economic decline of the coup years.
—Eliminate the flood of Haitian migrants seeking economic and political sanctuary on our shores.
—Conduct free and fair local, parliamentary and presidential elections.

PRESIDENT CLINTON'S promise to the American people regarding Haiti is being realized:

When President Clinton ordered over 23,000 U.S. troops to Haiti on September 19, 1994 to lead the multinational Operation "Restore Democracy," he stated the mission would be limited in scope and duration.

On March 31, 1995, the U.S.-led Multinational Force was transitioned (or was reduced) to the 6000-man United Nations Mission in Haiti (UNMIH), 2500 of whom were Americans. The 2500 U.S. soldiers began their redeployment from Haiti in December, 1995. U.S. operational participation in UNMIH ended when the original U.N. mandate expired on February 29, 1996. The bulk of U.S. UNMIH troops now have returned to their home stations in the United States. The President just visited Fort Polk, Louisiana where he greeted returning forces. The remainder will be home by mid-April.

U.S. troops and their civilian and international military counterparts have given the people of Haiti the chance to restore their democracy and work toward a more secure and prosperous future. Specifically, they have:

- Confiscated or bought-back more than 30,000 firearms and individual explosive devices;
- Maintained a secure and stable environment as the brutal FAd'H (Haiti's former military) was disbanded;
- Provided security, technical expertise, and logistical support for democratic elections nationwide; and
- Supported the development of the new, civilian police force to assume security and law-enforcement responsibilities throughout Haiti.

Today, as U.S. military participation in UNMIH comes to a close, the Government of Canada has stepped forward to take charge of the mission under United Nations auspices. This new, smaller UNMIH military component will remain in Haiti for an additional four months, until the end of June.

President Préval and the democratically elected Haitian Parliament have affirmed his commitment: to sustain and extend the development of a professional and uncorrupted police and security establishment; to intensify judicial reforms; and to put into place sound economic development plans that will benefit the Haitian people and attract foreign and domestic investment as well as assistance from the international donor community.

Under the leadership of President Préval and his government, the Haitian people now face the challenges of building a better future for themselves and their country. The United States is proud to have played an important role in enabling the Haitian people to face these challenges, and will continue its support for Haiti's restored democracy and critical economic growth.

THEN AND NOW

Haiti has made remarkable progress since the U.S.-led Multinational Force deployed to Hispaniola in September 1994. The difference between then and now is dramatic:

BEFORE September 1994, Haiti was ruled by a brutal, corrupt military regime that preyed upon its own people. NOW, the peaceful, democratic transfer of power on February 7 from President Aristide to his elected successor, René Préval, was an historic event that will further cement Haiti's place among the community of democratic nations. Since the September 1994 arrival of the Multinational Force, Haiti has conducted three rounds of national elections—for local governments, for Parliament, and for President.

BEFORE, Haiti's military dictators ruled through terror. Rape, torture and murder were routine instruments of governance. NOW, the Haitian people have a government committed to respecting basic human rights, and is developing the kind of law enforcement and judicial structures necessary to ensure the Rule of Law prevails. The Haitian military has been disbanded and the feared paramilitary organizations such as FRAPH have been eliminated. With U.S. help, a new, civilian police force is being trained and deployed to protect and serve the Haitian people, rather than to exploit and abuse them.

BEFORE, thousands of refugees risked their lives at sea to get to the United States in an effort to escape Haiti's oppression. NOW, the flow of migrants from Haiti has decreased dramatically. The serious crisis prompted by massive waves of Haitian refugees has been eliminated.

BEFORE, the Haitian economy was in decline. In the last year alone of the dictatorship, GDP declined 11 percent, inflation rose to 40 percent, and the public sector deficit skyrocketed to 6 percent of GDP. NOW, Haiti's economy is slowly recovering from the coup years. In the first twelve months after the restoration of Haiti's democratically elected government, the economy expanded by over 5 percent. Inflation has been cut almost in half. Export assembly operations, which were completely closed down in September 1994, came back to life and now employ over 12,000 people.

A CHRONOLOGY OF SUCCESS:

—December 16, 1990: Jean-Bertrand Aristide is elected President of Haiti in a free election.

—September 29–30, 1991: A coup topples the Aristide government and installs a brutal military regime.

—October 1, 1991 to September 18, 1994: Thousands of people are killed by or with the complicity of the coup government.

—September 19, 1994: The American-led Multinational Force (MNF) launched Operation Restore Democracy in Haiti.

—October 15, 1994: President Aristide returns to Haiti accompanied by U.S. Secretary of State Warren Christopher, U.S. Congressional leaders and other foreign dignitaries for welcoming ceremonies in Port-au-Prince. Aristide calls for reconciliation among all Haitians.

—October 21, 1994: The Haitian Senate passes a bill outlawing paramilitary groups.

—November 30, 1994: The MNF reports it has collected 14,943 weapons; 1,72O Haitians had graduated from the Interim Public Security Force (IPSF) police training courses; 8,670 U.S. troops remain in Haiti.

—December 1994: The Haitian Government takes several important steps to reform key institutions, including the appointment of a new supreme court, and the separation and reorganization of police and army units.

—December 21, 1994: The Government of Haiti announces the appointment of the last of nine members of the Provisional Electoral Council (CEP), which opens the way for Haiti to begin the election process for legislative, municipal, and local elections.

—January 4, 1995: MNF Commander, General Meade, declares that a secure and stable environment exists in Haiti, one of the requirements necessary to transition from the MNF to the United Nations Mission in Haiti (UNMIH).

—January 17, 1995: President Aristide officially dismisses the remainder of the Haitian army. U.S. Secretary of Defense Perry pronounces Haiti secure and stable for turnover to the UNMIH forces, which will replace the MNF by March 31, 1995.

—January 30, 1995: The U.N. Security Council passes Resolution 975 to transfer the Haitian peacekeeping mission from the MNF to UNMIH effective March 31, 1995.

—January 31, 1995: In Paris, the World Bank and international agencies from 20 countries pledge $1.2 billion in assistance for Haiti's economic recovery.

—March 31, 1995: President Clinton and other dignitaries attend ceremonies in Port-au-Prince transferring operations from the MNF to UNMIH. Major General Joseph W. Kinzer, USA, assumes command of all U.S. and U.N. forces in Haiti.

—June 4, 1995: President Aristide and Secretary of State Christopher address the first 357 graduates of the Haitian National Police training program and announce that the program to train new police will be doubled in order to field over 5,000 police officers by March, 1996.

—June 5, 1995: The Organization of American States (OAS) General Assembly begins its session in Port-au-Prince, demonstrating regional support for democracy in Haiti.

—June 25, 1995: Haiti holds first round of national elections for which more than 3.5 million Haitians registered to vote for some 10,000 candidates to fill over 2,000 local and national offices.

—August 13, 1995: Haiti holds make-up elections in 21 towns including Port-au-Prince. Voter turnout isn't high, but procedural complications have declined since the June 25 round.

—September 17, 1995: UNMIH forces provide security and logistical support to the conduct of run-off elections throughout Haiti. 68 Parliamentary races are contested, 60 for the Chamber of Deputies and 8 for the Senate. Elections are violence-free and improved administratively, though voter turnout is low.

—October 15, 1995: To commemorate the first anniversary of President Aristide's return to Haiti, Vice President Gore attends ceremonies in Port-au-Prince and visits UNMIH troops.

—December 12, 1995: The last class of Haitian National Police candidates to receive training at Fort Leonard Wood, Missouri graduates 758 members.

—December 17, 1995: Haiti holds its presidential election. René Préval is elected to succeed President Aristide.

—February 7, 1996: René Préval is inaugurated as the new President of Haiti, the first peaceful transfer of power from one civilian leader to another in Haiti's 192-year history.

—March, 1996: The U.N. Security Council votes to extend the UNMIH mandate in Haiti for four months under Canadian military command and control. United Nations Special Representative Lakdhar Brahimi is replaced by Enrique Ter Horst of Venezuela. U.S. Major General Kinzer changes military command to Canadian Brigadier General Daigle and U.S. forces terminate operational missions as part of UNMIH.

—March 18, 1996: President Clinton travels to Fort Polk, Louisiana to welcome U.S. troops home from Haiti and present military awards to representative service members.

—March 19–21, 1996: President Préval and delegation travel to Washington for an official working visit and meet with President Clinton at the White House.

APPENDIX H

U.N. Security Council Resolution 940 (1994)

Adopted by the Security Council at its 3413th meeting, on 31 July 1994

The Security Council,

Reaffirming its resolutions 841 (1993) of 16 June 1993, 861 (1993) of 27 August 1993, 862 (1993) of 31 August 1993, 867 (1993) of 23 September 1993, 873 (1993) of 13 October 1993, 875 (1993) of 16 October 1993, 905 (1994) of 23 March 1994, 917 (1994) of 6 May 1994, and 933 (1994) of 30 June 1994,

Recalling the terms of the Governors Island Agreement (S/26063) and the related Pact of New York (S/26297),

Condemning the continuing disregard of those agreements by the illegal de facto regime, and the regime's refusal to cooperate with efforts by the United Nations and the Organization of American States (OAS) to bring about their implementation,

Gravely concerned by the significant further deterioration of the humanitarian situation in Haiti, in particular the continuing escalation by the illegal de facto regime of systematic violations of civil liberties, the desperate plight of Haitian refugees, and the recent expulsion of the staff of the International Civilian Mission (MICIVIH), which was condemned in its Presidential statement of 12 July 1994 (S/PRST/1994/32),

Having considered the reports of the Secretary-General of 15 July 1994 (S/1994/828 and Add.1) and 26 July 1994 (S/1994/871),

Taking note of the letter dated 29 July 1994 from the legitimately elected President of Haiti (S/1994/905, annex) and the letter dated 30 July 1994 from the Permanent Representative of Haiti to the United Nations (S/1994/910),

Reiterating its commitment for the international community to assist and support the economic, social, and institutional development of Haiti,

Reaffirming that the goal of the international community remains the restoration of democracy in Haiti and the prompt return of the legitimately elected

President, Jean-Bertrand Aristide, within the framework of the Governors Island Agreement,

Recalling that in resolution 873 (1993) the Council confirmed its readiness to consider the imposition of additional measures if the military authorities in Haiti continued to impede the activities of the United Nations Mission in Haiti (UNMIH) or failed to comply in full with its relevant resolutions and the provisions of the Governors Island Agreement,

Determining that the situation in Haiti continues to constitute a threat to peace and security in the region,

1. Welcomes the report of the Secretary-General of 15 July 1994 (S/1994/828) and takes note of his support for action under Chapter VII of the Charter of the United Nations in order to assist the legitimate Government of Haiti in the maintenance of public order;

2. Recognizes the unique character of the present situation in Haiti and its deteriorating, complex, and extraordinary nature, requiring an exceptional response;

3. Determines that the illegal de facto regime in Haiti has failed to comply with the Governors Island Agreement and is in breach of its obligations under the relevant resolutions of the Security Council;

4. Acting under Chapter VII of the Charter of the United Nations, authorizes Member States to form a multinational force under unified command and control and, in this framework, to use all necessary means to facilitate the departure from Haiti of the military leadership, consistent with the Governors Island Agreement, the prompt return of the legitimately elected President and the restoration of the legitimate authorities of the Government of Haiti, and to establish and maintain a secure and stable environment that will permit implementation of the Governors Island Agreement, on the understanding that the cost of implementing this temporary operation will be borne by the participating Member States;

5. Approves the establishment, upon adoption of this resolution, of an advance team of UNMIH of not more than sixty personnel, including a group of observers, to establish the appropriate means of coordination with the multinational force, to carry out the monitoring of the operations of the multinational force and other functions described in paragraph 23 of the report of the Secretary-General of 15 July 1994 (S/1994/828), and to assess requirements and to prepare for the deployment of UNMIH upon completion of the mission of the-multinational force;

6. Requests the Secretary-General to report on the activities of the team within thirty days of the date of deployment of the multinational force;

7. Decides that the tasks of the advance team as defined in paragraph 5 above will expire on the date of termination of the mission of the multinational force;

8. Decides that the multinational force will terminate its mission and UNMIH will assume the full range of its functions described in paragraph 9 below when a secure and stable environment has been established and UNMIH has adequate force capability and structure to assume the full range of its functions; the determination will be made by the Security Council, taking into account recommendations from the Member States of the multinational force, which are based on

the assessment of the commander of the multinational force, and from the Secretary-General;

9. Decides to revise and extend the mandate of the United Nations Mission in Haiti (UNMIH) for a period of six months to assist the democratic Government of Haiti in fulfilling its responsibilities in connection with:

(a) sustaining the secure and stable environment established during the multinational phase and protecting international personnel and key installations; and

(b) the professionalization of the Haitian armed forces and the creation of a separate police force;

10. Requests also that UNMIH assist the legitimate constitutional authorities of Haiti in establishing an environment conducive to the organization of free and fair legislative elections to be called by those authorities and, when requested by them, monitored by the United Nations, in cooperation with the Organization of American States (OAS);

11. Decides to increase the troop level of UNMIH to 6,000 and establishes the objective of completing UNMIH's mission, in cooperation with the constitutional Government of Haiti, not later than February 1996;

12. Invites all States, in particular those in the region, to provide appropriate support for the actions undertaken by the United Nations and by Member States pursuant to this and other relevant Security Council resolutions;

13. Requests the Member States acting in accordance with paragraph 4 above to report to the Council at regular intervals, the first such report to be made not later than seven days following the deployment of the multinational force;

14. Requests the Secretary-General to report on the implementation of this resolution at sixty-day intervals starting from the date of deployment of the multinational force;

15. Demands strict respect for the persons and premises of the United Nations, the Organization of American States, other international and humanitarian organizations, and diplomatic missions in Haiti, and that no acts of intimidation or violence be directed against personnel engaged in humanitarian or peacekeeping work;

16. Emphasizes the necessity that, inter alia:

(a) all appropriate steps be taken to ensure the security and safety of the operations and personnel engaged in such operations; and

(b) the security and safety arrangements undertaken extend to all persons engaged in the operations;

17. Affirms that the Council will review the measures imposed pursuant to resolutions 841 (1993), 873 (1993), and 917 (1994), with a view to lifting them in their entirety, immediately following the return to Haiti of President Jean-Bertrand Aristide;

18. Decides to remain actively seized of the matter.

APPENDIX I

Command-and-Control Relationships

The diagram illustrating these relationships appears on the following page, courtesy of the U.S. Government's Training and Audiovisual Support Center, Fort Eustis, Virginia.

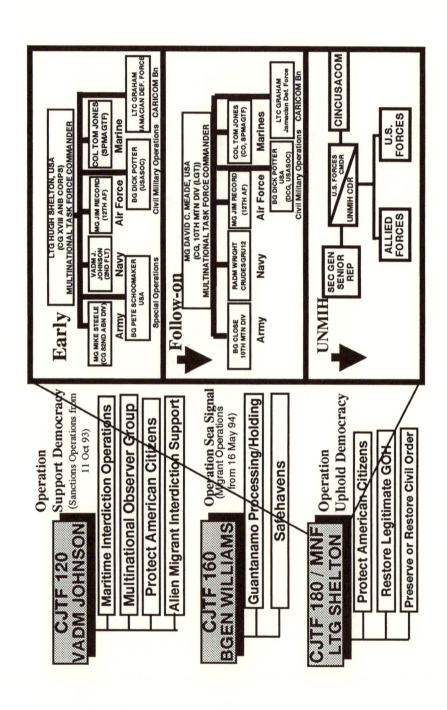

Glossary

AFB	Air Force Base
AIDS	Antibody Immune Deficiency Syndrome
AMIO	Alien Migrant Interdiction Operation
AOA	Area of Operations
ARG	Amphibious Ready Group
ATF	Bureau of Alcohol, Tobacco, and Firearms
BCT	Brigade Combat Team. An army term used to identify a task organized unit of several battalions, normally commanded by a colonel
BEC	local electoral committee
CARICOM	Caribbean Community. The organization of Caribbean states
CAT	Crisis Action Team
CBC	Congressional Black Caucas
CCE	Coalition Coordination Element
CEP	Provisional Electoral Committee
CINC	Commander-in-Chief. Normally a four star officer commanding a U.S. unified command
CINCFLEET	Commander-in-Chief, Fleet. The senior commander of the Royal Navy
CINCUSACOM	Commander-in-Chief, United States Atlantic Command. During operations in Haiti, the the CINCUSACOM was first Admiral Paul D. Miller, then General John J. Sheehan; Admiral Harold M. Gehman took command of USACOM in September, 1997
CJCS	Chairman of the Joint Chiefs of Staff, the senior military officer in the United States. For operations in Haiti, the CJCS position was filled by General John Shalikashvili. General Henry Shelton assumed the position as CJCS in October, 1997

CJTF	Commander, Joint Task Force
CMO	Civil–military operations. CMO are conducted worldwide, primarily by special operations forces, to ensure that civilian needs and issues are properly integrated into military actions
CMOC	Civil–Military Operations Center. CMOCs are clearing houses and coordination centers for CMO
CNG	Conseil nationale du government. The CNG is the advisory council of the Haitian government
CNN	Cable News Network
COMNAVBASE	Commander, Naval Base
COMSECONDFLT	Commander, Second Fleet. A vice admiral commanding the naval striking force of USACOM
CP	Command Post
DAO	Defense Attaché Office. The DAO serves as a part of an ambassador's staff advising on military matters and coordinating with U.S. military agencies
DC	Deputies Committee
DEC	Departmental electoral committee
D-day	The day that major operations commence during a military campaign
DOD	Department of Defense
DOJ	Department of Justice
DOS	Department of State
EXCON	Executive Committee
EXORD	Execution Order. A message approved by one of the two members of the U.S. national command authority, either the Secretary of Defense or the President, authorizing the commencement of military operations
FAd'H	Forces Armées d'Haiti. The Haitian armed forces, including the Haitian army, Haitian police and the Haitian navy
FRAPH	Front pour l'Avencement et le Progrès d'Haiti
Gourde	The basic unit of the Haitian national currency
HAG	Haiti Assistance Group. The organization authorized by the United Nations to facilitate the retraining of the FAd'H after the planned return of President Aristide in 1993
HMS	Her Majesty's Ship. The designation of a Royal Navy ship similar to the designation "USS" for U.S. Navy ships
HNP	Haitian National Police. Formed after the return of President Aristide
HUMVEEs	A medium-sized, U.S. military personnel and light-cargo vehicle, the replacement for the Jeep
ICITAP	The International Criminal Investigation and Training

	Assistance Program. Managed by the Department of State, and used in Haiti to retrain the HNP
ICM	International Civilian Mission. United Nations observers assigned to monitor human-rights violations
IOM	International Organization for Migration
IPC	Interagency Planning Cell
IPM	International Police Monitor
IPSF	The Interim Police Security Force created after the start of Uphold Democracy to maintain law and order in Haiti during the initial training of the new Haitian national police
IWGs	Interagency Working Groups. Low-level coordination bodies within the U.S. government, researching issues and developing potential options for review by national policy-makers
JFACC	Joint Force Air Component Commander. The senior air commander within a joint force charged with execution of aerospace tasks by the joint force commander
JFPs	Joint Force Packages. Groups of service forces tailored to a specific mission tasking
JIB	Joint Information Bureau
JOA	Joint Operations Area. The area assigned to a joint force commander for operations
JOC	Joint Operations Center
JOPES	The Joint Operations Planning and Execution System. A system of automated data-processing tools, planning procedures, and decisionmaking processes for joint warfighting
JSOTF	Joint Special Operations Task Force. The special operations component of a joint force
JTF	Joint Task Force. A specially organized grouping of forces from two or more U.S. military departments
KONAKOM	Komité Nasyonal Kongrès Oganizasyons Démokratik
LANTCOM	The original acronym title for the U.S. Atlantic Command, changed to USACOM in 1993
Lavalas	The name of President Aristide's political organization
LSV	Landing Ship Vehicle
MAGTF	Marine Air–Ground Task Force
MATs	Ministerial Advisory Teams
Mech	Mechanized. A designation used to identify army units primarily organized around tanks and armored personnel carriers/fighting vehicles
MEU	Marine Expeditionary Unit. A task-organized, Marine air–ground task force commanded by a colonel

MIO	Maritime Intercept Operations. Naval operations used in sanctions enforcement
MNF	Multinational Force
NCA	National Command Authority. The President and the Secretary of Defense or their legally designated successors
Négritude	A cultural-pride movement in Haiti based on the strong heritage of African descendants
NGO	Nongovernmental Organization. See Appendix F for a listing of organizations in Haiti
Noirist	Member of a black-pride organization
NSA47	National Security Act of 1947
NSC	National Security Council
OAS	Organization of American States
OPLAN	Operation Plan. A formal plan written through deliberate coordination among a variety of defense agencies, normally focused on major combat operations
OPORD	Operation Order. Operation orders are operation plans, refined and updated to current situations, ready for execution
PAO	Public Affairs Office. The military organization that deals with the Press and media issues
POLAD	Political Adviser. A Department of State official assigned for duty with a military commander
PSYOPs	Psychological Operations. Actions aimed at supporting military operations through the dissemination of information
PVO	Private Volunteer Organization. See Appendix F for a listing of organizations in Haiti
RO/ROs	Roll-on Roll-off. Ships designed to rapidly load and unload wheeled vehicles as cargo
ROE	Rules of Engagement
SECDEF	The U.S. Secretary of Defense. During early Haiti operations, the SECDEF was William Perry
SOF	Special Operations Forces. Army, Navy and Air Force forces trained and equipped for special operations under the combatant command of the Commander-in-Chief, Special Operations Command
SPMAGTF	Special Marine Air–Ground Task Force. A Marine unit of smaller than MEU size specially configured for a given task
TPFDD	Time-Phased Force Deployment Database. The collection of required unit and routing information needed to flow military forces from homebases to the area of operations in a controlled manner

UCP	Unified Command Plan
UNMIH	United Nations Mission in Haiti
UNSCR	United Nations Security Council Resolution
UNSMIH	United Nations Support Mission in Haiti
USACOM	U.S. Atlantic Command after 1993. The strategic headquarters for operations in Haiti
USAID	United States Agency for International Development
USCG	United States Coast Guard
USFORHAITI	United States Forces in Haiti
USNS	United States Naval Ship. Military support ships crewed largely by civilians, under the direction of the U.S. Transportation Command
USSPTGPHAITI	United States Support Group Haiti
VSN	Voluntaires de la securité nationale. The proper name of the Tonton Macutes
VTC	Video-teleconference. Two-way video and audio communications
WBB	Weapons Buy-Back Program
WWMCCS	Worldwide Military Command and Control System

Bibliography

ARTICLES AND PAPERS

Albright, M. K. (1994, Oct. 17). "Reinforcing Haitian democracy." *U.S. Department of State Dispatch,* 99–100.

————. (1995, February 13). "Keeping faith with the people of Haiti." *U.S. Department of State Dispatch,* 93–94.

Archambault, R. III. (1995, Nov.). "Joint operations in Haiti." *Army,* 22–29.

Aristide, J.-B. (1996, Spring). "Passing milestones: Political and economic renewal in Haiti." *Harvard International Review,* 42–43, 77–78.

Bryan, A. P. (1995, Feb.). "Haiti: Kick-starting the economy." *Current History,* 65–70.

Casa, K. (1995, July/Aug.). "Iraq embargo toll now surpasses war's horrors." *The Washington Report on Middle East Affairs,* 14, 10–11.

Cleaver, C. (1994, Jan. 17). "Notes from the hell that is Haiti." *New Leader,* 5–7.

Clinton, W. J. (1994, June 27). "Establishing the basis for a successful conclusion to the crisis in Haiti." *U.S. Department of State Dispatch,* 424–429.

————. (1994, Oct. 1). "Invasion of Haiti canceled." *Vital Speeches of the Day,* 740–741.

————. (1994, Oct. 1). "The possible invasion of Haiti." *Vital Speeches of the Day,* 738–740.

Clinton, W. J., & W. H. Gray. (1994, June 27). "Establishing the basis for a successful conclusion to the crisis in Haiti." *U.S. Department of State Dispatch,* 424–429.

Constable, P. (1996, Feb.). "A fresh start for Haiti?" *Current History,* 65–69.

Crowley, J. F. (1963). "An argument for administrative occupation of Haiti: A case in point." Unpublished student paper, Armed Forces Staff College.

Dobbins, J. F. (1995, July 17). "Elections in Haiti: An important milestone." *U.S. Department of State Dispatch,* 567–569.

Doughty, R. A., & H. E. Raugh, Jr. (1991, Spring). "Embargoes in historical perspective." *Parameters,* 21, 21–30.

Fauriol, G. (1988, Fall). "The Duvaliers and Haiti." *Orbis,* 587–607.

French, H. W. (1993, Jan. 9). "Visiting U.S. general warns Haiti's military chiefs." *New York Times,* p. 5.

Headley, B. D. (1992, Feb.). "Why we won't see an American-led invasion of Haiti" *Monthly Review,* 29–34.

Henderson, N. C. (1996, May–June). "Civil affairs and logistics in Haiti." *Army Logistician,* 21.

Hollis, P. S. (1995, Apr.). "Projecting America's military might." *Field Artillery,* 6–9.

Kidder, T. (1994, Oct. 24). "Uncle Sam, super cop: Iraq, Haiti and the growing challenges to a smaller military." *U.S. News and World Report,* 30–42.

———. (1995, Apr. 17). "The Siege of Mirebalais." *The New Yorker,* 72–95.

Killebrew, R. B., & D. H. Petraeus. (1995, Apr.). "Winning the peace: Haiti, the US, and the UN." *Armed Force Journal International,* 40–41.

Klepak, H. (1996, June 12). "Keeping democracy on schedule in Haiti." *Jane's Defense Weekly,* 33–35.

Maingot, A. P. (1992, Feb.). "Haiti and Aristide: The legacy of history." *Current History,* 65–69.

———. (1995, Feb.). "Haiti: The political rot within." *Current History,* 59–64.

Marshall, R. (1987, Jan.). "Haiti: Evolution or revolution?" *Defense and Foreign Affairs,* 40.

Martin, E. M. (1981, Summer). "Haiti: A case study in futility," *SAIS Review,* 410–516, 6980–6989.

Mendel, W. W. (1994, Jan.). "The Haiti contingency." *Military Review,* 48–57.

Merrill, J. (1996, Winter/Spring). "Vodou and political reform in Haiti: Some lessons for the international community." *Fletcher Forum of World Affairs,* 31–52.

Nicholls, D. (1996, Oct.). "Haiti: The rise and fall of Duvalierism." *Third World Quarterly,* 1239–1252.

Reding, A. (1996, Spring). "Exorcising Haiti's ghosts." *World Policy Journal,* 15–26.

Rotberg, R. I. (1988, Fall). "Haiti's past mortgages its future." *Foreign Affairs,* 93–109.

Rotberg, R. I., & J. Sweeney. (1996, Spring). "Was intervening in Haiti a mistake?" *Foreign Policy,* 134–151.

Siegel, A. B. (1996, Aug.). "The intervasion of Haiti." Center for Naval Analyses, Professional Paper 539.

Silverberg, D. (1994, Nov.). "The Haitian malaise." *Armed Force Journal International,* 7–8.

Smith, G. (1995, Feb.). "Haiti: From intervention to intervasion." *Current History,* 54–58.

Talbot, S. (1995, Mar. 13). "Promoting democracy and economic growth in Haiti." *U.S. Department of State Dispatch,* 185–189.

Thompson, M. (1994, July 18). "Invasion target: Haiti." *Time,* 22–23.

Valenzuela, A. A., & T. S. Russell, Jr. (1995, June). "Operation UPHOLD DEMOCRACY: The 10th Mountain Division Artillery in peace operations." *Field Artillery,* 26–30.

Zakheim, D. (1994, Oct. 10). "Haiti deployment has many costs." *Defense News,* 23–24.

Zimmerman, T., & A. A. Auster. (1994, July 18). "Caribbean cruise." *U.S. News & World Report,* 33–35.

BOOKS

Abbott, E. (1988). *Haiti: The Duvaliers and Their Legacy.* New York: McGraw- Hill.

Allard, K. C. (1995). *Somalia: Lessons Learned.* Washington, DC: National Defense University Press.

Aristide, J.-B. (1993). *In the Parish of the Poor: Writings from Haiti.* New York: Maryknoll.

Clausewitz, C. von. (1976). *On War,* ed. and trans. M. Howard & P. Paret. Princeton, NJ: Princeton University Press. (Original work published in 1832.)

Davis, H. P. (1936). *Black Democracy: The Story of Haiti.* New York: Dodge Publishing.

Diederich, B., & A. Burt. (1969). *Papa Doc: The Truth about Haiti Today.* New York: McGraw-Hill.

Dupuy, A. (1997). *Haiti in the New World Order: The Limits of the Democratic Revolution.* Boulder, CO: Westview Press.

Fauriol, G. A. (Ed.). (1994). *Haitian Frustrations: Dilemmas for U.S. Policy.* Washington, DC: Center for Strategic & International Studies.

Fishel, J. T. (1997). *Civil–Military Operations in the New World.* Westport, CT: Praeger Publishers.

———. (Ed.). (1998). *"The Savage Wars of Peace."* Boulder, CO: Westview Publishers.

Gingras, J.-P. O. (1967). *Duvalier, Caribbean Cyclone: The History of Haiti and Its Present Government.* New York: Exposition Press.

Hayes, M. D., & G. F. Wheatley (Eds.). (1996). *Interagency and Political–Military Dimensions of Peace Operations: Haiti—A Case Study.* Washington, DC: National Defense University Press.

Healy, D. (1976). *Gunboat Diplomacy in the Wilson Era: The U.S. Navy in Haiti, 1915–1916.* Madison: University of Wisconsin Press.

Heinl, R. D., & N. G. Heinl. (1978). *Written in Blood: The Story of the Haitian People, 1492–1971.* Boston: Houghton Mifflin.

Leyburn, J. G. (1966). *The Haitian People.* New Haven, CT: Yale University Press.

Logan, R. W. (1941). *The Diplomatic Relations of the United States with Haiti.* Chapel Hill: University of North Carolina Press.

———. (1968). *Haiti and the Dominican Republic.* New York: Oxford University Press.

Manigat, L. F. (1964). *Haiti of the Sixties: Object of International Concern (A Tentative Global Analysis of the Potentially Explosive Situation of a Crisis Country in the Caribbean).* Washington, DC: Washington Center for Foreign Policy Research.

Manwaring, M., D. E. Schulz, R. Maguire, P. Hakim, & A. Horn. (1997). *The Challenge of Haiti's Future.* Carlisle Barracks, PA: U.S. Army Strategic Studies Institute.

Marcella, G. (1994). *Haiti Strategy: Control, Legitimacy, Sovereignty, Rule of Law, Handoffs, and Exit.* Carlisle Barracks, PA: U.S. Army Strategic Studies Institute.

McCrocklin, J. H. (1956). *Garde d'Haiti, 1915–1934: Twenty Years of Organization and Training by the United States Marine Corps.* Annapolis, MD: U. S. Naval Institute Press.

Millspaugh, A. C. (1931). *Haiti Under American Control, 1915–1930.* Boston: World Peace Foundation, 1931.

Moore, E. O. (1972). *Haiti: Its Stagnant Society and Shackled Economy.* New York: Exposition Press.

Nicholls, D. (1979). *From Dessalines to Duvalier: Race, Colour and National Independence in Haiti.* London: Cambridge University Press.

Oakley, R. B., & D. Tucker. (1997). *Two Perspectives on Interventions and Humanitarian Operations.* Carlisle Barracks, PA: U.S. Army Strategic Studies Institute.

Oakley, R. B., M. J. Dziedzic, & E. M. Goldberg. (1998). *Policing the New World Disorder: Peace Operations and Public Security.* Washington, DC: National Defense University Press.

Perusse, R. I. (1995). *Haitian Democracy Restored, 1991–1995.* Lanham, MD: University Press of America.

Plummer, B. G. (1992). *Haiti and the United States: The Psychological Moment.* Athens: University of Georgia Press.

Powell, C. L., & J. E. Persico. (1995). *My American Journey.* New York: Random House.

Ridgeway, J. (Ed.). (1994). *The Haiti Files: Decoding the Crisis.* Washington, DC: Essential Books.

Rodman, S. (1954). *Haiti: The Black Republic.* New York: Devin-Adair.

Rotberg, R. I. (1971). *Haiti: The Politics of Squalor.* Boston: Houghton Mifflin.

Schmit, H. R. (1971). *The United States Occupation of Haiti, 1915–1934.* New Brunswick, NJ: Rutgers University Press.

Schulz, D. E. (1996). *Whither Haiti?* Carlisle Barracks, PA: U.S. Army Strategic Studies Institute.

————. (1997). *Haiti Update.* Carlisle Barracks, PA: U.S. Army Strategic Studies Institute.

Scott, J. C. (1972). *Comparative Political Corruption.* Englewood Cliffs, NJ: Prentice-Hall.

Tyson, G. F., Jr. (Ed.). (1973). *Toussaint L'Ouverture.* Englewood Cliffs, NJ: Prentice-Hall.

Weinstein, B., & A. Segal. (1992). *Haiti: The Failure of Politics.* New York: Praeger.

INTERVIEWS

Barnes, Thomas E., Lieutenant Colonel, USA, interview with John R. Ballard, Feb. 5, 1997, Norfolk, VA.

Barnhill, Paul C., Major, USMCR, interview with John R. Ballard, May 29, 1997, Norfolk, VA.

Byron, Michael J., Major General, USMC, interview with William R. McClintock, January 17, 1995, Norfolk, VA.

Fargo, Thomas B., Rear Admiral, USN, interview with William R. McClintock, Feb. 10, 15, Mar. 22, 1995, Norfolk, VA.

Fisher, George A., Major General, USA, interview with J. Burton Thompson, May 8,1995, Schofield Barracks, HI.

Garner, Robert J., Colonel, USMC, interview with John R. Ballard, Nov. 4–5, 1997, Norfolk, VA.

Gehman, Harold W. Jr., Rear Admiral, USN, interview with Alexander G. Monroe, Jan. 28, 1994, Norfolk, VA.

Hartzog, William W., Lieutenant General, USA, interview with William R. McClintock, July 18, Oct. 24, 1995, Norfolk, VA.

Heyl, Phillip, Commander, USCG, interview with John R. Ballard, Nov. 13, 1997, Norfolk, VA.

Kinzer, Joseph, Major General, USA, interview with William Neale, Dec. 4, 1995, Port-au-Prince, Haiti.

Langdon, John, Colonel, USMC, interview with John R. Ballard, Jan. 18, 1996, Norfolk, VA.

Maxim, Robert M., Political Advisor to USACOM, interview with William R. McClintock, July 7, 1995, Norfolk, VA.

Meade, David C., Major General, USA, interview with Dennis P. Mroczkowski, Oct. 27, 1994, Port-au-Prince, Haiti.

Miller, Paul David, Admiral, USN (Ret.), interview with William R. McClintock, Jan. 19, 1995, Charlottesville, VA.

Prendergast, Timothy "Spike" E., Captain, USN, interview with William R. McClintock and Ralph J. Passarelli , Nov. 23, 1994, Norfolk, VA.

Pulley, James G., Colonel, USA, interview with William R. McClintock, Nov. 19, 1993, Norfolk, VA.

Seely, Edgar C., III, Lieutenant Colonel, USA Reserve, interview with John R. Ballard, Mar. 13, 1997, Norfolk, VA.

Shadley, Robert D., Brigadier General, USA, interview with William R. McClintock, Apr. 25, 1995, Norfolk, VA.

Sheehan, John J., Lieutenant General, USMC, interview with William R. McClintock, Mar. 17, 1993, Norfolk, VA.

Stull, Jon, Colonel, USMC, interview with John R. Ballard, Nov. 19, 1997, Norfolk, VA.

Tyrrell, John, Colonel, USAF, interview with John R. Ballard, June 23, 1995, Norfolk, VA.

GOVERNMENT DOCUMENTS

10th Mountain Division. (1996). *10th Mountain Division "Operation Uphold Democracy" After-Action Report, Operations in Haiti August 1994 through January 1995.* Fort Eustis, VA: Training and Audio Visual Support Center.

Cole, R. H., & W. R. McClintock. (1996). *"Chronology of Operation Uphold Democracy: The Role of the Chairman of the Joint Chiefs of Staff DuringPlanning and Execution of U.S.-Led Multinational Force Operations in Haiti, 11 Oct 93–31 Mar 95."* Washington, DC: Joint History Office.

Cole, R. H., W. S. Poole, et al. (1995) *The History of the Unified Command Plan, 1946–1993.* Washington, DC: Joint History Office.

Department of Defense. (1995, Dec. 1). *Operation Uphold Democracy: An Assessment of Intelligence and Communications Systems and Networks.*

Grumelli, M. L. (1995) *"Rules of Engagement Employed in Operation Uphold Democracy, September 1994–March 1995."* Norfolk, VA: U.S. Atlantic Command.

Hayden, C. L. (Ed.). (1996). *JTF-180 Uphold Democracy Oral History Interviews.* Fort Bragg, NC: XVIII Airborne Corps, X.

———. (1996). *JTF-190 Oral History Interviews: Operation Uphold Democracy.* Fort Bragg, NC: XVIII Airborne Corps, X.

Hirrel, L. P. (1998). *United States Atlantic Command Fiftieth Anniversary, 1947–1997.* Norfolk, VA: U.S. Atlantic Command.

McClintock, W. R. (1997). *Establishment of USACOM, 1 October 1993.* Norfolk, VA: U.S. Atlantic Command.

———. (1997). *"Working Chronologies Caribbean Campaign: Operations Support and Uphold Democracy and UN Mission in Haiti and Sea Signal in GTMO, 1 Apr 93–1 Jun 97."* Norfolk, VA: U.S. Atlantic Command.

McClintock, W. R., & A. G. Monroe. (1998). *Operation GTMO, 1 October 1991–1 July 1993.* Norfolk, VA: U.S. Atlantic Command.

Marion, F. L. (1997) *Development of a Haitian Public Security Force, September 1994–March 1995.* Norfolk, VA: U.S. Atlantic Command.

———. (1997). *Captured Weapons and the Weapons Buy-Back Program in Haiti, September 1994–March 1995.* Norfolk, VA: U.S. Atlantic Command.

Trask, R. R., & A. Goldberg. (1997). *The Department of Defense, 1947–1997: Organization and Leaders.* Washington, DC: Historical Office, Office of the Secretary of Defense.

U.S. Atlantic Command. (1995). *Operation UPHOLD DEMOCRACY, Joint After-Action Report (JAAR).* Norfolk, VA: U.S. Atlantic Command.

———. (1997). *Migrant Camp Operations: The Guantanamo Experience.* Hampton,VA: OC, Inc.

————. (1997, May). *Operation UPHOLD DEMOCRACY: US Forces in Haiti.*

U.S. Congress. (1994). *Haiti: The Agreement of Governor's Island and its Implementation. Hearing before the Subcommittee on Western Hemisphere Affairs of the Committee on Foreign Affairs, House of Representatives. July 21, 1993.* Washington, DC: U.S. Government Printing Office.

————. (1994). *U.S. Policy Toward, and Presence in, Haiti. Hearings and Markup before the Committee on Foreign Affairs, House of Representatives. September 13, 27 and 28, 1994.* Washington, DC: U.S. Government Printing Office.

————. (1994). *Situation in Haiti. Hearing before the Committee on Armed Services, United States Senate, September 28, 1994.* Washington, DC: U.S. Government Printing Office.

————. (1996). *Haiti: The Situation after the Departure of the U.S. Contingent from UNMIH. Hearing before the Subcommittee on Western Hemisphere Affairs of the Committee on International Relations, House of Representatives. February 28,1996.* Washington, DC: U.S. Government Printing Office.

————. (1996). *Public Papers of the Presidents of the United States, William J. Clinton, 1995, Book I—January to June 30, 1995.* Washington, DC: U.S. Government Printing Office.

U.S. Joint Chiefs of Staff. (1995, Jan. 10). *Joint Pub 1, Joint Warfare of the Armed Forces of the United States,* X.

————. (1995, Feb. 24). *Joint Pub 2-0, Unified Action Armed Forces,* X.

————. (1995, Feb. 1). *Joint Pub 3-0, Doctrine for Joint Operations,* X.

————. (1995, Apr. 13). *Joint Pub 5-0, Doctrine for Planning Joint Operations,* X.

————. (1996, Oct. 9). *Joint Pub 3-08, Interagency Coordination During Joint Operations,* vol. 1, X.

————. (1996, Oct. 9). *Joint Pub 3-08, Interagency Coordination During Joint Operations,* vol. 2, X

Index

About the Author

JOHN R. BALLARD is Professor of Military History and Strategy at the Armed Forces Staff College of the National Defense University in Norfolk, Virginia. He served as a member of the U.S. Atlantic Command staff and was deployed to Haiti as part of the Multinational Force that returned President Aristide to power in 1994.

ISBN 0-275-96237-7

90000>

EAN

9 780275 962371

HARDCOVER BAR CODE